Justice Daniel Cohalan 1865–1946

American patriot and Irish-American nationalist

Justice Daniel Cohalan.
(Source: Library of Congress)

Justice Daniel Cohalan 1865–1946

American patriot and Irish-American nationalist

MICHAEL DOORLEY

CORK UNIVERSITY PRESS

First published in 2019 by
Cork University Press
Boole Library
University College Cork
Cork
T12 ND89
Ireland

Library of Congress Control Number: 2019949088
Distribution in the USA: Longleaf Services, Chapel Hill, NC, USA

British Library Cataloguing in Publication Data
A CIP record for this book is available from the British Library.

ISBN: 978-1-78205-352-1

Printed by Gutenberg in Malta.
Print origination & design by Carrigboy Typesetting Services
www.carrigboy.com

www.corkuniversitypress.com

This book is dedicated to
Justice Peter Fox Cohalan

Contents

Acknowledgements

THIS BOOK HAS HAD A LONG GESTATION. I first recognised the need for a biography on Judge Daniel Cohalan following the completion of my book on the Friends of Irish Freedom organisation in 2005. Cohalan was such a central figure in the transatlantic Irish-American relationship in the early decades of the twentieth century and yet, as Professor Francis Carroll points out in the foreword to this book, his life has been 'something of a mystery'. This book will not only help us better understand Cohalan, warts and all, but will also contribute to our knowledge of the relationship between the United States and Ireland during a tumultuous period in American and Irish history.

I would like to acknowledge the immense help I have received over the years in the completion of this publication. My visits to the American Irish Historical Society (AIHS) in New York City, where Cohalan's papers are stored, were efficiently facilitated by Library and Archives Curator Georgette Keane. As a result of this research, I completed a number of preliminary articles on different aspects of Cohalan's life. These included a biographical article on Cohalan which appeared in the *New Hibernia Review* in 2015. With the encouragement and support of Jim Rogers, editor at the *Hibernia Review*, I have incorporated many of my research findings from this short article into this publication.

I also gained critical insights into Cohalan's role in the Irish Rising of 1916, following a conference I attended at NYU's Glucksman Ireland House in 2016 entitled *America and the 1916 Easter Rising*. I would like to pay special tribute to Miriam Nyhan Grey, Associate Director Glucksman Ireland House NYU, who helped organise this conference and who also edited the subsequent publication *Ireland's Allies* (2016) which has again very much informed this work. Miriam herself has been a staunch ally of my project on Cohalan and I am indebted to her for her assistance and kindness.

I owe a deep debt of gratitude to Professor Francis Carroll, Professor Emeritus at the University of Manitoba, who not only read and commented extensively on each chapter but also wrote an elegant foreword to this book. I would also like to note how other scholars in the field of Irish-American history have helped me refine my understanding of the American social and economic environment that so profoundly influenced Daniel Cohalan's 'Americanism'. Such scholars include David Brundage, Marion Casey, Kevin Kenny, Tim Meagher, John McCarthy, William Manz, Brian Hanley, David Doolin, Patrick Maume and Bob Schmuhl. Karen Heil from the Middletown Thrall Library provided information on relevant historical sources available in New York State and my former colleagues from the University of Illinois at Chicago, Leo Schelbert and Jim Sack, also provided much encouragement and support.

In 2016 I was fortunate to be introduced to retired New York State Supreme Court Justice Peter Fox Cohalan and his partner Eileen Kremers. Peter Fox Cohalan is a grandnephew of 'The Judge' and is himself a historian. Peter provided me with vitally important background material on Daniel Cohalan's family and his role in the complex world of New York politics. Moreover, Peter proved to be an excellent proofreader of my manuscript, combing out the many errors or 'nits', as he called them, which he found along the way. All errors and omissions that remain are, of course, my own. We have done our utmost to ensure that all photos and visual images have been captioned correctly and that all rights have been chased up and we are keen to hear from you with any additional comments or corrections that can be addressed in future reprints.

Peter Fox Cohalan also informed me of the work of the Robert D.L. Gardiner Foundation, which promotes the history of New York City and New York State. This foundation provided a generous grant to St Joseph's College, New York, to enable me to present a lecture series and mount a digital exhibition covering Daniel Cohalan's contribution to New York history during the course of his lifetime. Professor Mark Hessler, Coordinator of Innovative Instruction at St Joseph's College, provided invaluable assistance to me in the preparation of the lecture series and exhibition, and the research that I undertook for that project has very much influenced the contents of this book.

Daniel Cohalan maintained a summer home in Glandore in west Cork which he visited frequently. Given his Cork connections, it was only natural that I should approach a Cork publisher, Cork University

Press (CUP), to publish this work. I would especially like to thank CUP editor Maria O'Donovan for her assistance and advice throughout the process. Other individuals based in County Cork have also contributed to my understanding of the west Cork dimension to Cohalan's life. These include John Borgonovo at University College Cork, Don Healy and Fachtna Hickey of the Rosscarbery and District History Society and John Hamilton from the *Southern Star* newspaper. Eileen McGough, whose own magnificent biography of Diarmuid Lynch provided a model for this work, also shared much-needed insights into Cohalan's links to Glandore.

Closer to home, numerous colleagues and friends have assisted me in preparing the manuscript for publication. My old friends Pat Long and Pat Brereton read several drafts and provided many invaluable editorial suggestions. Thanks to Ken Finlay for his assistance with photo research and likewise Richard Howlett and Olivia Hearne from Concept 2 Print. Piotr Sadowski provided welcome advice on the publication process. Frank Boucher-Hayes gave excellent insights into the problems facing the new Irish Free State in the 1920s and also provided important sources on this critical period. I would also like to express special thanks to my colleague Jennifer Shepherd, Faculty of Arts and Social Sciences at the Open University, for her encouragement and support of my continuing research work on the Irish diaspora in the United States.

Grateful thanks to the staff at the following institutions: the American Irish Historical Society; the British Library; *Das Politisches Archiv des Auswärtigen Amts* [Diplomatic Archive of the German Ministry for Foreign Affairs]; the National Library of Ireland; the New York Public Library; the National Archives of Ireland and the National Archives of the United Kingdom; the UCD Archives Department. A special word of thanks to the staff of dlr LexIcon library and in particular James O'Sullivan, County Hall Archives in Dún Laoghaire. My sincere appreciation also to the Cushwa Centre for the Study of American Catholicism who facilitated the publication of this book through a Hibernian Research Award in 2017. Finally, I would like to thank my wonderful daughters Nora and Joanna for their encouragement and my wife Marian for her untiring patience with what must have seemed like an endless project. I finally got there in the end with their tolerance and support.

Abbreviations

AANC	All America National Council
AARIR	American Association for the Recognition of an Irish Republic
AOH	Ancient Order of Hibernians
APA	American Protective Association
FOIF	Friends of Irish Freedom
GAA	Gaelic Athletic Association
IAAC	Irish-American Athletic Club
IPL	Irish Progressive League
IPP	Irish Parliamentary Party
IRA	Irish Republican Army
IRB	Irish Republican Brotherhood
MP	Member of Parliament
RIC	Royal Irish Constabulary
TD	Teachta Dála
UILA	United Irish League of America
UVF	Ulster Volunteer Force
WASP	White Anglo-Saxon Protestant

Sources, Archives and Libraries

AIA	Archives of Irish America
AIHS	American Irish Historical Society
BMH	Bureau of Military History
CBS	Crime Branch Special
DIFP	*Documents on Irish Foreign Policy*
DLRCA	Dún Laoghaire Rathdown County Council Archives
MCIHP	Maloney Collection of Irish Historical Papers
NAI	National Archives of Ireland
NARA	National Archives and Records Administration (USA)
NAUK	National Archives of the United Kingdom
NLI	National Library of Ireland
NYPL	New York Public Library
PAAA	Politisches Archiv des Auswärtigen Amts
UCDA	University College Dublin Archives

Foreword

JUSTICE DANIEL F. COHALAN was a dominant figure in the Irish-American community in the early twentieth century and he was particularly influential in the efforts in the United States to organise support for the Irish independence movement from 1914 to 1921. But he has also been something of a mystery – powerful, shrewd, wealthy and independent. Much of the historical scholarship that mentions Justice Cohalan has centred on his spectacular clash with Éamon de Valera, President of Dáil Éireann, in 1920 over control of the Irish-American nationalist movement, the marshalling of support across America, and the raising of money for Ireland. Not surprisingly, much of the literature about the Irish War of Independence, and particularly those studies concerned with de Valera's extended trip to the United States in 1919 and 1920, portrays Cohalan as a malign force. Why did he publicly challenge the elected leader of the Irish people, someone he ostensibly should have supported, thereby opening the door to a split in the Irish-American movement at its most critical moment?

Dr Michael Doorley has written a masterful biographical study of Justice Cohalan based on research in all of the relevant manuscript collections on both sides of the Atlantic and all of the current scholarship. In doing so he has confronted these questions about Cohalan. The result is a sympathetic, but not uncritical, study of this complex man, a study that gives us, for the first time, a penetrating insight into Cohalan's aspirations and intentions. Dr Doorley explores the multiple facets of Cohalan's career: lawyer, judge, politician, churchman and family man, in addition to being a major Irish-American nationalist leader. Doorley brings to light many important, but largely unknown, details that are part of the life story that help make sense of this complex man: his great-grandfather was an aide-de-camp for the Marquis de Lafayette during the American revolutionary war, giving Cohalan a sense of ownership of an American heritage in the face of what he perceived as 'Anglo-American' attempts to sideline the Irish role in America's foundation and history. He followed his father into the Clan na Gael as a young man, thus stepping into a revolutionary nationalist family tradition. A son and grandson of Famine survivors, Cohalan became, in the words of New York journalist Forrest Davis, the 'Squire of Glandore' in west Cork, close to where his family had roots and where he entertained Douglas Hyde and Patrick Pearse, giving him a presence in the new Ireland. He was a successful legal advisor to Tammany Hall in New York City and a prominent State Supreme Court Justice, providing him with upper middle-class wealth and status. His nomination to the United States Senate in 1911 was blocked by upstate New York Democrats led by Franklin D. Roosevelt, leaving him with a sense of resentment towards the official Democratic Party. His hostility to imperialism was not directed exclusively at the British but was equally critical of American and French imperialism. So Cohalan's actions regarding Britain or President Woodrow Wilson or Éamon de Valera or the League of Nations become more understandable when seen in the context of these values and experiences.

Doorley is particularly skilful in guiding us through Cohalan's work in the Irish-American nationalist movement. By 1900 he had emerged as a leading figure, assisting John Devoy in reuniting the Clan na Gael, which held the revolutionary movement together during the era in which home rule seemed triumphant. Moreover, in the crisis of 1914, Cohalan quickly made arrangements for Roger Casement to meet with the German ambassador to the United States and to facilitate Casement's plans to secure German assistance for an Irish rebellion. Doorley, as he has done in his earlier work, *Irish-American Diaspora Nationalism* (2005), shows Cohalan to be instrumental in organising the Irish Race Convention in March 1916, which founded the Friends of Irish Freedom. This organisation became the leading Irish-American nationalist body in the United States. It provided support for Ireland after the rising and was the group that rallied behind the revolutionary government of Dáil Éireann in 1919. The Friends of Irish Freedom raised over one million dollars that underwrote the work of the American Commission for Irish Independence in Paris, financed de Valera's tour of the United States, lent the funds to start the Dáil Éireann bond certificate campaign, and also fought the prospect of United States membership of the League of Nations.

As is well known, in the course of these events in 1919 and 1920 Cohalan and de Valera and their followers disagreed so completely that a new nationalist organisation was created – the American Association for the Recognition of the Irish Republic – controlled specifically by de Valera. Dr Doorley is brilliant in threading his way through this tangled narrative. His Cohalan is an experienced lawyer and politician who is sensitive to language and its implications and to the need to be flexible, and is conditioned to think a step ahead about political possibilities. De Valera's plans to raise funds by selling 'bonds' in the name of an unrecognised government is a case in point – a less financially secure instrument, 'bond certificates', had to be used to conform to the law. Cohalan was prepared to accept a special relationship between Ireland and Britain, but de Valera's specific reference to Cuba's relationship with the United States showed that the Irish leader had not grasped how one-sided that relationship actually was. De Valera's pre-empting Cohalan at the 1920 Republican Party convention, insisting on a platform plank that called for the recognition of the Irish republic, showed a failure to understand the limits to which 'friendly nations' can go in commenting on the internal affairs of other nations. While supporting Irish independence, Cohalan never lost sight of his conservative vision of America's international role, an issue not appreciated by de Valera and his followers. Finally, Doorley shows Cohalan's realistic acceptance of the Anglo-Irish Treaty and the Irish Free State on the basis of a recognition of Michael Collins' statement that it gave the Irish 'the freedom to achieve freedom'. As Doorley shows, Cohalan supported Collins and later William T. Cosgrave for practical reasons, quite apart from mere hostility to de Valera, but he continued to push for a more independent Ireland, independent of both Britain and the League of Nations.

Daniel Cohalan lived on into the 1940s. As Doorley notes, although Cohalan returned to Glandore, was welcomed by the Irish Free State government, and even attended the Eucharistic Congress in 1932, he stepped back from continued leadership in the Irish-American world. However, he continued to fight with the Democratic Party, he opposed the nomination of Franklin D. Roosevelt in 1932 and 1936, he fought the proposal that the United States join the World Court, and he resisted American support for Britain after the outbreak of war in 1939. Cohalan saw 'internationalism' as a trap that would tie the United States to British imperialism and keep Ireland marginalised; today he would be called an 'isolationist'. As for Cohalan's role in the leadership of the Irish nationalist movement in the United States from at least 1914 to 1921, Dr Doorley's book will be the definitive source.

Francis M. Carroll

INTRODUCTION

American Patriot and Irish-American Nationalist

Daniel Florence Cohalan (1865–1946) remains a relatively unknown figure in Irish and American history. Save for an unpublished master's degree completed in 1968 and a few short articles, no biography has ever been completed on his life.[1] This is surprising since, in the first quarter of the twentieth century, Cohalan exercised considerable influence in both New York politics and Irish-American nationalist circles. Today, Daniel Cohalan, or 'The Judge' as he was known to friend and foe alike, is best remembered for his tempestuous relationship with Irish nationalist leader Éamon de Valera during the latter's mission to the United States in 1919–20.[2] Yet de Valera's famous remark about Cohalan – 'Big as the country is, it was not big enough to hold the Judge and myself' – is testament not just to the rivalry between both men but also to the stature of Cohalan during this tumultuous period in Irish and American history.[3]

Crucially, Cohalan's role in American and Irish affairs long predated and outlasted his conflict with de Valera in 1920. During the period 1908–11 he was 'Grand Sachem' or associate leader of the Democratic political machine in New York City otherwise known as Tammany Hall.[4] As a result of his close connections to Tammany boss Charles F. Murphy, Cohalan became a New York State Supreme Court Justice in 1911, a position he held until 1924. On a national level, in alliance with Idaho Republican Senator William Borah, Cohalan also played a significant part in the campaign against American involvement in the League of Nations. Cohalan's papers in the American Irish Historical Society (AIHS) in New York reveal a close advisory relationship with leading American political figures of his day. These included Missouri Democratic Senator James Reed, Bainbridge Colby who served as Secretary of State for President Woodrow Wilson, and labour lawyer Frank Walsh who led the American Commission on Irish Independence to the Paris Peace conference in 1919. Again, in the early 1930s, Cohalan became a leading figure in New York politics as an advisor to Tammany boss John Francis Curry.[5] He was also prominent at the Democratic convention in 1936, where he and other conservative Democrats attempted to prevent the re-nomination of Franklin Roosevelt as a candidate for the upcoming presidential election.[6]

Paradoxically, alongside his role in American politics and the judiciary, Cohalan occupied a position of great influence in the Clan na Gael, a secret Irish-American nationalist organisation devoted to the establishment of an Irish republic by revolutionary means. John Devoy from County Kildare, who had served time in British prisons for his involvement in the 1867 Fenian Rising, was the organisation's acknowledged leader. However, in the first two decades of the twentieth century, Cohalan and Tyrone-born Joe McGarrity, a Philadelphia businessman, exercised considerable influence in Clan decision-making. Cohalan's papers in the AIHS and Devoy's papers in the National Library of Ireland (NLI) provide evidence of Cohalan's influential role in the Clan and his lifelong friendship with Devoy.[7] In contrast, Cohalan's relationship with McGarrity broke down after the latter took de Valera's side in the bitter dispute that wracked the Irish-American nationalist movement in the United States in 1920.[8]

In March 1916, Cohalan played an instrumental role in launching and then leading the powerful Friends of Irish Freedom (FOIF). He and the FOIF adopted a low profile when the United States entered the war on Britain's side in April 1917, but the period from the end of the First World War in November 1918 until his open break with de Valera in November 1920 marked the high point of Cohalan's career. By 1920, the FOIF numbered 275,000 regular and associate members and achieved a national profile in its efforts to win US recognition for Irish independence and in its campaign against the League of Nations.[9] Despite the fact that the Irish-born and those with Irish parents numbered five million in 1900, this was still a significant figure given that the vast majority of Irish-Americans did not normally become involved in Irish-American nationalist organisations. Ward in his work *Ireland and Anglo-American Relations* has described the FOIF as one of the most effective propaganda machines in Irish-American history.[10]

From the end of the First World War in November 1918 and before his break with de Valera in November 1920, Cohalan, as leader of the FOIF, represented the public face of Irish-American nationalism, commonly described by his political supporters as the leader of the 'Irish Race' in America.[11] However, behind the scenes, Cohalan faced stiff opposition from other Irish nationalists in the United States such as Clan leader Joe McGarrity and Sinn Féin 'envoy' Patrick McCartan, who vehemently disagreed with his tactics and strategy.[12] Cohalan's conflict with de Valera brought these tensions into public view and this delivered a heavy blow to his reputation. Yet despite this turmoil, Cohalan's interest in Ireland continued after the establishment of the Irish Free State. As evidenced in Cohalan's correspondence in the AIHS and Irish diplomatic correspondence serialised in *Documents on Irish Foreign Policy*, vol. 1, 1919–22, he played a hitherto unreported role in advising the new government of William T. Cosgrave on Irish interests in the United States.[13]

In a biographical sketch on Cohalan that appeared in the Ancient Order of Hibernians' (AOH) publication the *National Hibernian Digest* in 1948, John J. Sheanan headed his article 'Daniel F. Cohalan, Defender of American Principles and an Ardent Lover of Ireland'.[14] This loyalty to both Ireland and the United States characterised Cohalan's life and actions. Accordingly, this biography will explore Daniel Cohalan's role as an Irish-American nationalist as well as aspects of his American political life which shaped his Irish nationalist outlook. Indeed, it would be impossible to cover his career as an Irish-American nationalist without reference to his American political objectives and how he sought to achieve these. In turn, Cohalan's very 'Americanism' and his American political connections made him a valuable asset to Irish nationalists in the United States. However, his dual allegiance to both the Irish nationalist cause and the United States led to tensions. His aim to uphold the interests of the Irish-American Catholic group and safeguard the interests of the United States against what he perceived as insidious threats from the British Empire did not always sit well with the interests of Irish nationalists, who were naturally motivated by purely Irish considerations. A biography of Cohalan thus offers an opportunity to study how both Irish events and the American social and political environment shaped the ideology of a leading Irish-American nationalist. This in turn helps to deepen our understanding of the forces which shaped Irish-American nationalism during a tumultuous period in Irish history.

Throughout his political career, Cohalan aroused both admiration and condemnation in equal measure. Corkman and 1916 veteran Diarmuid Lynch remained an unwavering supporter of 'The Judge' to the end. In his unpublished manuscript on the history of the Friends of Irish Freedom, Lynch wrote flatteringly of Cohalan: 'It is universally acknowledged that in every phase of human endeavour, certain individuals, because of devotion to principle, distinguished service, force of character, ability, experience and general equipment to advance a cause, always attain a commanding influence with their fellow men.'[15] Irish poet and playwright Padraic Colum, who came to know the leaders of the American Clan in 1915, has also painted a sympathetic portrayal of Cohalan. In an article which appeared in the *Irish Times* in 1964, Colum noted: 'As a lawyer and politician he was a persuasive speaker and a practised manager of men. He was also a man of deep feeling: I saw him cry when he was being harried by partisans of a newcomer in the American political field.'[16]

Of course, other Irish nationalists such as de Valera became strongly critical of Cohalan. De Valera felt particularly aggrieved by Cohalan's opposition to his newspaper interview where he had stated that the security relationship between Cuba and the United States could serve as a model for the relationship between an independent Ireland and Britain. In a report on this event to the Irish cabinet in Dublin in 1920, de Valera noted that Cohalan was a 'tricky police court lawyer' and 'guilty of a wilful misrepresentation of my whole attitude'.[17] Harry Boland, who acted as de Valera's secretary in the United States, also believed that Cohalan exercised an inordinate role in Irish-American nationalist affairs and dominated the ageing Clan leader John Devoy. In a public statement issued to the press in October 1920, severing relations between the Irish Republican Brotherhood (IRB) and the New York-based Clan, Boland declared: 'We have been reluctantly compelled to sever our connections between the Clan na Gael and the parent body in Ireland until such time as the will of the members of the executive becomes operative and not the will of Justice Cohalan.'[18]

Not surprisingly, the British government took a dim view of Cohalan's activities and believed him to be a dangerous menace. Royal Irish Constabulary (RIC) reports in the National Archives of Ireland indicate Cohalan's role as a 'Clan na Gael delegate' distributing funds to the Irish Republican Brotherhood during his many vacations in his holiday home in west Cork.[19] The British government's report entitled *Documents Relative to the Sinn Féin Movement*, which investigated the 1916 Rising, contains a copy of an intercepted message between Cohalan in New York and the German war office in Berlin calling for naval attacks on England and the landing of German officers in Ireland so as to coincide with the rising. A German academic, Reinhard R. Doerries, in his work *Prelude to the Easter Rising: Sir Roger Casement in Imperial Germany*, has also uncovered this and other messages from Cohalan to Germany in German archives in Berlin.[20] In September 1917, after the United States had entered the war, the American authorities released transcripts of Cohalan's message to the American media but, despite rumours of impeachment, Cohalan survived the crisis and restored his political reputation after the war. Nevertheless, the existence of such documents suggests that Cohalan, although a New York State Supreme Court Justice in one jurisdiction, was perfectly willing to become an Irish rebel in another.

As one might expect, American opinions on Cohalan varied during his lifetime. At the height of Cohalan's power, in October 1919, the well-known newspaper editor Arthur Brisbane noted: 'Powerful in intellect and of inflexible integrity, Cohalan stands as one of the great Americans of our time.'[21] Also in 1919, Henry Cabot Lodge, Republican chairman of the powerful Senate Foreign Relations Committee, praised Cohalan as 'one of the ablest men who ever came to Washington to plead a cause. The citizens of Irish blood are fortunate in having him as a leader.'[22] In contrast, President Woodrow Wilson's animosity towards Cohalan stretched back to the Democratic convention in Baltimore in 1912 where Cohalan and Tammany boss Charlie Murphy had attempted to block his nomination for the presidency in favour of the alternative candidacy of congressman Champ Clark of Missouri, who was well known for his anti-British views.[23]

Wilson also despised Cohalan for his well-known German sympathies and doubted his loyalty after American intervention in the First World War. In March 1919, Wilson's Irish-American secretary Joseph Tumulty urged the president to meet with a Cohalan-led delegation from the Irish Race Convention in Philadelphia, who were then pressing the American government to allow Irish representatives to attend the Paris Peace Conference. As Tumulty put it: 'Regardless of what we may think of Cohalan and his crowd, there is a deep desire on the part of the American people to see the Irish question settled …'[24] In the end, Wilson agreed to meet the delegation but just before the meeting was scheduled to take place he told Tumulty that Cohalan had five minutes to remove himself: 'If in that time the rest of them want to come I will receive them; if not, I will go to the dock.' In response to Tumulty's warning that the exclusion of Cohalan would make a 'terrible impression' on his followers, Wilson replied: 'That is just what I want it to do, Tumulty; but I think it will make a good impression on decent people.'[25]

This biographical study of Cohalan's life and work on behalf of Ireland and Irish-America will include many examples of the various political controversaries that characterised his life. In so doing, it will help throw new light on the activities of Irish-American nationalists during a crucial phase in Irish and American history. While Cohalan's personality played a factor in such controversies, it is important to stress that he was a product of his time and very much influenced by the social and political milieu in which he found himself. This work will show how Cohalan's sense of Irish nationalism was influenced by his reaction to events in Ireland, by the evolving position of the Irish-American community within American life and by political events in the United States. As we shall see, Cohalan considered the furthering of the Irish nationalist cause in America and Ireland to be of primary importance but he also linked this objective to safeguarding the Irish-American ethnic group and defending the United States from both domestic and international threats.

The development of Irish-American nationalism has attracted much debate among historians. Contrasting perspectives range from Thomas Brown's seminal work *Irish-American Nationalism*, which argued that a hostile American cultural environment reinforced a Catholic Irish sense of communal identity and contributed to the formation of Irish-American nationalism, to comparative works such as Matthew Frye Jacobson's *Special Sorrows: The diasporic imagination of Irish, Polish, and Jewish immigrants in the United States*, which emphasised how the culture of the migrants themselves and developments in the country of origin have influenced the development of diaspora nationalism.[26] Meanwhile, David Brundage, in his work *Irish Nationalist in America: The politics of exile, 1797–1998*, has explored not only the global and transatlantic nature of this phenomenon but also its dynamic nature as it became intermeshed with the experience of the Irish diaspora in different areas of Irish settlement.[27]

My previous work, *Irish-American Diaspora Nationalism: The Friends of Irish Freedom, 1916–1935*, focused on the history of a specific Irish-American nationalist organisation which grew in numbers against the background of the Anglo-Irish war. On a theoretical level, *Irish-American Diaspora Nationalism* argued that the nationalist ideology of the FOIF, given its broad support base, was influenced as much by the American social and political environment as by Irish events. Developments such as American entry into the First World War and the bitter post-war controversy over whether the United States should become a member of the League of Nations shaped its policies and objectives. This biography of Daniel Cohalan adopts a similar approach in that it highlights the importance of an American social and political environment shaping Cohalan's nationalism. Cohalan was, after all, born in the United States and deeply immersed in its political life. Yet it is important to note also that his Irish heritage played an important role in shaping his nationalist outlook. This dimension to Cohalan's nationalism was not covered in *Irish-American Diaspora Nationalism*, given that the focus of that work was on the development of the FOIF organisation rather than Cohalan himself, who had close family ties to Ireland and visited there frequently.

Kerby Miller in his work *Emigrants and Exiles: Ireland and the Irish exodus to North America* has highlighted how Irish emigrants to the United States often saw themselves as involuntary 'exiles' forced out of Ireland by British oppression and misgovernment, even though the vast majority made rational decisions to emigrate as a result of structural changes in the Irish economy. Miller argues that such feelings of exile made Irish emigrants especially receptive to appeals from Irish nationalists to support the establishment of an independent Irish state which would put an end to the evils of emigration and ensure Irish prosperity.[28] This may well have been true of some Irish emigrants, especially after the Famine period. However, this work will show that Cohalan and other leading Irish-American nationalists did not view themselves as 'exiles'. Cohalan was fully immersed in all aspects of American life and took pride in his American identity. Nevertheless, like many Irish-American nationalists, he believed that Ireland was a victim of British imperial misgovernment and that an independent Ireland modelled on American democratic and economic principles would deliver Irish prosperity. As we shall see, Cohalan was never short of advice to Irish leaders on how this could be achieved.

Cohalan's interactions with Ireland were made possible by an increasingly globalised world. By the turn of the twentieth century, telegraphic and postal communications allowed messages to be transmitted more rapidly. Irish-Americans were now more informed about Irish events, compared to previous generations. Irish-American newspapers such as the *Gaelic American* and the *Irish World* reported on events for their Irish-American readers, though, admittedly, these events were interpreted in different ways, depending on the nationalist ideology of particular editors.

Meanwhile Irish people, with the expansion of literacy from the nineteenth century, were themselves familiar with American culture and society. The improvement in transport and telegraph communications meant that travel between Ireland and the United States had become much more commonplace, while Irish newspapers reported extensively on American political and social developments. By the turn of the century, the United States was a less alien environment for Irish emigrants compared to the Famine period.

Cohalan frequently visited Ireland and maintained a summer home in Glandore, west Cork, until the 1930s. These visits were often noted by the Cork press, such as the *Southern Star*. Besides his own family links with west Cork, his wife Hanna, who he met in New York, came from the same locality. Again, Hanna was no 'involuntary exile' and did not see herself as such. As explored by Gerardine Meaney, Mary O'Dowd and Bernadette Whelan in their work *Reading the Irish Woman: Studies in cultural encounter and exchange, 1714–1960*, Irish women, because of developments in literacy and transatlantic communications, were aware of the opportunities available to them in the United States and were familiar with American cultural norms.[29] Hanna, who had been educated at the Sacred Heart Convent in Killarney, was, according to her daughter Aileen's memoirs, the intellectual equal of Daniel. She fitted seamlessly into the Upper East Side social circles which they both inhabited and also kept in close touch with events in Ireland. According to the *Gaelic American* newspaper, she was 'equally at home in discussing American and Irish affairs'.[30]

Timothy J. Meagher, in a chapter on Irish nationalism in his work *The Columbia Guide to Irish American History*, makes the point that Irish-American nationalism was 'unique' within the Irish diaspora in its level of militancy and radicalism. Unlike other areas of Irish settlement within the British Empire such as Canada and Australia, Irish nationalists in the United States could operate freely and could also link the Irish struggle to America's own republican traditions and anti-colonial struggle. This comparison between the Irish and American revolutions certainly featured in Cohalan's speeches and writings. He advocated the complete separation of Ireland from the British Empire, and as an active member of the Clan and the Gaelic League in New York, his many trips to Ireland were more than a sentimental visit to the land of his forebears. His immersion in Irish nationalist activities in the United States was partly shaped by his family's Cork heritage and cultural and political developments in Ireland, and this dimension to his nationalism will represent an important theme in this work.

Prior to the 1916 rebellion in Ireland, Irish nationalists of all hues visited the United States on lecture tours and in search of funding for various nationalist and cultural projects. Joe Lee, in a foreword to *Ireland's Allies* (2016), a book devoted to an analysis of the American contribution to the 1916 Rising, argues that Irish revolutionary nationalism in Ireland could not have survived without the support it received from Irish-American organisations such as the New York-based Clan na Gael.[31] Lee's claim could be said to overstate the importance of the American connection since, as we shall see in later chapters, developments in Ireland created the conditions for the rising and even the Clan leaders were not notified of the exact date until just a few months before it took place. Nevertheless, it is important to stress that there were significant connections between Irish-American nationalist organisations such as the Clan na Gael and the indigenous IRB in the years prior to the rising and this biography will naturally explore Cohalan's role in these efforts.[32]

Historians such as Kevin Kenny, in his work *The American Irish: A history* (2000), have highlighted how Irish nationalism became a mass movement after the executions which followed the rising in Dublin. Kenny compares the mood within Irish-America during the Anglo-Irish war of 1919–20 to that which existed during the Irish Land War of the 1880s.[33] One could also argue that the Irish in the United States occupied a more important role in Irish nationalist ambitions after the rising than before it. The collapse in support for Redmond's Parliamentary Party at the 1918 election and the subsequent rise of Sinn Féin dramatically altered the nature of the Irish question. Sinn Féin's focus on enlisting financial and diplomatic support for the Irish cause in the United States meant that Cohalan, because of his leadership of the FOIF and his American connections, occupied a pivotal position in their American strategy. Bernadette Whelan, in her work *United States Policy and Ireland: From empire to independence 1913–1929*, has explored how the Irish question became significant in American politics especially in the post-war period.[34] Cohalan's interactions with the Wilson administration and leading American political figures of the day and his leadership of the FOIF certainly helped to ensure this.

One might have expected a close working relationship between Cohalan and the leaders of Irish nationalism from Ireland, but this was not the case and this work will explore the reasons for the many disputes which arose. While personality played a role in these disputes, other ideological factors involving a clash of two types of nationalism, Irish and Irish-American, were also at play. These disputes became even more complicated as the Sinn Féin movement in Ireland itself became divided over the terms of the Anglo-Irish Treaty, which brought Ireland's War of Independence to an end. For reasons that will be explained, Cohalan supported the treaty and did what he could to promote the new Irish Free State among Irish-Americans. However, his relations with the leaders of the Irish Free State, though cordial, were not without friction, especially with regard to Ireland's membership of the League of Nations and Anglo-Irish relations. In this context, Cohalan's correspondence with leading figures in the new Irish state such as Executive President William T. Cosgrave and Minister for Labour Joseph McGrath represent a fascinating insight into the relationship between the new Irish Free State and Irish-America. Tellingly, this relationship mirrored the efforts of later Irish governments to harness the power of the Irish-American diaspora to further Ireland's geopolitical and economic standing in the world.[35]

The impact of the American environment on Cohalan's nationalism will surface throughout this work. At the time of his birth in Middletown, New York, to Irish Catholic immigrant parents in 1865, the United States was still predominantly Protestant. The American Protective Association (APA), a secret society founded in 1887, advocated discrimination against Catholics 'in all spheres of life: political, occupational and educational'.[36] But by the beginning of the twentieth century, Irish Catholics in the United States had made much social progress since the Famine period and the APA was a spent force. However, they still faced discrimination and hostility even into the 1920s, as witnessed by the anti-Catholic hostility directed at Al Smith in his campaign for the presidency in 1928. As Kevin Kenny also points out in *The American Irish*, 'Anti-Catholicism had been a major component of the successful drive for immigration restriction in the early 1920s, and the virulently anti-Catholic Ku Klux Klan claimed anywhere between three and five million members in the 1920s.'[37]

Cohalan was a devout Catholic and was very much aware of the inferior position of the Irish Catholic community in the United States. He involved himself in many Catholic organisations and this work will show how his friendships with the leading Catholic churchmen of his day impacted on his role as a prominent figure in Irish-American nationalism. Though Cohalan claimed to speak for all Irish-Americans, in practice he tended to conflate the interests of Irish-America with those of the Irish Catholic group and he saw institutions such as Tammany Hall and the Catholic Church as mechanisms to defend and promote Irish Catholic interests.

Aside from religious discrimination, Irish Catholics also faced racial discrimination which was related to their perceived 'Celtic' origins. A common cultural affinity between the US and Britain had existed since the foundation of the colonies in North America. However, towards the end of the nineteenth century, social Darwinist ideas became popular. Contemporary political scientist John Burgess (1844–1931) described the Anglo-Saxons as the most highly developed racial and ethnic group in the world and argued that this justified their domination over the 'beaten men of beaten races'. Burgess blamed so-called 'inferior races' such as the Celts and the Slavs for America's social problems.[38]

Matthew Guterl points out in his work *The Color of Race in America, 1900–1940* that the Irish in the United States saw themselves, and were seen by others, as a distinct racial community 'predicated on the belief that the Irish and the Anglo-Saxon were biologically, culturally, and historically different'.[39] It is important to stress in this context that Irish-Americans, unlike Chinese and Japanese at this time, were regarded as legally white and the level of discrimination experienced by non-white groups such as African-Americans was far greater than that experienced by the Irish. Nevertheless, social discrimination and stereotypical representations of the Irish in America persisted and inevitably shaped Irish attitudes towards their American host environment. This in turn influenced Irish-American nationalist ideology.

In his book, Guterl highlights Cohalan's role in challenging the dominant Anglo-Saxon conception of American identity in the early twentieth century and his call for a more pluralist America that would recognise the contributions of all the different racial groups to the growth of the United States.[40] As we shall see in later chapters, Cohalan continually expressed fears about the dominance of 'Anglo-Saxonism' in American life to the exclusion of other groups. However, in common with other prominent Irish-Americans during this period, his writings and speeches are notable for their lack of references to the plight of non-white groups in American society such as Native Americans or African-Americans. Instead, Cohalan, in keeping with his Irish-American nationalist ideology, focused on defending the Irish 'race' and in several interviews and speeches tried to counter what he believed were cultural pressures to assimilate the Irish into an Anglo-Saxon Protestant cultural norm. In an interview with *The Metropolis* magazine in 1921, he declared: 'The man or group of men who set out to make this land into an Anglo-Saxon country, servile imitator of England and things English, is as great an enemy of our country as the one who would attempt to do similar work as to Germany and things German.'[41]

In this regard, Cohalan's views can be seen as typical of many other middle-class Irish-Americans who emphasised racial pride and respectability in the face of Anglo-Saxon assimilationist pressures. Alison Kibler, in a recent work entitled *Censoring Racial Ridicule: Irish, Jewish and African American struggles over race and representation, 1890–1930*, highlights how the Irish, though legally white, 'still occupied a middle ground in terms of popular culture and some scientific classification'.[42] In an earlier article entitled 'The Stage Irishwoman' (2005), she described how vaudeville theatre productions, which became popular in American cities in the first decades of the twentieth century, depicted the Irish as prone to drinking and brawling and in the words of one critic as 'but one degree [removed] from the baboon'. Meanwhile Irish women typically featured as inept and 'manly' domestic servants who could not be controlled by their Anglo-Saxon mistresses.[43] Kibler describes how Irish-American organisations such as the Ancient Order of Hibernians contested such racial stereotypes by staging protests and 'riots' both inside and outside theatres. In one such production called *The Irish Servant Girls*, staged at the Orpheum Theatre in New York in 1907, Irish-American protestors pelted the male performers, who were impersonating Irish female domestic servants, with lemons and eggs.[44]

There is no evidence to suggest that Cohalan was personally involved in such protests, though the Clan na Gael, of which he was a prominent member, was behind many of these demonstrations. Instead, Cohalan chose to focus on other means to enhance the standing of the Irish community in the United States and his involvement as fundraiser for the American branch of the Gaelic League will be explored in this context. Úna Ní Bhroiméil, in her work *Building Irish Identity in America, 1890–1915: The Gaelic revival* (2003), describes how Cohalan saw the work of the Gaelic League as more than just reviving the Irish language and Gaelic games. The nurturing of an Irish-American understanding of Irish culture and traditions could help awaken a sense of ethnic pride among the Irish in America and also combat what he perceived as Anglo-Saxon prejudice.[45] In a speech to the Harlem Gaelic Society in 1904, he argued that the goals of the league should focus on banishing 'such monstrosities as the stage Irishman' and correcting the 'falsifying of American history'.[46] Kibler too notes how the Gaelic League 'celebrated Celtic traits, Irish manhood and the Celtic contribution to America as a means to de-Anglicize American culture'.[47]

Cohalan, like other prominent Irish-Americans, was especially sensitive to allegations that the Irish were not fully loyal to the American nation. As part of his mission to correct, as he saw it, the falsification of American history, Cohalan took an active role in the American Irish Historical Society. While the AIHS never exceeded 2,000 members nationwide, its membership was influential and included prominent political figures such as Congressman Bourke Cockran and President Theodore Roosevelt Jr. The AIHS celebrated the Irish role in America's early foundation and history and challenged the then established view that England was the 'motherland of America'.[48] In this instance the contributions of all Irish, both Protestant and Catholic, were celebrated. Drawing on the work of the AIHS, he continually highlighted in his speeches and writings the heroic role of the Irish in defending the American nation.[49] This too would become an issue in his dealings with Irish nationalists in Ireland who tended to overlook this dimension to Irish-American nationalism.

In *Machine Made: Tammany Hall and the creation of modern American politics*, Terry Golway has described how the Irish-American Catholic response to White Anglo-Saxon Protestant (WASP) cultural dominance of American society also had a political dimension. Golway describes how Irish-Americans created ethnic institutions which sought to promote and defend the interests of the Irish Catholic community in the United States, and the actions of the Tammany system in New York can be viewed in this context. It not only dispensed benefits to the Irish and other immigrant groups but also served as a 'vehicle for expressing Irish resistance and grievances'.[50]

Cohalan directly benefited from the Tammany system and his beliefs often reflected traditional Tammany ethnic and religious defensiveness towards WASP America. In this regard, he often made common cause with other prominent Irish-Americans like Bourke Cockran and John Quinn, who did not share his adherence to revolutionary Irish nationalism.[51] Bourke Cockran served as a Democratic congressman for New York for a number of terms. He was also Grand Sachem of Tammany Hall and chief advisor of Boss Murphy until replaced by Cohalan in 1908. Unlike Cohalan, he supported John Redmond's efforts in Ireland to secure home rule. Likewise, fellow Irish-American lawyer John Quinn supported Redmond but worked with Cohalan in promoting Gaelic League activities in the United States and was for a time involved in Tammany politics.

Cohalan's preoccupation with American politics extended from the local to the global. As a loyal and patriotic American, he took a keen interest in the position of the United States in the international order. His speeches and writings contain many references to the international problems of the day. At the time of Cohalan's birth in 1865, the United States had just emerged from the terrible internecine conflict of the Civil War and was considered a rural backwater by the Great Powers of Europe. However, by the time of Cohalan's death in 1946, the United States dominated the world's stage and its dominant role looked set to continue. Ever-increasing social and political ties between the US and Britain marked the rise of American internationalism in the first half of the twentieth century.

As evidenced in his letters and speeches, Cohalan reacted negatively to these increasing Anglo-American ties as well as the massive transformation of American power in the twentieth century. Prior to the First World War, he campaigned against pre-war arbitration treaties aimed at improving relations between Britain and the US. His campaign for American neutrality in the war, his campaign against the League of Nations and later the World Court, and finally his campaign to preserve US neutrality in the Second World War can be seen as a consistent effort to prevent the US from becoming embroiled in what he termed 'Old World struggles' which he believed would only benefit the British Empire.

Cohalan opposed all forms of imperialism and believed that the United States should refrain from involvement in imperialist adventures abroad. As he explained in a pamphlet published in 1925 entitled *Democracy or Imperialism, which?*, 'if imperialism grows, it grows at the expense of freedom. If democracy grows, it grows at the expense of imperialism.'[52] Though a member of the Democratic Party, Cohalan accused the two most internationalist Democratic presidents of the twentieth century, Woodrow Wilson and Franklin D. Roosevelt, of abandoning traditional American isolationism towards European affairs. In his writings and speeches, Cohalan attributed such policies to the perceived pro-British leanings of these presidents and the work of individuals and groups such as the Carnegie Institute, who promoted greater links between Britain and the United States.

Cohalan felt that these growing ties between the US and Britain ran contrary to the intentions of the founding fathers of the United States whose determination to remain free of Britain represented true 'Americanism'. This was a dominant theme in his speeches and writings and appeared to have dominated his thinking from an early age. As he later pointed out, in 1916:

> From an early boyhood, I have been taught to believe that the only country whose enmity, the only country whose hostility, the only country whose wiles America need fear at all was the country from which Washington and the revolutionary heroes delivered it … I have as life has gone on, and as I have had an opportunity of forming opinions and convictions for myself, I have been convinced more and more from a study of American history, and from a study of English history, that that thing which was taught to me in early boyhood was the truth.[53]

Cohalan's attitude towards President Woodrow Wilson can also be examined in the context of his fears about increasing British influence in shaping American foreign policy. Cohalan, like Devoy, believed that the president's decision to enter the First World War and his later ambition to create a League of Nations were motivated by Wilson's known Anglophile sympathies. These beliefs have been shared by some Anglophobe historians such as Charles Tansill. In his work *America and the Fight for Irish Freedom*, Tansill argues that: 'The very fact that Cohalan was anti-English was enough to damn him in Wilson's eyes.'[54] Meanwhile, Carl Wittke in *The Irish in America* has argued that, during the Wilson administration, a perception emerged that the president was 'at heart a Britisher masquerading in American colors'.[55]

As we have seen, strong cultural ties existed between Britain and the United States but this work will argue that Cohalan tended to overstate the impact of such ties on American foreign policy. Other more geopolitical factors drew both countries together in the first half of the twentieth century. In his work *The Great Rapprochement: England and the United States, 1895–1914*, Bradford Perkins has pointed to an alignment of diplomatic, political, military and economic interests between the United States and Britain in the years before the outbreak of the First World War.[56] As Britain faced a resurgent Germany, closer ties to the US allowed it to focus more closely on its vital European continental interests. Britain's decision to withdraw its naval squadron from the Caribbean in 1903 so as to bolster its own naval power in Europe illustrates this shift in its foreign policy. This played perfectly into America's own expansionary inclinations in the western hemisphere. Following America's defeat of Spain in the Spanish–American War of 1898, the US gained temporary control of Cuba and acquired Puerto Rico and the Philippines as well as other Spanish possessions. Britain adopted a position of benevolent neutrality towards these acquisitions.[57]

Adopting a similar approach, Robert Hannigan, in a more recent work entitled *The Great War and American Foreign Policy*, has argued that President Woodrow Wilson's actions, as distinct from his rhetoric, represented a continuation of a benevolent policy towards Britain pursued by the three previous American administrations of William McKinley, Theodore Roosevelt and William Howard Taft. According to Hannigan, while the 'distinctive qualities and style' of each administration differed, all agreed with the 'essential elements' of the existing British-centred international order and looked forward to an eventual US domination of Latin America and China and the peaceful displacement of Britain as the leading world power. All three previous administrations had pursued treaties of arbitration with Britain in order to settle outstanding disputes peacefully. In keeping with this broad policy, Hannigan argues that Wilson favoured Britain during the period of American neutrality and that his reluctant decision to enter the war was designed to safeguard American interests against German domination of Europe. Hannigan also argues that Wilson's plan for a League of Nations after the war, in co-operation with Britain, can be seen in the context of a continuation of his desire to stabilise the international order in the interests of the United States.[58]

John Milton Cooper in his work *Breaking the Heart of the World: Woodrow Wilson and the fight for the League of Nations* has placed greater emphasis on Wilson's internationalism and his goal of building post-war global institutions to safeguard peace and international stability. Cooper argues that Wilson believed that these institutions would evolve over time and would involve the active commitment of the United States and other states to preserving peace. This would suggest that Wilson's 'internationalism' represented a departure from the more isolationist policies of his predecessors.[59]

Irrespective of whether Wilson was motivated by realpolitik considerations or by a genuine internationalism, it is clear that he saw Britain's co-operation as vital to his overall mission of constructing a League of Nations and creating a stable post-war international order. This policy was motivated by American interests rather than British, and did not mean that Wilson was anti-Irish or anti-Catholic. Bernadette Whelan in *United States Foreign Policy and Ireland* has pointed out that Wilson had long been sympathetic to Irish national demands. He admired British Prime Minister William Gladstone's attempts to settle the Irish question in the 1880s and also supported Prime Minister Herbert Asquith's efforts to introduce home rule in 1912.[60] Wilson encouraged Britain to reach a satisfactory settlement to the Irish question but he had no intention of forcibly applying his much-vaunted principles of self-determination to Ireland for fear of jeopardising Anglo-American relations. As a Democratic president, he also included a number of Irish-Americans in his administration, such as his private secretary Joseph Tumulty. Bainbridge Colby, who was also sympathetic to Irish nationalism, served as secretary of state during the last year of Wilson's administration. This more complicated analysis of Wilson's motivations would challenge Cohalan's belief that the president's Scots-Irish heritage and known Anglophile sympathies shaped American policy. Nevertheless, these beliefs often featured in Cohalan's speeches and publications and were also shared by many Irish-American nationalists at this time.

Cohalan's deeply felt American patriotism was advantageous to Irish nationalists. A patriotic American of Cohalan's stature, with links to local and national US politics, and at the head of a 275,000-strong Irish-American lobby group, stood a much better chance of mobilising American support for the Irish cause than some *arriviste* Irish political exile unfamiliar with the workings of American institutions. Yet Cohalan's very Americanism caused difficulties. His attachment to American isolationist principles and his determination to uphold what he perceived as the vital interests of the Irish-American ethnic group sometimes clashed with the objectives of Irish nationalists, who were naturally more preoccupied with the struggle to establish an independent Irish state.

In explaining such disputes, this biography will emphasise how Cohalan, like many other prominent Irish-American nationalists, was motivated by a deeply felt American patriotism and a genuine desire to protect the United States from foreign intrigue.[61] There is evidence to suggest that even de Valera recognised this. In a February 1920 letter to Arthur Griffith, then acting leader of the Irish cabinet in Dublin, and contained in *Documents on Irish Foreign Policy*, vol 1, 1919–22, de Valera acknowledged that: 'Fundamentally Irish-Americans differ from us in this – they being Americans first would sacrifice Irish interests if need be to American interests – we, Irish first, would do the reverse.'[62] Yet instead of trying to accommodate these differences, de Valera, with the full backing of Dublin, robustly attempted to assert Irish control over Cohalan and his FOIF movement. This policy tended to exacerbate existing divisions and finally led to an open breach between Cohalan and de Valera in November 1920.

The legacy of this Cohalan–de Valera dispute, which took place at the height of the Anglo-Irish war, has very much defined Cohalan's reputation, at least in Ireland. As we shall see in later chapters, many Irish nationalists in the United States and later historians and commentators viewed Cohalan's opposition to de Valera's strategy and tactics as 'obstructionism' and believed his actions were driven by personal jealousy and political ambition. However, at least one historian has noted how the American dimension to Cohalan's Irish nationalism was the ultimate source of the 'problem' with him. In 1957, the eminent Irish historian F.S.L. Lyons, in a review article on Tansill's *America and the Fight for Irish Freedom*, noted the 'dual allegiance' felt by many Irish-Americans who supported the Irish cause in the US. Referring to the split in 1920 within Irish-America, Lyons commented perceptively on Cohalan's angry protestations to de Valera that his 'only allegiance is to America', arguing that:

> Perhaps it is not altogether fanciful to discern in these phrases something of the tragedy of the exile. However nostalgically he may look back to the mother-country, however generously he may respond to her needs, he cannot help from forming fresh attachments and striking deep roots in a new soil.[63]

Daniel Cohalan deserves more attention than his much-publicised conflict with de Valera. His papers in the American Irish Historical Society in New York testify to a political career that spanned several decades. These papers have some inevitable gaps. They do not include his known contacts with German officials in the United States prior to the 1916 Rising. They are also quite sparse with regard to his involvement in Tammany politics. As this book will explore, Cohalan was involved in a number of political scandals, and fears of investigation by federal or state authorities may explain the absence of such records. Nevertheless, his papers at the AIHS and other archives in the United States, Germany, Ireland and Britain provide more than sufficient evidence for a critical assessment of the broader trajectory of his political life that goes far beyond his dispute with de Valera.

There is no doubt that while Daniel Cohalan devoted much of his time and energy to the Irish nationalist cause, he also struck deep roots in America's soil. From one perspective, Cohalan may be seen as part of a long line of Irish-American nationalist leaders ostensibly dedicated to supporting the Irish nationalist cause. From another, one can see Cohalan as an Irish-American leader dedicated to furthering the interests of the Irish 'race' in a then Anglo-Saxon America and patriotically defending the interests of the United States as he saw them. These goals were not always compatible with Irish interests and a study of Cohalan's life offers a vehicle with which to explore how these competing objectives shaped Irish-American nationalism in the first decades of the twentieth century.

1

The Making of an American-Irish Nationalist, 1865–1903

DANIEL FLORENCE COHALAN was born in Middletown, upstate New York, in December 1865 and died on 12 November 1946. If he had not involved himself in Irish nationalism, he would still be remembered today as a prominent jurist and as an influential figure in New York and US national politics. Yet Cohalan pursued strongly held Irish nationalist objectives and, with characteristic energy, devoted much of his life to activities which sought to translate such objectives into reality. This chapter will explore how an Irish family heritage steeped in the tradition of physical force nationalism imbued Cohalan with a strong degree of nationalist fervour. It will also explore how the position of the Irish in the United States, American social and political developments and international factors also shaped his sense of nationalism, a brand of American-Irish nationalism shared by many Irish-Americans of his day.

A key influence in Cohalan's nationalist zeal lay in his close family connection with Ireland, especially County Cork. His grandfather, John Cohalan, owned a farm in the coastal area of Courtmacsherry and left Ireland at the height of the Great Famine in 1848. According to a 1967 interview with Daniel Cohalan's son Monsignor Florence Cohalan, Daniel's grandfather left the southern port of Cobh (then Queenstown) the 'father of four motherless children: three young daughters and a twelve-year-old son'.[1] This boy, Timothy, would later become Daniel Cohalan's father.

The Skibbereen area in west Cork was particularly badly hit by the Famine. In the 1841 census the population of the Poor Law Union of Skibbereen numbered 43,266. Approximately 17 per cent of the

Daniel Cohalan's grandfather, John P. Cohalan (1788–1872).
Born Courtmacsherry, County Cork, Ireland. Died Middletown, New York.
(Source: Cohalan family records: Peter Fox Cohalan, Sayville, New York)

population, a total of 7,332 people, died in the period September 1846 to September 1847.[2] Many of those who died came from the lower social ranks of Irish society and included small farmers and landless labourers. Compared to the many who died or emigrated to England or Scotland, the Cohalan family must have had some means, since only those with significant resources for the journey could have afforded to emigrate to the United States.[3] Cormac Ó Gráda, in his discussion of the demography of the Famine, noted that already by February 1847 'in the Skibbereen area the larger farmers were saving up the proceeds of selling corn' and planning to emigrate to America at the first opportunity. The Cohalan family appear to have been part of this group of relatively prosperous farmers and this is confirmed by Peter Fox Cohalan, a descendant of Daniel Cohalan who has done much research on the Cohalan family history.[4]

While the Famine may not have had a direct impact on the family, it nevertheless became part of Cohalan family folklore. The *Gaelic American*'s obituary of Daniel's father, Timothy Eugene Cohalan, noted that he was old enough to remember the horrors of the Famine, which he blamed on British policy in Ireland. These beliefs had some justification. The British Conservative government of Sir Robert Peel had provided considerable aid initially, but, as the Famine wore on, the Liberal government of Lord John Russell, who took office in June 1846, was much less ideologically inclined to continue these aid efforts.[5] In late 1846, the local *Cork Examiner* newspaper commented negatively on the ideological free market mindset of the British Liberal government which determined its response to the crisis: 'Political economy has slain enough of victims; it has raised hecatomb upon hecatomb of fathers, mothers, children, to its cruel, bloody policy …'[6] The lack of an effective British aid effort during the Famine crisis generated much criticism in Ireland and would fuel Irish nationalist sentiment both in Ireland and among the Irish diaspora abroad.

Irish nationalist politician T.P. O'Connor, when meeting those Irish in the United States in the 1880s who had experienced or witnessed Famine evictions, commented that: 'It was these clearances and the sight of wholesale starvation and plague, far more than racial feelings, that produced the hatred of English government which strikes impartial Americans as something like frenzy.'[7] However, as O'Connor explained, this hatred of Britain was directed more at the workings of the British Empire rather than a hatred towards the British people. Daniel Cohalan upheld this view in his later writings and speeches. In a 1919 pamphlet, appropriately entitled *The Indictment*, he argued that the British government was responsible for the Famine and, having 'systematically broken down every effort made to develop its industries', had used Ireland as 'a great dairy farm' for its own economic interests.[8]

The immigrant Cohalan family formed part of the great Irish exodus to the United States in the nineteenth century. Out of a population of approximately eight and a half million in 1840, Donnelly estimates that

1.2 million left Ireland between 1845 and 1855 and about 900,000 in the next five years. Emigration continued in the following decades. In 1900 the US census indicated that 4,826,904 Americans were either Irish-born or had Irish parents.[9] This almost equalled the population of Ireland at this time.

The Cohalan family first settled briefly at Pierrepont in upstate New York but within a few months had moved on to Middletown, Orange County, then a growing town lying in New York's Hudson Valley region. Industrialisation was getting under way in the American north-east at this time and the Cohalans benefited from the resulting economic expansion. The US Federal Census of 1860 indicates that John Cohalan, now sixty-five, had not remarried and had established himself as a grocer. Meanwhile, like countless other Irish migrants to America, his son Timothy, now aged twenty-two, had entered the construction trade. In the same census he is listed as a 'master mason', a skilled occupation which enabled him to secure continuous employment in the thriving economy of Orange County. Later newspaper reports indicate that he went on to establish a successful glass business.[10]

Despite increasing prosperity, the Cohalans retained a strongly nationalist Irish identity. Indeed, the family's links with Irish and even American nationalism long predated their arrival in America. John Cohalan's wife Catherine MacCarthy, Daniel's grandmother, had died before the family had left Ireland in 1848, but her father, Captain Eugene MacCarthy, had been a soldier of fortune who had served as an aide-de-camp to the Marquis de Lafayette during the American Revolution, after which he returned to his native Cork.[11] This memory became a source of comfort to Daniel Cohalan, who prided himself on his loyalty to both Ireland and the United States. In an introduction to Cohalan's work *The Indictment* (1919), James McGurrin, president-general of the American Irish Historical Society, described Cohalan as an 'American of Irish blood whose family history goes back to the battlefields of the revolution'.[12]

According to Timothy Cohalan's obituary in the *Gaelic American*, another Eugene MacCarthy, an uncle on his mother's side, had taken part in the Young Ireland Rebellion of 1848. This rebellion had taken place during the Famine but attracted little support due to the demoralised condition of the peasantry at that time. The best-known battle took place at Ballingarry, County Tipperary, in 1848 where an ill-armed party of rebels attempted to storm a police barracks. The rebels were beaten back, and according to the *Gaelic American*, Eugene MacCarthy had a 'thumb shot off' in the ensuing firefight with police.[13]

Given this colourful Irish nationalist heritage, it is perhaps unsurprising to find that Timothy Cohalan became involved in the American Fenians in the 1860s. This movement devoted itself to the achievement of an Irish republic by 'physical force means'. Reflecting the importance of the Irish diaspora to Irish-American nationalism, the Fenian movement was founded in Ireland in 1858 as the Irish Republican Brotherhood and then in New York in 1859. The term Fenianism was henceforth used to describe Irish republican nationalism on both sides of the Atlantic, though the movement in Ireland retained its official title of the IRB.[14]

In Ireland the IRB staged the so-called Fenian Rising in 1867. Though relatively easily suppressed by the British authorities, the rising again symbolised the importance of the Irish diaspora in America as a support base for radical nationalism at home. Some Irish veterans from the American Civil War took part in this rising and unsuccessfully attempted to land American arms. Meanwhile, the so-called senate wing of the Fenian movement in the US, drawing on the Civil War experience of many of its members, launched ill-fated invasions of British Canada in 1866 and 1870.[15] Timothy Cohalan did not participate in these invasions, though, according to the *Gaelic American*, he became for a time a trusted advisor to Fenian leader John O'Mahony and helped fund the *Irish People* newspaper, then the main organ of the American Fenians. In a later report, the *Gaelic American* commented that Timothy formed part of the guard of honour at O'Mahony's funeral in 1877.[16]

Further evidence of Timothy's involvement with the Fenians and in American politics is provided in an obituary on his son Michael J. Cohalan (Daniel's brother) which appeared in *The Journal of the American Irish Historical Society* in 1926. According to this report, Timothy entertained well-known Irish nationalists in his home in Middletown. These included the famous Union general Thomas Francis Meagher, who for a time led the Irish Brigade during the American Civil War. Interestingly, this article also indicated that Timothy Cohalan preferred to work with the Republican Party on behalf of the Irish nationalist cause, unlike most other Irish nationalists, who favoured the Democratic Party. Timothy was particularly impressed by former Republican governor Oliver P. Morton of Indiana who in 1867, as chairman of the Foreign Relations Committee of the Senate, told him that 'the influence of voters of Irish birth or

Daniel Cohalan's father, Timothy E. Cohalan (1835–1909). Born Courtmacsherry, County Cork, Ireland. Died New York City, New York. (Source: Cohalan family records: Peter Fox Cohalan, Sayville, New York)

descent was limited by the fact of their being all, or nearly all affiliated with, one of the political parties [Democratic Party] in the United States'. Significantly, the article pointed out that Timothy continually sought to impress this perspective on others. As we shall see in later chapters, Daniel frequently formed close political relationships with prominent members of the Republican Party and seemed closer ideologically to that party's values in his final years.[17]

With the failure of the invasions of Canada and of the 1867 rising in Ireland, the Fenian movement in the United States became plagued with factionalism. In its place a new secret revolutionary organisation known as

Clan na Gael emerged after 1867 and later established formal links with the IRB in Ireland. The Clan represented the same revolutionary principles of Fenianism but aimed to create a more disciplined organisation that would better serve the Irish republican cause in the United States. Compared to the Fenians, the Clan had the advantage of having a more forceful and dynamic leader, John Devoy. Earlier, Devoy had been arrested by the British authorities in Ireland in 1865 for attempting to enlist Irish soldiers from the British army into the movement. After his release in a general amnesty for Fenian prisoners in 1871, he then made his way to the United States. For the next seventy years, Devoy became the dominant voice of Irish revolutionary nationalism in the United States and an implacable enemy of the British Empire, forever plotting its downfall.[18] Operating in a relatively free American environment, the Clan supported the IRB with financial and material support. As Devoy pointed out in his memoirs, the revolutionary movement 'was maintained almost entirely by moral and material support from the Clan na Gael'.[19]

Many Irish-American nationalists such as Timothy Cohalan, disillusioned with the divisions within Fenianism, transferred their allegiance to the Clan, but the Irish republican objectives and revolutionary principles of both organisations overlapped. In its 1909 obituary of Timothy Cohalan, the *Gaelic American* noted that he 'never wavered in his allegiance to the principles of Fenianism and died a member of the New York Napper Tandy Club of Clan na Gael which he joined soon after its foundation in 1867'.[20]

Timothy Cohalan devoted much of his time and energy to the cause of Irish republicanism, but as with all Irish emigrants in the United States, he needed to build a new life in an unfamiliar and often inhospitable environment. Not unusually, Timothy sought solace among other Irish immigrants from his own native county of Cork. In 1861 he married Ellen O'Leary, his second cousin, from Lislevane, near his own Cork birthplace. Ellen, who was born in 1842, had come to the United States as an orphan in 1853. She lived for a time with her uncle, the Rev. John McCarthy of Greenpoint, Long Island, who established the first Catholic parish in Suffolk County.[21] This would suggest that Ellen was part of the first wave of Catholic Irish immigration to this part of New York State. Ellen's marriage to Timothy proved to be a happy one but, in the conditions of the day, child mortality was high and the couple's first two children did not survive infancy. However, their third child, Daniel, born on 21 December 1865, proved to be a healthy and robust child, the first of a large family of five sons and two daughters.[22]

Such marriages among Irish migrants from the same Irish locality were not uncommon. Since both parents came from the same Irish-speaking area in Cork, Irish was spoken freely in their house and Daniel Cohalan is reputed to have been fluent.[23] Such an environment undoubtedly infused the young Daniel with a love of Cork and its customs and this may later on have made him receptive to the ideas of the Irish cultural revival of the early twentieth century. According to Daniel's daughter Aileen, her father had a strong singing voice 'and was especially fond of Irish and Scottish folk songs and dances'.[24]

Cohalan's family were part of a great Irish exodus – itself part of a wider nineteenth-century movement of different peoples from Europe – to an America still largely Protestant and Anglo-Saxon. In a sense, one can see the Irish settlement in America as part of a broader white racial expansion of European peoples into different parts of the globe. However, there were differences in how such European immigrants adapted and were integrated into American life. Despite being recognised as legally white, Irish Catholic immigrants often faced discrimination and hostility.[25] In contrast, as William van Vugt points out, British Protestant migrants were, by and large, viewed as 'invisible immigrants in the sense that they had a comparatively rapid assimilation and were not seen as true foreigners'.[26] The fortunes of the Irish in America were therefore dependent to a great degree on the cultural character of the American host culture. Fully aware of this, Irish-Americans formed associations to protect and advance their own interests, and as we shall see, many of Daniel Cohalan's political objectives in life would be inextricably bound up with Irish-American efforts to gain recognition for the Irish contribution to the building of the American nation.

The Cohalan family formed part of a very small Catholic community in the largely Protestant Middletown. According to his obituary, Timothy became the life of the Catholic congregation and through his efforts a priest was finally assigned to the parish. In its obituary of Timothy Cohalan, the *New York Times* claimed that the first mass celebrated in Middletown Orange County was hosted in the Cohalan household.[27] But the minority status of Catholicism within the United States had its darker side. The Cork newspaper the *Southern Star* points out that in the 1850s, when the anti-Catholic Know Nothing movement became popular in some parts of the US, 'men like Cohalan had to gather together to defend their churches, their clergy, their families and their lives from the savagery of sectarian and race bigotry'.[28]

Hostility towards Catholics diminished following the American Civil War, but growing up in Middletown, Daniel would have been aware of the minority status of Irish Catholics in a sea of white Anglo-Saxon Protestants. His family background, and the position of Irish Catholics in American society generally, influenced his later efforts to broaden the scope of American identity to encompass those of an Irish Catholic background and, as he later explained in a press interview, to 'put to an end the claim that England, or any other single country, is the motherland of America'.[29] Throughout his life, Cohalan became involved in a host of Catholic societies and organisations and had close links with leading Catholic figures in the United States.

So far, the story of the Cohalans typified the experience of many thousands of other Irish families who left Ireland during the Famine and post-Famine period. The improvement in the family's status reflected the gradual improvement of living standards for many Irish-Americans in the post-Civil War era. Timothy succeeded in building up a successful glass business in Middletown and the family prospered as a result.[30] This prosperity enabled Daniel and his four brothers to attend the local Wallkill Free Academy, where the young Daniel proved to be an exceptional scholar, gaining a good grounding in the classics which was to serve him well in his later legal studies.[31]

Cohalan, along with his brothers, attended Manhattan College in New York and all five later entered the legal profession, thus highlighting the enhanced social standing of the family at this time. The choice of college was not surprising for prosperous Catholics such as the Cohalans. Irish-American historian Terry Golway argues that in the then Protestant-dominated American culture, Catholic Irish-Americans founded a 'parallel society' of schools, churches and benevolent institutions. Manhattan College was one of many such Catholic institutions which enabled Irish-American upward social mobility.[32] Cohalan appears to have excelled in his studies. According to a later *New York Times* article, he earned a reputation as a capable baseball player with the college team. The report mentions that his team defeated Yale and even contested a game with the New York Giants.[33] Yet despite his acknowledged skills in baseball, a steady career in law held more of an attraction. In 1885

Cohalan graduated from college and in 1888 he was admitted to the New York Bar.[34]

In the late 1880s, the entire family moved to New York, the definitive American metropolis, which, unlike Middletown, offered a choice of professional opportunities for Daniel and his brothers.[35] According to Kerby Miller, of the city's 1.5 million inhabitants in 1890, over a third were either Irish or second-generation Irish.[36] In the parallel society which Golway describes, many such residents were more likely to turn to an Irish lawyer for assistance than a lawyer of another nationality.

After briefly working for an established law firm, Cohalan set up his own practice opposite City Hall. According to a later newspaper report, he 'went after the big cases and swiftly built up a large practice'.[37] This legal background enhanced Cohalan's oratorical skills, which would become vital in later years. His privileged background also infused Cohalan with a tremendous pride in the workings of the American political and legal systems. While he inherited his father's Irish republicanism, he believed that a free Ireland shaped particularly by American commercial principles would bring prosperity to its people once, as he saw it, the dead hand of British control had been removed.[38]

New York became Cohalan's home for the rest of his life, where his qualifications and talents defined a future far removed from the rural life of his grandfather in Courtmacsherry. Indeed, Cohalan formed part of a growing 'lace curtain' middle-class Irish community which was generally conservative on social issues.[39] Nevertheless, he still retained a visceral attachment to his Irish heritage and a particular affinity for Cork and its people. He reinforced this connection to his ancestral county through his marriage to Hanna O'Leary in 1899.

Hanna was a niece of Monsignor John O'Leary of Clonakilty in west Cork and a second cousin on Daniel's mother's side. According to the memoirs of Aileen Cohalan, Hanna had been visiting New York in 1898 when the couple met. Daniel proposed just 'two weeks after her arrival' at the entrance to New York's Central Park. Reflecting his close attachment to County Cork, the couple later married in St Peter and Paul's Church in Cork city and had their honeymoon in Glengarriff in the west of the county. After their return to New York, the couple bought a large house on the Upper East Side of Manhattan located at 23 East 94th Street.[40]

Hanna O'Leary exemplified the expansion in female education that had taken place in Ireland in the late nineteenth century.[41] Educated emigrants like Hanna were fully prepared for the challenges that adapting to American society would bring. She had been educated at the Sacred Heart Convent in Killarney and Aileen considered her the intellectual equal of Daniel. Aileen also describes how Hanna expertly managed lavish dinner parties at the Cohalan's East Side residence in New York to which the city's elite were invited.[42]

Hanna also had impeccable nationalist credentials. Her uncle the monsignor, unlike most of his clerical colleagues, remained a strong supporter of Charles Stewart Parnell after the Parnellite split.[43] He also served as chairman of the board of the *Southern Star* for many years, a newspaper which often included accounts of Cohalan's frequent visits to County Cork.[44] Thus through marriage, Cohalan's links with the county of his parents were reinforced. The pair went on to have seven children. Reflecting the family's Catholic ethos, their son Florence became a monsignor, Patrick became a Jesuit priest, while daughter Aileen entered the Society of the Sacred Heart of Jesus convent at Kenwood, Albany, in upstate New York.[45] Other sons Dan Junior and Conn (Cornelius) maintained the links to the legal profession and became attorneys. The family also actively supported the American Irish Historical Society, devoted to the research and study of the Irish contribution to American history. Monsignor Florence Cohalan led the society for over fifty years while Cohalan's other daughter, Kathleen O'Leary, served as the society's librarian.

In 1909 the family bought a summer home in Ireland, which again helped to solidify their connections to County Cork. The house, located in Glandore in the west of the county, was not far from the townland where his grandfather and father were born and had been occupied by a local notable, Dean Reeves of the Church of Ireland. Situated on a hill overlooking Glandore Harbour, the house provided spectacular views of the beautiful scenery of west Cork. In her memoirs, Cohalan's oldest daughter Aileen recalls that ordinarily the family spent the summer in Glandore and this is also borne out by evidence from ships' passenger lists.[46] Cohalan built a golf course and tennis courts on the estate and Aileen recalls idyllic summers spent playing tennis and handball and horseback riding in the surrounding countryside and learning Irish from 'Mr Donohue', the headmaster of the Glandore national school.[47]

According to local Glandore historian Fachtna Hickey, Cohalan was well known for his support for the Irish language movement in the area.

The archives of the *Southern Star* contain a photograph of Judge Cohalan and his family at the opening of the Irish language summer school Coláiste Chairbre in Glandore in 1910. According to James Coombes' work *Utopia in Glandore* (1970), the area became one of the leading centres of Gaelic culture in the south following the establishment of Coláiste Chairbre and Glandore attracted many 'illustrious visitors' including Patrick Pearse and Gaelic League leader Douglas Hyde.[48] As we shall see, the presence of Cohalan in the area also provided a motivation for these visits.

Aileen also recounts the family visiting cousins and aunts in the area. During these visits, which continued until the mid-1930s, Daniel Cohalan maintained friendly relations with his cousin and namesake Bishop Daniel Cohalan of Cork and Hanna's uncle Monsignor John O'Leary.[49] Father Daniel Cohalan became auxiliary bishop of Cork in May 1914 and following the death of Bishop Thomas O'Callaghan he served as the diocesan bishop of Cork from August 1916 until his death in August 1952. Aileen records in her memoirs how Bishop Cohalan 'often came down for tea and stayed with us sometimes to say mass in the parlor'. Cohalan appears to have kept up these ties with his cousin throughout his life, as evidenced in his family correspondence in the AIHS. The *Southern Star* centenary edition, produced in 1989, contains a photograph of Cohalan with his uncle Bishop Cohalan in the grounds of Glandore House in the 1930s.[50]

Given Monsignor O'Leary's close connections to the *Southern Star*, the paper is a useful source on Cohalan's popularity in west Cork during his long summer breaks from the US. In September 1912, in an article headed 'Departure of Judge Cohalan', the *Star* reported how a large number of local dignitaries accompanied Cohalan to Queenstown before he set sail for New York:

> The Judge was accompanied to Queenstown by many friends, who saw him off, including Sir James Long, Mr. F. J. Healy, BL, Mr. J M Burke BL, … Mr. H. K. Cruikshank, US Consul, Queenstown … On leaving here he got a cordial send-off from his friends while prominent Americans aboard expressed the pleasure they felt at having him as a fellow passenger.'[51]

Given his close links to Ireland and growing up in a deeply nationalist household, Cohalan was naturally drawn to Irish political separatism. Not long after his arrival in New York as a young student, Cohalan followed his father into the Napper Tandy Club of the Clan na Gael. According to an account by Diarmuid Lynch, later a member of the IRB and a participant in the 1916 Rising, Captain James Murphy, who had been behind the Fenian bombing of Clerkenwell jail in London in 1867, swore Cohalan into the Clan. This bombing had attempted to free a Fenian prisoner, Richard Burke, but the attempt failed and twenty people died in the resulting explosion.[52]

Cohalan identified with the 'physical force' nationalist tradition of the Clan. Even though he later became a New York State Supreme Court Justice and upheld the law of the United States, he did not believe that British rule in Ireland or throughout its empire was legitimate. The Clan contained many such men of high social standing, including several judges, who believed that revolutionary methods were justified against the British Empire, either in Ireland or in any of the British colonies. Justice John Goff (1848–1924), a close colleague of Cohalan on the New York Supreme Court bench, had been involved with Devoy in the rescue by ship of six Fenian prisoners from Australia in 1875. This rescue had done much to enhance the reputation of John Devoy and the Clan among Irish-Americans.[53]

Despite such favourable publicity, the Clan, like the Fenians, was frequently riven by factionalism. In the 1880s, Devoy had opposed the bombing of British cities carried out by the Chicago wing of the Clan led by Alexander Sullivan, though this was more for tactical than moralistic reasons.[54] This and other differences with Sullivan led to deep divisions within the Clan. Eventually, after Sullivan's death, Devoy helped to forge a reunification among all the divergent Clan factions at a convention in Atlantic City in July 1900.[55] In this task of reconciliation, the powerful Clan leader in Philadelphia Joseph McGarrity played a key role. However, Devoy also called upon Daniel Cohalan to help in this process.

Cohalan's debating skills were honed in many courtrooms, his commitment to physical force nationalism, and his powerful personality provided ideal attributes for the difficult task of bringing the Clan together. As part of the reunification process, both factions of the Clan agreed upon a clear directive which restated that Irish independence would be achieved by 'physical force alone'. The Clan later distributed this statement of policy to all members in a circular of October 1900. According to Brown, Cohalan helped to draft this document and its legalistic language would certainly indicate this. The circular also recalled the 'great Convention of last July' where 'every expression on the subject was that our men should not touch any other than the revolutionary movement and that our policy should be one of physical force alone'. It stated that the convention had adopted a 'Declaration of Principles' and included extracts from this 'Declaration' in quotation marks:

> The object of the Organization is 'the complete independence of the Irish people and the establishment of an Irish Republic', and to accomplish that, to unite 'all men of our race in all lands who believe in the principles of Wolfe Tone and Emmet'.[56]

The circular also contained a 'pledge' which had been agreed at the convention. Reflecting Cohalan's anti-imperialist ideology, the pledge linked the cause of Irish freedom to that of other struggling nationalities within the British Empire. 'We pledge ourselves to the principle that physical force is the only engine a revolutionary organization can consistently and successfully use to realize the hopes of lovers of freedom in lands subject to the bonds of oppression.'[57]

Cohalan's organisational talents within the Clan soon became well known. Although not a member of its executive, he exercised considerable influence on its policies through his close association with Devoy. According to a later account by a prominent member of the executive, James Reidy, the Clan executive consulted Cohalan 'when important decisions had to be made'.[58] The strong-willed Devoy knew his own mind but he was nevertheless willing to take advice from Cohalan, especially on American and international issues. Judging from the correspondence between the two men, it is clear that Devoy often sought such advice.[59]

By 1900, Cohalan had become district officer for the Clan in the New York area and presided over the Clan's biennial conventions as chairman from 1902 to 1910.[60] Tom Clarke, who had served a long prison sentence in Britain for his role in the Fenian bombing campaign there, also commented on Cohalan's organising talents. Clarke had joined the Clan in New York in 1900. In a letter to a member of the IRB in Ireland, Major John McBride, he expressed his admiration for Cohalan's work: 'Things are now humming in the district. Not a jar [out of place] and physical force alone is the word that gets stronger day by day. Cohalan is doing magnificent work. He won't stand for any nonsense.'[61]

Cohalan was also involved in numerous other organisations, which no doubt increased his value as a fundraiser for the Clan. Such involvement included his presidency of the Manhattan College Alumni Association and he also served on the board of directors of the Irish-American Athletic Club (IAAC), which ran Celtic Park sports ground in New York. It is likely that some of the funds collected at Celtic Park made their way into the coffers of the Clan na Gael. In his biographical sketch of Cohalan for the AOH publication the *National Hibernian Digest*, Sheanan, commenting on Cohalan's dynamism and commitment to the Clan, noted that he 'spent his nights attending and speaking at Irish meetings in the New York metropolitan area – sometimes he spoke at three or four meetings in one night – and by his eloquence, tireless energy and example brought many new and influential members into the various clubs'.[62]

Devoy also valued Cohalan's links with the corporate world. In 1913, at a time when Cohalan had fallen ill, Devoy wrote to Joseph McGarrity about the absence of wealthy men at a Clan reunion. Devoy lamented that 'none of the rich men were there and we will have to get after them. Cohalan's sickness was a bad blow to us as he was going to tackle a lot of the moneyed men.'[63]

In 1900, the now reunited Clan was estimated to possess over 40,000 members. However, this represented only a small fraction of the estimated 4.8 million Americans who were either Irish-born or had Irish parents.[64] Meanwhile, the majority of those Irish who did demonstrate an interest in Irish nationalism tended to favour constitutional home rule as the only practical solution to the Irish question. In Ireland, John Redmond (1856–1918), who now led the Irish Parliamentary Party in the British House of Commons, represented this policy. Redmond sought to achieve a limited measure of self-government, or 'home rule', after which Ireland would still remain within the empire and have no control over its foreign policy.

Redmond's Irish Party dominated the Irish political landscape outside of unionist Ulster and was virtually guaranteed victory in election contests prior to the First World War. Moreover, Redmond could also count on a majority of Irish-American nationalist opinion. A United Irish League of America (UILA), led by Michael Ryan, acted as an effective fundraising arm for Redmond in the United States. The main Irish-American newspaper, the *Irish World*, also wholeheartedly supported Redmond's constitutional approach and denigrated that of the Clan.[65]

Like Devoy, Cohalan despised Redmond's brand of constitutional nationalism, and as an accomplished public speaker effectively promoted the Clan's policy of using 'physical force' to attain Irish freedom. This is evident in Cohalan's speech at a 1903 Clan na Gael gathering at the Hoffman House in New York. The *New York Times* also covered the speech, which is an indication of Cohalan's growing stature as spokesman for radical Irish nationalism in the city. The Clan held this meeting to welcome the return of Chicago Clan leader John T. Keating to the United States after a visit to Ireland. Keating was then on the Clan executive. While in Ireland, Keating had participated in demonstrations against the visit of King Edward VII.[66] Highlighting the Clan's approach to the Irish question and linking it to the revolutionary strategy of the American Revolution, Cohalan stated 'that Ireland was sure to be free of England, and it would be by arms in the way that the United States had won its freedom'. In a strident attack on constitutional nationalism, Cohalan claimed that:

> The experience of seven centuries has taught us that England will never willingly give to Ireland the power to repair the wreck and havoc wrought by English rule, that if through stress of circumstances or to avert imminent national danger she should at any time concede a measure of home rule, she would follow her invariable precedent and break the compact at the first opportunity.[67]

While publicly Cohalan continued to denounce home rule, there was a real fear among the leadership of the Clan that its brand of revolutionary Irish nationalism was being overshadowed by constitutional nationalism. On a practical level, this meant defections by members of the Clan to the UILA. As the New York district organiser, Cohalan issued strident directives condemning attempts by the UILA to poach Clan members. One directive, signed by Cohalan and announcing a Clan meeting in Brevoort Hall, Manhattan, noted that:

> On the same evening an attempt will be made in another hall in New York to put the Irish people on record as favouring efforts to secure independence by talking in the British House of Commons, and to again put Ireland in the position of a beggar among the nations by sending the hat around for funds to support a Parliamentary Party.

> To show that you have no sympathy with such a movement and that you are a firm believer in the doctrine that Ireland's independence, like that of all other nations, can never be won except by physical force, we urge upon you the duty of attending the meeting in Brevoort Hall, where the doctrines of Wolfe Tone, Emmet and Fitzgerald will be taught and Irishmen urged to make themselves worthy of liberty by fighting for it.[68]

The emergence of an Irish cultural revival in the late nineteenth and early twentieth centuries offered the Clan an opportunity to counter the attractions of constitutional nationalism. This revival witnessed a renewed interest in the Irish language, literature and cultural activities such as the ancient Celtic games of hurling and football. While these objectives were not in themselves political, movements associated with the revival, such as the Gaelic League (1893) and the Gaelic Athletic Association (GAA), vehemently opposed the Anglicisation of Ireland and denounced the Irish Parliamentary Party as West-British. Many of those attracted to cultural nationalism later became involved in physical force nationalist movements such as the IRB and the revival was also increasingly popular in the United States.[69]

Diarmuid Lynch, who in 1908 joined the IRB and later fought in the 1916 Rising, first became prominent in Irish cultural activities in New York. Lynch had emigrated from Cork to the United States in 1896 and when the Gaelic League extended its activities to New York, Lynch became its branch president.[70] In a later work on the history of the IRB, he provided an insight into the thinking of the Clan on the cultural revival. According to Lynch, the Clan welcomed the Celtic revival, not due to any burning interest in the revival of the Irish language and Gaelic culture, which was then in decline in Ireland, but as a counterweight to the Irish Parliamentary Party. Referring to the then Clan leadership, which included Cohalan, Lynch argued that:

> They did not then appreciate the fact that the winning of political freedom would have to await a favourable opportunity and that if the 'opportune time' did not come in their day it could be availed of by a future generation. Whereas if the language (then dying) were allowed to disappear, it could not be restored even by a free Ireland.[71]

In an account on his first years in the United States, prior to his return to Ireland, Lynch has left us with a fascinating record of his early encounters with Daniel Cohalan where he tried to enlist Cohalan's support in reviving the Irish language. According to Lynch, Cohalan did not at first display any enthusiasm, even though, as we have seen, he was favourably disposed to the Irish language due to his family heritage.[72]

No doubt Lynch's west Cork origins helped him to cement an initial friendship. In his first encounter with Cohalan, Lynch admitted that he had 'pestered' Cohalan to provide a Clan guard of honour for the body of Irish author Fr Eugene O'Growney prior to the removal of his remains to Ireland by sea on the SS *Campania.* Father O'Growney (1863–99) had been based in Los Angeles and had written many texts on the teaching of Irish grammar.[73] Cohalan had at first slyly denied that he had any such influence in the Clan but to Lynch's surprise a guard of honour suddenly 'materialised' at the appointed time.[74]

In what Lynch later amusingly describes as 'missionary work' on behalf of the Gaelic League in America, he writes of how he converted Cohalan to the cause of Irish cultural nationalism. In 1903, Lynch gave a speech at the Greenpoint Gaelic Society in Brooklyn. Apparently, he knew that Cohalan would be there and, knowing his power and influence in Irish circles, had directed his speech with this in mind. As both men shared a cab on the way back from the meeting, and later over lunch at Cohalan's lawyers club, Lynch claims that he convinced Cohalan that such cultural work on behalf of the Irish language would 'instead of hindering the objective of the Clan, [be] essential to its achievement'.[75] As Lynch hoped, the dynamic Cohalan was not content to be an ordinary member and became chairman of the finance committee of the Gaelic League Fund in the United States. Along with fellow Irish-American lawyer John Quinn, Cohalan later played a key role in organising League President Douglas Hyde's successful tour of the United States in 1906.[76]

Cohalan's increasing interest in the Gaelic revival is also evident in his involvement, along with John Devoy, in the establishment of the *Gaelic American* newspaper in 1903.[77] Both men decided that the paper should be run as a publishing company, in which outsiders held stock. It is likely that Cohalan, with his legal background, played a key role in this decision. In the company's articles of incorporation, Cohalan is listed as president of the board of directors of the Gaelic American Publishing Company and his name also appears on the share certificates. A circular promoting the *Gaelic American* stressed that the paper would give special attention 'to the Gaelic revival, which is the surest sign of the resurgence of the old race and the old spirit of Ireland'. The inclusion of the word 'Gaelic' in the title of the newspaper, in ancient Celtic script, clearly indicates sympathy with the aims of this revival. The newspaper both championed Irish cultural events in its columns and endorsed fundraising efforts on behalf of the Gaelic League.[78]

There were of course other pressing political reasons for the establishment of a newspaper that would represent the voice of radical Irish republicanism in the United States. While many of the Clan's public meetings were covered in the mainstream press, it still had no media voice of its own. Devoy argued that the Clan needed 'a defender in the press, and a public voice to enunciate its principles'.[79] These principles consisted of not only supporting the Irish nationalist cause but also upholding what Devoy perceived as the interests of the Irish ethnic group in the United States and defending America's interests.

Devoy became the editor of the *Gaelic American*, a task which he relished given his earlier editorial experience on the *Irish Nation* newspaper, which had failed in the 1880s. In his own account of the establishment of the paper, Devoy claimed that he had wanted to call the new newspaper the *Irish Nation*. However, he admitted that he had been overruled by Cohalan, who favoured the title *Gaelic American*.[80] The fact that the usually obstinate Devoy backed down is an indication of his respect not only for Cohalan's counsel but also his growing interest in cultural nationalist issues.

Typically, Cohalan threw himself into the task of promoting the *Gaelic American*. As a district organiser, he was also behind the Clan's efforts to encourage Clan members and other prominent Irish-Americans to buy stock in the paper.[81] His business links and his contacts with wealthy middle-class Americans proved to be a great asset for the fledgling publishing company. At a Clan meeting in Rhode Island, where Cohalan appeared as principal speaker, Clan member John Gannon, who was also a wealthy businessman, reported to Devoy that Cohalan emphasised the power of the *Gaelic American* and the necessity of giving it their support. In subsequent correspondence with Devoy, Gannon made several donations to the newspaper, one amounting to over 2,000 dollars on 27 November 1905.[82] Cohalan's efforts in support of the *Gaelic American* undoubtedly helped to make it a commercial success. By 1907, it had achieved a circulation of 14,956 and by 1913 this had increased to 30,000. This was no small achievement, since its more long-established rival the *Irish World* had a circulation of 60,000 in 1912.[83]

Given that Cohalan had initially framed the name of the newspaper, it is important to spell out its objectives in more detail as an illustration of his Irish-American nationalist concerns. The full title thus read: *The Gaelic American: A journal devoted to the cause of Irish independence, Irish literature and the interests of the Irish race.*[84] In feature articles, which often appeared on its front page, the paper promoted the revolutionary tradition of earlier Irish republican movements, such as that of the United Irishmen and the Fenians.[85] Simultaneously, the paper took a highly critical view of Redmond's policy on home rule. From the *Gaelic American*'s point of view, home rule, even if it was secured, would mean continued Irish membership of the British Empire and British control over Ireland's economic and foreign policy. Following the Liberal Party's victory in the 1906 election the prospect of the British government introducing home rule in some form brightened. However, the *Gaelic American* remained sceptical and in 1909 declared:

> The Irish people have tired of parliamentary methods and the promises of the Irish party no longer gain credence. 'Hope deferred makes the heart sick' and the prophesies that Home Rule was coming, coming next year and when next year came it was coming the year after, have discredited the prophets. A critical people now argue that the kind of Home Rule that England may by some chance grant would not be worth the having.[86]

The focus of the newspaper on promoting the 'interests of the Irish race' also conformed to Cohalan's traditional defence of the Irish-American group in the United States. As discussed in Kibler's work *Censoring Racial Ridicule* (2015), the use of the word 'race' to describe the Irish in America in the first decades of the twentieth century was not unusual. Indeed, other white ethnic groups used the term 'race' to describe their own sense of ethnicity and the term was also used widely by so-called Anglo-Saxons, those of British heritage in the United States. A Clan circular written by Cohalan, promoting the *Gaelic American* and encouraging members to purchase stock in the company, is itself revealing of his fear that the Irish race in America would lose their own sense of identity in an Anglo-Saxon environment:

> We want to reach out to young men and women of Irish race who are fast falling away from Irish ideals. We want to reach the children of Irish-American families so that they may be taught that they belong to a race that was great in war, in literature, in art and in music before the barbarous Anglo-Saxons emerged from the primeval forests.[87]

In helping to found the *Gaelic American*, Cohalan saw its value not only as a means of instilling radical nationalist beliefs in its readers but also as a means to encourage Irish-Americans to take an interest in their 'literature', history and culture. Irish-American nationalists claimed to speak for twenty million Americans of Irish descent, yet they also recognised that comparatively few Irish-Americans took an interest in Irish affairs.[88] By encouraging and maintaining a distinct Irish-American identity, the Irish race could become a real force in American affairs.

Prior to his appointment to the State Supreme Court bench in 1911, Cohalan sold his stock in the company. However, Patrick McCartan, a member of the Irish nationalist organisation Sinn Féin, but with long associations to the Clan, noted in 1917 that Cohalan still worked closely with Devoy in determining the paper's 'editorial attitude'.[89] In this context, the general stance of the *Gaelic American* on US and international affairs in particular is itself a good indication of Cohalan's thinking on such issues. Many of the articles on US foreign relations and the threat posed by the British Empire have no listed author but their general focus is reflected in Cohalan's speeches elsewhere and it is likely that Cohalan would have influenced or certainly approved of their content. In subsequent controversies involving Cohalan, the *Gaelic American* always remained his staunch defender.[90]

Through an examination of Cohalan's early life, one can already see the different influences shaping his Irish nationalism, notably in the context of family heritage, his close association with the Clan na Gael in the United States, his rejection of constitutional nationalism and his growing interest in Irish cultural activities in the US. However, there was also an American dimension to this nationalism which was already apparent in Cohalan's circulars promoting the *Gaelic American*. Cohalan, motivated by a desire to see Irish-Americans fully accepted into American life, challenged what he perceived as a prevailing Anglo-Saxon dominance in American society. Cohalan, in the words of F.S.L. Lyons, struck 'deep roots in American society'. His immersion in US society and politics and in the politics of Irish-America would inevitably shape his approach to Irish nationalism, and it is to these American roots that we must now turn.

2

Defending the Irish Race in America, 1903–11

As already noted, Irish-Americans like Cohalan possessed a 'dual allegiance' to both the cause of Ireland and the United States. Benjamin Reid in his biography of Cohalan's friend John Quinn, *The Man from New York: John Quinn and his friends*, has noted that Cohalan, like other prominent Irish-Americans of the early twentieth century, such as Quinn himself, Bourke Cockran and Bainbridge Colby, were from an 'Americanized generation, a qualified Irishry'.[1] All shared an intense loyalty to American principles and institutions but were also willing to sacrifice much of their time and energy to further what they saw as the best interests of the 'old land'. Opinions among these men differed as to what these interests should be. Quinn, Cockran and Colby supported Redmond's objective of home rule for Ireland within the empire while Cohalan supported Devoy's vision of an Irish republic achieved by physical force means. Yet there is no doubting the genuine devotion of these men to Ireland. All were in their own way American-Irish nationalists and, while they differed on issues related to Ireland, they often co-operated in defending what they perceived as the interests of the Irish 'race' in America.

Of course, not all Irish-Americans displayed such an interest in Ireland's welfare. In 1931, Forrest Davis, the staff writer of the *New York World-Telegram*, pointed out that for many of Cohalan's Irish-American colleagues, their attachment to Ireland was remote and sentimental.[2] In contrast, Cohalan's devotion to Ireland took a more pronounced and radical form. As we have seen in the previous chapter, Cohalan's nationalism drew on impulses from his own family heritage and ongoing developments in Ireland. However, it was also shaped by the American political and social environment in which he found himself.

In 1902, Daniel Cohalan, while still a young attorney, joined the Democratic Party in New York.[3] The Democrats would have been an obvious party of choice for an ambitious young Catholic Irish-American, though as we shall see in later chapters, he was also willing to support Republican presidential candidates and members of Congress if he felt they would better serve the interests of the United States and Irish-America. His father Timothy had after all been an active member of the Republican Party in Orange County.

At this time the Democratic Party organisation in New York was commonly referred to as 'Tammany Hall'. It attracted the support of not only large numbers of Irish Catholics but other ethnic groups as well. In the early years of the twentieth century, it was the Irish who dominated its leadership positions. One could thus describe Tammany as an Irish ethnic institution, since it tended to favour primarily the interests of the Irish ethnic group and saw itself as a counterweight to a perceived WASP (White Anglo-Saxon Protestant) influence in American politics nationally.[4]

Prior to Roosevelt's New Deal in the 1930s, the Tammany system brought welfare and work benefits to Irish immigrants often in return for votes. For the progressive reformers of early twentieth-century America and for much of the mainstream media such as the *New York Times*, such practices exemplified Tammany Hall nepotism and corruption. In 1903, the New York journal *The Outlook* denounced Tammany (and other Irish-dominated political machines) as 'not only un-American in its methods', but as 'distinctly un-American in its ideals'. It also described Irish-dominated city politics as a symbol of 'the broad distinction between what may be called Anglo-Saxon ideals of character and public service, and the Celtic ideals'. At the same time *The Outlook* celebrated the Anglo-Saxon contribution to the founding of the American nation as providing the United States with the 'instinct of freedom and spirit of liberty'.[5]

Such views were widely held. In attacking the excessive role played by foreign immigrants in city government, some of New York's urban reformers drew on a work by James Bryce, a British member of parliament who later became British ambassador to the United States. Terry Golway explains how Bryce's work *The American Commonwealth*, which contained an indictment of the Tammany system, 'was greeted with raptures of praise

Daniel and Hanna Cohalan purchased their Irish summer home in 1909. The house overlooked Glandore Harbour in West Cork. The house was sold in 1945 to the Sacred Heart Order and became a Novitiate for the training of Catholic nuns until its sale to a private buyer in 1999. (Photograph taken by author, June 2012)

from New York's Anglo-Protestant Reformers'.[6] Bryce had argued: 'There is no denying that the government of cities is the one conspicuous failure of the United States.'[7]

There was some truth in these allegations. Tammany bosses knowingly accepted large pay-offs from contractors who did business with the city. In return for political favours, they also received bribes from saloon keepers and the owners of brothels and gambling dens. In the 1870s, such was the scale of Tammany corruption that Boss Tweed and his so-called Tweed Ring were investigated for defrauding the city of millions of dollars and Tweed died in prison. Tweed's successors 'Honest John' Kelly and Richard Croker were equally controversial but more circumspect in their affairs. Avoiding the fate of Tweed, Boss Croker retired to Ireland with an immense fortune, which enabled him to purchase the large Glencairn estate in south County Dublin and raise racehorses.[8]

When Cohalan joined Tammany, Charles Murphy, or 'Boss Murphy' as he was better known, had taken over the leadership from Croker. Golway points out that, while Murphy typically protected his friends in the Tammany fashion, he also introduced social legislation to protect the poor.[9] There were practical political motivations behind this policy. Tammany, under mainly Irish-American leadership, sought to build coalitions with other ethnic groups such as Jews, newly arrived Eastern Europeans and African-Americans. In the absence of a fully developed welfare state, these groups wanted more social policies implemented on factory safety, child labour and tenement reform. The Tammany system responded to such demands in return for votes, so while the system aroused the ire of urban reformers it nevertheless maintained tacit support among working-class New Yorkers.[10]

Boss Murphy soon recognised Cohalan's organisational strengths. Within a short time, Cohalan became his trusted legal and political advisor. Indeed, the *New York Times* later went so far as to describe Cohalan as the 'brains of Murphy'.[11] Given the nature of the Tammany system, Tammany politicians and their officers could amass considerable fortunes and Cohalan would not have been an exception in that. As Gustavus Myers points out in his history of Tammany Hall:

> A few years previously, Cohalan was an obscure lawyer, but as the friend and advisor of 'Boss' Murphy, his practice had grown to large and lucrative proportions; it was a practice principally dealing with

> matters concerning municipal affairs. In 1908 Mr Murphy had caused Mr Cohalan to be chosen Grand Sachem of the Tammany Society.[12]

During this period of his life, Cohalan became a very wealthy man. His ties to Murphy won his legal practice lucrative contracts, which also benefited his brothers. According to a 1911 report in the *New York Times*, the city paid 113,195 dollars in contracts to the Cohalan brothers in the previous three years.[13]

Cohalan's prosperity thus enabled him not only to maintain his family in a large house in New York's prestigious Upper East Side but also to keep a summer home at Glandore in County Cork. On a more practical level, his visits to Ireland also enabled him to keep in touch with developments there in a way which would not have been possible for the vast majority of his colleagues in the Clan. Devoy had not visited Ireland since 1879, and then only as a clandestine visitor, as the terms of his release from a British prison stipulated that he would remain a permanent exile.[14]

These visits to Ireland further deepened Cohalan's interest in cultural nationalism. Eileen McGough points out in her biography of Diarmuid Lynch that within the extensive gardens of Cohalan's house in Glandore there is a 'Pearse Walk' in honour of Patrick Pearse, who took a principal part in the 1916 Rising but was also a leading figure in the Gaelic revival. McGough writes that 'locals claim that Patrick Pearse stayed here as a guest of the Cohalans'.[15] This is confirmed by James Coombes' short work of local history, *Utopia in Glandore*, which points out that Cohalan entertained both Patrick Pearse and Gaelic League leader Douglas Hyde in his house.[16] Aileen Cohalan also notes in her memoirs that Pearse was much loved by the Cohalan family: 'When he visited us at Glandore, we children had great reverence for him.'[17]

Cohalan's home in New York also became well known for its hospitality. In her memoirs, Aileen Cohalan notes how she often assisted teams of servants in preparing for such events, which were all expertly supervised by her mother Hanna. As journalist Forrest Davis pointed out, Cohalan, like an eighteenth-century squire, held court in both New York and Glandore:

> Here and abroad, he keeps a sort of salon where piety, wit and learning make the best of it together. His board here seats fourteen.

> You may find there George Russell, 'Æ', some of the Irish players, Jim Reed, a stray Jesuit metaphysician; Denny Lynch, biographer of Tweed, and Bainbridge Colby, all at one sitting.[18]

Visiting nationalists from Ireland knew of Cohalan's increasing political importance in the city and of his considerable financial resources. Cohalan's contacts with Irish-American organisations and American politicians throughout the United States proved invaluable for visitors such as Patrick Pearse, who in 1914 conducted a lecture tour of the United States in aid of St Enda's, his struggling Irish school in Dublin. Cohalan's papers contain letters soliciting financial support for the school. In July 1913, Bulmer Hobson – a member of the IRB in Ireland but also an Irish correspondent for the *Gaelic American* – wrote to Cohalan soliciting such help on behalf of Pearse, stressing the value of the school to the cause of radical nationalism:

> You will probably have by this time received a letter from P. H. Pearse of St. Enda's school .... He is thinking of going out to America in the autumn in the hope of raising sufficient funds .... St Enda's is the only college preparing boys for the universities that is really and intensely national in tone ....[19]

In the event, Pearse went in April 1914 and met with Cohalan in New York. Cohalan's papers contain an appreciative letter from Pearse thanking him 'for his generous subscriptions' to St Enda's school and for his 'unceasing and successful efforts to put me in touch with other good friends'.[20]

Cohalan shared his passion for assisting the Irish cultural revival with fellow lawyer John Quinn.[21] However, Devoy did not appear to share the same enthusiasm, seeing such cultural activities as a distraction from the physical force nationalist goals of the Clan. He was particularly incensed by J.M. Synge's play *The Playboy of the Western World*, which he believed presented the Irish 'as a lawless and brutal people'. Devoy's reaction was not unusual. As already discussed in the introduction in relation to Alison Kibler's work *Censoring Racial Ridicule*, many Irish-Americans had long campaigned against stage representations of the Irish as a violent and half-civilised race. Devoy incorrectly interpreted Synge's romantic portrayal of the Irish in this context and attacked the play in several editions of the *Gaelic American*.[22] He also resented Douglas Hyde's support for the play and in a thinly veiled criticism of the amount of time Cohalan was devoting to Gaelic League business complained: 'The time of our men is constantly taken up with raising money for the League, to the neglect of our own work. Hardly anybody does anything, and yet everything is done to please those who are hostile and indifferent and every recommendation made by us or our friends is ignored.'[23]

Cohalan did not pay any attention to this controversy. In contrast, the urbane and literary-minded John Quinn criticised Devoy for his opposition to the *Playboy*. In an eight-page letter to Cohalan in early 1913, he lambasted Devoy for his support of the protestors who had disrupted the play on its American tour, claiming that: 'I used to respect and admire him [Devoy]. Now I can't help feeling that his usefulness is ended.'[24] Cohalan diplomatically maintained a close relationship with both men, though he appears to have sided with Quinn on the question of the *Playboy*. Significantly, he continued his work as treasurer of the Finance Committee of the Gaelic League in New York and there is no doubt that Hyde valued Cohalan's 'good advice' on American matters.[25]

Cohalan's work with the Gaelic league overlapped with his other mission to defend the interests of the Irish race in America. He saw the language movement in the United States and other Irish cultural activities as a means to reawaken a sense of ethnic pride among Irish-Americans.[26] In a speech to the Harlem Gaelic Society on 18 June 1904, Cohalan stressed that the work of the Gaelic League in America had both Irish and American objectives. These American objectives were based on his view that the Irish in America were still treated in a discriminatory way by an Anglo-centric America. Cohalan argued that the League should campaign 'to correct such abuses as the falsifying of American history. To introduce Irish history into the parochial and public schools, to foster and promote in every way possible Irish industries, music, dances and pastimes and in this manner to create a strong, healthy, irresistible public opinion in favor of a free Ireland.'[27]

Meanwhile, Cohalan continued with his work in Tammany. His position as Grand Sachem allowed him to develop contacts which would serve the interests of radical Irish nationalism in the United States in later years. As Grand Sachem, Cohalan exercised influence in the selection of Democratic candidates for office. Reid recounts how Boss Murphy and Cohalan approached John Quinn and pressed him to accept the chairmanship of the Democratic National Committee for the East. Quinn turned down the post but remained active in Democratic politics. Drawing on Quinn's papers in the New York Public Library, Reid describes how Cohalan accompanied Quinn and Murphy to the Democratic National Convention in Denver, Colorado, in 1908. Under Quinn's tutelage the experience provided Cohalan with an intensive introduction to the Byzantine world of US Congressional politics.[28]

Cohalan proved adept in the political arts and Murphy appreciated his talents. In 1911, Cohalan narrowly missed out on an opportunity to become a senator at a time when senators were elected by the legislature for New York. A small group of 'insurgent' Democratic legislators in Albany led by none other than Franklin Delano Roosevelt (FDR) opposed Murphy's first choice of candidate, William F. ('Blue-eyed Billy') Sheehan of Buffalo. The young Roosevelt, seeking to curry favour with other reformers, saw Murphy's attempts to install Sheehan as an example of Tammany nepotism, which he campaigned against.[29] In order to break the deadlock, Murphy then asked the insurgents via an 'emissary' if they would accept one of three possible candidates: New York Supreme Court Justice Victor J. Dowling; Justice James O'Gorman who also served on the New York Supreme Court bench; and Daniel Cohalan. Roosevelt immediately indicated that he would not accept Cohalan, seeing him as too close to Murphy. Given that Dowling withdrew his name from the contest, the Roosevelt 'insurgents' then accepted O'Gorman, who was subsequently elected as New York senator.[30]

Roosevelt's much-publicised opposition to Sheehan and Cohalan won him the support of many reformers and demonstrated that the might of the Tammany machine could sometimes be challenged from within the Democratic Party. Murphy later cleverly restored relations with Roosevelt, who in turn came to appreciate the political benefits of a close association with Tammany. However, according to the *New York Times*, Cohalan 'never forgot' this slight to his ambitions. In a later chapter, we will see how Cohalan became an implacable opponent of Roosevelt's New Deal and of his administration's foreign policy in the 1930s. No doubt the memory of this earlier 'slight' contributed to Cohalan's animosity.[31] However, ideological factors especially with regard to contrasting ideas on the role of government, as well as Roosevelt's perceived pro-British foreign policy stances, would also determine Cohalan's anti-FDR position.

O'Gorman's appointment had, however, a silver lining for Cohalan in that it created a vacancy on the Supreme Court bench. According to Reid, Murphy initially offered this to Cohalan's friend and fellow attorney John Quinn but Quinn did not want the job. Instead, Quinn, illustrating the close alliance between both men, campaigned successfully among Tammany's chiefs on Cohalan's behalf and thus helped to secure the latter's appointment in May 1911.[32]

For the establishment and the reformist-leaning press, Cohalan's appointment smacked of the usual corruption associated with the Tammany system. The *New York Times* thundered:

> We should be most reluctant to believe that Gov. Dix had of his own volition nominated Daniel F. Cohalan to the Supreme bench. But it is vastly worse that he should have permitted himself to be cudgelled into making the nomination. It is very evident that he did make it under the application of the Tammany cudgel. Mr Murphy's Senate would not confirm the Governor's other appointments until the name of Cohalan was sent in, and the Governor weakly yielded.[33]

While the failure to secure a Senate seat represented a disappointment to Cohalan's ambitions, his appointment to the State Supreme Court was still a prestigious prize. Even the *New York Times* recognised this and in a somewhat backhanded compliment argued that his appointment might serve to weaken what they saw as corruption in City Hall:

> Mr Cohalan, according to a general belief, is a much abler man and a better lawyer than most of the Tammany Judges now on the Supreme Court bench. He has long been very near to Murphy, he has been the brains of Murphy. For that reason, his appointment to the bench has been favored by many who would on other grounds oppose it, because they insisted that it would promote the public welfare to take away Murphy's brains.[34]

Ostensibly, this prediction assumed that Cohalan would sever his ties with the Murphy machine and the *New York Times* held out the possibility that this might take place:

> Mr Cohalan is now in a position where he can turn his back on Murphy. If he is fit for the judicial office he will do that, he will

> henceforth have nothing to do with Murphy or with Tammany politics. He can live down his Tammany past only by holding aloof from the organisation and maintaining, as every worthy and honourable Judge should maintain, his entire independence.[35]

Given the nature of the Tammany system, Cohalan was not in a position to sever his relations with Tammany and his advisory relationship with Murphy continued, though not in an official capacity. Later, in November 1911, Cohalan stood for election in his own right for this Supreme Court post and had the full backing of the Tammany machine. Cohalan was subsequently elected for the full fourteen-year term. With the support of Murphy, he also attended the Democratic National Convention in Baltimore in 1912 as a New York delegate. In the nomination process for the Democratic presidential candidate for 1912, Cohalan and Murphy supported Congressman James Beauchamp Clark of Missouri, or 'Champ' Clark, by which he became better known. Clark had earned notoriety for his inflammatory anti-British speeches on Canada the previous year when he had declared on the floor of the House: 'I look forward to the time when the American flag will fly over every square foot of British North America up to the North Pole.'[36] Clearly such sentiments would have been music to the ears of Cohalan and the Clan. However, even though Clark had been favoured to win, the nomination went to Governor Woodrow Wilson of New Jersey, who subsequently went on to win the presidency.

Murphy and Cohalan opposed Wilson, in part for his association with reform-minded Democrats and for his declared intention to reform local politics, which would have been detrimental to the Tammany machine. However, Cohalan's opposition went deeper than this. In his writings, Cohalan consistently took an isolationist line on American foreign policy, arguing that the United States should refrain from involving itself in what he described as Europe's eternal wars.[37] In this context his fears of Woodrow Wilson's perceived internationalism had some justification. At a St Patrick's Day banquet in New York in 1909, Wilson spoke of America coming out 'upon a stage of international responsibility, from which we cannot retire'.[38] His later decision to enter the war on the Allied side as well as his support for a League of Nations indicated that these words were not empty rhetoric.

Cohalan also associated Wilson with a dominant Anglo-Saxon elite in American society that identified with the interests of Britain as much as the United States. As argued in the introductory chapter, it seems more plausible that Wilson would have put American interests before those of Britain, but his admiration for British institutions was well known even before he became president. One of his best works, *Congressional Government* (1885), drew on the writings of Walter Bagehot on English politics to show how British principles of government formed the basis of American democracy.[39] Later, as president of Princeton University, he declared in an after-dinner speech in New York in 1904: 'The Anglo-Saxon people have undertaken to reconstruct the affairs of the world, and it would be a shame upon them to withdraw their hand.'[40]

Moreover, Wilson's favourable attitude towards Britain was widely held. In a speech at Harvard University in 1898, US Secretary of State Richard Olney went on to describe Americans as 'part of one great English-speaking family whose proud destiny it is to lead and control the world'.[41] Such language was commonly used by advocates of American imperialism at this time, with many public commentators drawing favourable contrasts between democratic Britain on the one side and autocratic Germany and Russia on the other.[42]

Meanwhile in Britain many influential writers and industrialists called for a closer relationship between the United States and Britain, given this shared cultural and political history. Contemporary writer William Stead, in his work *The Americanization of the World* (1902), argued that a merger between the British Empire and the United States would unify the English-speaking world and help Britain to 'continue for all time to be an integral part of the greatest of all World-Powers, supreme on sea and unassailable on land, permanently delivered from all fear of hostile attack, and capable of wielding irresistible influence in all parts of the planet'.[43] The Scottish-born Andrew Carnegie, who had made a fortune in steel production in the United States, was also enthusiastic about this goal and funded many projects aimed at improving Anglo-American relations. In an article entitled 'A Look Ahead', which appeared in the influential *North American Review* in 1893, Carnegie also called for a 'union' of the English-speaking peoples.[44]

As already discussed in the introductory chapter, such racial rhetoric was common in both Britain and the United States at this time but this did not imply that cultural considerations shaped American foreign policy objectives. Hannigan points out that, while American and British elites shared feelings of kinship, American policy-makers were guided by the geopolitical interests of the United States. He also argues that, while the United States wished to see British influence in the western hemisphere reduced, it also wished to see the more open trading system of the British Empire maintained elsewhere. Drawing on the same 1898 speech by Secretary of State Olney cited above, Hannigan refers to Olney rhetorically asking: 'are we so likely to gain new outlets for our products as through that of a Power whose possessions girdle the earth and in whose ports equal privileges and facilities of trade are accorded to the flags of all nations?'[45]

Nevertheless, suspicion of British intrigue in the United States characterised Cohalan's pronouncements. In one of his first public speeches, in 1900, he denounced American imperialism in the Philippines, believing that it was inspired by Anglophile tendencies in the US Department of State. In the same speech, he declared that the Department of State had become so Anglophile that it 'feared to express the hope entertained by nine tenths of the people of America that the two struggling republics of South Africa should be victorious in their magnificent fight for existence lest the feelings of England should be ruffled'.[46]

In this context, Cohalan, along with other Irish-Americans, stressed that they were as loyal if not more loyal to the US compared to WASP Americans. The celebration of the Irish contribution to the United States and warnings of British intrigue in the country became a perennial theme in the *Gaelic American* and in Cohalan's writings and speeches. As the editorial of the first edition in 1903 warned:

> Our people have been the sturdiest champions of American principles of government, because they are the principles for which the race has fought and struggled for centuries. We find these principles assailed at the very fountain head by an organized movement to destroy the old American spirit and substitute for it a servile dependence on England. This movement aims to place in the hands of pro-British sycophants the direction of the foreign policy of this republic, to get control of the army, the navy and the schools of the United States, as it has already secured control of a portion of the popular press.[47]

This editorial echoed Cohalan's belief that America's Anglophile elite were the real hyphenates in the United States, who were determined to drag the US into British schemes to maintain their empire. Many of the articles in the *Gaelic American* warned against this British threat to American interests. In 1911 and 1912, the paper, on behalf of the Clan, launched a campaign against a proposed arbitration treaty aimed at resolving territorial disputes between the United States and Britain.[48] In an opening salvo against this proposal, the *Gaelic American* reprinted a speech by Republican Senator Henry Cabot Lodge of Massachusetts which argued that the proposed treaty would conflict with the powers of the Senate in influencing American foreign policy.[49] In this fight, the *Gaelic American* had many allies. Its main rival, the *Irish World*, which supported Irish home rule, also vociferously opposed the treaty. The Clan's opposition to the treaty thus represented widespread opposition within Irish-America which enabled it to mount a more broad-based campaign under the general umbrella of the United Irish Societies. The Clan also combined with German-American societies to fight the measure. The United German-American and United Irish-American Societies of New York dispatched a joint petition to the Senate which included the following: 'The propaganda carried on in favour of the Treaty is essentially pro-English and offensive to citizens of other races, who now constitute a majority of the population of the United States … '[50]

In its campaign, the *Gaelic American* singled out steel magnate Andrew Carnegie as posing a particular threat to American democracy. In a February 1912 edition it declared: 'Carnegie's real object in spending millions for arbitration and "peace" is to insidiously destroy popular government in this country and make it the "Re-United States of the British-American Union".'[51] The British ambassador James Bryce also became the object of particularly venomous attacks by the paper. During the controversy over the arbitration treaty, Bryce had attacked the power of the United States Senate over American foreign affairs. In response the *Gaelic American* in November 1913 poured scorn on both Andrew Carnegie and Bryce. It complained: 'No soft-soaping of Carnegie and his millions, or the flapdoodle twaddle of a misfit Ambassador will make liberty-loving Americans sycophants of a decayed monarchy.'[52] Cohalan and Devoy had relevant extracts of Bryce's writings distributed to each member of Congress.[53]

Ultimately, the Senate modified the bill to such an extent that President William Howard Taft refused to sign it. It would be difficult to gauge whether Irish-American and German-American pressure influenced the Senate's decision but those senators representing large Irish-American and German-American communities must surely have taken this well-orchestrated campaign against the treaty into account.[54] Devoy certainly seemed to think so. In March 1912 he sent a cable to the IRB's newspaper *Irish Freedom* which read: 'On the fifty-fifth anniversary of the Fenian Rising, the American-Irish have won a notable victory over England. The Senate cut the Arbitration Treaty to pieces … and followed exactly the Irish lines of opposition.'[55] *Irish Freedom* dutifully reprinted the article, though it is doubtful if they understood the significance of the defeat of this measure for the Irish-American press. Meanwhile, the *Irish World* exulted in this Senate outcome and in August 1911 declared: 'Owing to the fact that the Monroe Doctrine and other cherished traditions will be endangered, the ratification of the Arbitration Treaty has been held up by the United States Senate.' Underneath this statement, the paper ran a front-page cartoon of a disappointed John Bull tied up by a banner with the inscription 'Beware of Foreign Alliances, G. Washington'.[56]

Despite this apparent victory, Cohalan believed that Irish-America needed to be constantly vigilant against future attempts by a pro-British elite to ensnare the US into an alliance with Britain. In a later speech in 1916 supporting American neutrality during the war in Europe, he articulated these fears and saw the efforts of Irish-America in 1911–12 as a template for future co-operation with other ethnic groups: 'If it were not for the efforts of the people of our race and of the other races, aside from those of English blood … these men might succeed and might again to all intents and purposes make these United States a part of the British Empire.'[57]

Cohalan believed that Wilson's denial of the role Irish-Americans played in the foundation of the United States misrepresented American history in such as way as to deny Irish-Americans their rightful place in US society. Wilson's speech at the unveiling of a monument to Wexford man Commodore John Barry in May 1914, who Irish-Americans considered as one of the founders of the American navy, caused the *Gaelic American* grave offence. In his speech, Wilson had pointed out: 'Some Americans need hyphens in their names, because only part of them has come over …

This man was not an Irish-American; he was an Irishman who became an American.'[58] The *Gaelic American* described the president's speech as 'mean minded' and argued that 'the occasion called for some recognition of the priceless services to the United States of the race to which Jack Barry belonged, in the revolution, the war of 1812, the Civil War, to say nothing of its work in the building up and development of the Republic from the Revolution to the present day'.[59]

In order to combat what he saw as a pro-British bias in American society, Cohalan's speeches and writings opposed the idea of assimilation to an Anglo-Saxon norm which would only serve to make American institutions such as the press, judicial system and system of government even more vulnerable to British wiles. Instead of erasing ethnic differences, the contribution of each 'race' to American civilisation needed to be celebrated. In particular, Cohalan focused on the contribution of the Irish to America's armed services. According to Cohalan, the Irish were 'a fighting race'. As he pointed out in one speech, 'No men of any race have shed their blood more freely, or even recklessly, than have the men of our breed.'[60]

Matthew Guterl has pointed out in his work The *Color of Race in America* that Cohalan advocated a type of 'cultural pluralism' where the contributions of each race to America's history would be recognised and not just the English contribution.[61] As part of his efforts to promote a proper understanding of the true contribution of the Irish to America, Cohalan became a prominent figure in the New York chapter of the American Irish Historical Society. The members were mainly drawn from the upper middle class and included both Protestants and Catholics. Other prominent members included Congressman Bourke Cockran, who, though a supporter of Redmond's Irish Parliamentary Party, found common cause with Cohalan in upholding the aims of this society.

The AIHS was founded in Boston in 1897 but it later relocated to New York in 1904. It declared its main aim as 'to make better known the Irish chapter in American History', especially the contribution of the Irish to the American Revolution and defence of the Union in the Civil War. The AIHS documented this contribution in its yearly *Journal of the American Irish Historical Society*. The 1908 edition lists Cohalan as one of its New York members in a membership roll of approximately six hundred members. By 1914 membership had grown to 1,168, with members mainly concentrated in the north-east of the United States. The 1941 edition of the journal lists a membership of 2,260 nationwide and this membership level has been maintained to the present day.[62]

Through the efforts of its researchers, the society challenged a perceived Anglo-Saxon bias in the history of America's foundation and in the wider society generally. Over three-quarters of the articles published by the society dealt with the heroic Irish contribution to American colonial history, especially Irish service in the revolutionary war. By so doing the society hoped to achieve an 'awakening and appreciation of their [Irish-Americans] worth as citizens'.[63]

The society's chief historiographer, Cork-born Michael J. O'Brien, wrote many celebratory articles on the Irish contribution for the society's *Journal of American Irish History*. His article 'How the Descendants of Irish Settlers in America Were Written into History as Anglo-Saxons and Scotch Irish', which appeared in the society's journal in 1919, represented a typical example.[64] The *Gaelic American*, no doubt with the encouragement of Cohalan, often included shortened versions of these articles.[65] In one edition, O'Brien recounted the heroic revolutionary war story of the 'brilliant capture of the British fort at Stony Point, in which Irishmen are shown to have played the most prominent part'.[66] Other O'Brien articles highlighted the Irish role in the colonial settlement. In a piece on the Irish settlement in the Carolinas, O'Brien pointed to the 'host of Irish names to be found in the early records' and argued that such evidence did much to 'controvert those pro-English writers who claim that the American people are of Anglo-Saxon origin'.[67] Cohalan also contributed to the journal, as in an article on Irishman General John Sullivan who fought in the Continental Army during the American revolutionary war.[68]

This celebration of the Irish contribution to the foundation of the United States was not just an academic exercise. The work of the AIHS had a political objective aimed at challenging the dominant belief that the United States was an Anglo-Saxon country. Cohalan often peppered his speeches with references to such Irish heroism in America's wars and drew heavily on O'Brien's research in his own publications, such as in his own work *Andrew Jackson: Hero of New Orleans* (1930). Cohalan also believed that a greater Irish-American awareness of their contribution to the founding of the United States would make the Irish in the United States better Americans. As the *Gaelic American* declared in an editorial:

'We are stimulating their patriotism and fitting them to become more loyal citizens of the country of their allegiance.'[69]

In the years before the First World War, Cohalan and Devoy became particularly concerned about how the racial ties between America's White Anglo-Saxon Protestants (WASPS) and Protestant Britain were becoming a cause of celebration. Both believed that this was politically motivated and designed to pave the way for a British alliance. In 1913, in an exchange of letters, Devoy expressed fury at the prospect of a proposed Anglo-American peace centenary celebration in 1914, which was intended to celebrate one hundred years of peace between Britain and the United States.[70] Devoy argued that leading American political figures such as Theodore Roosevelt and William Jennings Bryan were behind plans that advocated textbooks in schools which emphasised Anglo-American friendship, 'a free commemorative bridge over the Niagara river, a great free building in New York or some other city, and the purchase of the original Washington estates in England with a number of celebrations thrown in'. Devoy also blamed what he described as 'Anglomaniacs' in the United States such as steel magnate Andrew Carnegie for financing this propaganda. In an editorial in February 1911, the *Gaelic American* declared: 'The amount of English money spent in organized efforts to Anglicize the American people must be enormous.'[71] The *Irish World* shared this Irish-American disquiet. In a May 1911 edition, the paper declared: 'The Peace Society of New York has Multi-Millionaire Carnegie for its president. Ostensibly its mission is to promote the cause of peace; in reality it is an organisation whose main object just now is to bring about an Anglo-American alliance.'[72]

Devoy pointed out to Cohalan that battling such schemes would give the Clan work for years but that this campaign, given the near unanimity of Irish-American opinion on this issue, would work best through an 'open public American organization'.[73]

Though the Clan held public meetings which were reported in the press, it was also a secret organisation. The battle against the arbitration treaty had taught the Clan the value of working with other groups in a more public manner. A more open organisation would also be much better placed to counter Redmond's UILA and rally Irish America behind the banner of physical force nationalism. This organisation would also have other more American goals, such as the defence of Irish-America and the protection of the interests of the United States. Given Cohalan's increasing stature and range of political skills, one suspects from this correspondence that Devoy already knew who would lead such an organisation.

It would be impossible, in a single volume, to comprehensively cover Cohalan's role as a State Supreme Court Justice and document his involvement in Tammany politics while still leaving sufficient space to address his contributions to Irish-American nationalism. Yet these American dimensions to his career inevitably impacted on his work on behalf of Irish nationalism in the United States. His involvement in Tammany politics provided Cohalan with a platform on which to articulate the cause of Irish independence to an American audience largely ignorant of Irish affairs. Cohalan can thus be seen as a forerunner of later American power brokers friendly to Ireland but also as deeply immersed in an American political world. Furthermore, the Tammany system undoubtedly helped to further his legal career, particularly with regard to gaining lucrative city contracts and to his appointment as a Supreme Court Justice. This wealth and status enhanced his role in promoting the Irish-American nationalist cause, which visiting Irish nationalists and the Clan leadership were only too willing to exploit. Cohalan too saw the value of the Tammany system in protecting and enhancing the interests of Irish-America while remaining deeply suspicious of the efforts of WASP urban reformers such as FDR. Finally, like many prominent Irish-Americans, Cohalan possessed a sincere patriotism, and saw his involvement in politics as a means of defending American interests against the actions of an Anglophile elite bent on dragging the United States into an alliance with Britain. Cohalan believed that all these goals were intertwined and progress in achieving one goal would naturally lead to success in the others. Tumultuous events in the United States, Europe and Ireland itself would soon demonstrate that this was not always the case.

3

State Supreme Court Justice and Irish Rebel, 1911–16

In the years after his judicial appointment, Cohalan faced considerable challenges both in his own family life and in his legal career. In the latter instance, his position as a State Supreme Court Justice appeared for a time in doubt. Despite these difficulties, he still kept a careful eye on international developments both in Ireland and elsewhere. In July 1914, events in the Balkans finally produced the European war and a powerful potential German ally, which Cohalan had long hoped for. Redmond's support for the British war effort also allowed the Clan to unify Irish-American opinion in a way that would not have been possible beforehand. At considerable risk to his own reputation, Cohalan would play a pivotal role in harnessing these developments for the benefit of Irish-America and for the Irish nationalist cause in the United States.

At the time of his judicial appointment, Cohalan's status in New York society typified that of a successful Irish-American lawyer with a happy family life. To celebrate his judicial appointment, and with an eye to the forthcoming judicial election later that year, the *Gaelic American* ran a short item on his family in their May 1911 edition complete with an illustration of Cohalan, his wife Hanna and his now seven children.[1] His first-born, Aileen, was now ten, Conn (Cornelius) was eight, Kathleen seven, Daniel F. Junior six, Patrick five and Florence and Dermot, twin boys, were aged two.[2]

Just when all appeared to be going well for the Cohalans, tragedy struck their household. In June 1911, Hanna died giving birth to another child. In a further tragic twist, the child, who had already been named Gerard, also died. It would take Cohalan many months to recover from

The Cohalan family as portrayed in an illustration which appeared in the Gaelic American shortly after Daniel Cohalan's appointment as New York State Supreme Court Justice. Hanna would die in childbirth just one month later. (Source: *Gaelic American*, 27 May 1911, Joseph McGarrity Collection. Digital Library@Villanova University)

this loss and his daughter Aileen noted in her memoirs: 'For quite some time Father became more and more serious.'[3]

Hanna's funeral, covered extensively in the *New York Times* and the *Gaelic American*, provides an indication of Cohalan's growing stature in American public life at this point in his career. At the funeral, leading judicial and political figures rubbed shoulders with leading members of the Clan.[4] The *Gaelic American* noted that 'all the judges of the court and all the public men of the city' attended and suggested that it was the largest Irish funeral in the city since the funeral of Fenian leader John O'Mahony in 1877. Political leaders in attendance included New York Governor John Dix, Democratic Senator James O'Gorman and of course Tammany Boss Charles Murphy. Given Cohalan's close connection to the Cork area, the *Southern Star* reprinted the *Gaelic American* report in full.[5] Meanwhile, Hanna's sister, Madge O'Leary, came over from Cork to look after his distraught children.

The following summer, the family paid their yearly visit to Glandore. In a sympathetic article in August 1912 entitled 'Judge Daniel Cohalan: An impression', the *Southern Star* alluded to Cohalan's continuing sadness over his wife's death but also his well-known reputation for hospitality:

> A hospitable man, for though the shadow of an unforgotten sorrow has clouded his life, though he ever yearns for the vanished hand and longs to hear the voice that is still, yet he likes to see others relishing the joys of life and making a harvest of the day, and he finds infinite pleasure in presiding over the company of guests at his lavish table.[6]

Only by 1913 had the stress of his bereavement begun to lift. Paradoxically, his recovery from a serious operation for appendicitis may have helped to ease his grief. Devoy, in an April 1913 letter to Joe McGarrity, the Clan chief in Philadelphia, reported on visiting Cohalan, who was then recovering in hospital. In an indication of the close friendship between the two men, Devoy hoped that his recovery from this operation might also lead to a recovery from his longstanding grief.[7]

> He is doing splendidly but must stay in bed another ten or fourteen days. He had a close call. I saw him today just as the children were leaving him and he was in fine condition and spirits. I think it will take him out of the gloom he has been in since his wife died.[8]

While still in mourning for Hanna in 1913, Cohalan faced yet another crisis, this time involving his controversial links with Tammany. Given his appointment to the Supreme Court judiciary, he no longer officially offered advice to Tammany leader Boss Murphy. However, his Tammany past now came back to haunt him when he became embroiled in a controversy involving his alleged receipt of corrupt payments from John Connolly, an Irish-American heating contractor. The *New York World* initially broke the story on 25 May 1913 and the *New York Times*, which had long called for reform of the Tammany system, eagerly followed up on the scandal. Certainly, the controversy had all the hallmarks of Tammany corruption. The contractor Connolly claimed that Cohalan had received 55 per cent of the profits he made on heating contracts with the city during 1903 and 1904.[9] These payments had amounted to almost 4,000 dollars. Cohalan was then a trusted legal advisor for Murphy, though he had not yet been appointed Grand Sachem of Tammany.

Connolly further alleged that in 1909, when his business was not going well, he had given Cohalan a promissory note for a further 4,000 dollars so that Cohalan could use his influence with Tammany to secure Connolly an appointment to public office. After Cohalan allegedly failed to secure him such an appointment, Connolly passed on the corrupt payment allegations to the *New York World* in May 1913. Following this public disclosure, the Bar Association of New York launched an enquiry into Cohalan's fitness to practise as a judge.[10] This came as a shock to Cohalan, as he was preparing for his 'summer sojourn' in Glandore when news of the enquiry broke. Cohalan immediately postponed his vacation plans in order to deal with the crisis. These allegations represented a serious threat to his career. If substantiated, he faced being removed from the judicial bench and declared unfit to practise law. This would not only be disastrous for Cohalan and his family but would also seriously undermine his effectiveness as a spokesman for radical Irish-American nationalist opinion.

As one might expect, Cohalan enjoyed the full support of the *Gaelic American*. On 14 June 1913, the paper reported how Cohalan sent his children to Ireland and remained 'to fight blackmailers and grafters'. He also enlisted the help of his friend and fellow lawyer John Quinn in defending his case, and Quinn's papers offer an insight into how Irish-Americans, who often differed in their attitudes towards Ireland, could find common cause in their defence of the perceived interests of the Irish ethnic community. As Irish-American Democrats, both men had a stake in the Tammany system and distrusted the Bar Association, which they perceived as dominated by upstate WASP American lawyers. On Quinn's advice, Cohalan refused to appear before the grievance committee of the Bar Association. Instead Quinn persuaded him to demand an investigation by the Judiciary Committee of the State Legislature, seen as more sympathetic to Tammany. According to Reid, this ultimately helped to save Cohalan, though the committee took several weeks to reach their verdict.[11]

The *New York Times*, welcoming the opportunity to expose Tammany, devoted extensive coverage to the Judiciary Committee's investigation into Cohalan. The committee heard complex testimony from both sides but, in summary, Cohalan argued that he did not receive any percentage of Connolly's profits and that the 4,000 dollars promissory note was simply payment for legal advice. He also claimed to have returned the note so as to ensure that Connolly did not cause a scandal. Cohalan grimly described the return of the money in this context as giving in to Connolly's 'blackmail' and admitted that 'it was the gravest mistake of his life'.[12] Connolly, in turn, agreed that he had received the money back but that this had come about due to pressure from Boss Murphy rather than due to any change of heart on the part of Cohalan. Interestingly, the committee did not call the media-shy Murphy as a witness, who might have either substantiated or refuted this claim.

Cohalan responded to Connolly's charges robustly. His defence team argued that these allegations were a classic example of 'government by newspaper' and a deliberate attempt by the establishment Anglo-dominated press to ruin Cohalan.[13] In support of this claim, they argued that a contract existed between Ralph Pulitzer, publisher of the *New York World*, and Connolly. They also alleged that Pulitzer had promised Connolly money and a job 'in return for substantiating his charges against Cohalan'.[14] As the case drew to a conclusion, Cohalan denied promising Connolly a job in return for the money and claimed that Connolly was 'suffering from hallucinations'. To back up this allegation, Cohalan presented dramatic evidence that Connolly had at one point been admitted to an insane asylum. As if to confirm Cohalan's claim, Connolly broke down after six hours' cross-examination. Meanwhile, the *New York Times* noted that Cohalan, still wearing black mourning since his wife's death, presented a 'cool denial' of the charges in an eloquent and forceful manner.[15]

Defence team accusations of press harassment and Connolly's public breakdown worked in Cohalan's favour and the Judiciary Committee unanimously recommended Cohalan's acquittal in July 1913.[16] Despite this acquittal, though, the case provided useful ammunition for the enemies of Tammany. The *New York Times*, which had long campaigned for a reform of the judicial appointments system, saw the case as indicative of the corruption that pervaded local government in New York. In an article entitled 'Not a Vindication', the paper grudgingly accepted Cohalan's acquittal but added that:

> Justice Daniel F. Cohalan is acquitted, not exonerated. The burden of the Bar Association's charges still rests upon him. His reputation is not cleared. He stands apart from other Judges on the bench as one at whom the accusing finger still points ....
>
> The broader moral of this miserable, sordid business is one that has a very direct bearing upon which the judges of our courts are chosen. The acts charged by Connolly, the acts admitted by Judge Cohalan, are the familiar methods of the Tammany system. Such things have been going on for generations, they are going on now all about us.[17]

Not surprisingly, such criticism of Cohalan in the *New York Times* did not undermine his position in Irish-American circles. His stout performance before the legislature drew praise and he emerged from the crisis unscathed. The *Gaelic American* saw the affair in the context of its long-running criticism of an 'Anglomanic press'. It described the actions of the *New York World* as 'a mere frame-up, arranged between a ruffian who is a disgrace to Ireland and a disreputable newspaper which is a disgrace to American journalism'. It also viewed the whole case as not only an attempt to ruin Cohalan and undermine the power of the Irish ethnic group in local politics but also as a challenge to American democracy:

> There is much more at stake than the character of a man. The interests and good name of the Irish Race are deeply involved and incidentally the interests of the whole community. A combination of dishonest newspapers menaces the public interest in more ways than one.[18]

Cohalan's acquittal came as a huge relief for the wider Cohalan family. All his brothers (including John, with whom he had a strained relationship) attended the committee hearing to lend him their support.[19] After the verdict, he immediately set sail to join his family in Glandore, west Cork, a place far removed from the tense dramas which he had just endured before the state legislature.[20]

Despite family tragedy and the recent crisis confronting his career, Cohalan still retained a deep concern for Ireland's welfare and in the summer of 1913 he had much to be concerned about. While he had immersed himself in the work of the Gaelic League and the Clan in the United States he, like Devoy, remained frustrated at the popularity of home rule nationalism in Ireland. To a degree, this popularity had much to do with Redmond's apparent achievements at this time. In the years before the First World War, Redmond, because the Irish Party possessed the balance of power in the House of Commons, had won the support of the Liberal Party to the cause of home rule. Despite the opposition of the Conservative Party and the Ulster Unionists, the Liberal Party introduced a Home Rule Bill in the House of Commons in 1912. Though the bill would not become law for two years due to the opposition of the Lords, home rule finally seemed to be within nationalist Ireland's grasp after decades of constitutional struggle.

The popularity of the home rule cause in both Ireland and the United States frustrated the Clan. As Clan leader William Carroll pointed out gloomily to Devoy in 1913:

> The dark side of the prospect here and overseas is not so much what Lloyd George, Redmond and [Michael J.] Ryan propose, but the fact that there and here the Irish people accept and applaud their betrayal of everything national they once professed to advocate.[21]

According to Francis Carroll, Redmond's popularity had a negative impact on the IRB. By 1910 it had declined to between 1,500 and 2,000 members, many of whom were now elderly men.[22] The Clan, while still suffering defections to Redmond's UILA in America, remained the stronger of the two groups and made every effort to keep the IRB sustained. As Devoy pointed out in his memoirs, the revolutionary movement in Ireland 'was maintained almost entirely by moral and material support from the Clan na Gael'. Every year, sums amounting to between 600 and 1,000 pounds were sent to the Supreme Council of the IRB.[23] The Clan used some of its trusted members to forward this money to Ireland. Cohalan himself, a frequent visitor to Ireland, appears to have sometimes played the dangerous role of Clan courier and this brought him to the attention of the police authorities. An RIC police 'Crime Branch Special' report for August 1906 pointed to Cohalan as a likely dispenser of Clan funds:

> The Irish Republican Brotherhood has been showing increased activity during August. The Clan na Gael delegate D. F. Cohalan was in Ireland for the greater part of the month and it is highly probable that funds for organizing purposes have been received through him.[24]

In line with Clan opposition to what the *Gaelic American* described as Redmond's 'Bogus Home Rule', Cohalan tried to ensure that the IRB kept faith in the tradition of physical force. The same police report of 1906 which had referred to Cohalan's activities in Ireland noted that:

> The hostility of the Clan na Gael to parliamentary agitation is still very active. The leaders of the American and Irish secret societies appear to be determined that no parliamentary compromise will be permitted to interfere with their own policy of a completely independent Ireland.[25]

In 1907, the old Fenian Tom Clarke, who had been on the staff of the *Gaelic American*, decided to return to Ireland with the full approval of Devoy. Historians have argued that it was Clarke who did most to revitalise the IRB in the following years and in this task he had the full support of Devoy's Clan.[26] However, other political forces would also come to challenge Redmond's dominance of nationalist Ireland.

In 1905, a new political party, Sinn Féin, emerged in opposition to the Irish Party. Led by Arthur Griffith, Sinn Féin represented the political voice of cultural nationalism in Ireland. The party linked Ireland's social and economic decay to what it saw as Redmond's policy of Anglicisation. According to Sinn Féin, Anglicisation demoralised the Irish people and made them more susceptible to British values and ways of thinking.[27] At this point the party did not advance a republican platform but rather the idea of a dual monarchy as then existed in Austria-Hungary. However, its 'Irish Ireland' ideals proved attractive to many members of the IRB and nationalists recently arrived from the United States such as Patrick McCartan and Diarmuid Lynch.

Since the IRB was not a political party, the Clan welcomed the emergence of Sinn Féin as a counterweight to the Irish Party and subsidised its newspaper, also called *Sinn Féin*. Cohalan, Devoy and McGarrity also tried to cultivate the emergence of an open Sinn Féin

League of America, though this made little headway given the popularity of Redmond's UILA. Cohalan hoped that circumstances might change which would allow for the successful mobilisation of a more broad-based Irish-American movement supportive of the Clan.[28]

Cohalan was realistic enough to know that even if the Clan enjoyed majority Irish-American support, the achievement of full independence for Ireland depended on the actions of the Irish in Ireland and the support of a foreign power. If such support could be obtained, then an uprising in Ireland, combined with support from the Irish diaspora, might very well succeed. Cohalan voiced this philosophy in a speech in New York in 1902:

> Ireland's true interests will therefore be best served by a steady resolute and progressive policy of organisation among her own people the world over and the cultivation of alliance with England's enemies with a view to the eventual reconstruction and re-establishment of an Irish nation – the founding of a true Republic – on the ruins of the British Empire.[29]

Cohalan put forward these views at Clan meetings around the country. At one such meeting in 1905, in Providence, Rhode Island, local Clan member John Gannon wrote to Devoy complimenting Cohalan on his speech:

> Dan made a very able and clear address on England's position showing the small hold she had on some parts of her dominions and the discontent in other parts. Her standing as a military power, each part of which he defined in a masterful manner.[30]

For Cohalan, any enemy of England could also be Ireland's friend and, in this regard, he adopted the policy of successive generations of Irish rebels. Devoy himself had been involved in a failed attempt to enlist Tsarist support for an Irish rebellion when relations between Russia and Britain were tense in the 1870s.[31] It was not surprising, therefore, that in 1900, when Britain was involved in a war in South Africa, Cohalan declared his support for the rebel Boers. In a speech before an Irish-American audience at the Hoffman House in 1900, Cohalan expressed the hope that 'the two struggling republics of South Africa should be victorious in their magnificent fight for continued existence'.[32] Cohalan, with his interests in international affairs, also recognised that the Germany of Kaiser Wilhelm II represented a much more formidable opponent to Britain's ambitions than Boer farmers in South Africa. As relations between Germany and Britain deteriorated in the early twentieth century due to increasing economic and naval rivalry, the *Gaelic American* began to take a pro-German stance. A clash between the rival alliances seemed likely and in any such clash Britain might well be defeated, thus paving the way for a free Ireland.

This German alliance had a domestic orientation too. The Clan had made common cause with the leaders of German-American groups in their battle against the arbitration treaty and Cohalan had formed friendships with some Germans involved in the campaign, such as journalist George von Skall. Von Skall would later write articles for the *Gaelic American* justifying Germany's position after war had broken out in Europe. The German-American campaign was funded by the German government through its embassy and officials and these contacts would prove valuable later as the Clan sought to enlist German support for an Irish rebellion. Meanwhile, German officials in the US looked with favour on Irish-Americans such as Devoy and Cohalan as a potential means of keeping America neutral in any future conflict.

While international tensions in Europe escalated, tensions also began to grow in Ireland. Ironically, in the years before the outbreak of the First World War, the spirit of rebellion seemed more prevalent among unionists after the Liberal government of Herbert Henry Asquith (1852–1928) introduced a Home Rule Bill in 1912. Due to the opposition of the conservative-dominated House of Lords, the bill was not due to become law until 1914. This allowed unionists led by Edward Carson to form an Ulster Volunteer Force (UVF) to oppose any implementation of the measure, by force if necessary. To show their determination, the UVF imported arms from Germany in April 1914. The formation of the UVF led in turn to an equivalent force of Irish nationalists in 1913. This came about at the instigation of a prominent cultural nationalist and university professor, Eoin MacNeill. MacNeill envisaged that this force would serve as a counterweight to Carson's force and would bolster a weak-willed British government in facing down the UVF and introducing home rule.[33]

The emergence of both the UVF and the Irish Volunteers, paired with the inaction of Asquith's government, introduced a revolutionary potential to the situation in Ireland which the Clan welcomed. With the UVF actively determined to resist home rule, the possibility of an armed conflict breaking out had very much increased. Moreover, the leadership of the Irish Volunteers rested in a committee which was dominated by IRB men such as Tom Clarke and Patrick Pearse.

Devoy and the Clan welcomed the spread of the Irish Volunteers, which, by the summer of 1914, numbered 180,000 members. In July 1914, the *Gaelic American* also reported excitedly on reports that the Irish Volunteers had received a cargo of arms from Germany, dramatically brought ashore from the sailboat *Asgard* at Howth near Dublin. Roger Casement, then on a fundraising mission for the force in the United States, had played a key role in organising and financing the shipment.[34] Casement was an unlikely Irish rebel: he was an internationally known figure, who, some years earlier, while serving with the British foreign office, had obtained a knighthood for his role in exposing the horrors of Belgian rule in the Congo. Though born in County Dublin, Casement was raised as a northern Protestant within a typically unionist environment. Nevertheless, he had embraced the Irish nationalist cause. Staying at Joe McGarrity's house in Philadelphia when news of the shipment arrived, he received a rapturous welcome by Clan supporters. McGarrity, in a letter to Devoy, described him as the 'reincarnation of Tone'.[35]

The landing of arms had not been without incident.[36] Frustrated British troops, unable to intercept the weapons, fired on a crowd of jeering Dublin civilians, killing three. In the US, the *Gaelic American* publicised details of the shooting in lurid headlines and this helped raise funds for the Volunteers.[37]

Ireland now seemed on the brink of war but dramatic events in Europe interrupted this escalating tension. The assassination of the Austro-Hungarian Archduke Franz Ferdinand in Sarajevo by a Serbian nationalist triggered an all-out conflict between the two rival alliance systems in Europe. As Germany came to the aid of Austria-Hungary and attacked France through Belgium, Britain decided to honour the earlier commitments it had made to France and Russia and entered the war on 3 August 1914.

Following this British declaration of war, Redmond, believing that home rule was secure, generously offered the Irish Volunteers to defend Ireland. Later, in a significant speech in Ireland on 20 September, he asked Irish Volunteers to 'go wherever the firing line extends'. This in effect meant encouraging Irishmen to enlist in the British army and participate in the war on Britain's side. This generosity on the part of Redmond was not reciprocated by Asquith's Liberal government. While the government did place home rule on the statute book, its implementation was suspended for the duration of the war and the government attached an amending bill which made the prospect of some type of partitionist solution to the crisis highly likely.[38]

Redmond's support for the British war effort caused a split in the Volunteer movement. A majority of the Volunteers, approximating 170,000 men, sided with Redmond and these became known as the National Volunteers. Meanwhile, a minority of about 11,000, under the command of Eoin MacNeill, maintained a separate force of Volunteers to be held in readiness to oppose Britain in the event of attempts to round up the Volunteer leadership and introduce conscription. The leadership of the latter faction, which retained the title of Irish Volunteers, was dominated by the IRB. Unknown to MacNeill, the supreme council of this body now made the momentous decision to take advantage of international conditions to stage a rising. In order to preserve secrecy, a Military Council, representing just a few members of the IRB leadership and including Tom Clarke, pressed ahead with their plans. As we shall see, Devoy, McGarrity and Cohalan would later play a crucial role in these plans.

In the summer of 1914, Cohalan and his family made their usual summer visit to Glandore in County Cork. As with his previous vacations, this was not just a sentimental visit to the land of his parents. As a close confidant of Devoy, he was anxious to learn more about the evolving political situation and its implications for the revolutionary movement in Ireland. Given the febrile political atmosphere, Tom Clarke, his old associate from the *Gaelic American*, travelled down from Dublin to the port of Queenstown in Cork to meet with Cohalan as he arrived from the United States. Things initially did not go to plan, as Clarke spelled out in a letter to Devoy on 7 July 1914: 'When I got there, I discovered the boat was not expected to arrive until late that night. It was impossible for me to remain over so I arranged with D.C. Cove to meet Dan and attend to the matter. I saw Dan on Sunday and got the news etc. from him.'[39]

Clarke's letter highlights Cohalan's importance as a communications link between the Clan and the IRB but Cohalan was not content to merely report on events. The *Irish Independent* newspaper, under the heading 'Irish-American Judge at Volunteer Review', had a photograph of Cohalan addressing a Volunteer meeting at Skibbereen. According to Aileen Cohalan's memoirs, Cohalan allowed the grounds of Glandore to be used for drilling purposes.[40]

While Redmond's support for the British war effort had caused dismay among Irish-Americans, it nevertheless created an opportunity which the Clan could now exploit in the interests of promoting their more radical version of Irish nationalism. In its headlines, the *Gaelic American* highlighted Redmond's 'Open Betrayal of Ireland'. The paper also gave front-page coverage to a large Irish-American demonstration, held in Celtic Park, New York City, on 9 August in opposition to Redmond and attended by 10,000 people. As a member of the board of Celtic Park, Cohalan helped to facilitate this event. In the same edition, the paper pointed out how a German victory over Britain would mean freedom for not only Ireland but also for Poland, Finland, India and Egypt.[41] Meanwhile, the *Gaelic American*'s campaign against Redmond's actions was now supported by the *Irish World*, which argued that for Redmond to 'fritter away any part of her [Ireland's] military resources would be treason of the blackest kind'.[42]

Casement had long been an admirer of Germany and, like the leaders of the Clan and the IRB, believed that a German victory in the war could spell the destruction of the British Empire and gain Irish freedom at last. On his own initiative, Casement decided that he would go to Germany to try to enlist support for the Irish cause. In order to accomplish this, he first needed to obtain the help of the Clan in getting him there and he needed the German government to approve the mission.

Cohalan's papers in the National Library of Ireland and McGarrity's papers in the NYPL indicate how Cohalan became involved in the web of subterfuge surrounding Casement's mission. A note in McGarrity's papers indicates that Casement attended a meeting in Cohalan's house on 5 October 1914. McGarrity and Devoy also attended and, along with Cohalan, decided that 3,000 dollars would be provided by the Clan for Casement's mission to Berlin. The men also agreed to arrange an interview with the German ambassador Count Heinrich von Bernstorff as soon as possible so as to facilitate Casement's mission and to secure a German declaration in favour of Irish independence.[43]

The German ambassador proved very responsive to such requests. Cohalan's papers in the NLI contain a letter from Casement dated

8 October 1914 suggesting a meeting in Cohalan's house at 7 p.m. the following day before meeting with German officials in the German Club at 9 p.m.

> My Dear Judge
>
> I write to suggest that we meet at your house tomorrow Friday at say 7.00. That would give us time for an exchange of views before reaching the club at 9.00. You can phone to the *Gaelic American* office if this does not suit, otherwise I shall call on you at 7.00 Friday.[44]

McGarrity's papers in the NYPL indicate that the meeting at Cohalan's house lasted from 7 p.m. to 8.15 p.m. Again, McGarrity notes that Cohalan, Casement and Devoy attended. The four men then made their way down to the German Club for the 9 p.m. meeting. McGarrity also notes that those who attended the meeting on the German side were Captain Franz von Papen, Dr Bernhard Dernburg, and Count von Bernstorff. Dernburg would become much better known in the American media the following year when he defended the German sinking of the *Lusitania* by claiming that the ship was a 'war vessel'. He was then described by the *New York Times* as a former German colonial minister and Emperor Wilhelm's 'personal agent in this country'.[45]

The presence of these high-ranking officials denotes that Germany took the Irish-American proposals seriously. This is also confirmed by German diplomatic files. A German academic, Reinhard R. Doerries, has translated the correspondence sent from German officials in the United States to the German Foreign Office in Berlin. One message from von Bernstorff dated 15 October reads:

> I am pressed constantly by Casement and other Irish [the Clan leadership] that the Imperial Government should declare that in case of victory, it would support the Irish. Casement himself wants to travel to Germany this week .... Looked at from here, nothing could be said against a [German] declaration in the way the Irish wish it. Moreover, the mood against us in England appears to be so thoroughly embittered that it can't get any worse. German declarations for the Irish, the Poles, the Jews, the Finns, etc could only have a positive effect here ....[46]

Von Bernstorff was obviously looking at such a declaration from a German perspective. German policy was intent on securing American neutrality in the current struggle and such declarations in favour of subject peoples would at least help to ensure that some sections of America's diverse ethnic communities would not be against a German victory.

McGarrity has also left us an account of a final meeting with Casement at Cohalan's house before he left for Germany. This time all the forged documents had been prepared for Casement. He was to travel with a passport under the name of Landy, an American businessman. Apparently, the real Landy was complicit in this arrangement and had even lent Casement his glasses and his Sons of Veterans badge to complete the disguise. According to McGarrity's account, both he and 'The Judge' helped to school Casement in the role of an American businessman. McGarrity provides an amusing account of this lesson in impersonation which was ultimately successful:

> I suddenly asked him [Casement] what his mother's name was. He answered O'Mara. The Judge said 'Oh, no. That is your wife's name. Your mother's name was Joyce.' We came to the conclusion that only by being recognised would he be taken.[47]

In the event, Cohalan and McGarrity's prediction proved correct. The Royal Navy stopped Casement's ship in a routine search and even removed some passengers for further questioning. However, the clean-shaven man in an American businessman's suit and glasses escaped attention.[48]

Cohalan's papers in the National Library of Ireland also contain a further letter from Casement on notepaper from the Continental Hotel in Berlin. This one was addressed to Cohalan's New York home address at 23 East 94th Street and dated 12 November. The letter indicates Casement's pleasure at securing a German declaration in favour of Irish independence. Arthur Zimmermann, the undersecretary for war at the German Foreign Office, had just published a declaration that if 'the fortunes of war should lead German troops to the shores of Ireland, they would land there not as a force of invaders … but as armed forces of a befriended government'.[49]

Knowing Cohalan's animosity towards the British Empire, Casement indicated his hope that a German declaration in favour of Irish independence would actually encourage other suppressed peoples:

> I forgot to say the first declaration (to appear next month) will be officially commn [communicated?] to all the German embassies and delegations throughout the world for issue there and also to the press here from the foreign office. It will also be specifically sent to Turkey, Egypt and India if possible.[50]

From Cohalan's perspective, Casement's mission to Germany at first seemed to be going very favourably. Meanwhile, back in the United States, the decline in Redmond's status there offered Cohalan an opportunity to exploit mainstream Irish-American opinion in favour of the Clan's vision of an independent Ireland. However, both Cohalan and Devoy recognised that this would need to be done through an open organisation and not a secret oath-bound body such as the Clan na Gael. Such an organisation would inevitably have an agenda reflecting Cohalan's isolationist preoccupations. Cohalan now seized this opportunity with both hands.

4

The First Irish Race Convention and 1916 Rising

REDMOND'S SUPPORT FOR the British war effort in 1914 helped to discredit the cause of Irish home rule in the eyes of many of his Irish-American followers. In the coming years, Cohalan would seek to channel this disenchantment with Redmond into a new broad-based organisation. Known as the Friends of Irish Freedom, it reflected Cohalan's own America-centred Irish nationalism in not only upholding Irish independence but also in defending Irish-American interests and the United States itself. Meanwhile, Cohalan, as a leading member of the Clan, would become directly involved in the web of subterfuge which led directly to the 1916 Rising in Ireland. Under Cohalan's leadership the FOIF would seek to exploit the emotion generated by the rising for both Irish and American ends. However, increasing international tensions between the United States and Germany would have domestic repercussions and impinge on this endeavour.

On a personal level, Cohalan's gloom over the death of his wife Hanna had eased by 1914. In an indication of his new-found optimism, he married Hanna's sister Madge in New York in February 1915. Madge had looked after his children since Hanna's death in 1911 and Cohalan had become increasingly devoted to her. The Rev. Patrick O'Leary, the bride's brother and a close friend of the family, celebrated the wedding mass held in St Francis de Sales Church on East 96th Street not far from the Cohalan residence on 94th Street.[1]

While this was a joyous event for the entire Cohalan family, 1915 also brought tragedy just months later with the death of Cohalan's six-year-old son Dermot from complications arising from appendicitis. Such deaths, from what are today preventable illnesses, were all too frequent during this era and struck Cohalan, who idolised his children, a severe blow. Yet his deep religious faith appears to have helped him come to terms with the tragedy.[2]

The ongoing war in Europe also impacted on the Cohalan family, who remained in the United States for the duration of the conflict. Cohalan did not want to put his family at risk by sailing to Ireland in wartime conditions. According to Aileen Cohalan's memoirs, the family rented a summer home on Lake Placid in upstate New York. Cohalan chose this house on the advice of his close friend Victor Herbert, who lived in the area.[3] Herbert was at this time a famous composer and conductor renowned for his successful operettas.

According to Aileen, Cohalan and Herbert frequently played golf in the area. Herbert's links to Ireland were tenuous. Though his mother had Irish heritage, he was born on the island of Guernsey and spent most of his formative years in Germany. Nevertheless, as Marion Casey points out in her article on Herbert in *Ireland's Allies* (2016), Herbert chose to identify himself as an Irishman and he became involved in Irish-American nationalist activities. Some of his best works, such as his operetta *Eileen*, had a strong Irish nationalist tone. Both Cohalan and Herbert were lifelong friends and, following Herbert's death in 1924, Cohalan wrote to Mrs Herbert indicating his intention to write a memorial for Herbert for the *Journal of the American Irish Historical Society* (1925).[4] As we shall see later, Herbert would become the first president of the Friends of Irish Freedom. Meanwhile, Cohalan followed closely the ongoing war in Europe. In line with Clan policy, he had long hoped that the British Empire would be defeated by another Great Power thus paving the way for Irish independence.[5] Indeed, as Germany held its own in Europe and inflicted immense casualties on the Allies, a British defeat seemed a distinct possibility. The *Gaelic American*, reflecting Cohalan and Devoy's pro-German stance, ran feature articles on individual German generals and seized upon Allied setbacks as portents for the destruction of the British Empire.[6]

Cohalan's pro-German stance alienated John Quinn, one of his closest friends, and all communication between them ceased for the duration of the war.[7] However, Quinn's pro-British stance was now less popular among Irish-Americans even though Redmond still enjoyed considerable support in Ireland itself. This may have been partly due to a traditional anti-British sentiment within Irish-American opinion, but newspapers such as the *Gaelic American* and the *Irish World* helped to fan this anti-Redmond sentiment. In contrast, nationalist newspapers in Ireland such as the *Irish Independent* and the *Freeman's Journal* continued to celebrate the Irish contribution to the war effort.[8] In a reversal of the usual Irish financial dependence on American money, Redmond's support organisation in the US, the United Irish League, had to be supported with funds from Ireland.[9]

In this changing environment Devoy saw an opportunity to form a new, more broad-based Irish-American movement more in line with Clan thinking on Irish and Irish-American interests. Following a Clan convention in New York in 1915, where both Cohalan and Devoy condemned Redmond's actions, Clan members called for the formation of just such an organisation. Richard McGinn, a senior member of the Clan, impressed by Cohalan's articulation of the anti-Redmond position, remarked:

> The convention that the U.B. [United Brotherhood or Clan na Gael] held in NY [New York] recently was a fine thing and [has] done much to enthuse the members; if that convention had been an open one and the same speeches delivered as those by Cohalan and yourself it would have a marked effect upon our people as a race, instead of a few thousands of dollars that will be raised by that appeal it would have reached a million.[10]

Devoy recognised that Cohalan, a State Supreme Court Justice with political contacts across the United States, would be the ideal candidate to organise such an 'open' convention. His appreciation of Cohalan's advice is revealed in his letter to Clan member Joseph McLaughlin on 6 December 1915, where Devoy referred to Cohalan as:

> … strongly pointing to the advisability of sounding a number of men of prominence whose names would add weight to such a gathering and then getting a number of such men together with the representatives of the societies known to be favorable, for the purpose of planning the larger conference and issuing the invitation thereto.[11]

Cohalan's role in organising the convention is further evidenced in the minutes of a meeting of the Clan executive on 11 December 1915. Here Devoy recorded the decision of the executive to hold a preliminary meeting to which leading figures such as Robert Ford, editor of the *Irish World*, and Judge John Goff would be invited so as to thrash out the details of the convention in advance. As noted in the minutes of the meeting, the Clan executive accepted Cohalan's advice as to how the meeting should be organised:

> The conclusion reached was that a recommendation be made to the DO's [district officers] ... that we approve of the calling of a conference under the conditions named by D.F.C. [Daniel Florence Cohalan]. Namely, that a small private conference be held on Sat Dec 18 to lay down the lines of action to be submitted to it, the organization and individuals to be invited and the time and place of the meeting.[12]

The acceptance of Cohalan's recommendation is further evidence of his ability to influence the direction of the Clan organisation, especially in relation to reaching out to mainstream Irish-American opinion. Under Cohalan's influence, this preliminary meeting decided that the convention should be as broad-based as possible and that it should be held in New York the following March. A subsequent Clan circular in December 1915 promoting the convention declared that 'men of standing in the community' and those 'former followers of Mr Redmond who have left him on account of his unpatriotic attitude' would be invited. The circular also underlined the importance of the forthcoming convention: 'It is hardly necessary to point out to you that such a conference, if successful, will afford a rallying point for the union of the entire Irish race at home and abroad and that on the result of its action will probably depend the whole future of the Irish cause.'[13]

In February 1916 the Clan sent out an official invitation to the convention entitled 'To the Men and Women of the Irish Race in America'.[14] This invitation asked those invited to consider four so-called 'problems' and reflect on what steps needed to be taken 'towards their solution'. These 'problems' constantly feature in Cohalan's later speeches and publications and they reflect the different components of his America-centred approach to Irish nationalism.[15]

Firstly, the invitation called on 'Americans of Irish blood' (a term frequently used by Cohalan), 'with their inherited love of liberty and their knowledge of English guile and cant', to consider how best 'the teachings and practices of Washington and Jefferson, of Jackson and Lincoln may continue to prevail'. As later outlined in Cohalan's convention speech, these presidents had advocated that the United States should always refrain from involvement in Europe's wars.

Secondly, the invitation highlighted the convention's support for the Irish-American ethnic community in its call for Irish-Americans to consider 'how best to destroy the British influences which misrepresent America to Ireland and Ireland to America'. Cohalan had already sought to promote such goals through his work in the American Irish Historical Society, in the Gaelic League in America and through his promotion of the *Gaelic American.*[16]

Thirdly, the invitation reflected the upholding of Irish national interests in its call for Irish-Americans to consider how best 'to preserve for Ireland the remnant of her manhood' and prevent England from sending young Irishmen to death or captivity on foreign soil. This perceived 'problem' tapped into the disillusionment felt by many Irish-Americans at Redmond's support for British army recruitment.

Finally, the invitation looked towards Ireland's position in the post-war period. Irish-Americans were asked to ponder another 'problem':

> How best to act so that at the Congress of the Nations which, at the end of the war, will remake for generations the map of Europe, the legitimate claims of Ireland to separation from England – to which race, geographical position and interest entitle her – may receive the fullest measure of consideration, and that after her age-long sufferings she may again take her place among the nations of the world.[17]

After months of preparations, in which Cohalan took a leading part, the first 'Irish Race Convention' took place on 4 and 5 March 1916 at the Hotel Astor in New York. It was considered one of the largest and most representative of such gatherings in Irish-American history so far held, as over 2,300 people from across the United States attended. Cohalan's contacts in the judiciary and the American corporate world ensured that many 'men of standing' did indeed attend. In his later work, *Recollections of an Irish Rebel* (1929), Devoy proudly pointed out: 'At no previous Irish Convention was there even one [State] Supreme Court Justice; there were five at this, besides several other judges of lesser rank, and a large number of lawyers.'[18]

The convention speeches reflected the key 'problems' which confronted Irish-America as set out in the invitation to the gathering. These speeches also offer an insight into the subsequent policy of the FOIF which emerged from the convention. Cohalan's colleague on the State Supreme Court bench Judge John Goff delivered the keynote speech. In line with Clan policy, Goff declared that he refused to believe that hostility to England, which had been 'maintained for centuries in the face of famine and persecution', had suddenly given way to 'zealous loyalty for an empty formula labeled home rule'.[19]

In his own keynote speech, which took place at the close of the event, Cohalan focused on Irish-American loyalty to the United States and typically the threat posed from within to American institutions by an Anglo-American elite bent on subverting America's policy of neutrality. In a rousing speech he argued that:

> America could never be overcome, that American institutions could never fail unless it were by British force from without or by British wiles from within. There has always been, there always will be, in this country, a group of people who have sympathized not with those who won in the Revolution, but with those who lost in the Revolution.[20]

As intended by Cohalan, the Clan harnessed the goodwill generated by the successful conference to form a new open organisation, which would live on long after the speeches at the convention had been forgotten. In a dramatic gesture, Robert Ford, editor of the *Irish World*, proposed the name of the new organisation as the 'Friends of Irish Freedom' and this was seconded by John Devoy of the *Gaelic American*.[21] Given that both men had attended the pre-convention meeting organised by Cohalan some months previously, this gesture between old rivals was not spontaneous and must surely have been pre-arranged. Nevertheless, the move symbolised a greater level of unity within Irish-American opinion which would have been unthinkable just two years previously.

The convention selected Cohalan's close friend Victor Herbert, the renowned Irish-American composer, as president of the FOIF. This highlighted the respectability of the new organisation. However, though Herbert made several speeches in promoting the ideals of revolutionary Irish nationalism to middle-class Irish-Americans, the real power over the FOIF resided in an executive committee.[22] Of the seventeen men on this executive, fifteen were Clan members. Daniel Cohalan remained the dominant member and was the acknowledged leader of the FOIF

Curiously, John Devoy chose not to be on the FOIF executive committee. He may have decided that he did not want his name too closely identified with a movement that sought to appeal to a broad spectrum of Irish-American opinion and he could, after all, exercise his influence through his leadership of the Clan. He also trusted Cohalan completely and allowed him free rein in managing this new open organisation.[23]

The promotion of the Irish cause in the United States loomed large in the FOIF's constitution, which stated that it dedicated itself 'to encourage and assist any movement that will bring the national independence of Ireland'. The convention also laid down a 'Declaration of Principles and Policy' which Cohalan helped to draft. According to the *Gaelic American*, the new nationwide organisation was 'mandated' to carry out this declaration and, given Cohalan's leadership role, it would be his responsibility to ensure that such a declaration would be implemented.[24] The declaration reflected the key themes of the invitation and convention speeches. It insisted that the United States should not enter the war as England's ally and demanded that 'our neutrality laws be enforced with fairness and impartiality'. Echoing Cohalan's closing speech, the declaration also recalled historic British treachery towards Ireland which now menaced the United States.

> We have followed with closer attention than many of our fellow citizens of other strains of blood, the course of American History, and have seen the same hand which has crushed Ireland ever stretched out in constant menace against America.[25]

For Cohalan and Devoy, the maintenance of American neutrality satisfied both Irish and American interests. In the first instance, it would make British defeat more likely and this in turn would ensure the emergence of an independent Ireland out of the ruins of the British

Empire.[26] Secondly, they believed that US intervention would cost American lives and resources in an unnecessary foreign war and bolster the pro-British movement in the United States. Commenting on the founding of the FOIF, the *Gaelic American* declared that 'the pro-British movement is now confronted by an organized Irish race throughout the land'.[27]

Following the successful convention, the Clan now had a public organisation in place to maximise the expected propaganda effects of the impending rising. Cohalan would make full use of the FOIF to press home the cause of revolutionary Irish nationalism in the United States. However, in line with his often stated aim of countering Anglo-Saxon influence in American life and defending American interests, it was inevitable that the resulting FOIF organisation would also reflect these objectives.

While Cohalan and other Irish-American leaders congratulated themselves on the success of the convention and the launch of the FOIF, the mainstream press did not demonstrate the same enthusiasm. The *Brooklyn Citizen* argued that the version of Irish nationalism displayed at the convention was at 'variance with Ireland's elected representatives in Ireland' who supported the British war effort.[28] To a large degree, these observations had validity. The version of Irish nationalism put forward by Cohalan and the other delegates to the convention did not correlate with the constitutional nationalism held by the majority of Irish nationalists in Ireland. However, Irish nationalist opinion in Ireland was not static and the coming years would see a dramatic shift in favour of the type of nationalism which the Clan advocated.

The FOIF provided Cohalan with a national propaganda machine to secure objectives which he had long campaigned for. Organised on a national basis with members of the Clan forming the backbone of the organisation in different parts of the country, the FOIF appealed to all sections of Irish-America. Organisations such as the Ancient Order of Hibernians and the Friendly Sons of St Patrick could affiliate to the FOIF and the members of these organisations could enjoy 'Associate' status in the FOIF. Women could also join and many, such as Mary McWhorter, president of the Ladies' Auxiliary of the AOH, also played a significant role in FOIF activities.[29] Not surprisingly, the organisation was strongest in those areas with a strong Irish community, especially on the east coast. According to Diarmuid Lynch, who later became national secretary at the

1918 convention, eighty-seven branches were established in 1916 and, of these, twenty-six were located in the greater New York area while twenty-five were established in Massachusetts.[30]

The establishment of the FOIF came at a propitious time as far as its Irish objectives were concerned. The convention occurred just six weeks prior to the Easter Rebellion in 1916. Cohalan, Devoy and McGarrity already knew of the impending rising. On 5 February 1916 Devoy had received a coded message by courier from the Military Council of the IRB indicating that a rising was about to take place on the following Easter Sunday and also requesting German assistance. The following day, in Cohalan's home, Devoy informed both Cohalan and McGarrity of this dramatic news.[31]

As a trusted and valued member of the Clan, Cohalan therefore knew of the anticipated rising, but what of his own involvement? As already discussed in the previous chapter, Cohalan had played a role in facilitating Casement's mission to Germany and his house had been used as a venue for planning that mission and co-ordination with German officials in the United States. Following Casement's departure for Germany, the Clan's contacts with these German officials and Germany itself intensified. It communicated with Casement and forwarded IRB messages to Berlin, using the New York offices of German commercial attaché Wolf von Igel. Devoy, as leader of the Clan, was at the centre of these contacts and was a frequent visitor to von Igel.[32] Cohalan also played a role in these communications. Reinhard Doerries, a German academic, who has drawn on German archives to explore Casement's role in the rising, has reprinted several translated German documents containing Cohalan's name. One undated message from Casement to Cohalan (probably November 1914) reads:

> Landy's identity discovered by enemy who are greatly alarmed and taking steps [to] defend Ireland and possibly arrest friends. They are ignorant of true purpose of my coming [to] Germany but seek evidence at all cost.
>
> Here everything favourable. Authorities helping warmly. Send messenger immediately to Ireland full instructed verbally. No letters on him. He should be a native-born American citizen, otherwise arrest likely. Let him dispatch priest here via Christiana quickly. German legation there will arrange passport.[33]

Unknown to the Clan, British naval intelligence had broken the German codes and could read such transmitted messages between Casement and Cohalan. Indeed, the above message later appeared in the British government white paper published in 1921 and entitled *Documents Relative to the Sinn Fein Movement.*[34]

The British ability to crack German codes enabled them to notify their American counterparts that German spies operated from von Igel's offices in New York. Some of these spies had engaged in sabotage operations against British supply ships in American docks, though the Clan itself did not take part in these operations. On 18 April, just days before the rising broke out, the American authorities raided these offices and discovered documents indicating the date of the planned Irish rebellion and details of a German arms shipment scheduled to arrive in Ireland on the eve of the revolt.[35] One message seized indicated that Cohalan had been in touch with the German high command requesting their support for the rebellion. The captured cable read:

> The Irish revolt can only succeed if assisted by Germany; otherwise, England will be able to crush it, although after a severe struggle. Assistance required. There would be an air raid on England and a naval attack timed to coincide with the Rising; followed by a landing of troops and munitions and also of some officers, perhaps from an airship. It might then be possible to close the Irish harbors against England, set up bases for submarines and cut off food exports to England. A successful rising may decide the war.[36]

At the time of the raid, the US authorities informed the American press that a raid had taken place but did not disclose the substance of the seized documents. The American government only released a transcript of the above document in September 1917 when the US itself had joined the war as Britain's ally. In response, Cohalan denied the veracity of this message and claimed that it had been forged in an attempt to discredit him.[37] However, the presence of this document, along with other Cohalan messages in the German archives, provides overwhelming evidence that he made this last-minute, desperate appeal before the Irish rebellion began.

While Cohalan's role as a New York State Supreme Court Justice makes such an appeal highly unorthodox, the request must be set against the background of ongoing Clan efforts to enlist German support for the

Irish cause. In this context, Cohalan's appeal was largely a restatement of an earlier request from the IRB to the Clan for German arms and capable officers to be sent to Ireland to coincide with the revolt.[38] Echoing this request from the IRB, the Clan leader in Philadelphia, Joe McGarrity, pleaded with Casement to put pressure on the Germans to get a small force of German troops to Ireland:

> Can nothing be done to get a small force with a quantity of arms to Ireland? A small force with a quantity of arms would I believe get such support as would enable them if not to free Ireland at least to keep the field until peace would be declared which with Germany the victor would or should mean Ireland independent.[39]

The German High Command, recognising the dominance of the Royal Navy, did not take seriously Cohalan and McGarrity's requests to send troops, no doubt believing that it would be impossible to send sufficient numbers to affect the outcome of any revolt. Germany did, however, resolve to dispatch weapons to Ireland by ship, disguising it as a neutral Norwegian vessel renamed *Aud*. However, due to confusion over the date of the landing, no Irish Volunteers had been present to meet the ship. After a fruitless wait, the ship was eventually discovered by the British navy off the Irish coast. In a further dramatic twist, Casement, disillusioned by the failure of the German authorities to provide sufficient weapons, had also landed in Ireland by German submarine with the intention of preventing what he perceived as a suicidal rebellion taking place. He too was captured.[40]

Despite the interception of the arms ship and the arrest of Casement, and still lacking sufficient arms and men, Tom Clarke and the other members of the Military Council decided to press ahead with the rebellion on Easter Monday. The IRB notified the Clan accordingly. Cohalan was involved in this communication though it is not clear who in New York received this news first. According to Cronin, based on a study of McGarrity's papers in the NYPL, members of the Kerry IRB transmitted this message to Cohalan via Valentia coastguard station. Alternatively, as claimed by Donard de Colgan in a *History Ireland* article in 1993, it may have first gone to Devoy who then informed Cohalan who in turn notified McGarrity. In his memorandum on 1916, McGarrity claims that he received the news in Philadelphia via a telephone call from Cohalan in New York, so it is clear that Cohalan was one of the first to get the news that the rising was going ahead.[41]

In the absence of German support, and given the rebel tactics of defending public buildings rather than engaging in guerrilla warfare, the rising stood no chance of success against well-trained and numerically superior British forces. By the end of Easter week, after much destruction and loss of life, the surviving rebels surrendered. As contemporary commentators and historians have often noted, the British government's response to the rising, rather than the rising itself, had a more significant impact on Irish-American and Irish nationalist opinion.[42] In a move described by the *New York Times* as 'incredibly stupid', General Sir John Grenfell Maxwell, charged with putting down the revolt, ordered the executions of the main rebel leaders. These executions, which dragged out over several days, undermined support for Redmond among nationalists in Ireland and enhanced the standing of the FOIF movement in the United States.[43]

Cohalan recognised how the propaganda value of these executions could be used to further undermine Redmond's already weak standing among Irish-American nationalists. In a speech in Pittsfield, Massachusetts, on 30 April, recorded in the *New York Times*, Cohalan declared: 'Can one imagine a more contemptible figure than that which has been cut by Redmond? Lost to all sense of decency, he alone has been acting as the chief recruiting sergeant for England in Ireland.' In keeping with his deep-rooted anti-imperialism, Cohalan also saw how the rising could serve as an example to other oppressed nationalities within the British Empire. In the same speech, Cohalan declared that: 'The rising in Ireland is the greatest and most effective blow that has ever been struck at England.' He argued that news of the rising 'will spread all over the British Empire with Gallipoli and Kut-el-Amara, win the Indians, hearten the Egyptians and show Japan upon what a weak reed she leans'.[44]

Cohalan called for nationwide meetings protesting against the British executions of the rebel leaders, to take place on 8 May. At one such meeting in San Francisco, over 6,000 people attended.[45] An alarmed British ambassador in Washington, Sir Cecil Spring Rice, noted Cohalan's involvement in this Irish-American 'excitement' and in a report to the London Foreign Office in May 1916 quoted Cohalan as saying that: 'If the arms going to Ireland had ever gotten there, the mere sample of warfare which was shown by the handful of revolutionaries would have been a real revolution.'[46] In contrast, in a report to Berlin in December 1916, the German ambassador to the United States Count Bernstorff noted approvingly 'the ruthless [British] procedure against Ireland since the Easter Rebellion of which a well-directed press service of American Irish keeps public opinion constantly informed'.[47]

Cohalan as leader of the FOIF also sent appeals and petitions on behalf of Irish prisoners to both Congress and the president. Since 1916 was an election year, senators and congressmen anxious to curry favour with their Irish-American voters were receptive to such appeals. In May 1916, Thomas Gallivan of Chicago and Murray Hulbert of New York introduced congressional resolutions appealing to the British government 'to exercise restraint with the Irish Prisoners'. At state level, resolutions were also introduced in the Massachusetts House of Representatives demanding that there be no more executions of Irish prisoners. Such agitation combined with reports from the British ambassador may well have moderated the British response to the rebellion, though this came too late to have any moderating effect on Irish-American opinion.[48]

Cohalan's talent for oratory helped the FOIF to publicise support for the Irish cause in the wake of the failed rebellion. As part of this campaign, Cohalan spoke at receptions for so-called 'emissaries' from Ireland. These included prominent individuals such as Liam Mellows, who had taken part in the Easter Rising in Galway, Nora Connolly, the daughter of executed leader James Connolly, and Hanna Sheehy-Skeffington, the widow of Dublin pacifist and journalist Francis Sheehy-Skeffington, who had been murdered by a British officer during the rising itself. Cohalan also made time to meet lesser-known figures such as Frank Robbins, who had been a member of James Connolly's Citizen Army and who had come to New York after his release from prison in England. In a later book, Robbins recalled meeting Cohalan at a reception hosted by the Clan. Typically, such exiles called upon Cohalan's hospitality in different ways. Robbins, who sang rebel songs at such meetings, recalled Cohalan's efforts to introduce him to Victor Herbert in order to help him develop his singing voice.[49]

Cohalan recognised that Irish-American sympathy for the civilian victims of the rising could be harnessed for fundraising purposes, and in

May 1916 he helped set up an Irish Relief Fund for the 'relief of suffering in Ireland'. Once again, his leadership skills are evident in the make-up of the fund's organising committee. He took central stage as chairman. John D. Moore, national secretary of the FOIF, became secretary and Thomas Hughes Kelly, treasurer of the FOIF, also became treasurer of the fund.[50] By mid-July 1916 the fund amounted to 100,000 dollars. On 8 July, two representatives of the fund, John A. Murphy and John Gill of New York, travelled to Ireland to distribute the monies and, to the discomfort of British ambassador Spring Rice, reported back to the American press on the 'desperate conditions' in Ireland.[51] When Thomas Kelly later attempted to land in Ireland, the British authorities, suspecting that the relief fund was not entirely non-political as Cohalan claimed, refused him entry.

Cohalan's leadership role in the Irish Relief Fund, like that of his leadership role in the Irish Race Convention and the 1916 Rising itself, demonstrates that his attachment to Ireland was more than sentimental. He cleverly used his status as a Supreme Court Justice and drew on his political connections to further the Irish cause in the United States in ways that drew the admiration of Irish nationalists in both Ireland and the US. His creation, the FOIF, would eventually become, as historian Alan J. Ward put it, 'the most effective propaganda machine in Irish-American history'.[52] However, in the months ahead, as the United States faced the prospect of entry into the Great War then raging in Europe, Cohalan would be presented with difficult choices which would call into question his dual allegiance to both Ireland and the United States. Irish nationalists did not always fully understand these conflicting pressures, thus paving the way for the first of several battles over Cohalan's America-first priorities.

5

Defending American Neutrality and the Flag, 1914–18

While much of Cohalan's efforts were devoted to publicising the Irish cause in the United States, he also pursued more American-oriented objectives in line with his isolationist ideology. Throughout 1916 and early 1917, Cohalan used the FOIF in a national campaign to maintain American neutrality towards the war in Europe. As tensions between Germany and the US gave way to all-out war, Cohalan would be faced with a difficult choice. Continuing the FOIF campaign against British policy in Ireland left him open to charges of disloyalty by a pro-Allied public opinion. Alternatively, if he scaled back FOIF activities, he risked incurring the wrath of those who wished to pursue a more energetic campaign on behalf of the Irish cause. In the months ahead, Cohalan sought to steer a middle path between these conflicting pressures but this was a difficult manoeuvre in a time of growing nativist sentiment. For a time Cohalan's career – and even his freedom – would hang in the balance. Meanwhile, Cohalan would have to deal more directly with Sinn Féin representatives in the US itself and come to recognise that their approach to defending the Irish cause did not always coincide with his own.

After war broke out in 1914, Cohalan, in line with the isolationist policies of the FOIF, the Clan and the *Gaelic American*, had called for American neutrality. The *Gaelic American* and many leading members of the FOIF had also been vocal in their desire for a German victory.[1] On 15 August 1914, the *Gaelic American* praised the German kaiser, proclaiming: 'We hope and pray for his success.' Typically, Cohalan's call for neutrality was tinged with anti-imperial sentiment and a belief that

Britain was working behind the scenes to enlist the United States as an ally in its life and death struggle with Germany. As Cohalan declared in a speech in Pittsfield, Massachusetts: 'With the United States out, England must herself fight as she has never done. She would use us [the American people] to pull her chestnuts out of the fire.'[2]

Cohalan's fears about British intrigue in the United States had some basis in fact. Shortly after the war began, the British government established a War Propaganda Bureau, known as Wellington House, with the objective of enlisting American support in the war against Germany and her allies. According to David Welch, in *Propaganda, Power and Persuasion*, the Wellington House campaign was 'almost invisible' and 'targeted America's elite with material with which they might make up their own minds, in the belief that this would, in turn, influence the larger public'.[3] Cohalan's FOIF sought to counteract this pressure by issuing press releases and holding demonstrations in favour of American neutrality. Yet while large numbers still attended such demonstrations, FOIF membership remained low. According to its records, the FOIF listed only 2,891 members for the year 1916 to 1917, of whom 1,495 were based in New York.[4]

An American environment hostile to any overt displays of ethnic identity may explain this relatively low membership, despite the emotional Irish-American reaction to the 1916 Rising. Historian John Higham has argued that the period of the Great War produced the 'most strenuous nationalism and the most pervasive nativism' that America had ever known.[5] In this climate, Americanisation drives took place which urged all citizens to shed their allegiance to their country of origin and become fully American. President Wilson seemed especially focused on the need for national solidarity. In a speech to Congress in October 1915, he questioned the loyalty of so-called hyphen-Americans and declared that they had 'poured the poison of disloyalty into the very arteries of our national life'.[6]

A numerically inferior FOIF, therefore, limited the effectiveness of Cohalan's neutrality campaign but he persisted in his efforts with his usual dogged determination. In this context he judged the prospect of another presidential term for Woodrow Wilson as highly dangerous to American neutrality. As discussed in the introduction, Cohalan was convinced that Wilson, because of his Anglophile tendencies, would embroil the United States in a European war on Britain's side. Among Cohalan's papers at the AIHS are several extracts from Wilson's publications and speeches indicating the president's reverence for British democracy and culture and his scepticism about the Irish character. As an illustration of Cohalan's belief that Wilson identified with his English 'mother country', one file contains several quotations from Wilson's book *Mere Literature*, published in 1896. Emphasising his obsession with Wilson's ideological leanings, Cohalan has even underlined certain words such as 'we', 'us' and 'thought', as in the example below.

> In the middle of the last century, two Irish adventurers crossed over into England – Edmund Burke and Oliver Goldsmith. For their sakes alone, we can afford to forgive Ireland all the trouble she has caused us. (pp 104–5)
>
> No man belongs more thoroughly to England than does Edmund Burke, indubitable Irishman though he was. His words, now that they have cast off their brogue, ring out the authentic voice of the best political thought of the English race. (pp 105–6)[7]

Ironically then, Cohalan shared Wilson's fear about the disloyalty of 'hyphen-Americans', but for Cohalan, the real hyphenated Americans were the pro-British Anglo-Saxon elite who would sacrifice the interests of the United States in support of their own mother country, England. Cohalan, in an interview with the *Boston Daily Advertiser*, stated that 'only the Irish-Americans and German-Americans could save the United States from the sinister and perfidious domination of English interests'.[8]

As discussed in the introductory chapter, Cohalan had long distrusted Wilson's 'internationalism' and Anglo-Saxonism.[9] Wilson also represented the reformist wing of the Democratic Party and had never been comfortable with how Tammany operated. Cohalan and Boss Murphy had after all attempted to block his nomination at the Baltimore Convention in 1912. Yet Cohalan exaggerated the extent to which Wilson's emotional attachment to Britain shaped his domestic and foreign policy. Wilson was guided by what he perceived as the interests of the United States and not by the interests of Britain. Moreover, several Irish-Americans served in the Wilson administration, including his Irish-American secretary Joseph Tumulty, who had served him loyally since his term as governor of New Jersey.[10] The British ambassador to the United States, Sir Cecil Spring Rice, who was himself of Anglo-Irish background, recognised this.

In a later message to his superiors in London, Spring Rice noted: 'The President is by descent an Orangeman and by education a Presbyterian. But he is the leader of the Democratic Party in which the Irish play a prominent part …'[11]

Nevertheless, as historical analysis often illustrates, perceptions shape actions and there is no doubt that Cohalan perceived Wilson as pro-British and his defeat in the 1916 election thus became a vital goal. As the *Gaelic American* pointed out, Wilson, 'if re-elected would try to plunge the country into war on the side of England, his Mother's country. The surest way to avert such a calamity is to defeat Wilson at the polls.'[12] According to Patrick McCartan, who later served as a Sinn Féin 'envoy' in the United States, Cohalan used the FOIF as a 'national machine' in a co-ordinated campaign to prevent Wilson's re-election and in support of Republican presidential candidate Charles Evans Hughes. In FOIF rallies, Cohalan portrayed Hughes as more committed to American interests compared to the 'pro-British' Wilson.[13] This decision to support Hughes must have been a difficult one. After all, Cohalan, like many New York-based Irish-Americans, owed his career to the Tammany system.[14] But in other respects this was a logical choice and was again consistent with his traditional devotion to American isolationism.

In the election campaign itself, both candidates appealed to the ethnic vote, though Wilson tapped into public fears that the war in Europe would cause a conflict of loyalties among America's different cultural groups. At one stage in the campaign, Wilson's attacks on 'hyphenism' provoked an angry response from Jeremiah O'Leary, a member of the FOIF executive committee and also president of the American Truth Society. O'Leary had founded this society to counteract mounting Anglo-Saxon influence in American life. While Cohalan shared these aims, he disagreed with O'Leary's more strident methods. During the campaign, O'Leary in a telegram angrily warned Wilson that he would lose votes if he did not support the Irish nationalist cause. In a celebrated response, which garnered Wilson much support, including that of the *New York Times*, Wilson replied: 'Your telegram received. I would feel deeply mortified to have you or anybody like you vote for me. Since you have access to many disloyal Americans and I have not, I will ask you to convey this message to them.'[15]

A booming economy and a campaign which celebrated the fact that 'he had kept us out of the war' helped Wilson win the 1916 presidential election but the margin was close. Wilson defeated Hughes by 9,129,606 votes to 8,538,221 and by 277 electoral college votes to 254.[16] The *Gaelic American* argued that this narrow victory highlighted the power of the Irish vote and many Irish-American politicians may have believed such claims. However, in a ward by ward analysis of Irish-American voting patterns, William M. Leary has argued that ethnic Irish voters still voted overwhelmingly Democratic despite Wilson's anti-hyphen campaign. According to Leary, Irish-Americans, while they sympathised with their cousins in Ireland, were more motivated by domestic bread and butter issues in this election. The Irish working class was especially impressed by Wilson's Child Labor Act and the Adamson Eight-Hour Act, which he had only recently introduced.[17] The British consul general in New York, Joyce Broderick, lends further credence to this view. In a report to his superiors in London on Irish-American voting patterns in the 1916 election, Broderick noted that 'loyalty to the Democratic Party gave them [Irish-Americans] a fairer prospect of personal profit direct and indirect'.[18] This evidence would underline the limitations on Cohalan's power to convince Irish-Americans to vote against their own economic interests.

Undaunted by this result, Cohalan stepped up his neutrality campaign in early 1917. He continually warned Irish-Americans that US participation in the war would only bolster the British Empire. In a New York speech on 4 February 1917, at a public meeting of the FOIF, Cohalan declared that if the country fought on the side of the Allies, it 'would be fighting for the combined subjection of Ireland, India, and Egypt to English rule. It would be a war against Germany and would keep Ireland, whose sons fought for America in their way, under the heel of England.'[19]

The escalating tensions between the United States and Germany in the spring of 1917, especially with regard to the resumption of unrestricted German submarine warfare that targeted American shipping, and the publication of the Zimmermann note, a German proposal to Mexico that it should declare war on the United States, further limited Cohalan's power to influence events. Finally, in the face of such tensions, the United States declared war on Germany on 6 April 1917.

As discussed in the introduction, the reasons behind Wilson's decision to enter the war has provoked much historical debate. Many historians take the view that Wilson made every effort to avoid American involvement in the war in the face of considerable provocation by Germany.[20] Justus D. Doenecke argues that 'it was Germany that forced the administration's hand' and the American press and a majority in Congress supported Wilson's decision.[21] In contrast, Robert Hannigan's work *The Great War and American Foreign Policy* (2016) argues that Wilson's policies represented a continuation of a benevolent attitude towards Britain pursued by the three previous American administrations of W. McKinley, T. Roosevelt and W.H. Taft. Hannigan suggests that it was in the interests of the United States that Britain should win the war, thus making way for an international order which the US would ultimately dominate. While such an analysis would conform to Cohalan's view that Wilson's policies were pro-British and anti-German, it would nonetheless see these policies driven by cold *realpolitik* considerations reflecting the growth of American power rather than by the president's known Anglophile sympathies.[22]

The entry of the United States into the First World War represented a blow to Cohalan's hopes for a German victory. Yet it also provided him with an opportunity. President Wilson, reflecting his vision of a post-war order which would ensure lasting peace, stated in his 'Declaration of War' speech to Congress that the United States would fight 'for the rights and liberties of small nations, for a universal dominion of rights by such a concert of free peoples as shall bring peace and safety to all nations and make the world free at last'.[23]

As the United States went to war against Germany, Cohalan did not shirk from publicly calling on Irish-Americans to rally to the national flag as they had always done since the American Revolution. In April 1917, in an interview with the Catholic newspaper the *Brooklyn Tablet*, he argued that Irish-Americans would always be 'present in defense of the flag and support of American institutions'.[24] Cohalan's patriotic call to action was even picked up by the unionist-leaning *Irish Times* newspaper in Ireland, which cited a New York speech where Cohalan stated that: 'I am for America first, last and all the time. When the United States entered the war, I turned against Germany.' The *Irish Times* headed their article 'A Prominent Sinn Féiner Faces Facts' and used his speech to rally support for the war effort.[25]

The actions of his own family reflected this American patriotism. Aileen Cohalan, in her memoirs, records how the Cohalans, like a lot of other New York Upper East Side families, held large dinner parties where guests had to pay for dinner tickets. The proceeds were collected in a 'war chest' and then donated to the war effort. Aileen Cohalan, with her father's approval, also organised garage sales, raising 'hundreds of dollars' in support of the troops fighting in France.[26] Such actions typified the natural loyalty of most Irish-Americans to the war effort and suggest that Cohalan's patriotism was sincere, despite his previous campaign to preserve neutrality and his belief that American entry into the war had been a profound mistake.[27]

Cohalan's initial response to the war also sought to balance traditional Irish-American loyalty to the American nation with calls for Irish freedom. At a Carnegie Hall meeting in New York attended by 3,000 people, just days after the US declaration of war, he urged Irish-Americans to support the war effort: 'Whatever our opinions were as to the merits of the controversy, we have but one duty. To remember that we are, above all, Americans.' Cohalan linked this open declaration of support for the United States to claims that the war was being fought for the freedom of oppressed nationalities. In a speech which according to the *New York Times* evoked a 'storm of cheers' Cohalan declared: 'This Republic [United States] is now in a position to demand from England the independence of Ireland. England professes to be fighting for the small nationalities and for the faith of treaties. Ireland is as much entitled to her freedom as Belgium, Serbia, Montenegro or Rumania.' At the same meeting, it was agreed that an appeal should be sent to Congress to 'take such action as will secure the independence of Ireland, not at the end of the war when scraps of paper may be safely torn up, but now when America's intervention will count for more than at any time in the future'.[28]

Cohalan's reaction to the British-inspired 'Irish Convention' of all the political parties in Ireland typically illustrates his twin-track policy of supporting the American war effort and upholding Irish independence.[29] The idea of such a convention was the brainchild of David Lloyd George, who had replaced Henry Asquith as prime minister in December 1916. American pressure may well have motivated Lloyd George to attempt to reach a political settlement of the Irish question or at least to appear to be doing so. In April 1917, not long after the US entry into the war, the prime minister had received a congressional declaration signed by over 200 members of the American Congress stating that: 'Nothing would add more to the enthusiasm of America in the war than a settlement now of the Irish problem.'[30] Anxious to give the impression that the British government was working towards a solution to an issue that might hamper future co-operation with the United States, the Irish Convention began its proceedings in July 1917. Yet from the beginning the prospects of reaching any agreement seemed slight. While a home rule settlement was on the table, full independence was not. Sinn Féin, now rapidly becoming the most popular nationalist party in Ireland in the wake of the 1916 Rising, decided to boycott the proceedings. Meanwhile, the Ulster unionists remained resolutely opposed to any home rule-type settlement.[31]

Taking the Sinn Féin view, Cohalan, in an interview with the *New York Times*, attacked the convention as an 'affront to the self-respect of Ireland and an insult to the intelligence of America'. He also suggested that Lloyd George's home rule proposals were being made 'in bad faith'.[32] John D. Moore, national secretary of the FOIF, echoed Cohalan's comments and in an article in the *Gaelic American* claimed that the US had entered the war 'for the rights of small nations great and small ... and to make the world safe for democracy'. Again, drawing on Wilson's principles, Moore claimed that 'the American people expected England to apply the principles of real democracy to Ireland'.[33]

As Cohalan and many commentators anticipated, the convention failed to reach an agreement. From a British perspective it may well have served to distract American opinion for a time. Lloyd George correctly anticipated that once US engagement in the war deepened, the Irish question, never at the forefront of American politics, would inevitably recede from the headlines. In Ireland itself this signalled yet another nail in the coffin of an already declining Irish Parliamentary Party and contributed to the increasing popularity of Sinn Féin, who had opposed the convention from the very beginning.[34]

Cohalan welcomed the increasing popularity of Sinn Féin, all the more so since it stood for a form of republican nationalism which the Clan had traditionally advocated. Sinn Féin, in turn, recognised the increasing importance of the United States in determining the post-war peace settlement. Not surprisingly, they looked to Irish-American nationalists such as Cohalan and Devoy to help ensure Irish representation. Indeed, from a Sinn Féin perspective, Cohalan, with his undoubted organising ability and political and corporate connections, was potentially a much more significant ally than the reclusive and aged Devoy.

With the aim of securing American recognition for Irish independence in mind, Sinn Féin dispatched Dr Patrick McCartan to the United States as a so-called 'envoy' of the Irish republic in early 1917. In Sinn Féin eyes, the republic had been declared at the start of the 1916 Rising and had been sanctified by the blood of the executed leaders, despite the obvious fact that it had no international recognition. McCartan was an obvious choice as envoy. He had previously lived in the United States and was well known to Joe McGarrity in Philadelphia. Both men came from the same part of County Tyrone.[35]

McCartan carried with him a 'memorial' signed by twenty-six 'recently released prisoners' who had been arrested following the 1916 Rising. The statement, which McCartan hoped to present to the American president, referred to Wilson's claims that the US was fighting 'for the liberty, self-government and undictated development of all peoples …'.[36] Upon arrival in the United States, McCartan, with the help of Cohalan, McGarrity and Devoy, compiled a memorandum deemed an expression of the national 'aspirations of the Irish people'. In his work *With de Valera in America*, McCartan recounts how he accepted Cohalan's slight changes to the phraseology of the document.[37]

With Cohalan's full approval, McCartan went directly to the White House accompanied by James Maguire, chairman of the FOIF executive committee, and national secretary John D. Moore. Unwilling to offend Britain, Wilson refused to speak with McCartan directly, though his staff accepted the prisoner's petition and memorandum.[38] This negative reaction did not augur well for the future. Nevertheless, both Sinn Féin and the FOIF held out the hope that political pressure could be brought to bear on a reluctant Wilson to apply his democratic principles to Ireland irrespective of his desire for close relations with Britain in shaping a post-war peace settlement.

In making its demands, the FOIF had to contend with an oppressive wartime atmosphere where those ethnic groups perceived as favourably disposed to Germany as well as socialists and radicals were deemed a threat to the stability of the United States. In this context, any attack on British policy in Ireland could thus be seen as an expression of disloyalty to the United States. In June 1917, Hanna Sheehy-Skeffington, then in the United States on an FOIF-sponsored tour to publicise the Irish cause, recognised this shift in public opinion. In a letter to Devoy, she expressed alarm at hostile US press reaction to her lecture tour in the American west, which denounced her as a 'traitor' for spreading pernicious doctrine about 'our ally' Britain. She also claimed that: 'The pro-British here are clamouring for my internment and repression (a vague term, which may mean anything).'[39]

Cohalan reacted to the increased wartime hysteria by scaling back FOIF activities. This was even noted by the British ambassador, who informed his colleagues in the Foreign Office in London of 'a diminution of public activity which was perceptible to most close observers of the Irish-American community'.[40] The cancellation of an Irish race convention which had been scheduled for August 1917 symbolised Cohalan's caution.[41] A month previously, he had pointed out in a letter to James McGuire: 'As to the Convention, you asked my opinion … it would be folly and poor judgment to convene such a gathering.' Cohalan felt that such agitation would call into question Irish-American loyalty to the US war effort. As he went on to explain to McGuire, such pleas for action from New York 'would simply make certain the re-election of the present incumbent [New York Mayor John Mitchel] and the securing triumph of all he represents'.[42]

This message to McGuire is revealing in the extent to which domestic American political considerations dominated Cohalan's thinking at this time. Cohalan was aware of the coming New York mayoral election which would be held in November 1917. The incumbent, Mayor John Mitchel, was a reform Democrat and avid supporter of the war and the president's international policy. In the mayoral campaign, Mitchel was running as an independent candidate and was challenged by Judge John Hylan, who had the backing of Tammany Hall and the Hearst press.[43] Morris Hillquit, who opposed the war, was also running as a socialist candidate. Cohalan favoured Hylan, who took a more ambivalent position on the war and focused on local issues in his campaign. In turn, Cohalan feared that Mitchel would exploit Irish-American agitation so as to demonstrate his patriotic credentials and thus sideline Hylan's domestic-orientated campaign.[44]

Cohalan's caution made him vulnerable to criticism by more radical voices within the broader spectrum of the Irish-American nationalist movement. These included Jeremiah O'Leary, who continued to protest American participation in the war. In July 1917, O'Leary wrote to James

McGuire arguing that the Irish in America should take a stand against further government harassment of the Irish community in the US. O'Leary complained of Cohalan's passivity:

> Shall the future history of the American Republic say that the Irish in America submitted to this without protest? Justice Cohalan seemed to think that they should. In fact, he said so in so many words, for in a conversation with me, he conveyed the impression that it would be unwise and unpatriotic, if you please, to make any protest against such a radical departure from American traditions.[45]

In August 1917 some of the more radical members in the FOIF staged a large FOIF anti-British demonstration in New York which attracted over 6,000 people. John D. Moore and another senior figure in the organisation, Peter Golden, organised the meeting. In response, the New York police took a heavy-handed approach, with Mayor Mitchel declaring that 'treason and sedition are preached at the open-air meetings of the Friends of Irish Freedom'. The *Gaelic American* reported that John D. Moore was arrested as soon as he began to criticise England, though he was later released. The paper also accused Mayor Mitchel of acting at the behest of 'New York's pro-Britishers', declaring that: 'Mitchel's war against the Irish race is on.'[46]

McGuire now pressed for the holding of a convention to clarify FOIF policy. In the face of such pressure, Cohalan finally relented and agreed that a convention should be held, though on an unspecified date. A terse report which appeared in the *Gaelic American* in September 1917 reported that: 'The Irish Race Convention will be held in New York City at some date to be hereafter fixed between November 15th and December 15th next.'[47]

Meanwhile, the FOIF August demonstrations and the coming mayoral elections may have persuaded the authorities to move against Cohalan. In September 1917, the Committee on Public Information released to the press the papers of the German agent Wolf von Igel, which the FBI had seized in April 1916 just prior to the Easter Rising in Ireland. As noted earlier, these documents contained damning evidence that Cohalan had called for German attacks on England and a landing of German troops in Ireland to coincide with the rising. But while it seems certain that

Cohalan sent these messages given their presence in German archives, it is important to stress that he made such requests when the United States was still neutral.[48] Their sudden release in September 1917, when the United States was at war, seemed an obvious attempt to discredit him.[49] The *New York Times*, never on good terms with Cohalan, seized upon the newly released documents to depict what they considered as treasonable activities by Irish nationalist leaders. In a front-page headline following the release of the documents, the paper declared: 'Cohalan and other Irish Leaders Named in New Exposé of German Plots: von Igel papers bared conspiracy'. In addition, the *New York Herald* in a stark headline declared: 'Justice Cohalan Named as Kaiser's Adviser'.[50]

In what appears to have been a co-ordinated move, the British government released to the *New York World* a copy of a message that its intelligence services had intercepted between the German ambassador Count von Bernstorff and the German Foreign Office. Again, the message was dated 23 August 1916, well before the United States entered the war. In his message, von Bernstorff enclosed a request from the Clan leadership in New York that Germany should use its influence at the Vatican to support the appointment of Assistant Bishop Daniel Cohalan for the vacant bishopric of Cork following the death of Bishop Thomas O'Callaghan. A portion of the message read: 'Assistant-Bishop Cohalan is a cousin of Judge Cohalan and strongly Nationalist and pro-German .... It would have a great moral effect in Ireland if Cohalan were appointed. If Germany can exert any influence to bring about this result it would defeat the English intrigue aimed against its interests.' This report appeared in the *New York World* on 4 October 1917 just a week after the von Igel revelations. By 1917, Cohalan's cousin had indeed been appointed to the bishopric of Cork and this message was undoubtedly sent by the Clan but there is no evidence that his appointment was down to German influence at the Vatican. As auxiliary bishop, he was popular with the clergy and his appointment was a logical choice. Yet this message, alongside the von Igel revelations, created the impression that his appointment was in some way a reward for Cohalan's services to the kaiser during the Easter Rising.[51]

According to McCartan's work *With de Valera in America*, these revelations caused Cohalan serious anxiety and appear to have brought him close to a nervous collapse. Doubtless, he remembered the Connolly case in 1913 which had come close to ending his career. McCartan recounts how

Cohalan received help from an unexpected quarter in the fight to prove his innocence. Scottish-born Dr William Maloney had operated a practice in New York before enlisting as a captain in the British army when war began in Europe in 1914. He had later resigned his commission when he was wounded. Returning to the United States in 1917, and in the wake of the 1916 Rising, he had embraced the Irish cause and had become a firm friend of fellow doctor Patrick McCartan. In his book, McCartan includes a vivid account by Maloney of a meeting in Cohalan's house where Cohalan, looking haggard and ill, constantly paced the floor of his library moaning that: 'He would be impeached, he was destroyed, they would have his life.'[52]

According to McCartan, Maloney offered Cohalan a possible lifeline out of the crisis. British diplomats in the United States were aware of Maloney's interest in Irish matters, and a few months previously, in May 1917, they had invited him to a meeting in the British embassy in Washington to discuss Irish-American affairs. As a former British officer and wounded war veteran, Maloney was assured of a warm welcome by the British ambassador Sir Cecil Spring Rice. Maloney journeyed to the embassy with Shane Leslie, who was at this time an active supporter of John Redmond's United Irish League of America. Leslie, from an Anglo-Irish background, was well connected to the British establishment and a cousin of Winston Churchill. At this meeting in the embassy, the increasing radicalisation of the Irish in America following the 1916 Rising was discussed. However, Leslie had 'minimised Irish-American opposition' and claimed that enough evidence existed to 'silence Cohalan'.[53]

Shortly after the embassy meeting in May 1917, Maloney had informed Cohalan of this conversation but had thought nothing further of it. Now, with the release of the von Igel papers in September, he reminded Cohalan of the conversation he had had with Leslie and suggested that Leslie must have been aware of Cohalan's alleged transmission to Germany calling for support for the 1916 Rising. In his discussion with Cohalan, Maloney assumed that this message was a forgery, though as we have seen, it seems certain that Cohalan had indeed sent this message given its presence in German archives. Nevertheless, the timing of the release of this message to the media, now that the United States was in the war, suggests that the British authorities had been waiting for an opportunity to cause maximum damage to Cohalan's reputation.[54]

Relations between Cohalan and Maloney would sour after the war as the latter took de Valera's side in the dispute which engulfed Irish-American nationalism. Cohalan would later brand Maloney a British spy, while Maloney would denounce Cohalan for betraying the Irish cause for his own political interests. However, at this point in time, Cohalan valued Maloney's advice and, according to McCartan, Maloney helped Cohalan draft a press release defending his position. In a response which he released to the press, Cohalan stated that: '… I was warned by one who had an entrée to the British Embassy that the British authorities were determined, if possible, to destroy me, as they would like to destroy every well-wisher of Ireland'. In addition, Cohalan professed his loyalty to the American nation: 'In my opinion, as an American who yields to no man in devotion to this country of ours, a grave error of judgment has been made by those who attack the loyalty of citizens of Irish blood. This is a time for unity and not disruption.'[55] In a further interview with the *Gaelic American*, Cohalan compared the allegations against him to the Piggott forgeries that had been unsuccessfully used by the London *Times* newspaper to implicate Charles Stewart Parnell in the so-called Phoenix Park murders of the chief secretary for Ireland, Lord Frederick Cavendish, and the permanent under-secretary for Ireland, T.H. Burke in 1882.[56]

In his statement to the *New York World*, Cohalan went on to mention those who had attended the meeting, including Leslie. According to McCartan, Leslie, in turn, 'sent a letter to the press, admitting his presence with others at the British Embassy on the date mentioned, but asserting he was plotting to save, not to destroy, Irishmen'.[57] These developments embarrassed the British embassy, which now refused to comment on the entire affair.

The von Igel revelations became a topic for debate in the mayoral contest. Just prior to the election, Mayor Mitchel issued a press statement declaring that, behind Judge Hylan, 'you will find … every force of enemy intrigue of sedition and disloyalty that today curses our country … Cohalan, Jeremiah O'Leary … Devoy are all fighting for the election of Judge Hylan'.[58] In the event, these attacks did not help Mitchel, and Cohalan's vigorous defence may have helped to mitigate the damage which these revelations had caused to Hylan's campaign. Fighting on local issues, and with the support of the Tammany machine, Hylan won the mayoral election on 6 November 1917.

Initially at least, the American authorities appeared to treat the allegations against Cohalan seriously. In their 'Enemy Activities File', the United States War Department compiled a report on Cohalan entitled 'Justice Daniel F. Cohalan Named in New Exposé of German Plots'. Interestingly, the report indicated that: 'Justice Cohalan has long been prominent in Irish-American circles but has never been directly identified with violent action.' This file, complete with a photograph of Cohalan in his judicial robes, is available in the American National Archives.[59]

Despite this investigation and calls by the New York press for his impeachment, no charges were brought against Cohalan.[60] This decision by the authorities not to proceed with such charges remains a mystery. They may well have anticipated that a prosecution would have been difficult to sustain given that Cohalan had sent these messages to Germany while the United States was still neutral. Also, Cohalan still had powerful allies in Tammany and the New York judiciary. The federal authorities would have had to divert wartime resources into what could have been a costly and lengthy investigation which would have had to rely on the co-operation of Mayor Hylan, a known Cohalan ally.

The federal authorities seemed content in any case to allow the release of the documents to serve as a warning. Cohalan seems to have absorbed this point, since he urged that the FOIF adopt a relatively low profile for the rest of the war. Cohalan believed that this tactic would avoid outright suppression and allow the FOIF to re-emerge intact after the end of the war. This policy can be illustrated by the calling off of the planned convention scheduled for November and December. This again outraged O'Leary, who believed that Cohalan and Devoy were behind this decision. In his later work, *My Political Trial and Experiences*, O'Leary claimed that: 'The calling off of the convention was unauthorised. No meeting was held at which such a decision was reached. The convention date was simply ignored by the Irish leaders.'[61]

In a further illustration of government repression which was tinged with a degree of moderation, Irish-American newspapers such as the *Gaelic American* and the *Irish World* were banned from the mails in February 1918. This was a blow to the *Gaelic American*, but while copies of the newspaper could not be purchased by mail subscriptions, it could still publish and be offered for sale at newsstands. In the summer of 1918, Devoy launched a fund appealing to readers and supporters to help rescue the paper and this too was permitted. By September the fund had reached 10,000 dollars and in an article in the *Gaelic American*, Devoy proudly stated: 'It [the fund] has exceeded all expectations and it is the most effective answer to the tyrannical bureaucrats of the Post Office Department who sought to strangle the paper in the interests of England.'[62] Meanwhile, Jeremiah O'Leary did not fare as well and in June 1918 he was indicted on treason and espionage charges on account of his continuing contact with German agents in the United States.[63] Clearly, Cohalan wanted to avoid this fate, which would not only have ruined his career but also undermine the effectiveness of the Irish-American nationalist movement after the war.

While the majority of the FOIF agreed with Cohalan's moderate stance, a minority faction founded a new organisation known as the Irish Progressive League (IPL). Poet and singer Peter Golden became general secretary and leader of the organisation. The IPL adopted a more radical approach to the Irish question and the war but also took a more radical stance on social and political issues such as women's suffrage. For instance, it supported the socialist anti-war candidate Morris Hillquit for the mayor of New York in the summer of 1917. Its membership consisted of many Irish nationalists in the United States disillusioned with the inactivity of the FOIF. These included Hanna Sheehy-Skeffington; Nora Connolly, a daughter of executed rebel leader James Connolly; and Liam Mellows. Mellows had fought in the 1916 Rising and had then fled to the US. He had been taken on to the staff of the *Gaelic American* but was ideologically closer to Golden and the IPL than he was to Devoy and Cohalan.[64]

Despite its small size, the IPL established an Irish National Bureau in Washington in an attempt to influence the policy-making process. As part of its campaign, it sent letters to members of Congress so as to assess their stance on the Irish question. It also engaged in agitation to secure Irish representation at the post-war peace conference. This bureau served as a type of proto 'Irish embassy' for Irish interests in the United States and worked closely with Sinn Féin envoy Patrick McCartan. Given the wartime atmosphere, there were obvious limits as to what it could achieve but the newly elected president of Sinn Féin, Eamon de Valera, appreciated its contribution to the Irish cause in the United States. In February 1918, in a letter to McCartan, de Valera complimented the work of the league in 'placing before the free citizens of the United States the true position of Ireland and its relation with England'.[65] Joe McGarrity, the Clan leader in Philadelphia, also supported the league's activities and, to Devoy's frustration, founded a rival newspaper to that of the *Gaelic American* known as the *Irish Press*. McCartan edited this newspaper, which covered the activities of the league closely.[66]

The establishment of the IPL represented a challenge to the work of Devoy and Cohalan. Both had worked for years to demonstrate the loyalty of Irish-Americans to the United States. Both now feared that the Wilson administration could use the activities of the IPL to repress the wider Irish-American nationalist movement as represented by the Clan and the FOIF. In this regard, Cohalan may have incorrectly assumed that the president was motivated by personal antipathy towards him. In reality, Wilson was increasingly preoccupied by the war effort, and the federal authorities, as demonstrated by their half-hearted approach to the *Gaelic American*, were more focused on dealing with the threat posed by socialist and anarchist groups than by Irish nationalists.[67]

Hanna Sheehy-Skeffington, now an active member of the IPL, was particularly scathing towards Cohalan's cautious approach. In January 1918 she presented President Wilson with a petition which asked him 'to consider our claims as a small nation governed without consent'. In a thinly veiled attack on Cohalan's hesitant policy, she wrote to Devoy: 'It is apparently no treason to the US to plead for Ireland, otherwise the President would not receive me or the petition.'[68]

Now under pressure from the Irish Progressive League, from Irish nationalists in America and even from some senior members of the Clan and the FOIF such as McGarrity and McGuire, Cohalan and Devoy agreed to hold the long-awaited Second Race Convention on 18–19 May 1918. Events in Ireland also dictated that a convention should be held. On 16 April 1918, the British government, facing collapse on the western front as a result of a massive German offensive, introduced a law to impose conscription on Ireland. All nationalist parties in Ireland opposed the measure and a resurgence of conflict seemed possible.[69] Given the nationalist hostility the measure produced and the failure of the German offensive, conscription was never enacted, yet in the spring of 1918 it seemed a distinct probability and Irish nationalists in the US called on Irish-Americans to support their campaign.

Like the first convention, the Second Race Convention took place in New York, but now the atmosphere was very different. Instead of the hopeful air of expectation which characterised the First Race Convention, the mood was more depressed and fearful. This time the invitation to delegates reflected Cohalan's cautious approach and noted 'the splendid services of the Race to this Republic from the Revolution down through every crisis of the nation's history'.[70]

Predictably, the convention looked ahead towards the end of the war and called on President Wilson to permit the attendance of Irish representatives at the post-war peace conference. This took the form of a petition which urged the United States government 'to exert every legitimate and friendly influence in favour of Self-Determination for the people of Ireland'. While all the delegates to the convention could readily agree to this, the convention also brought to the surface tensions over policy which had been building for months. It soon became clear that a vocal minority of those present did not agree with Cohalan's cautious policy, even though it had Devoy's support. In a rousing speech, Liam Mellows told delegates that: 'America, by its silence on the question of Irish Independence, has been and is still, until it speaks out, tacitly acquiescing in England's domination. The state of affairs at home is so desperate that you people are acting like a lot of curs if you do not speak out now…' Mellows went on to state that: 'Those who say it is disloyal to speak the truth on behalf of Ireland, those people are not American. They are pro-British.'[71]

Taking a moderate line, Cohalan, in his own speech, urged delegates 'not to lose their heads'. Instead, he put forward the case that Irish-Americans, by displaying loyalty to the war effort, could win the gratitude of America in the post-war peace settlement. Referring to Wilson's promise of self-determination for oppressed nationalities, Cohalan declared that: 'I believe solemnly that the President and the Congress of the United States are determined to see that Ireland shall be included with the other countries.' Again, Devoy took Cohalan's side on this issue and, in the *Gaelic American* report on the convention, Devoy referred to 'unfounded fear on the part of some that the resolutions and the utterances of the speakers might be too tame for the present situation'.[72]

Father Peter Magennis took over the presidency of the FOIF from Victor Herbert at the convention, though this was not due to any ill-feeling since both Herbert and Cohalan remained good friends. However, in other respects, the Second Race Convention symbolised an emerging factionalism which would plague the Irish-American nationalist movement in the months and even years ahead. Perhaps anticipating such trouble, Cohalan seized the opportunity to take firmer control of the organisation. Some months prior to the convention, national secretary John D. Moore had resigned his position. In a letter to Cohalan, Moore complained that his expenses as secretary of the Irish Relief Fund had not been paid. It also seems likely that he was unhappy with the general approach of the FOIF as witnessed by his involvement in the FOIF demonstration in August 1917.[73] Following the convention, 1916 veteran Diarmuid Lynch, recently deported to the United States by the British authorities, became the new national secretary. As noted earlier, Lynch had formed a close friendship with Cohalan during his time as president of the Gaelic League in New York and before his return to Ireland in 1907. From Cohalan's perspective, Lynch was an obvious candidate for the position of national secretary. As can be seen from the Friends of Irish Freedom Papers in the AIHS, he was a methodical worker and possessed good organisational skills, vital attributes for any administrator. One of his first acts was to revise the membership records and, under his stewardship, the organisation launched a membership drive which began to yield dividends at the end of the war. Most of all, Lynch was loyal to Cohalan and he felt that disunity played into the hands of anti-Irish elements in the United States. An indigent Liam Mellows, in a letter to Golden, noted that he had been reprimanded by Lynch, who had stressed the need for 'discipline' and 'obedience'.[74]

This demand for 'obedience' to Cohalan did not, of course, satisfy those within the IPL who wanted a more spirited campaign attacking British policy, especially with regard to the possible imposition of conscription on Ireland. In response to Cohalan's urgings of caution, Mellows, who was active in this campaign, wrote to Peter Golden complaining that 'the gang', that is, Cohalan and Devoy, 'opposed and sabotaged' their efforts 'by threats and underhand means'.[75] Yet while the IPL's stand was a courageous one, its appeals to members of Congress to oppose Irish conscription at a time when the US was itself conscripting its own young men largely fell on deaf ears. As Carroll points out: 'Although there were some exceptions, the replies indicated clearly that Irish nationalist activities in the United States during the war were widely regarded as seditious.'[76]

The American war crisis created unprecedented challenges for Cohalan, who had long celebrated his dual allegiance to both the United States and a free and independent Ireland. Though he believed that America's entry into the war had been a mistake, he also felt duty bound to rally to the flag and demonstrate his loyalty to the American nation. If he had done otherwise and followed the path of Jeremiah O'Leary, his ability to exercise any influence in American politics after the war would have been seriously undermined. Irish nationalists from Ireland and the more radical voices within the IPL did not fully understand this cautious approach in 1918 but, for Cohalan, their perspective still represented a minority view within Irish nationalism in the United States.

Even before the war ended, Cohalan recognised that Wilson's wartime call for self-determination for oppressed nationalities could prove very beneficial to the Irish nationalist cause. Interestingly, his cousin Bishop Daniel Cohalan of Cork, in a sermon to the Cork Young Men's Society on 22 October 1918, made a similar plea which linked Irish independence to a generous post-war peace settlement that recognised Ireland's right to liberty:

> I hope that we will win liberty for Ireland without sacrificing any more lives, but I refer to the situation as one fact that the Great Powers should keep in mind .... Looking into the future I say that if the question of Ireland is not settled in a generous way, settled in a way that will meet the sentiments of the younger people, it will not be a lasting settlement … .'[77]

Bishop Cohalan's speech received wide publicity and Charles Hathaway, the American consul in Queenstown, reported the speech in full to his superiors in Washington.[78] There is no evidence to indicate that the bishop had co-ordinated his statement with his cousin in New York despite similar appeals made by the FOIF at this time. Yet his sermon is an indication of an increasing realisation among Irish nationalists in Ireland that the fate of Ireland could be linked to the post-war settlement and that the United States would play a key role in the outcome of these negotiations. As the war ended with an Allied victory in November 1918, Cohalan had every reason to hope that Irish-American nationalists and Irish nationalists in Ireland could now present a united front in calling for 'self-determination' at the coming peace conference. Unfortunately for Cohalan, the time of discord was only just beginning.

6

Supporting Irish Self-Determination but Opposing the League of Nations, 1919

IN THE AFTERMATH OF THE First World War, Cohalan sought to link Irish national demands to President Wilson's stated policy on securing self-determination for the oppressed nationalities of Europe. In pressing home this message, Cohalan successfully expanded the Friends of Irish Freedom movement, which became a significant pressure group in American politics. Sinn Féin in Ireland, aware of the important role that the US would play in the post-war peace settlement, now looked to Irish-America for help in 'leveraging' US support for Irish independence.[1] However, differences in opinion on strategy soon emerged. Cohalan had other priorities not always shared by Irish nationalists from Ireland or by other voices within Irish-America. For Cohalan and Devoy, President Wilson's vision of a post-war League of Nations seemed yet another attempt to embroil the United States in a British-inspired alliance and much of the resources of the FOIF would be devoted to defeating this measure. In contrast, Sinn Féin nationalists in the United States would view this campaign as counter-productive and a distraction from what they considered to be the interests of Ireland. Cohalan would be at the centre of this controversy.

Now that the conflict in Europe had ended, Irish-American nationalists such as Cohalan were no longer subject to allegations that they were allied to America's enemies. As if to illustrate this change in public atmosphere, Cohalan, in December 1918, successfully sued the *New York Evening Mail* for libel arising from the German plot charges made against him in September 1917 and received 5,000 dollars in damages. Cohalan's Irish-American supporters seemed well pleased by his apparent vindication and his files in the AIHS contain several letters from well-wishers congratulating him on this award. These include a letter from the influential Cardinal William O'Connell of Boston, who wished Cohalan 'Heartiest Congratulations'.[2]

The ending of the war at once removed a major source of tension which had weighed heavily on Irish-American efforts to put the Irish nationalist case before a pro-Allied public opinion. This impacted favourably on membership figures for the FOIF. Already, by the end of February 1919, regular membership had grown to 6,000. This represented a five-fold increase on the barely 1,000 members listed for December 1918.[3] Political events in Ireland also contributed to this organisational growth. In the December 1918 election held across Britain and Ireland, Sinn Féin secured 105 Irish seats while the once-powerful Parliamentary Party of home rule held on to just six.[4] In Sinn Féin eyes, the Irish people had spoken and a majority had voted in favour of an Irish republic. Revolutionary Irish-American nationalism advocated by the Clan and the IRB was now in the ascendant on both sides of the Atlantic. In January 1919, the Irish Republican Army (IRA) commenced a military campaign against British forces in Ireland and news of this conflict helped to further garner Irish-American support for the FOIF throughout 1919 and 1920.[5]

Cohalan now sought to weld the FOIF and other Irish societies into a cohesive body which would act as an Irish-American nationalist pressure group in American politics. Along with other FOIF leaders, Cohalan believed that Wilson would prefer to wash his hands of the Irish question in the interests of greater co-operation with Britain in constructing a post-war international world order. In a letter to Cohalan, Matthew Cummings, FOIF leader in Boston, spelled out what Cohalan already knew: 'It is plainly evident that Wilson will ignore the Irish question except his hand is forced by public opinion.'[6] In this context, Cohalan recognised that an appeal had to be made to wider American opinion and not just Irish-America. In a 1919 interview with the *Dearborn Independent*, Cohalan exemplified this strategy:

> The Irish question is not a question of English domestic politics – it is an Irish question. It is an American question. It is one of the outstanding international problems of the present day and will

> continue to be so until it is settled with justice to the people of Ireland, and without regard to the effect such sentiment may have on English party questions. There is no single question of international politics with which we as Americans are more deeply concerned.[7]

In typical dynamic fashion, Cohalan attempted to bring this message home to the American people. During the week of 8–15 December 1918, the FOIF held 'Self-Determination for Ireland' rallies across the United States in which Cohalan took a prominent part. Over 25,000 people attended one of the largest such meetings, in New York's Madison Square Garden. Here Cohalan shared the same platform as Cardinal William O'Connell of Boston and Republican governor Charles Whitman of New York.[8] The active participation of such high-profile individuals lent an air of respectability to Irish demands. Referring to Wilson's principles of self-determination for oppressed peoples in the context of the bloodshed of the war, Cardinal O'Connell declared that: 'The war can be justified only by the universal application of those principles. Let that application begin with Ireland.'[9]

Cohalan's ability to enlist Cardinal O'Connell's support illustrates his political skills. Due to clerical infighting, the administrator of the New York archdiocese, Monsignor Joseph Mooney, had been reluctant to invite the Boston cardinal to New York. Cohalan not only succeeded in persuading the cardinal to come but also the monsignor to extend the necessary invitation from the New York archdiocese. Following O'Connell's lead, most of the leading American Catholic bishops now endorsed 'self-determination' for Ireland. At the Madison Square meeting, Cohalan linked his own speech to Wilson's principle of self-determination and also advocated that a plebiscite be held on this issue as part of a post-war peace settlement.[10] By so doing, Cohalan hoped to persuade American opinion that the Irish demand for self-government was no different from that of other peoples in Europe such as the Poles or Czechs.

The support of such Catholic dignitaries also illustrated Cohalan's rehabilitation after his political isolation in late 1917. In particular, O'Connell was fulsome in his praise. At a similar 'Self Determination for Ireland' meeting, in Fenway Park in Boston, the cardinal declared: 'When Ireland gains her liberty, she will owe it to Judge Cohalan more than to any man of his generation.'[11] For Cohalan, the Madison Square Garden event helped to rejuvenate his spirits after the dark days of the war. In a letter to John J. Splain, a senior figure in the FOIF, Cohalan triumphantly wrote that the Madison Square rally represented 'the greatest meeting ever held in America for the cause of Ireland'.[12]

Under Cohalan's direction, the FOIF targeted members of Congress to discover where they stood on the Irish question. In particular, the FOIF sent questionnaires to those congressmen who represented areas where 'citizens of Irish blood formed a large percentage of the population'.[13] In response, some members of Congress, and others running for public office in the November elections of 1918, openly declared their support in the press for Irish self-determination.[14] Further evidence of congressional support for the Irish cause can be illustrated by the introduction in December 1918 of a congressional resolution before the House Committee on Foreign Affairs by Thomas Gallagher, Democratic congressman of Illinois. The resolution called upon the United States delegates at the post-war peace conference in Paris to present 'the right of Ireland to freedom, independence, and self-determination'.[15] Gallagher represented a large Irish-American population in Illinois and the evidence suggests that he was influenced by the FOIF campaign, going so far as to keep Devoy fully informed of the proceedings.[16]

Over sixty Irish-American witnesses testified before congressional hearings on the Gallagher resolution. While Cohalan did not himself appear due to illness, senior FOIF figures such as Diarmuid Lynch and Richard Dalton represented his views. Dalton's testimony echoed Cohalan's speech in Madison Square Garden when he called for the application of self-determination to Ireland and argued that 'it is essential that the Irish question be settled, and it can only be settled by reference to a fair plebiscite of the adult population of Ireland'. It would take several months before the resolution came to a vote, and in the meantime it would be watered down considerably.[17] Yet this testimony helped to air the Irish issue in Congress and among the wider American public. Even the *New York Times* admitted that these hearings 'reactivated Irish-America after the war'.[18]

From the point of view of rallying mainstream American opinion to the Irish cause, Cohalan's stress on the Wilsonian term 'self-determination' made perfect sense. However, the use of this phrase alarmed Sinn Féin envoy Patrick McCartan. In Ireland itself, the term 'self-determination' could be taken to mean a limited form of home rule independence which the now discredited home rule party had previously advocated. After all, the leaders of the 1916 rebellion had sacrificed their lives for an Irish republic and Sinn Féin had run on a republican platform in the 1918 election.

Following the Sinn Féin election victory in December 1918, McCartan asked Cohalan to organise FOIF rallies across the country celebrating the new Irish republic. For publicity purposes, McCartan pressed Cohalan to send a cable to Éamon de Valera, then leader of the Sinn Féin party in Ireland, congratulating him on the establishment of this republic.[19] However, Cohalan, with an eye towards American public opinion and congressional support, stuck with the term 'self-determination'. His cable to de Valera contained no mention of a republic and instead stated that: 'Ireland's overwhelming verdict in favor of President Wilson's policy of self-determination for all peoples will greatly strengthen her position with lovers of liberty throughout America.'[20]

Despite this difference of opinion over the issue of self-determination, Cohalan and other FOIF leaders went ahead with plans for a Third Irish Race Convention, intended to symbolise the unity that now existed across the Irish-American nationalist movement. Cohalan intended that the convention, like the congressional hearings still taking place, would, as Matthew Cummings pointed out, 'bring the [Irish] question into the press and before the public'.[21] This time the convention was held in McGarrity's stronghold of Philadelphia but FOIF branches from across the United States and affiliated societies such as the AOH and the IPL also attended.[22]

The convention went ahead on 22 February 1919 with an attendance of over five thousand delegates from across the United States. These included over thirty bishops and archbishops as well as Cardinal James Gibbons of Baltimore.[23] The presence of Gibbons, one of the most influential Catholic churchmen of his time, represented an enormous coup for Cohalan. He had been a staunch supporter of John Redmond's home rule policy and it took all of Cohalan's considerable charm to persuade him to attend. The cardinal's presence ensured massive media coverage across the US and internationally.[24]

Remembering the discord that had plagued the second convention, Cohalan exercised tight control over the proceedings. This caused resentment in some quarters, with Washington FOIF delegate Rossa Downing complaining of Cohalan's dominance of the FOIF. In a later report, Downing took particular umbrage at Cohalan's role in the selection of the three-hundred-member FOIF National Council: 'The fact is, however, that the National Council was not elected, but selected by somebody or a group of somebodies, the chief of whom was Daniel F. Cohalan.'[25] As Downing continued:

> One of the members of the National Executive is Daniel F. Cohalan ... and this is the only office he holds in our organisation. Yet his influence is such with this national executive that he is in a position to dictate the activities of the Friends of Irish Freedom.[26]

Representatives of Sinn Féin in the United States also believed that Cohalan possessed untrammelled power over the institutions of the FOIF. McCartan, in his work *With de Valera in America*, claimed that the FOIF had become 'his personal machine under his complete control'. In a further point, perhaps revealing his anti-Cohalan bias, he declared that 'it became heretical to oppose his will'.[27]

Behind the scenes, opposing voices such as those of McGarrity, McCartan and Golden did indeed challenge Cohalan's will. The focus of this dispute once again centred on the issue of self-determination. Typical of this and later disputes, Cohalan and his allies were more concerned with the political situation in the United States, while his nationalist opponents, both American and Irish-American, were influenced more by events in Ireland. On 21 January 1919, Sinn Féin had convened a meeting of its elected representatives in a first 'Dáil' or parliament and had declared an Irish republic. McCartan as 'envoy' thus felt that Cohalan and other leaders of the Irish-American nationalist movement in the United States were now duty bound to plead for the recognition of this republic. McCartan had McGarrity's support in this regard but persuading Cohalan was a different matter. In dramatic prose, McCartan writes of an angry exchange with Cohalan on this issue: 'I put a proof sheet of *America*, containing Dáil Éireann's address to the nations of the world, before Cohalan, and pointed out that by demanding merely self-determination for Ireland we were not keeping step – as McGarrity phrased it – with the men in Ireland.'[28]

In reply, Cohalan pointed out that since the Irish republic did not yet exist and did not control an inch of territory, it would be foolhardy to ask the United States to recognise such a state as it would be effectively asking the US to 'declare war on England'. Referring to Gibbons' known home rule sympathies, Cohalan pleaded that Gibbons had informed him that he would only 'go as far as President Wilson and no further'.[29] Diarmuid Lynch takes Cohalan's side in his unpublished history of the FOIF, arguing that 'if the [convention] committee asked the Cardinal to propose a resolution calling for outright recognition of the Irish Republic, he certainly would have refused'. Although both sides avoided an open breach, Cohalan's explanation did not convince McCartan and in his later work he accused Cohalan of 'taking shelter behind the Cardinal's robes'.[30]

Overall, the Third Irish Race Convention proved a tremendous success; to outward appearances at least it created an impression of a unity of minds between Irish-American nationalism and Irish nationalism. Under Lynch's stewardship, FOIF membership grew tenfold in subsequent months from just 6,000 in February to over 70,000 in December 1919. Undoubtedly, this image of unity, together with increasing civil unrest in Ireland as the IRA engaged British military forces, generated much support.[31] Meanwhile, having such an organisation under his control enhanced Cohalan's profile as effectively the main spokesman for the 'Irish race' in America. Mary McWhorter, the national president of the Ladies Auxiliary of the AOH, wrote admiringly to Cohalan just prior to the convention, claiming: 'You are the guiding star and the inspiration of all that is best and truest in the ideals of our race … You have never faltered in your allegiance to our dear dark Rosaleen; you have never forgotten your dear Motherland.'[32]

The convention had appointed a delegation of twenty-five of its members to present Wilson with a resolution demanding self-determination for Ireland. The president had at this point temporarily returned to Washington from the Paris peace talks. Buoyed by the publicity generated by the convention, the delegation, led by Cohalan, travelled to Washington on 25 February 1919 hoping for an audience with the president.

Joseph 'Joe' Tumulty, Wilson's Irish-American secretary, had become fully aware of the publicity generated by the convention and by the ongoing congressional hearings on Ireland. Tumulty urged Wilson to meet the delegation but Wilson refused, claiming pressure of work. In a memo dated 1 March Tumulty tried again, pointing out to Wilson that not meeting the delegation 'will simply strengthen the Sinn Féin movement in this country'. Tumulty was also aware of Wilson's enmity towards Cohalan which stretched back to the 1912 Democratic convention. As pointed out in the introductory chapter, Cohalan and Boss Murphy had attempted to block Wilson's nomination in favour of Champ Clark.[33]

Wilson finally conceded to Tumulty's urgings and agreed on a meeting for 4 March in the New York Metropolitan Opera House, where a presidential speech had been scheduled. Sinn Féin in Ireland welcomed these developments and on the night prior to the meeting, Éamon de Valera cabled Cohalan the following message:

> The Executive of Dáil Éireann warmly appreciates the magnificent work for Ireland of the Irish Race in the United States of America and places the highest value on the active co-operation of the Irish Race Convention. The Executive welcomes the forthcoming reception of the Convention's delegates by President Wilson, whose clear enunciation of the true principle of international right has kindled throughout Ireland the firmest confidence in an early restoration of her inalienable liberties.[34]

Wilson intended to meet the delegation in a small opera clubroom after his speech but in a final dramatic twist he only agreed to meet the delegation if Cohalan was excluded. According to a report in the *Irish Times*, Wilson, 'through a secret service agent, gave Judge Cohalan five minutes to leave'. Taken aback by this development, the other members of the delegation loyally declared that 'they would leave sooner than have Justice Cohalan leave alone'. In a bid to ease the mounting tension, Cohalan announced: 'The cause is bigger than I am; for its sake, I will leave the room without question.'[35] The meeting then went ahead as originally planned.

Even without Cohalan's presence, the Irish-American delegation achieved little. With Frank Walsh now acting as chief spokesperson, the delegation asked Wilson to present the Irish case for self-determination at the Paris Peace Conference. Wilson took an evasive and noncommittal stance, stating that the Irish question was a British domestic matter over which he had no control.[36] The *Irish Times*, explaining Wilson's position to its mainly unionist readership, justified Wilson's actions in the following terms:

> Mr. Wilson may be an idealist, but he is also a politician, and the political situation required that he should give a civil hearing to the members of the Irish Race Convention. He promised nothing, however, and we are quite sure that, in his official capacity, he will do nothing. He knows perfectly well that the United States is no more entitled to bring Ireland before the Peace Conference than England is entitled to demand self-determination for Cuba and the Philippines.[37]

Not surprisingly, the *Gaelic American* took an entirely different view and described Wilson's treatment of Cohalan as 'shabby, venomous and wholly unjustifiable'. Indeed, the entire incident appeared to have enhanced Cohalan's reputation among Irish-Americans. Even McCartan noted, though with more than a hint of sarcasm: 'Soon our people were busy enthroning him [Cohalan] in their hearts … He was hailed as the chosen leader of our race.'[38]

Rather than focusing on Wilson's obvious dislike of Cohalan, the president's reaction to the delegation can be better explained by reference to his overall plan to establish a comprehensive peace settlement for the post-war world. As discussed previously, the establishment of a League of Nations was central to his post-war vision, and from Wilson's perspective this would provide a mechanism for the resolution of such questions as that presented by Ireland. Wilson saw Britain as a vital partner in constructing this international structure. He was, therefore, unwilling to offend Britain by interfering in the Irish question. Wilson may also have anticipated the so-called 'special relationship' that would shape Anglo-American relations in the coming decades and which would make future American administrations wary of involvement in the Irish question.

Just three weeks after the abortive meeting with Wilson, Cohalan moderated his stance on the issue of self-determination and publicly called for an Irish republic. In an obvious snub to Wilson, Cohalan deliberately chose the Metropolitan Opera House as a venue for his speech, where he declared: 'Today we are celebrating the fact that the Irish Republic has come into existence, but we pledge ourselves to carry on the fight until the existence of the Irish Republic is recognised by every country on earth including the country against which the fight has gone on for 750 years …'[39] Cohalan's speech was followed by a nationwide FOIF campaign, which began on 14 April 1919, pleading for recognition of an Irish republic.

In calling more explicitly for an Irish republic, Cohalan had obviously bowed to pressure from his Irish nationalist colleagues. He may also have felt that Wilson had now publicly demonstrated his insincerity in his call for self-determination for oppressed peoples. However, in private both Devoy and Cohalan still felt that for tactical reasons, the pursuit of self-determination seemed a more appropriate course of action in trying to convince ordinary Americans of the justice in Ireland's case. This is clear from an exchange of correspondence between Devoy and McCartan a few days after the FOIF nationwide campaign began. In a letter to Devoy on 19 April justifying the call for an Irish republic, McCartan argued that: 'Every conservative in Ireland … will do his utmost to interpret self-determination as colonial home rule.'[40] In his response of 21 April, Devoy echoed Cohalan's pragmatic belief that the calling for self-determination had a much greater prospect of winning American public support than any call for an Irish republic:

> The term Self-Determination has caught them [American public opinion], and holding it constantly up to him [Wilson] is the best means of getting him to do something. Recognition of the Irish Republic he could easily refuse, but making good his oft-repeated words is something of a different kind. He promised Self-Determination to all peoples; why should he deny it to Ireland?[41]

The passing of the Gallagher resolution by the US House of Representatives in early March, coincidentally coinciding with the Opera House meeting, appeared to be a positive step in this direction. The resolution, which had been winding its way through the House since the previous November, was passed by a majority of 216 to 45. While the original resolution had asked the American delegation at the peace conference to present Ireland's case for self-determination, the final wording of the resolution had been watered down and simply asked the conference 'to favorably consider the claims of Ireland to the right of self-determination'. As Ward points out, this was a 'declaration of support rather than a commitment to act'.[42] Yet the resolution reflected the pressure being brought to bear on Congress by Cohalan's campaign for

Irish-self-determination and this pressure would escalate in the coming months.

As part of the campaign to raise awareness of the Irish question in the United States, the Irish Race Convention had announced that three of the members of the delegation dispatched to meet Wilson would themselves journey to the Paris Peace Conference. Their mission – resourced by the Irish Victory Fund, which was inaugurated by the convention and which would be administered by the leadership of the FOIF – was to plead for a hearing for a delegation from Ireland and if that failed it was decided that they should then attempt to present the case for Ireland. An Irish delegation had already been assembled in Ireland comprising three senior Sinn Féin leaders: Éamon de Valera, Arthur Griffith and Count George Plunkett.[43]

Before the composition of the Irish-American delegation became known, President Wilson instructed his officials that, should Cohalan be one of its members, his passport would be refused.[44] Cohalan may well have anticipated such a move as he did not put his name forward as one of the delegates. The three men selected enjoyed high social standing in the US and two, perhaps intentionally, were well known to Wilson. Frank Walsh (1864–1939) had worked closely with Wilson during the war as a co-chairman of the National War Labor Board. Edward F. Dunne (1853–1937) had served as a Democratic mayor of Chicago and governor of Illinois. The third member, Michael J. Ryan (1862–1943), not known to Wilson, had been a former leader of Redmond's support organisation the United Irish League but had left it on account of Redmond's support for the British war effort. This three-man delegation, led by Walsh, described themselves as the 'American Commission on Irish Independence' and made their way to Paris in early April 1919.[45]

Meanwhile, Cohalan kept up the political pressure on the Wilson administration. Though Wilson remained in Paris for much of this time, he was still vulnerable to pressure from Congress and public opinion. In this campaign, Cohalan was not short of funds. Within a few months, the Victory Fund amounted to over one million dollars and Cohalan had considerable power over how this money should be spent. For instance, money from the fund allowed the FOIF to take over the Irish National Bureau of the Irish Progressive League (IPL), which had been highly critical of Cohalan during the war.[46]

Cohalan exercised tight control over the work of the bureau. Its director Daniel T. O'Connell was a devoted Cohalan loyalist. One of Cohalan's critics, Rossa Downing, later complained that Cohalan alone 'was the arbiter of the destinies of the Irish National Bureau' and O'Connell 'consulted with him and him alone'.[47] Control of the Irish National Bureau provided Cohalan with a platform in Washington and ready access to members of Congress, which he took full advantage of in order to press the Irish case. From July 1919, the bureau published a weekly *News Letter* which it distributed widely to newspapers, embassies, politicians and other prominent individuals in American society. The bureau also distributed pamphlets written by Cohalan such as *The Freedom of the Seas* (1919), which attacked Britain's imperial ambitions.[48]

In his work with Congress, Cohalan formed an especially strong alliance with Republican senator William Borah of Idaho. Borah led what would be called the 'Irreconcilables' within the Senate – those who opposed ratification of the League of Nations on any grounds. Borah and other anti-league opponents saw the Irish question as a useful means to expose many of the contradictions in Wilson's foreign policy, which on the one hand called for self-determination for oppressed peoples but on the other hand defended the territorial integrity of member states including that of the British Empire.[49]

On 29 May, in an illustration of how Cohalan's alliances with American politicians could deliver Irish dividends, Borah introduced a Senate resolution which called on the American delegation at the peace conference to secure a hearing for the Irish delegation of de Valera, Griffith and Plunkett. It also expressed sympathy for Irish self-determination. This resolution was more direct than the earlier Gallagher resolution and was passed by sixty votes to one, with thirty-five senators abstaining.[50] The massive majority in favour of the resolution is itself an indication of the success of Cohalan's campaign to make the Irish question centre stage in American politics.

The passage of this resolution, with such an overwhelming majority in favour, alarmed Wilson's secretary Joe Tumulty. In a telegram to the president, Tumulty expressed fears about the consequences of Wilson's perceived intransigence on the Irish question for his wider foreign policy. Tumulty argued:

> You cannot overestimate real intensity of feeling behind the Irish question here. It is growing every day and is not all confined to Irishmen. The passage of resolution of sympathy with almost unanimous vote in Senate last night is but slight evidence of interest here. I wish the President could do just a little for Ireland for I fear reaction here upon the League of Nations.[51]

Wilson chose to ignore Tumulty's advice and he soon found a useful pretext for inaction. The American commission had thus far made little headway in persuading the United States delegation to use their influence to secure safe conduct for the representatives of the Irish Dáil to plead their case in Paris. Cohalan had urged Walsh and the rest of the delegation to visit Ireland 'so as to enlighten American opinion' on the situation in Ireland.[52] The delegation, following Cohalan's advice, travelled to Ireland, where they received a rapturous welcome. In their travels around the country, the three men displayed little regard for British sensitivities and claimed 'unanimous support in America for the Irish cause'. These declarations outraged the British media and embarrassed the American delegation in Paris.[53] In a later meeting with Frank Walsh, upon the return of the American commission to Paris, Wilson claimed that he had almost cleared the way for the Irish delegation to present their case in Paris but that these 'scandalous speeches' in Ireland undermined his efforts. However, as Ward convincingly argues, the actions of Walsh and his colleagues provided Wilson with a convenient excuse to wash his hands of the entire affair.[54]

Tumulty correctly saw how the 'intensity of feeling over the Irish question' could have repercussions for Wilson's League of Nations battle. Many Republican opponents of the league seized on the unresolved Irish question as a means to discredit Wilson's claims that the league would give expression to oppressed nationalities. Article X of the league covenant committed future members of the league to respect and preserve 'the territorial integrity of other member states against external aggression'. In theory, this would safeguard British control over Ireland and other parts of its empire from any external interference.[55] Opponents of the league such as Borah used Article X to argue that American soldiers could be used to defend European empires.

Cohalan's alliance with Republicans in opposing Wilson's League of Nations plan was not just a tactical manoeuvre to be abandoned if Irish circumstances demanded. His opposition to the league reflected his own deep-seated American isolationism. He also believed it to be perfectly compatible with defending the cause of Irish independence, since, according to Article X, the US would be bound to uphold the integrity of the British Empire, of which Ireland was a reluctant member. Interestingly, other former Irish-American allies of Wilson such as Frank Walsh came to view the league in a similar light, seeing it as a mechanism to ensure the continued oppression rather than the liberation of oppressed peoples. Walsh's opposition can thus be seen in the context of the defection of other progressive reformers who felt that the league treaty was a betrayal of Wilson's more idealistic Fourteen Points.[56]

Cohalan's opposition to the league was sincere and heartfelt and also consistent with his earlier opposition to the pre-war Anglo-American arbitration treaties and his support for American neutrality during the Great War. For Cohalan, participation in the war had been a mistake and the US needed to return to its traditional isolationism. Cohalan also believed that the league would only benefit the British Empire. As Cohalan remarked in a speech in Brooklyn, New York, in March 1919: 'How clever the Englishman who devised the term, but oh, how much more strongly an appeal a "League of Nations" makes to mankind in general than a League for the preservation of the British Empire.'[57] At the Third Irish Race Convention, Cohalan orchestrated a resolution which demanded that any League of Nations should not infringe on American territorial security according to the Monroe Doctrine.[58]

Cohalan used the resources of the Irish National Bureau in Washington to run an effective campaign against the league. Indeed, the work of the bureau appeared very reminiscent of the propaganda work of the British-run Wellington House during the war, only this time the propaganda message was isolationist and anti-British. The bureau distributed FOIF leaflets and publications attacking the league to senators, congressmen and other leaders of opinion across the country such as churchmen and university professors. FOIF national secretary Diarmuid Lynch kept a tally on the numbers of leaflets produced and these included 100,000 pamphlets by Edward F. McSweeney entitled *America First*. However, given the context of the ongoing Anglo-Irish War of Independence, other leaflets had a more Irish focus and according to Lynch the bureau dispatched 700,000 leaflets entitled *The Irish Republic*

Can Pay Its Way and 500,000 coloured maps indicating Sinn Féin gains in the 1918 election.[59]

As the bureau was located in Washington, pressure could be brought to bear relatively easily on members of Congress. Cohalan devoted his customary energy to the battle. Daniel T. O'Connell, who headed the bureau, has left us a vivid account of Cohalan's campaign against the league: 'Each night, by long distance phone, we discussed our plan for the next day. Every Friday, Judge Cohalan left [New York] for Washington to confer with Senators. Rushing from office to office in taxis, telephoning and walking, this physical and mental marvel never tired.'[60]

In the battle against the league, Cohalan also forged alliances with prominent Republican members of Congress. These included Senator Henry Cabot Lodge, chairman of the powerful Senate Foreign Relations Committee and also leader of the so-called Senate reservationists. Reservationists, as the term suggests, had reservations about the League of Nations treaty but could be persuaded to favour the measure if certain amendments were attached.[61] While Cohalan clearly identified more with Borah's irreconcilable faction, he nevertheless welcomed Lodge's more moderate opposition, for tactical reasons. Lodge, in turn, welcomed Cohalan's support.[62]

On 30 August 1919, under Lodge's stewardship, the Senate Committee on Foreign Relations invited Cohalan and many other representatives of Irish-America to a series of public hearings on the Treaty of Peace with Germany. This treaty formed part of the Treaty of Versailles, which Wilson had personally negotiated in Paris. It also incorporated Wilson's plans for a League of Nations so the hearings, therefore, became a debate on the proposed league. Over thirty representatives from different Irish societies attended, with Cohalan acting as their chief spokesman. The members of the American Commission on Irish Independence made a separate submission. This suggests that from the point of view of the Senate committee, the Irish question played a significant part in their deliberations, as no other ethnic group received the same level of attention.[63]

Cohalan viewed the hearings as a golden opportunity to attack the league and put forward the case for Irish independence. For Cohalan these two issues were interlinked and a study of his arguments present yet another example of how his thinking on the Irish question was shaped by his own Americanism and by a deep-rooted anti-imperial sentiment. Extracts from his lengthy testimony, which ran to several pages of the congressional record, can be used to illustrate not only that the league posed a threat to the United States but also that the freedom of Ireland would be in America's best security interests.

Claiming to speak for 'the great bulk of the 20,000,000 of the Irish element in this country', Cohalan objected to the proposal 'to establish a superstate [League of Nations] to which shall be turned over powers that belong to the sovereign United States of America'. According to Cohalan, because of the demise of the other empires, Britain would have more control than other states over this superstate and would have 'control of the oceans of the world', thus contravening the Monroe Doctrine, which had traditionally secured American 'wealth, prosperity and power'. As Cohalan pointed out to the Senate committee: 'I believe that we went to war for the purpose of ending autocracy and all that means … and that it means not alone militarism, the control of the land but also navalism, the control of the oceans of the world.'

In his testimony, Cohalan cleverly linked American security interests to Irish independence. He pointed out that Ireland's geographical location meant that it controlled the approaches to Britain's western seaboard. According to this logic, 'England's continued control of the sea was dependent upon continued control of Ireland'. Because of these geographical facts, it was therefore in America's interest that 'England should give her consent to having the republican form of government which has been set up in Ireland recognised by herself and the nations of the world'. Cohalan also stressed that opposition to the league was consistent with America's traditional isolationist policy towards Europe: 'We Irish think that there should be no abandonment of the policy laid down by Washington in his farewell address of keeping away from permanent, entangling alliances with any of the countries of the OLD World.'[64]

Cohalan proved to be a valuable ally to Republicans such as Borah in the battle against the league. Organised on a national level, with supporters in every state, the FOIF mobilised against the league and drew on the considerable financial resources built up by the Victory Fund to fight their case. This proved useful in countering the president's nationwide tour of the country in support of the league in September 1919. FOIF branches took part in counter-demonstrations in those areas which the president visited and took out full-page advertisements attacking the league in the newspapers along his route.[65]

The Senate finally voted on the Treaty of Peace with Germany, which incorporated the League of Nations, in November 1919. The treaty failed to get the necessary two-thirds support and therefore failed ratification. This meant that, while a League of Nations did come into existence, the United States could not become a member.[66] An ecstatic Cohalan sent an immediate telegram to Senator Borah: 'Heartiest congratulations. Greatest victory for country and liberty since the American revolution largely due to you.' Borah was in turn fulsome in his praise for Cohalan: 'You have rendered in this fight a service which no other man has rendered or could have rendered.'[67]

The actual extent to which Cohalan's campaign contributed to the defeat of the league in the Senate is difficult to quantify. Predictably, the *Gaelic American* exaggerated Cohalan's role. Under a front-page banner headline entitled 'Senate's Action a Splendid Vindication of Americanism', the paper described Cohalan as the main architect of victory.[68] Perhaps of more substance is Wilson's own view. Robert Schmuhl, in his work *Ireland's Exiled Children: America and the Easter Rising,* argues that Wilson himself 'blamed the Irish for the failure to ratify the Paris Peace Treaty which incorporated the League of Nations'. Schmuhl refers to a letter from University of Chicago historian William Edward Dodd which recounted a meeting with Wilson in 1921 just before he left the White House. In his account of the meeting, Dodd noted that 'the President is sure a broken man' and that he 'insisted the Irish had wrecked the whole program for adoption of the work in Paris'. Dodd also recorded Wilson as saying despondently: 'Oh the foolish Irish … Would to God they might all have gone back home.'[69]

Wilson too may have exaggerated the role that the Irish played in the defeat of the League of Nations Treaty. There were other factors at play. As Cooper argues, Wilson's own 'self-righteousness and stubbornness', exacerbated by a stroke, alienated Senate reservationists who might otherwise have supported a modified treaty.[70] The Hearst press also opposed the league as did other factions, including ethnic groups from Eastern and Southern Europe and radical left organisations.[71] One could also reasonably argue that many Republican senators opposed the league for party political reasons rather than out of ideological conviction. This proved an effective strategy, since the whole debacle over the league undermined Wilson and paved the way for the return of a Republican administration in 1920. However, the case of Ireland offered all these opponents a ready example of the contradictions inherent in the treaty so even in this context one could still argue that the Irish issue loomed large in the defeat of the league. Cohalan's campaign played a role in bringing this question to public and congressional attention.

Another question that needs to be answered is whether Cohalan's antagonism to Wilson and the league had a detrimental impact on the Irish cause in the United States. In an article in the *Irish Times*, Sean Cronin claimed that the president's goodwill on the Irish question might have been forthcoming were it not for Cohalan's campaign and his alliance with prominent Republicans. Cronin argued that Cohalan should have suspended his campaign against the league in the interest of the Irish cause.[72]

Given that Cohalan saw his opposition to the league as perfectly compatible with Irish freedom, and that it was consistent with his long-standing isolationist approach to American foreign policy, there was little chance of this happening. Again, leaving aside the president's obvious dislike of Cohalan, it seems unthinkable that Wilson would have sacrificed his overall objective of a comprehensive peace settlement just for the sake of Ireland. Even Cohalan believed that this could come about only if his hand was forced by Congress and the court of public opinion.

In September 1919, Victor Herbert wrote to his friend Cohalan and marvelled at his achievements in such a short year. 'You have really done wonders for the cause and justly have gained the love and admiration of every true Irishman.'[73] Significant victories had indeed been won in the form of increased membership of the FOIF, a successful Irish Victory Fund, congressional resolutions in favour of Irish independence and the American Commission's much-publicised visit to Ireland. Cohalan had also won important congressional allies for the Irish cause through his campaign against the League of Nations. However, tensions already developing over Cohalan's America-centred approach to the Irish question would soon come into public view. The arrival of Sinn Féin leader Éamon de Valera in the United States would bring these tensions to a head and present Cohalan with one of the most significant challenges of his political career.

7

Cohalan and de Valera: 'The Judge' versus 'The Chief'

COHALAN'S DISPUTE WITH Éamon de Valera is perhaps the area of his life that has received the most historical attention. This is mainly due to the importance placed by Irish historians on de Valera's lengthy mission to the United States in 1919 and 1920. Explanations for Cohalan's tempestuous relationship with de Valera during this mission vary widely and often depend on the writer's own particular opinion of de Valera rather than any great knowledge of Cohalan's political motivations. Given Cohalan's relative obscurity, it is perhaps understandable for historians to have focused on personality factors or territorial power struggles in explaining the roots of this conflict between the leaders of Irish-American and Irish nationalism. This chapter takes the view that while such factors played a role, other, deeper ideological principles were chiefly responsible. It argues that a more American-rooted perspective shaped Cohalan's Irish nationalism while de Valera believed that Irish interests should take precedence over other considerations.

In June 1919, Éamon de Valera began his eighteen-month tour of the United States in search of American political recognition for the self-proclaimed Irish republic and funds for the ongoing political and military struggle for independence.[1] That de Valera decided to spend so long in the United States at such a momentous time is testament to the importance Sinn Féin placed on Irish-American support in achieving their objectives. Other Sinn Féin representatives preceded de Valera's visit. In May 1919, Harry Boland, one of Sinn Féin's most senior activists and a member of the supreme council of the IRB, arrived to prepare the ground for the 'Chief's' mission the following month.[2]

We have already explored the tensions over strategy that had arisen between Cohalan and Devoy on the one side and McCartan and McGarrity on the other. Some of these tensions related to the use of the Victory Fund, which had been launched at the Third Irish Race Convention and which would total almost one million dollars. At an April meeting of the executive committee of the FOIF, McGarrity advocated that these funds should be used entirely for Irish purposes. According to McGarrity's report of the meeting, Cohalan in response had argued forcefully that the money should be used for 'educational propaganda' in America. In a comment that would have repercussions for Cohalan's reputation at a later date, McGarrity observed that Devoy in a low voice said to Cohalan 'that he thought some money should go over, but the Judge was obdurate and the old man supinely kept silent'.[3] As we shall see in later chapters, such comments would later feed suspicions among Cohalan's critics that he somehow manipulated Devoy for his own political purposes.

These tensions escalated after Boland's visit. Cohalan's use of the Victory Fund in his battle against the league alarmed Boland who, like McCartan and McGarrity, felt that such monies could be better used in Ireland than in the United States.[4] Typically, Cohalan defended his position by reference to the threat posed by Britain to American sovereignty and arguing that opposing the league was compatible with Irish freedom. In a conversation with Boland in June 1919, Cohalan stressed the importance of mobilising the Irish-American community to counter this threat. According to Boland's report to the Dáil:

> The Judge [Cohalan] held that it is essential that the money be spent here and he has a very comprehensive scheme for linking up the Race so that they may be such a power in American politics that they could be used as one man against England's attempts to collar America and to this end, extensive propaganda must be carried out amongst the Irish here.[5]

Cohalan saw this objective as vital to the interests of Irish-America and received the full support of Devoy in this regard. However, for Boland the campaign against the league seemed a distraction from the main struggle then taking place in Ireland. Under pressure from Boland and McGarrity, Cohalan agreed that 250,000 dollars of the Victory Fund should be sent to Ireland after what Boland described as a 'very stiff fight'.[6] That Cohalan had to be persuaded about the importance of sending money to Ireland would again suggest his fixation on the league battle. However, his willingness to concede to Boland's request also demonstrates that he could adopt a pragmatic approach if circumstances demanded.[7]

Lynch, in his manuscript history of the FOIF, argues effectively that Boland's allegations that Cohalan misused the Victory Fund in pursuit of American objectives are overstated. As we have covered earlier, over one million dollars were collected in a relatively short space of time. Lynch points out that besides the 250,000 dollars dispatched to Ireland, FOIF money funded the expenses of the Sinn Féin envoy to Paris Seán T. O'Kelly and the American Commission in Paris. The fund also financed the various congressional campaigns on behalf of the Irish cause. As we shall see later, other funds would be used to finance de Valera's tour of the United States and provide seed money for the bond drive. The Victory Fund also helped finance the propaganda activities of the FOIF and the National Bureau in Washington. While much of this activity focused on battling the League of Nations, many propaganda pamphlets and leaflets published and distributed by the FOIF and the Irish National Bureau in Washington related to conditions in Ireland. These included *The Republic Can Pay Its Way* (1919) and Cohalan's pamphlet *The Indictment* (1919), an attack on British policy in Ireland in a historical context.[8]

At this point, criticism of Cohalan from within Sinn Féin ranks was limited to a small circle of Irish nationalists in the United States. In a letter in late June 1919, Sean T. O'Kelly, obviously aware that his mission to Paris was financed by FOIF funds, praised Cohalan for his work in organising the American Commission and for raising the profile of the Irish cause in the US.[9] Referring to the recent disputes with McCartan and Boland, O'Kelly informed Devoy: 'I hope the President [Éamon de Valera] will be able to settle that now that he is with you. If he cannot succeed in bringing those people to their senses, nobody will.'[10] A couple of weeks after his arrival, de Valera met Cohalan at the Waldorf Astoria Hotel in New York. In a display of unity, Cohalan and de Valera posed for a photograph on the roof of the building.

The *Gaelic American*, appealing to its mainly Irish-American readership, lauded de Valera for his role in the Easter Rising and paid special attention to his American birth.[11] The paper, in line with the mainstream media, also referred to de Valera as 'President of the Irish Republic' even though

Daniel Cohalan, Éamon de Valera, Justice John Goff and John Devoy at the Waldorf Astoria Hotel, New York, 23 June 1919. Photograph taken shortly after de Valera's arrival in the United States. (Source: Library of Congress)

technically he was president of the Irish Dáil or parliament and the Irish republic did not yet exist in international terms.[12]

In the eyes of the mainstream media, Cohalan continued to be viewed as the spokesman for the Irish cause in the United States. In July 1919, the *New York Times* carried a report on Cohalan's response to unionist leader Sir Edward Carson. The latter had warned the United States to stop interfering in Irish affairs, which he regarded as an internal British issue.[13] The *Times* indicated that: 'With Éamon de Valera in Chicago and his secretary Harry Boland confined to his apartment with a cold, Justice Daniel Cohalan was chosen yesterday by the Friends of Irish Freedom to reply to Sir Edward Carson's "hands off" ultimatum to America.' In a lengthy statement Cohalan pointed out:

> Sir Edward Carson forgets that America won the war and has, therefore, a right to dictate terms of peace. He forgets, too, that when we entered the war, which was won by the strength, vigor, and courage of America, we did so on grounds which pledge us to bring to the oppressed peoples of the earth the right to self-determination.[14]

Such comments enhanced Cohalan's status as leader of the Irish race in America but it is interesting to note that he directed such statements at mainstream American opinion rather than to an Irish-American audience. Typically, for tactical reasons, he still linked Wilson's professed claim to safeguard the rights of oppressed peoples to the Irish cause, using the president's own language of self-determination. Later in the interview, no doubt with the sensitivities of Irish nationalists in mind, he recalled the recent vote in Ireland in December 1918 which 'recorded that 50% of the population was in favor of a full republic'.[15]

The first signs of tension between Cohalan and de Valera emerged when the latter's fundraising plans for the United States became known. Shortly after his arrival, de Valera announced a scheme to raise money for the establishment of an Irish republic through the sale of bonds. Cohalan, drawing on his legal background, argued that the sale of such bonds would break America's 'blue sky' laws, since the Irish republic did not yet exist and had no international recognition.[16] In this context, Cohalan made a legal decision not motivated by any personal animosity towards de Valera. Others too questioned the legality of the bond drive. Congressman Bourke Cockran in a letter to Cohalan described the idea as 'preposterous'.[17] In the event, de Valera and his associates devised a scheme which overcame this legal obstacle. This involved selling Irish bond certificates rather than bonds themselves. It was intended that such certificates could be exchanged for real bonds when the Irish republic came into being.

McCartan, in his work *With de Valera in America*, claimed that Cohalan opposed the bond drive from the beginning and refused to co-operate in its administration. McCartan points out: 'There seemed to be a studied effort to prove to Boland that the project was impossible. No bank would agree to accept the money; no lawyer could surmount the legal difficulties, and offices suitable for headquarters could not be rented.'[18]

There is no evidence that Cohalan sought to put obstacles in the way of the bond campaign. While he believed the initial plan was illegal, he nevertheless agreed that the sale of bond certificates was within the law. One of his close allies in the FOIF, John J. Splain, even suggested to Bourke Cockran that Cohalan should be put in charge of the bond drive.[19] De Valera, already aware of the disputes between Boland and Cohalan over the use of the Victory Fund, insisted on keeping total control over the administration of the scheme. He appointed Frank Walsh, who had done so much valuable work leading the American Commission, to run the drive. However, de Valera, with customary caution towards all Irish-Americans, ensured that real control rested with James O'Mara, a Dublin businessman who had volunteered his services to Sinn Féin.[20]

Despite these initial tensions, the FOIF, under Cohalan's instructions, worked hard to make the bond drive a success. The organisation loaned 100,000 dollars from the Victory Fund to cover the expenses associated with setting up the drive. Money from the Victory Fund totalling 26,248 dollars, a considerable sum in 1919, financed de Valera's tour of the United States, which aimed to both promote the sale of bond certificates and secure recognition of the Irish republic.[21] Here the state-wide organisational infrastructure of both the FOIF and the Clan ensured that vast crowds turned out for his speeches along his route. Turnout was particularly high in those cities with large Irish-American populations and where the FOIF had a large presence. Over 70,000 people came to hear de Valera speak in Boston, while 50,000 heard the Irish 'President' speak in Chicago.[22]

Cohalan's decision to wind up the Victory Fund in August 1919 also helped ensure the success of the bond certificate drive. This meant that de Valera's fundraising efforts faced no competition from a rival Irish-American campaign. Diarmuid Lynch, FOIF national secretary, handed over the names and addresses of almost 70,000 FOIF members to de Valera. The FOIF encouraged its members to not only buy bond certificates but also assist in the sales campaign. John Splain, who still felt that Cohalan could have managed the bond drive more effectively, became chairman of the bond drive in Connecticut.[23] Members of the Clan also participated enthusiastically in the drive. Even McCartan noted that the Clan in New York sold over 600,000 dollars-worth of bonds. According to the *News Letter*, Cohalan personally played an instrumental role in launching the bond certificate scheme in Providence, Rhode Island.[24]

The bond drive, with the help of many ordinary FOIF members, collected over five million dollars. This far exceeded Sinn Féin expectations and ordinary rank-and-file FOIF members across the country played a significant role in making the drive such a success. Later de Valera, in a message to the Dáil, defended the expenditure of 1.5 million dollars in the United States on 'world propaganda' for the Irish cause. This would suggest that he too realised the importance of spending a substantial part of the bond money collected to promote the Irish cause in the United States.[25] Fitzpatrick, in his biography of Harry Boland, estimates that by the end of 1920, 'scarcely a million dollars of Bond-money (£200,000), one-fifth of the total subscribed, had been smuggled to Ireland'. This drew urgent requests from Michael Collins, minister for finance in the Irish Dáil and treasurer of the IRB, for more funds. In a somewhat lame explanation, Boland wrote to an exasperated Collins that de Valera was not yet satisfied that those at home could 'safeguard the money'.[26]

The above evidence indicates that de Valera had complete control over substantial sums of money and that he decided to spend and retain a large proportion of this money in the United States. This suggests that disputes over money should no longer have impacted on his relationship with Cohalan. Indeed, in September 1919 the initial conflict between de Valera and Cohalan appeared to have eased. In an optimistic note to Cohalan that month, even the normally taciturn Devoy noted that, after a 'straight' discussion with de Valera, the tensions between both camps appeared to have eased: 'I think the air will be cleared and that it will be plainer sailing in future.'[27]

Irish reaction to the Mason Bill, introduced by Republican congressman William Mason from Illinois in May 1919, provides further evidence of good relations between both sides. Mason, working closely with Cohalan, introduced a bill into the House of Representatives seeking the appropriation of government funds for 'the salaries of a minister and consuls to the Republic of Ireland'. This was a tactical move on Cohalan's part, since if Congress approved such a measure it would effectively recognise the existence of the Irish republic. Cohalan himself testified before the hearings on the bill in December 1919 and argued for the existence of such a state.

> More than 1,500 of the most active men and women in Ireland who believed in the establishment of the Irish Republic were under arrest and held without trial and without indictment in the jails of England. In spite of this, the Irish people by a vote of over 1,200,000 to 308,000, voted for separation from England and the establishment of the Irish Republic.[28]

McCartan writes that he rushed to shake Cohalan's hand to congratulate him for his performance after the hearings, 'and my enthusiasm he visibly appreciated. With Walsh and Cohalan to champion us, there would be nothing to stop us achieving final victory.'[29] Yet the outcome of the Mason Bill must have been a disappointment to Cohalan. Unlike previous resolutions, the bill was not reported to the committee, which suggested to Cohalan that its wording was too radical for the House of Representatives to contemplate.

Towards the end of 1919 and into 1920, a more fundamental difference between Cohalan and de Valera emerged over their varying attitudes to both Wilson and the League of Nations. As we have seen, Cohalan staunchly opposed the league, as much for American as for Irish reasons, and played a significant role in the defeat of the measure in the Senate in November 1919. In a rerun of the earlier debate, the measure failed in the Senate in March 1920. Again, Cohalan worked closely with Borah and other anti-league activists in convincing the Senate to reject the measure.

Cohalan's vehement opposition to the league appears to have unsettled de Valera. Like his Sinn Féin colleagues in Ireland, de Valera was not adamantly opposed to the league. Wilson's Fourteen Points had referred to the establishment of 'a general association of nations to be formed to guarantee to its members political independence and territorial integrity'. If a free Ireland could become part of such a league then its sovereignty could be protected. De Valera also worried that Irish opposition to the league might alienate the Democratic Party. After all, many Irish-American politicians were Democrats and Wilson enjoyed a great deal of popularity in Ireland and among other subject nations eager to shake off colonial bondage.[30]

In his tour across the country, de Valera publicly took an ambivalent approach to the league, though in private he was more positive about the proposal. As early as July 1919, just weeks after his arrival in the United States, he informed Arthur Griffith, who was then acting Sinn Féin leader in Ireland, that he was trying to let Wilson know that 'if he goes for his 14 points as they were and a true League of Nations, men and women of Irish blood will be behind him'.[31]

De Valera's increasingly positive attitude towards the league can also be illustrated by his response to the introduction of a congressional resolution on Ireland by pro-league Democratic senator Thomas J. Walsh of Montana. This resolution stated that, following ratification of the League of Nations Covenant and the peace treaty, 'the right of its people [the Irish] to self-government be presented by the United States to the Council or Assembly of the League'. This was immediately dismissed by Daniel O'Connell of the Irish National Bureau, who suggested that it would be 'ludicrous' to expect a British-dominated league to do anything for Ireland. However, de Valera, in a note to O'Connell, threatened to repudiate the bureau if O'Connell persisted in making such statements. O'Connell in response told de Valera 'politely' to 'mind his own business; that we proposed to save America against England and all those whom she could influence'.[32]

In the event, Senator Walsh's bill received little encouragement from Wilson. When Walsh finally introduced his measure on 17 October it was never brought before a committee or to a vote.[33] Nevertheless, this conflict over the work of the bureau reveals underlying tensions between de Valera's internationalist view of world affairs and Cohalan's American isolationism. For Cohalan, the League of Nations represented a threat to the United States but for de Valera a 'real' league could benefit small countries like Ireland and protect their sovereignty. De Valera maintained this stance throughout his mission and would be favourable to the league in his later political career. In a revealing message to Collins shortly after his return to Ireland, de Valera wrote: 'Though I was working directly for recognition in America, I kept in mind as our main political objective the securing of America's influence, in case she was to join a League of Nations, to securing us also a place within the League.'[34]

As early as October 1919, such disputes over American politics and the league caused de Valera to contemplate the formation of another, more broad-based organisation that would be under his complete control. The American Commission led by Frank Walsh already had control of the bond certificate drive but now de Valera considered extending its remit to take in anti-British propaganda activities on behalf of the Irish cause in the United States. This worried Devoy, who had long experience of the factionalism and division that had plagued Irish-American nationalist movements in the past. In an anxious letter to Cohalan, Devoy reported that Frank Walsh had told him: 'It has been suggested that the organisation [American Commission] be extended into a national organisation, on very broad lines, to include all those with Irish sympathies.' Referring to the 100,000 dollars which the FOIF had loaned for the bond drive, Devoy claimed: 'Evidently, that is what they want the $100,000 for, to use the money collected by the Friends to start an organisation to supplant it.'[35]

Through a resolution adopted by the National Council of the FOIF in November 1919, and reprinted in the *Gaelic American*, Cohalan now laid down a marker to de Valera. After urging FOIF members to continue co-operation with the bond drive, the resolution directed de Valera to confine himself to this task and leave the work of propaganda to the FOIF: 'We respectfully recommend to President de Valera that the men in charge of this work be instructed to devote their whole attention to it and leave to the Friends of Irish Freedom the work of organizing our people in America to combat English propaganda according to the plans laid down by the Race Convention in Philadelphia last February.'[36]

Following this 'respectful' rebuke, de Valera appeared to back down on his plans for a new Irish-American organisation. No doubt he recognised that any public quarrel would only disrupt the bond drive. Meanwhile, disputes over the League of Nations could be shelved for the moment given its imminent defeat in the Senate.[37] For de Valera, the dispute over the league underlined the necessity of having a nationwide organisation under his complete control but the time was not yet ripe.

At an FOIF National Council meeting in December 1919, de Valera adopted a conciliatory stance and praised the work of Cohalan and Devoy during the ongoing bond certificate campaign. In response to questioning by members of the National Council, de Valera also stated that no new organisation would be necessary. This announcement was reported approvingly in the *Gaelic American* under the heading 'De Valera Silences Mischievous Slanders'.[38]

Yet suspicions of de Valera's motives had not entirely disappeared, and in February 1920 the uneasy truce between Cohalan and de Valera came to a sudden end. The catalyst for this latest breakdown in relations related to a de Valera interview with a reporter from the *Westminster Gazette*, a London-based newspaper. In an attempt to counter suggestions that British security would be compromised in the event of Irish independence, de Valera cited the Platt Amendment, which governed relations between Cuba and the United States, as a possible model for relations between an independent Ireland and Britain. In line with the Monroe Doctrine, designed to protect US security interests in the western hemisphere, one of the amendment's provisions stipulated that Cuba could not make a treaty with any other foreign power which might impair its independence. De Valera indicated that he would have no objection if Britain adopted similar safeguards towards an independent Ireland. In his interview, de Valera argued: 'Why doesn't Britain declare a Monroe Doctrine for her neighbouring island? The people of Ireland, so far from objecting, would co-operate with their whole soul.'[39]

In the same interview, de Valera ignored other provisions of the Platt Amendment which gave the United States 'the right to intervene for the preservation of Cuban independence, the maintenance of a government adequate for the protection of life, property, and individual liberty …'.[40] The interview caused alarm within Sinn Féin circles both in the United States and in Ireland. McCartan writes that he had not been consulted prior to the interview, while several Sinn Féin members of the Irish Dáil expressed deep misgivings, with Countess Markievicz saying that the president 'spoke only for himself'.[41] Michael Collins, then spearheading the military campaign against British forces in Ireland, shut down all debate on the issue, and there things should have ended as far as Collins was concerned. Yet the *Gaelic American* showed no such reticence and throughout the next month published articles highly critical of de Valera. In one editorial, Devoy thundered: 'You cannot cite the Platt Amendment without bringing in the whole text of it, which gives the United States rights in Cuba which it would be suicidal to give England in Ireland.'[42]

This and other comments in the *Gaelic American* shocked de Valera. In a letter to Griffith, he argued that 'these attacks were a deadly attempt to ruin our chances for the bonds, and for everything we came here to accomplish'.[43] Given the level of support that Cohalan and the FOIF had already provided to the bond drive, this interpretation of the *Gaelic American* attacks seems unfounded. The newspaper, reflecting Devoy and Cohalan's anti-British imperialist ideology, had always taken a strident line in defence of American interests. Its view of de Valera's interview in this context should have come as no surprise.

In his letter to Griffith, de Valera recognised that Irish-American nationalists could have differing interests and objectives from that of Irish nationalists. However, he still believed that the interests of Ireland should be their primary concern:

> This organisation FOIF owes its life to the idea that it is an organisation to work for Irish freedom. It is not its primary object to secure in American life a promised place for our race here … Fundamentally, Irish-Americans differ from us in this – they being American first would sacrifice Irish interests if need be to American interests – we Irish would do the reverse.

Having admitted this, de Valera then made a somewhat contradictory claim in the same letter, stating that: 'The trouble is purely one of personalities. I cannot feel confidence enough in a certain man [Cohalan] to let him have explicit control over tactics here, without consultation and agreement with me.'[44]

Just three days after his letter to Griffith, de Valera took the unprecedented step of writing directly to Cohalan rather than Devoy to question the purpose behind the *Gaelic American* attacks on him. This would suggest that de Valera believed that Cohalan had somehow manipulated the aged Devoy into launching a campaign against him. After first emphasising that he *alone* was responsible to the Irish people 'for the trust with which I have been charged', de Valera stated that: 'It is my obvious duty to select such instruments as may be available for the task set me.' Using the same metaphor, de Valera also claimed:

> I see added force being applied, day by day, to the power end of the great lever of American public opinion, with which I hope to accomplish my purpose. I must satisfy myself as to the temper of the other end of the lever.
>
> The articles in the 'Gaelic American', and certain incidents that have resulted from them, give me grounds for the fear that, in a moment of stress, the point of the lever would fail me. I am led to believe that these articles in the 'Gaelic American' have your consent and approval. Is this so?

De Valera's reference to American opinion serving as a 'lever' for the Irish cause would again suggest that he expected Irish-Americans to act in the interests of the Irish homeland rather than in their own interests without any reciprocity from Ireland. In this context de Valera questioned Cohalan's loyalty in supporting his mission to seek 'recognition for the established Republic'. In a combative final question, which demanded Cohalan's 'urgent' response, de Valera pointedly asked: 'You are the officer of the Friends of Irish Freedom, who de facto, wields unchallenged the executive power of that organisation. It is vital that I know exactly how you stand in this matter.'[45]

De Valera had his letter hand-delivered by Harry Boland on 20 February. Cohalan responded two days later. His reply to de Valera is a valuable document in that it highlights once again the priorities that shaped his American-Irish nationalism. Cohalan initially noted that he was 'amazed' by the contents of de Valera's letter but: 'in spite of its tone, and because of the position which you occupy, I am responding to it'. After first declaring that he had no control over the contents of the *Gaelic American*, he highlighted Devoy's right 'to comment upon, or discuss your public utterances, or those of any man who speaks for a cause or a people'.

In a key passage which highlights Cohalan's own lifelong struggle against British imperialism, he alleged that de Valera supported a 'Monroe Doctrine' for Ireland:

> A British Monroe Doctrine, that would make Ireland the ally of England, and thus buttress the falling British Empire, so as to further oppress India and Egypt and other subject lands, would be so immoral, and so utterly at variance with the ideals and traditions of the Irish people, as to be as indefensible to them as it would be intolerable to the liberty-loving people of the world.

Cohalan also questioned de Valera's right, as a citizen of another country, to dictate policy to Americans and Irish-Americans:

> Are you not in great danger of making a grave mistake when you talk in your communication of selecting 'instruments' in this country, and of 'levers' and 'power end', and 'other end of the lever' through which you hope to accomplish your purpose here?
>
> Do you think for a moment that American public opinion will permit any citizen of another country to interfere, as you suggest, in American affairs? If so, I may assure you that you are woefully out of touch with the spirit of the country in which you are sojourning.

In making this statement, Cohalan took into account prevailing nativist American ideas that Irish-Americans were not fully loyal to the United States. Indeed, many Protestant Americans believed that Irish-American Catholics voted in accordance with the wishes of their priests and the pope and that this apparent willingness to follow the orders of a foreign potentate was antithetical to American principles.[46] Cohalan, like other prominent Irish-Americans, was especially sensitive to such allegations, hence his involvement in societies such as the AIHS, which sought to enhance the standing of the Irish in the United States. In this context, Cohalan believed that if Irish-Americans blindly followed the instructions of a foreign leader they would immediately leave themselves open to nativist criticism. In his letter Cohalan stressed: 'You point out that I have been called upon to speak not merely in the name of the Friends of Irish Freedom but in the name of the whole Irish Race in America. May I call attention to the fact that it was always as an American, and for my countrymen, that I spoke.'

In another key passage which highlights Cohalan's goal to win mainstream American support for the Irish cause, he declared:

> I respectfully suggest, in closing, that you would be well advised if you hesitate before you jeopardise or imperil that solidarity of opinion, and unity of action, among millions of American citizens, which you found here amongst us when you came, which have been the despair of England's friends, and have already accomplished so much for America and Ireland.[47]

In these closing remarks, Cohalan doubtless referred to not only the funds collected and congressional resolutions in favour of Ireland but also the recent defeat of the League of Nations, which he believed was compatible with Irish interests. This latter assumption would not have been shared by de Valera.

In spite of these very different perspectives on how the Irish question should be dealt with, both men wanted to avoid an open breach. This was evident at the New York St Patrick's Day parade on 17 March 1920. Cohalan had been selected as grand marshal of the parade, itself a measure of the prestige and status which he now enjoyed within Irish America. In a public display of loyalty to Ireland's elected 'President', Cohalan, as Tansill points out, 'yielded the place of honor on the reviewing stand to de Valera'. At a later Friendly Sons of St Patrick banquet, Cohalan, who was president of this society, introduced de Valera in glowing terms as a soldier and 'the elected head of the Republic of Ireland'.[48]

Behind the scenes, Cohalan sought to clarify matters. A couple of days after the St Patrick's Day banquet, he summoned a conference of leading Irish-American nationalists to debate the situation that had arisen. The meeting took place at the Park Avenue Hotel in New York on 19 March. According to McGarrity, de Valera had not been invited to the meeting. McGarrity then turned up unannounced and demanded that the Irish leader, the subject of the meeting, should be invited to defend his position. This was agreed and Harry Boland subsequently brought de Valera to the hotel.

McGarrity's account of the meeting, which became known in Irish nationalist circles as the 'Trial of de Valera', suggests that the atmosphere was tense. He noted that de Valera appeared to be under a great strain: 'His teeth were set, and he looked over the crowd, anxious, apparently to see the makeup of the same.' De Valera began by arguing that the *Gaelic American*'s interpretation of the *Westminster Gazette* interview gave it a meaning 'foreign to that which it was intended to convey'. Pointing out that these articles were doing considerable damage to the Irish cause, he asked Cohalan whether he agreed with 'the interpretation placed upon the interview by the editor of the *Gaelic American*'. De Valera's criticism of John Devoy was more muted. He praised Devoy for his long service to Ireland but, as summarised by Cronin, pointed out that 'a new generation had arisen in Ireland with but one object in life, and one allegiance in life and that allegiance was to Ireland only'. In a reiteration of the argument that he made to Griffith, de Valera stressed that his only interest was Ireland and 'he could not delegate to other, to American leaders, the trust given him by the people of Ireland to come and seek recognition and the other things necessary for Ireland's regeneration'.[49]

In response, Cohalan spoke of de Valera's 'utter ignorance of America' and complained of de Valera's willingness to be assisted by Americans but unwillingness to be advised by them. He also voiced suspicion at de Valera's reliance on Dr William Maloney's advice, describing Maloney as 'one of the ablest men of the British Secret Service'.[50]

There are conflicting accounts of what then happened at this meeting. McGarrity's version paints Cohalan in a critical light, accusing him of 'behaving like a prosecutor doing everything to irritate the President – walking close to him and pointing his finger, etc'.[51] Meanwhile, John D. Splain, a Cohalan ally, points to de Valera as the more belligerent party, indicating that: 'President de Valera himself became so excited that at one point he blurted out he had not been in America a month when he concluded that there was not room in the country for Justice Cohalan and himself.'[52] Another Cohalan supporter, Mayor John P. Grace of South Carolina, felt 'that President de Valera was that day revealed to me as laboring under some psychopathic condition or that the evil spirit himself had taken hold of the Irish movement'.[53]

After a heated discussion which lasted ten hours, all commentators agree that a compromise was finally reached and Bishop Turner of Buffalo led all those present in a prayer for reconciliation. De Valera agreed not to interfere in matters of American concern while Cohalan promised not to intervene in matters that were of purely Irish concern.[54] At the end of the marathon meeting, Cohalan shook hands with de Valera. No doubt both sides hoped that this would bring the dispute to a close. However, as we shall see in the next chapter, this truce only proved temporary and the tensions between both men would soon resurface.

It is clear from the exchange of letters and de Valera's more muted criticism of Devoy at the hotel meeting that de Valera believed that Cohalan had somehow manipulated Devoy to launch these attacks upon him. However, one could reasonably argue that de Valera overestimated Cohalan's influence over Devoy.[55] Diarmuid Lynch, in his manuscript history of the FOIF, makes the reasonable case that while Cohalan was a powerful figure in Irish-America, even he could not control what the independent-minded Devoy chose to write in the *Gaelic American*:

> Anybody acquainted with Devoy's previous career and writings knows full well that not alone was it unnecessary for Judge Cohalan or others to prompt the writing of those objections, but that no man or group of men (even if they wished to do so in this instance) could restrain John Devoy from expressing himself on a proposal which in his opinion was detrimental to the welfare of the Irish Republic, – towards the establishment of which he had by 1920 devoted himself indomitably over a period of well-nigh sixty years.[56]

As will also be evident in the next chapter, both sides overestimated the role of personality factors in the escalating conflict. De Valera and his colleagues blamed Cohalan's political ambitions and his supposed malign influence over Devoy. Cohalan and his supporters increasingly blamed de Valera, leaving aside the fact that tensions had already existed before de Valera arrived. In reality, the famous exchange of letters between Cohalan and de Valera and the so-called 'Trial of de Valera' reveal that each leader was motivated by a different set of priorities. De Valera believed that Irish-America could be used as a 'lever' to exercise influence on Ireland's behalf but that Irish-American leaders needed to acknowledge that 'he *alone* was responsible' for directing affairs. Cohalan, emphasising his own American identity, advocated that the Irish cause could best be served by Irish-Americans appealing to American interests and values rather than to purely Irish concerns. In the months ahead, these ideological differences would finally lead to a very public and bitter split which would impact upon the entire Irish-American nationalist movement and would have repercussions in Ireland itself.

8

Cohalan and the Split within Irish-America, 1920–1

THE APPARENT RECONCILIATION between Cohalan and de Valera in March 1919 would prove to be short-lived. While some of de Valera's actions tended to exacerbate an already tense situation, the root of the conflict was based upon a fundamental difference of opinion about how the relationship between Irish nationalists and Irish-American nationalists should work. De Valera, taking an Irish-centred view, was convinced that the majority of those who supported the FOIF were doing so because of 'sympathy for Ireland' and that Cohalan was seeking to exploit this sympathy for his own political ambitions.[1] This ignored Cohalan's Americanism and his genuine desire to defend the interests of the Irish-American community in the United States and defend the interests of the United States. Meanwhile, Cohalan, often preoccupied by American considerations, failed to understand that de Valera represented the views of other Sinn Féin members in the US and in Ireland itself and that it was not just de Valera's personality, or the actions of British spies, that caused the tensions. Cohalan's open split with de Valera would obviously undermine his hitherto high standing within the Irish-American nationalist community. However, he still enjoyed the loyalty of many of his followers.

Following the Park Avenue Hotel meeting, Boland, in a report on the meeting to Michael Collins, expressed the view that the 'air has been cleared' and that 'there is now no fear of a split'. At the same time, Boland admitted that the 'American-Irish leaders' would never submit to dictation from Ireland. 'It is practically impossible to harmonise the two points of view.'[2]

Prior to the Park Avenue meeting, de Valera and Boland had sought approval from the IRB in Ireland to assert control over the Clan and the FOIF in the United States if difficulties arose. These communications continued after the meeting, which suggests that while de Valera and Boland believed that a split with Cohalan had been avoided for now, the possibility of further disputes still remained. Focused on prosecuting the war against British forces in Ireland, and sharing de Valera's Irish-orientated view, the IRB did not challenge de Valera's account of the escalating tensions in America. Michael Collins, who occupied the dominant position of treasurer on the IRB's Supreme Council, assured Harry Boland that 'no matter what rumours were put out by certain people, your other colleagues and myself have unfailingly endorsed your actions and words even when they were not known to us'.[3]

In a further dispatch from Collins on 26 April, some weeks after the Park Avenue meeting, he tackled the sensitive question of whether the Clan and by implication the FOIF should be regarded as a 'subsidiary of the Organisation at home', or whether it should be treated as 'an independent Organisation'. In his dispatch, Collins unequivocally declared that the Clan should be:

> … an Organisation of Irishmen, in whatever land they live, bound by the same obligations, drawing their inspiration from Ireland, and having the purely Irish aspect as the first object of their existence … In operation this would mean direction from Ireland on big issues, accepting the policy and measures of the home Organisation even when it directed a course which might be considered as opposing the local interests of the subsidiary Organisation abroad.[4]

These dispatches from Collins also contained an 'ultimatum' for the Clan's executive to be presented at Boland's 'own discretion' in case of 'any further difficulties'. According to David Fitzpatrick, these instructions provided Boland 'with plenary powers to subjugate the Clan'.[5] He also argues that the IRB intended to reduce the Clan to the role of a 'collecting agency, with Harry [Boland] as manager and Collins as supremo'.[6] Following this logic, since the FOIF was the public face of the Clan, it too would need to be brought under Irish control.

The actions of Sinn Féin representatives in the US in the aftermath of the March meeting must therefore be seen in the context of Irish efforts to bring the Clan and the FOIF under the authority of the 'Home Organization' and, if this failed, to replace it by an organisation loyal to Dublin rather than to Cohalan and Devoy. An early example of this strategy can be seen in Irish efforts to gain control over the remaining portion of the Irish Victory Fund in April 1920. James O'Mara, overall director of the bond certificate drive, demanded an account of the remaining balance of the fund from Diarmuid Lynch, national secretary of the FOIF. In a strident tone, O'Mara declared that: 'Such money morally belongs to Ireland.' The National Council of the FOIF, acting with Cohalan's approval, rejected this request, stressing the objectives of the fund as outlined at the Third Irish Race Convention. While these objectives included a campaign to achieve recognition of a republican form of government in Ireland, other goals included the preservation of American ideals of government against false British propaganda and defence of American rights.[7]

Lynch, in his history of the FOIF, described O'Mara's claim as an attempt by de Valera to undermine Cohalan's power base through depleting the FOIF of its remaining resources. Given that funds from the bond drive would ultimately dwarf the Victory Fund by a factor of five, this suspicion appears well-founded. This motivation would also conform to de Valera's own agenda of asserting Irish control over the FOIF, which had now been sanctioned in Dublin.

De Valera's efforts to undermine Cohalan's position became more public in the row between both men at the Republican National Convention in Chicago in June 1920. On the surface, this row can be seen in the context of a tactical clash over how best to secure a Republican Party resolution in favour of Irish national claims. However, on a deeper level, its origins lay in de Valera's desire to assert his position as leader of the Irish movement not only in Ireland but also in the United States.

In explaining the roots of this latest clash, we first need to outline Cohalan's objectives. Typically, these had both an American and Irish focus. As 1920 was an election year, Cohalan, though a lifelong Democrat, looked forward to Wilson's replacement by a Republican president who would not only be more sympathetic to Irish national demands but would reassert traditional American isolationist values in the face of British intrigue.[8] To achieve this goal, Cohalan focused on securing the nomination of Hiram Johnson as Republican candidate for the presidency.

Johnson, an ally of Borah, had campaigned actively against the League of Nations and shared Cohalan's isolationist stance on American foreign policy. Following the second defeat of the league in the Senate in March 1920, Cohalan had cabled him his congratulations but also wished him success in his coming campaign to secure the Republican nomination: 'I hope for you in the near future the greatest honors which can come to an American.'[9]

On 6 June 1920, Cohalan journeyed to the Republican convention in Chicago hoping to enlist support for Johnson's candidacy and secure a policy plank in favour of Irish independence. Given the recent congressional rejection of the Mason Bill, Cohalan believed that a more moderate policy plank in support of Ireland had a greater chance of being adopted. Assisted by leading members of the FOIF, including Mayor John Grace of Charleston, Cohalan drafted a resolution in favour of self-determination for Ireland:

> Resolved; that this Republican Convention desires to place on record its sympathy with all oppressed peoples, and its recognition of the principle that the people of Ireland have the right to determine freely, without dictation from outside, their own government institutions and the international relations with other States and peoples.[10]

To Cohalan's astonishment, de Valera led another Irish delegation with the intention of presenting an alternative policy plank to the convention. Indeed, de Valera's delegation had established a campaign office in the city prior to Cohalan's arrival. According to McCartan's account, many of de Valera's allies, including Frank Walsh and Bourke Cockran, 'had advised President de Valera that it would be improper for him and dangerous to attend the Convention'. McCartan himself advised against it.[11] Cohalan appears to have been aware of this. In the minutes of a later meeting contained in McGarrity's papers Cohalan states: 'Mr. Bourke Cockran told him that it would be a tragedy; that it was the same as if Geddes [British ambassador] would appear before the Republican convention asking it to do something. A fact which would be resented by the American people. I had the notion that he might come out here and just look on.'[12]

De Valera, seeing himself as leader of the Irish cause in the United States, had no intention of simply 'looking on'. Instead, he made his presence felt in the city and organised demonstrations in favour of the Irish republic accompanied by torchlight parades, marching bands and banners. This caused some mirth in the press, with the *Chicago Tribune* assuring its readers that de Valera 'was not a candidate for the Presidency of the United States'.[13] In his work *With de Valera in America*, McCartan is critical of de Valera's tactics and noted that 'there was no chance of offending America that we did not take'.[14]

De Valera's team drafted a separate resolution much more radical than the one drafted by Cohalan's team, the last paragraph of which read: 'Therefore, we favor the according by our Government to the elected government of the Republic of Ireland full, formal, and official recognition by the government of the United States, thus vindicating the principle for which our soldiers offered up their lives.'[15]

McCartan recounts how a five-man Irish-American delegation led by Mayor Grace attempted to reach a compromise with de Valera on 8 June so that a joint resolution could be put forward to the Republican Party's resolutions sub-committee on the following day. Cohalan, aware of de Valera's dislike for him, did not take part in this meeting but the five men later reported back to the main Irish-American delegation at the Great Northern Hotel over which Cohalan presided.[16]

The minutes of this meeting, where the five delegates reported back to the main delegation, have survived and offer a fascinating insight into Cohalan's perception of de Valera. The larger meeting was attended by twenty-five prominent Irish-Americans. These included Bishop Michael Gallagher of Detroit, soon to be the new leader of the FOIF, and prominent Irish-American politicians from across the United States and Canada.

Interestingly, the minutes of this meeting are contained in McGarrity's papers and Joe McGarrity has included a handwritten note on this document: 'Copy of draft apparently minutes that came into the hands of de Valera'.[17] McGarrity appears to have surreptitiously obtained these minutes in order to build a case against Cohalan so as to charge him with disloyalty towards the Irish leader and involvement in a conspiracy to eject de Valera from the United States. Some passages in the report of the meeting are underlined so as to provide evidence for this charge. Yet the document is also revealing of an Irish-American perspective on de Valera's role at the Chicago convention which Cohalan shares.

Included in the document, and of particular significance, is a lengthy statement by Cohalan critical of de Valera's tactics to win support for Irish recognition from the Republican Party at Chicago:

> It was absurd to fall in behind a program of brass band methods that was intended to coerce delegates and party leaders. For months the American leaders of the Irish cause had planned and worked to secure assistance from party conventions. The plans were working out smoothly and effectively.[18]

The minutes of the meeting also reveal the preoccupations of the Irish-American leaders with their status in the United States. Here Mayor John Grace's report of his encounter with de Valera is especially revealing:

> I told the President with all due respect to him, we believed he had worked himself into a conception substantially, that he was not only the President of the Irish Republic but also of the Irish Race wherever they are. I informed him that we were running the American end of the question in this country with as much love for the race as he had. In order to be consistent here, to be loyal to the flag we were under, we must solve this question compatible with American interests.
>
> If we do otherwise, we would ostracise our cause and ourselves here ...[19]

Following this statement by Mayor Grace, Cohalan interjected by saying, 'the President's talk lends the impression that Ireland has annexed the United States'.

Another member of the group who met de Valera, John Archdeacon Murphy of Buffalo, now took up Cohalan's point.

> I tried to point out the impossibility of the situation he [de Valera] was trying to lead us into. If we were to follow him as President of the Irish Republic, all would become Irish citizens on the question and not American citizens. Thus, we would be doing just what our enemies are saying about us. He said that was what he wanted us to do. Finally, I asked him, 'Do I understand your position? Would you prefer to have defeated your Resolution, rather than victory upon Mayor Grace's Resolution?' He answered he would.[20]

Richard Wolfe, another member of the delegation who met de Valera, also criticised de Valera's obstinacy. 'His attitude of mind is that of a teacher over children – he is always right as we are absolutely wrong. We must try to bring harmony out of chaos or induce him to return to Ireland.' In response to this Cohalan suggested rather diplomatically: 'Perhaps the latter is the solution to the former. I am not recommending this in any way but merely commenting on Mr. Wolfe's statement.'[21]

Cohalan's reaction to the suggestion that de Valera should leave the United States is somewhat ambiguous and is not conclusive evidence that he was engaged in a conspiracy to eject the Irish leader.[22] Yet the following passage from the minutes of the meeting indicates that he feels de Valera's presence in the United States is harming the Irish-American cause and that such a course of action may be necessary. It also suggests that Cohalan recognises that de Valera does not understand legitimate Irish-American concerns.

> Because of our Irish blood, we are handicapped in America and consequently, have an interest in the freedom of the race. Therefore, we have the right to do what may be necessary to bring success to the movement. The case is a conflict of the European mind with the American mind. It is impeding progress and hurting in many ways.[23]

This hurt to the Irish cause would be amply demonstrated in the days which followed the Great Northern Hotel meeting. On 9 June, de Valera, aided by Frank Walsh, presented his resolution before the Republican sub-committee while Cohalan's team presented another. In the event a somewhat bemused sub-committee considered both resolutions. While rejecting de Valera's resolution by a margin of eleven to one, it approved Cohalan's resolution by a majority of seven to six. Hearing of this, de Valera disavowed Cohalan's plank and in a later press statement said:

> This declaration [Cohalan's] leaves the Irish question exactly where it was so far as America is concerned … There is no evidence in the declaration of the Resolutions Committee of any intention to act upon the principles embodied in the declaration. It is a pledge of intended action that is needed, not a statement of principles.[24]

The sub-committee, seeing that the Irish did not seem to know what they wanted, now decided to withdraw Cohalan's resolution and omit any reference to the Irish question in the Republican policy platform.[25]

The rejection of his resolution should not have come as a surprise to de Valera. He had pointed out earlier to Mayor Grace that he would prefer to see his own resolution defeated rather than victory to the Irish-American one. His rejection of Cohalan's resolution was consistent with this stance. True to his bi-partisan approach to American politics, he now journeyed to the Democratic convention in San Francisco but again the chances of securing acceptance of his resolution were very slim. Cohalan, having already committed himself to supporting Republican candidate Hiram Johnson and believing Wilson's influence over the Democratic Party's resolution committee would inhibit any action in favour of Ireland, did not even attempt to follow him. This proved a correct assessment and Wilson's influence prevented any resolution in favour of Ireland despite the best efforts of Frank Walsh.[26]

De Valera's behaviour at Chicago in rejecting Cohalan's measure needs further scrutiny. Since his own resolution was rejected, it would have made more sense for de Valera to allow Cohalan's resolution to stand. One could argue that any resolution in favour of Ireland was better than none. During the earlier debate over the Mason resolution, de Valera had indeed demonstrated such a willingness to compromise. This was picked up by Cohalan in an unpublished *Gaelic American* editorial also contained in McGarrity's papers, where he stated: 'The first substitute to the Mason Bill was personally drafted by President de Valera and given by him to Congressman Mason. Unyielding demand for flat recognition was thereby waived. It was good judgment and sensible.'[27]

The logic of de Valera's action is also brought into question by his later disclosure that his mission to secure American recognition of an Irish republic stood little chance of success. Shortly after his return to Ireland, as cited in Ward's *Ireland and Anglo-American Relations*, de Valera made a startling claim to a meeting of the Dáil: 'If I were President of the United States, myself, I could not and would not recognise Ireland as a Republic.'[28] McCartan notes in *With de Valera in America* that given the security situation, with many members of the Dáil on the run from British forces, this meeting of the Dáil took place in the private house of Walter Cole and only comprised twenty-four members. Piaras Béaslaí, in his work *Michael Collins and the Making of a New Ireland* (vol. 2, 1926), also refers to a letter from de Valera to Michael Collins where de Valera admitted that American recognition would only have been forthcoming in the event of a war between the United States and Britain.[29]

Given these factors, de Valera's actions in Chicago are best understood as a continuation of his efforts to assert control over the Irish-American movement, which had been sanctioned by Dublin. This took precedence over the winning of even a mild resolution in Ireland's favour. The passage of Cohalan's resolution and the rejection of his own would have served to enhance Cohalan's status as leader of the Irish race in America and undermined de Valera's mission.

The adoption of Cohalan's resolution would technically have committed the Republican Party to support some form of self-determination. Whether an American government would actually have pressed this is another question. Hiram Johnson failed to win the nomination. This went to Warren Harding, who had never been known to display any real interest in the Irish question. Nevertheless, Harding might have been forced to become more active on the Irish question if Cohalan's policy plank had been in place. Bishop Michael Gallagher, who became president of the FOIF in July 1920, certainly thought so and, in a later 'statement', claimed that the adoption of Cohalan's plank might have 'stayed the murderous hand of England' and its rejection 'was the signal for the opening of the saturnalia of arson, murder, lust and loot' in Ireland.[30]

There is some evidence for this, though it is inconclusive. Certainly, the infighting between the two Irish delegations in Chicago and the failure at San Francisco were watched with delight by the British ambassador, who reported the events in detail to London.[31] Shortly after, the British government ordered its troops in Ireland to behave 'as if on a battlefield'.[32] There were, no doubt, other factors which influenced such a policy but the failure to win even a mild resolution in Ireland's favour must surely have strengthened the hands of those in London who sought a purely military solution to the Irish conflict.

Following the debacle at Chicago, de Valera's plans to assert control over the Irish movement in the United States became even more overt. In August 1920, he made a direct appeal to the FOIF's new president, Bishop Michael Gallagher, to implement constitutional reforms. These proposals entailed the abolition of the Cohalan-dominated National

Executive and having FOIF monthly meetings in Detroit rather than New York, the centre of Cohalan's power base. In a letter to Gallagher, de Valera stressed his own view that the interests of Ireland needed to take precedence over all other objectives: 'As regards the FOIF, I have indeed thought that Ireland came first amongst the objectives of that organisation … It was on that assumption that I relied on it more than on any other organisation for the support of my mission here.'[33]

These latest moves by de Valera merely served to anger Cohalan and Devoy. Cohalan, in a letter to Devoy, seemed aware of this agenda, and referring to the 'visitor from Ireland', a term he used for de Valera, suggested that: 'They want America just as Redmond did to supply money.' Cohalan implied by this that Irish nationalists in Ireland wanted to control the Irish-American movement in the same way Redmond controlled the UILA, with all important decision-making resting in Dublin.[34]

Both Cohalan and Devoy were thus aware of de Valera's intentions to subjugate the Irish-American movement to Irish control. In a much-cited letter to Cohalan, Devoy claimed: 'D.V. [de Valera] is out to smash us, and he is nibbling away at the ramparts all the time … He is the most malignant man in all Irish History.' Devoy also argued that de Valera wanted to show 'that nobody in America amounts to anything and that he is the kingpin of the movement'.[35] Both Devoy and Cohalan attributed this to de Valera's ego. Indeed, Cohalan later explained de Valera's opposition to the Anglo-Irish Treaty in the same way, referring to de Valera as 'a jealous and disappointed egotist'.[36] However, while Devoy accurately assessed de Valera's intentions, he did not fully understand his motivations and his view underestimated the extent to which de Valera represented Irish policy already voiced by McCartan, Boland and the IRB in Dublin.

After further failed attempts at reconciliation, de Valera persisted with his campaign to assert control over the Irish movement in the United States and saw Cohalan alone as standing in the way of this task. In this mission, de Valera obtained the full support of the Irish Progressive League. As prominent IPL activist Helen Golden pointed out in a letter to her colleague Margaret Hickey: 'I am convinced that whatever the cost the most important thing is to give Dan [Cohalan] the knock-out blow. He must go and whatever the IPL can do to hasten his going I feel it is our duty to do.'[37]

At a stormy FOIF meeting on 17 September, de Valera sought to push through the earlier reforms he had suggested to Bishop Gallagher. As already noted, such reforms, if passed, would have undermined Cohalan's power over the FOIF. Given the tensions that now existed between both sides, these efforts were bound to fail. After what Rossa Downing described as 'tumultuous scenes', de Valera and his supporters walked out of the meeting. The following day, he declared his intention to form a new organisation which would be under the control of 'Ireland's elected government'. The new organisation became known as the American Association for the Recognition of the Irish Republic (AARIR).[38]

This act signalled the final break between Sinn Féin representatives in the United States and Cohalan's FOIF. This very public break with the FOIF also impacted on the IRB's relationship with the Clan. As noted in the introductory chapter, Boland, believing that even the seven-man Clan executive had become a tool of Judge Cohalan, publicly announced in October 1920 the IRB's severance of relations with the Clan: 'We have been reluctantly compelled to sever our connections between Clan na Gael and the parent body in Ireland until such time as the will of the members of the executive becomes operative and not the will of Justice Cohalan.'[39]

This action was a bitter blow to Cohalan, who had devoted so much of his life to the Irish nationalist cause. Membership in the FOIF fell dramatically from over 100,000 in November 1920 to just 20,000 by the end of the following year.[40] The Irish Progressive League, always a thorn in Cohalan's side, merged with the AARIR and its leader Peter Golden became the national secretary of the new organisation.[41] Meanwhile, membership of the AARIR expanded to a reputed 800,000, though this figure has been disputed.[42]

Cohalan's reputation as leader of the Irish race in the United States suffered considerable damage as a result of the split. Many rank-and-file members transferred their allegiance to the AARIR. However, the leadership remained solidly behind Cohalan. According to the records of the national secretary, of the original seventeen members of the executive council which made up the executive committee in 1916, only one, Joseph McGarrity, seceded in 1920. Meanwhile, of the 129 members of the National Council in 1930, 85 had held office since before the split.[43] Similarly, five of the seven members of the Clan executive remained loyal to Devoy, though this did not prevent Joe McGarrity from forming a new Clan known as Clan na Gael 'reorganised'.

Following the split, a widespread perception of Cohalan's disloyalty gained ground on both sides of the Atlantic. In a report read into the Dáil's official minutes, de Valera, shortly after his return to Ireland, accused both Cohalan and Devoy of not providing 'their whole-hearted support for the President' and attempting to 'force the President into a position of accepting their dictation in all matters of policy connected with his mission'.[44] Given Devoy's heroic status within the Irish nationalist movement, there was a reluctance to blame him for this perceived obstructionism. Instead, McGarrity's belief that Cohalan manipulated the aged and almost deaf Devoy gained ground. As we have seen, McGarrity had first expressed these views during the controversy over the disposal of the Victory Fund but de Valera now shared this perspective.[45]

De Valera's earlier exchange with Cohalan over the content of the *Gaelic American* following his Cuban interview reflected this belief in Cohalan's dominance over Devoy. This perception was misplaced. Devoy, though aged and infirm, was very much his own man. In an account of the dispute in the *Gaelic American* in July 1920, Devoy wrote that: 'I am responsible for my own personal action and was doing some things many years before Judge Cohalan was born and before he could wear trousers, but now the pet theory of the disruptionists is that I am a poor old fogey dominated by Judge Cohalan.'[46]

Despite such protestations from Devoy, the tensions that arose within the Irish-American movement in the United States impacted on Cohalan's reputation in Ireland. In the summer of 1920, in the midst of atrocities committed by British forces in the War of Independence, Bishop Michael Fogarty of Killaloe, in a letter to a fellow churchman in the United States, Monsignor James W. Power in New York, stated:

> One of Ireland's greatest afflictions at the moment is the behaviour of the Cohalan group in America. It is all dished up here in the daily papers to break the poor people's hearts. What a time they have chosen, these Friends of Irish Freedom, to round on us. We are being dragooned and shot like wild animals.[47]

Reports of Cohalan's supposed disloyalty to the Sinn Féin president also seems to have reached the tiny village of Glandore in west Cork. At this time, given his devotion to the Irish cause in the United States and the ongoing War of Independence in Ireland, Cohalan chose not to visit his Irish summer home. His mother-in-law, Mrs O'Leary, lived in the spacious house in their absence. Cohalan's family papers in the AIHS contain a hand-written copy of a typed 'threatening letter' dated 31 July 1920 and hand-delivered to the house apparently from the local IRB:

> Mrs. O'Leary
> You are hereby warned to remove yourself and any valuables you may possess from Glandore House. The Treasonable conspiracy against President de Valera engineered by your son-in-law D.F. Cohalan has forfeited his right to possess any property in Ireland. His house will be burned and his property confiscated.
> By Order
> IRB[48]

There is no evidence to suggest that the Sinn Féin leadership either in the United States or Dublin sanctioned this action. Furthermore, according to local historian Fachtna Hickey from the Rosscarbery and District History Society, the O'Leary family were well respected in the area. The local IRA may also have distinguished between Cohalan, who was disloyal to the Sinn Féin president in the United States, and those who were suspected of siding with Crown forces in Ireland. According to Fachtna Hickey, the houses of suspected Crown sympathisers were burned down in the nearby town of Union Hall, but Cohalan's house remained untouched.[49] Nevertheless, an anxious Mrs O'Leary forwarded a copy of the letter to her son-in-law in the United States and the letter must have caused some anxiety in the Cohalan family.

In the aftermath of the split within Sinn Féin, the FOIF published pamphlets justifying their stance during the recent dispute with de Valera. This included a fascinating pamphlet by FOIF president Bishop Michael Gallagher published in April 1921 and entitled *Statement Dealing with Matters which Arose out of the Visit to the United States of the Hon. Éamon de Valera.* This statement took Cohalan's side and accused de Valera of being an Irish 'colonist' in the United States. Gallagher described Cohalan and other members of the FOIF as 'American citizens who never intend to live in Ireland, who neither owe nor pay allegiance to the Irish Parliament or President thereof, but who, out of love for their race and loyalty to

American principles of liberty, work for the recognition of the Irish Republic ...'[50]

Gallagher tended to see the dispute in an ideological context and his statement supports this perspective. Yet most Irish-American supporters tended to see the dispute in personality terms. This was especially true of the old-style Tammany leaders. As Dr W.P. Slattery pointed out to Frank Walsh a month after the split: 'As for the choice between Mr Harry Boland and Judge Cohalan, give me Cohalan. The so-called Irish leaders that I have personally met and who are shooting off the hot air during this entire campaign, to my mind could not run a successful ward caucus.'[51]

In his work *With de Valera in America*, McCartan, with more than a hint of regret, described the dispute as one between two warring factions. Regarding the consequences of the Chicago debacle, he writes: 'We formed into camps of de Valeraites and Cohalanites. Each denouncing the other for the ruin of our hopes – To the scandal of America and our own degradation and until the frenzy lasted we forgot Ireland.'[52]

Certainly, there is no doubt that personality differences played their part in making the dispute between Cohalan and de Valera more bitter than it might have been. McCartan, generally supportive of de Valera and critical of Cohalan, admits that the Irish leader had leadership flaws, especially in his tendency to dictate to rather than influence Irish-American leaders. In a long letter to Joe McGarrity in July 1919 advising him not to invite de Valera to a particular meeting aimed at putting an end to the feuding, McCartan writes:

> My experience of him [de Valera] and Harry [Boland] is that they come to a conference not knowing what they want. Have an unconscious contempt or seem to have such for opinions of others. The Chief [de Valera] presides and does all the talking. Has a habit of getting on to side issues and shutting off people who wish to speak and thus makes a bad impression if not sometimes enemies. Tends to force his own opinions without hearing from the other fellows and thus thinks he has co-operation when he only gets silent acquiescence.[53]

Diarmuid Lynch, who remained a loyal national secretary of the FOIF until his return to Ireland in 1932, also points to flaws in Cohalan's leadership style. In his published work *The IRB and the 1916 Insurrection*,

Lynch points out that Cohalan was a 'masterful man of judicial habit and eloquent public speaker and forceful writer' but in diplomatic language hints at how his strong and dynamic personality could sometimes have a negative impact.

> If by 1919 he had acquired something of the mentality that he had a mission to advise everybody connected with the movement, it was one of the factors which created antagonism between him and Dr McCartan and later more disastrously, between him and de Valera.[54]

By 1919 Cohalan knew the American political system intimately and had experience of 'advising' not only Boss Charlie Murphy and the Clan but leading political figures such as Senator Borah. Moreover, as a 'masterful man', he was used to seeing his advice acted upon. In de Valera, he encountered a politician unwilling to accept advice so he tended to blame de Valera's intransigence on his personality rather than on an Irish nationalist ideology that wanted to concentrate all important decision-making in Dublin.

The minutes of the Chicago meeting, reinforced by correspondence between Cohalan and Devoy, indicate Cohalan's belief that if de Valera left the United States all would be well. This too failed to recognise that de Valera had not only the backing of other Sinn Féin representatives in the United States but also the Sinn Féin leadership in Ireland such as Michael Collins.

Not surprisingly, both Cohalan and Devoy felt bitter at the course of events, which undermined the power of the Irish-American movement and damaged their reputation in Ireland. As the *Gaelic American* pointed out: 'No better work for Ireland was ever done in living memory and yet those who did it are treated as the enemies of Ireland.'[55] But this isolation would not last long. The dispute within Irish-America would dwarf an even more bitter struggle within Irish nationalism over whether to accept or reject the Anglo-Irish Treaty aimed at bringing the Irish War of Independence to an end. Cohalan would have to choose sides in this dispute and his relationship with Ireland and Irish nationalism would now enter a new and equally controversial phase.

9

Supporting the Treaty and the Irish Free State, 1922–3

IN THE AFTERMATH OF THE bitter dispute which rocked Irish-America in 1920, one might have expected Cohalan to turn his back on Irish nationalism. This was not the case. As always, he followed the ongoing dramatic developments in Ireland with intense interest. This included the opening of negotiations between the Irish Dáil and the British government in the summer of 1921 and the heated debate within Irish nationalism over whether to accept the proposed Anglo-Irish Treaty which followed these negotiations. Cohalan's decision to support the treaty was certainly influenced but not preordained by de Valera's opposition to the measure. Cohalan would also base his decision on the same pragmatism that had characterised his policy towards winning American diplomatic recognition for Irish self-determination and on what he considered best for Ireland and for the United States. In this regard, Cohalan reflected the pro-treaty views of many prominent Irish-Americans eager to give the new Irish state a chance to rebuild its economy and work towards improving on the level of independence already achieved. In turn, the new Irish government saw Cohalan as a useful ally in its quest to gain influence in the United States. Cohalan would prove to be a supportive though not uncritical ally of the Irish Free State.

As the Anglo-Irish negotiations continued apace, the FOIF continued its propaganda campaign against British policy in Ireland and assisted the work of other Irish-American groups such as that of the American Committee for Relief in Ireland. This helped focus American attention on the Irish question during the ongoing conflict.[1] For the British, mounting domestic and international pressure and the inability to win outright victory convinced Prime Minister Lloyd George of the necessity of finding a political solution to the conflict. On 11 July 1921, the British government opened talks with the Sinn Féin leadership with a view to reaching a political settlement. A truce between both sides followed and in September Lloyd George invited Sinn Féin to send a delegation to London so that a lasting treaty settlement ending the conflict could be agreed upon. Controversially, de Valera did not take part in the final negotiations and Michael Collins, who had orchestrated the military campaign against British forces during de Valera's long mission to America, headed the treaty delegation to London.[2] However, as the negotiations progressed, it soon became clear that the British government would not concede the Irish republic which Sinn Féin and the IRA had fought for.

In the summer of 1921, Michael Collins surprisingly opened up communications with Devoy and Cohalan. Shortly before proceeding to London for the final negotiations, Collins met with James McHugh, 'an emissary' from Devoy and Cohalan.[3] According to McHugh's report of what took place, Collins spoke warmly of Cohalan but criticised Devoy for his 'intemperate remarks' about de Valera during the latter's American mission. Collins also defended de Valera's policy during the current treaty negotiations stating that he was 'playing the game just as he wants'.[4] Collins was at this time president of the IRB, an organisation that had officially 'written out' both Devoy and Cohalan. His feelers to Cohalan could, therefore, be seen as bypassing Boland and de Valera but it also seems likely that even at this stage Collins realised that some future compromise would have to be reached which would alienate some of his republican colleagues. In such a situation, Collins would need as many allies as possible. Indeed, as we shall see, Collins would come to value both Devoy and Cohalan's support in the coming months as the treaty negotiations caused tensions within Sinn Féin ranks and Boland and de Valera became his bitter enemies.

Following Lloyd George's threat of immediate and terrible war if the talks failed, the Irish delegation signed 'the articles of agreement for a Treaty' on 6 December 1921, though it still needed to be ratified by the Irish Dáil. There was much in the treaty which went beyond the proposed home rule settlement that had so divided Irish nationalism in the pre-war period.[5] Twenty-six counties of Ireland would gain dominion status similar to that already granted to Canada and Australia. Ireland would also have its own army. However, Britain's continued use of four Southern Irish ports constrained the Irish state's ability to exercise an independent foreign policy. The treaty settlement also envisaged the partition of Ireland. The six north-eastern counties, with a majority unionist population, had already been given a home rule parliament under the Government of Ireland Act of 1920 and would remain within the United Kingdom. Crucially, Southern Ireland would also remain within the British Empire and Irish members of parliament would still have to swear an oath of allegiance to the British monarch. As historians have noted, the position of the Crown rather than the proposed partition of the country dominated the subsequent treaty debates.[6]

Given Cohalan's long association with the Clan na Gael, a movement dedicated to the establishment of an Irish republic, one might have expected his vehement opposition to the agreement. In a noncommittal interview with the *New York Times* on 7 December 1921, the day after the Irish delegation had signed the treaty articles in London, he indicated 'his desire to wait until all the details have been made known'.[7] The following day, the FOIF released a press release which was very much in line with anti-treaty sentiment in Ireland: 'With Irish coastal fortifications under British control … with an Ireland swearing allegiance to a foreign king, the use of the term "Irish Free State" is an insult to the dead who died fighting for an independent Irish Republic.' Though written by Diarmuid Lynch, such a statement would never have been released without Cohalan's approval.[8] Again, at a National Convention of the FOIF on 10–11 December and reported in the *Gaelic American*, the meeting passed a resolution claiming that 'a free and independent Republic, separated from the Empire is the only solution to the Irish national problem'.[9] This evidence would suggest that the FOIF leadership initially opposed the treaty.

In the Irish Dáil, much bitterness and rancour characterised the treaty debates. Tensions emerged between those who advocated accepting the agreement as a compromise settlement and those who wanted to continue the struggle until the Irish republic had been achieved. The more pragmatic wing, headed by Michael Collins and Arthur Griffith, argued that the treaty would, as Collins famously put it, give Ireland the freedom to achieve freedom. Meanwhile, a more 'purist' wing, led by de

Valera and Boland, who had been so firmly aligned against Cohalan and Devoy during their mission to the United States, came out against the measure.[10] Again, much of the opposition to the treaty centred around the symbol of the oath of allegiance rather than the partition question. For its opponents, the existence of such symbols in the treaty seemed a betrayal of the republic proclaimed in 1916. Following a heated debate on the measure, the Dáil voted sixty-four votes in favour to fifty-seven against on 7 January 1922. The pro-treaty majority then went on to form the first so-called 'Provisional Government' of the Irish Free State.[11]

In the weeks which followed, Cohalan appeared to moderate his stance. On 22 January 1922, the FOIF National Council, over which Cohalan presided, decided not to oppose the treaty, declaring in the minutes of the meeting that:

> We as American citizens of Irish blood will do nothing to interfere with or obstruct any plans the result of which is to take the English army out of Ireland and put the powers of Government – limited and constricted though they be – into the hands of Irishmen.[12]

The reasons for Cohalan's change of heart on the treaty need explanation. It would be easy to explain his newfound support simply on the basis of his hatred for de Valera, that once de Valera came out in opposition to the treaty, Cohalan and his ally Devoy would inevitable support it. Historians have put forward this view in relation to Devoy, who tended to mirror Cohalan's attitude on most issues. Sean Cronin has argued that Devoy 'did not think much of the Treaty, which he probably accepted only because de Valera had rejected it'.[13]

There is contemporary source evidence available which suggests that de Valera's opposition to the treaty played a role in Cohalan's support for it, though as we shall see, there were other factors at play. In May 1922, the Provisional Government sent Denis McCullough to the United States as a special commissioner to try to unify Irish-American nationalist opinion in the wake of the bitter disputes. McCullough compiled a lengthy report for George Gavan Duffy, his superior in Dublin who was then serving as minister for external affairs.[14] McCullough believed that hostility to de Valera was the main reason for Cohalan's support of the treaty.

> I arranged an interview with Judge Cohalan and some of his friends and discussed matters fully and as frankly as possible. I found them inveterately opposed to de Valera and to all who took his side here; their bitterness was astonishing and I am afraid is implacable. I tried to argue away the disputes that occurred and to reason with them into a better frame of mind, but I found it literally impossible and I am afraid that there is not much hope of amity.[15]

Although pro-treaty, McCullough tried to present an even-handed account of the Irish-American situation for his superiors in Dublin. As he pointed out:

> I am going into this matter of Judge Cohalan at great length because he has been such a big figure in Irish matters here and may be again, that I think it necessary to furnish you with these details as a background to enable you to better understand the various currents that are flowing and the changes that are taking place in Irish circles here.[16]

McCullough had good reason to appear objective since, in his report, he stated his belief that opponents of the treaty in Dublin such as Austin Stack were highly suspicious of his mission and thought that he was in New York 'to purchase or secure the support of Judge Cohalan and his party for the Provisional Government'. No doubt anxious to scotch such rumours, McCullough's report contains some severe criticism of Cohalan's relationship with de Valera:

> When he [Cohalan] found that he could not work with de Valera who went over his head direct to the Irish people here, he fought him bitterly and in the fight all his cards were exposed. In the result, de Valera broke his power utterly and neither he nor his friends can forgive de Valera, nor those who helped him, particularly men like Joe McGarrity ...[17]

McCullough also reported that Cohalan believed that the treaty would cause a split within the AARIR organisation, which de Valera had helped set up before his return to Ireland, and that such divisions would 'reduce them to impotence, when he [Cohalan] will be left in possession of the field as the only strong Irish leader here, with a party. I believe he is correct in that forecast too.' Interestingly, in an otherwise astute interpretation of Irish-American opinion, McCullough's analysis of Cohalan's intentions was somewhat simplistic. He argued that Cohalan's support for the pro-treaty side was purely motivated by a hatred of de Valera and he suggested that Dublin needed to be cautious about accepting such support:

> … it is founded more on hate of de Valera than on love for those who are opposed to him – if de Valera was on the other side they would be the loudest against it – and because there is too large an element of selfishness in their purpose I would advise no direct affiliations with them from home for the present anyhow.[18]

McCullough's lengthy report correctly recorded Cohalan's hostility to de Valera and McGarrity. It also noted that his 'outlook is more American than Irish'. However, it neglected other factors which played a role in Cohalan's decision to support the treaty. In the first instance, Cohalan's support reflected his democratic instincts honed by his many years in American politics. He would undoubtedly have preferred the republic which had long been central to Clan objectives. At the same time, he recognised that the treaty had been approved in a democratic way in a Dáil vote. Furthermore, in elections in June 1922, those political parties who supported the treaty won an overall majority of seats, while business organisations, the labour movement and the Catholic Church also endorsed the settlement.[19]

Cohalan's American political pragmatism also influenced his approach to the settlement. He had already displayed such pragmatism in his handling of Irish affairs. At the Philadelphia Irish Race Convention in February 1919, he had championed 'self-determination' for Ireland over the protests of Sinn Féin, believing that it tied in with the American public's perception of Wilson's post-war plans. Again, at the Republican convention in Chicago in June 1920, Cohalan had advocated a moderate plank in favour of Irish self-determination knowing that de Valera's call for recognition of an Irish republic would be rejected.[20]

Cohalan's acceptance of the treaty mirrored that of most Irish-Americans and indeed American opinion itself. In a debate on the treaty in the Irish Dáil, even Harry Boland admitted that 'the great public opinion of America is on the side of this treaty' and he recognised that the American press had adopted a 'unanimous attitude in favor of it'.[21] Edward L. Doheny, the leader of the AARIR, and many rank and file members also came out in support of the measure. Doheny was then forced to resign and the AARIR went into rapid decline as many members left the organisation. By 1925 the AARIR had declined to 13,870 members nationwide with only 3,336 in New York.[22] As McCullough had correctly anticipated, the weakening of the AARIR enhanced Cohalan's standing once again in Irish-America, though he would never regain the degree of power he once wielded in 1919–20.[23]

While Cohalan had several reasons for supporting the treaty besides his hatred of de Valera, he had reservations about the measure. In line with his traditional anti-imperialist views, he remained wary of the constitutional ties which still bound the new Irish state to Britain. In instructions to Boston FOIF leader Matthew Cummings in March 1922, Cohalan expressed the view that while he preferred the leadership of Collins to that of de Valera, this did not mean that he would endorse everything that the Free State would do:

> I hope you will make it very clear in anything you say that while the Free State is regarded as a step forward on the road to independence, it is only that, and not in any sense an end in itself, or an achievement about which there will be any enthusiasm, if the result is going to be only to tie Ireland more closely to England. I think you should make it clear on every occasion that while as between Collins and de Valera, the real lovers of Irish liberty favor Collins, such favor is not an endorsement of any settlement with England ...[24]

Despite McCullough's warnings, Michael Collins, now chairman of the Provisional Government, welcomed both Cohalan's and Devoy's tacit support.[25] As early as February 1922, Collins in a letter to Devoy apologised for Boland's action in severing Sinn Féin ties with the Clan and the FOIF. Collins argued, somewhat lamely, that the Irish plan all along had been to 'set up a world-wide federation, each separate part working through the government, and in accordance with the laws of the country where it had its being'. In a barbed attack on de Valera and Boland, he added: 'Unfortunately, some of those we sent to America did not understand the vital principle of that idea.' In a further letter in early March, Collins assured Devoy, and by implication Cohalan, that 'your good opinion is of concern to us here'.[26]

Cohalan must have realised that Irish tactical considerations motivated the conciliatory approach of the Provisional Government, though he still displayed a warm regard for Collins' achievements. Following the outbreak of the Civil War in June 1922 between pro- and anti-treaty factions and Collins' death in a roadside ambush in August, Cohalan wrote a heartfelt obituary of the dead leader for *Pearson's Magazine* and indirectly blamed de Valera for his death:

> Shot down in his early thirties at the very moment of victory he has left behind him an inheritance that will steady and stabilize his people and make them with iron resolution put out the last fitful flashes of that flame of insensate fury with which the malignant vanity of de Valera has scourged a long-suffering people.[27]

Rather than seeing the Civil War as a struggle between pragmatists and republican idealists, Cohalan, like Devoy, saw de Valera as responsible for the conflict. While de Valera's opposition to the settlement stiffened anti-treaty opposition and prolonged the conflict, it is important to note that de Valera was one of many so-called 'anti-treatyites' who displayed an almost religious attachment to the Irish republic. As another prominent opponent of the treaty, Mary McSwiney, pointed out in a letter to Richard Mulcahy, minister for defence in the Provisional Government: 'If de Valera were on your side we would still fight on. We do not stand for men but for principles and we could no more accept your Treaty than we could turn our backs on the Catholic faith.'[28] Furthermore, after hostilities began, the military men on the anti-treaty side such as Liam Lynch and Rory O'Connor excluded de Valera from any decision-making, though they did accept his role in bringing about the end of hostilities in the summer of 1923.[29]

The Irish Civil War caused many Irish-Americans to turn away in disgust from the bitter conflict between erstwhile comrades in arms. Other Irish nationalists in the United States such as Dr William Maloney took a neutral stance and engaged in futile efforts to bring both sides together. This was not the case with Cohalan, who felt that it was now imperative that Irish-Americans should rally in support of the new Irish state in her hour of need.[30] Indeed, the assassination of Michael Collins solidified his determination to aid the new government in Ireland. In a letter to Bishop William Turner, Cohalan declared:

> The people of Ireland have decidedly expressed their approval of the plan [treaty] as a whole. This fact seems to make it imperative for us who have been, and who intend to continue to be interested in Irish matters, to revitalise and reconsolidate our friends in America in order to aid the people of Ireland in their advance to the goal of a real Irish Republic.[31]

By the spring of 1923, the pro-treaty side had achieved victory in the Civil War.[32] Though casualties were relatively small, the conflict left a bitter legacy with large sections of the population only reluctantly accepting the authority of the state. Moreover, many anti-treaty rebels made their way to the United States after their defeat, while those who remained behind looked to the Irish-American diaspora for funds to continue their political opposition. The new government was therefore anxious to demonstrate to the world and to the people at home that the Free State was an independent sovereign nation. Obtaining recognition from the United States could help achieve this goal. As Carroll points out, the Free State government 'turned first to the United States to have its envoy – Professor Timothy A. Smiddy – officially recognised as a minister plenipotentiary on 7 October 1924'.[33]

William T. Cosgrave, now the 'executive president' of the Irish Free State, recognised how Cohalan's goodwill could be harnessed as part of a wider goal of maintaining the support of the Irish diaspora in the United States. Firstly, Cohalan could help Irish diplomatic efforts by speaking in support of the Free State both to Irish and Irish-American opinion. Secondly, his political and corporate connections could be helpful in furthering Irish economic and political interests.[34] Indeed, the Irish government's relationship with Cohalan mirrors the relationship of later Irish governments with influential Irish-Americans in the US.

The Free State's determination to build better relations with the United States and Irish-America gave Cohalan's visit to Ireland on 12 August 1923, his first since 1914, added significance. Cosgrave, anxious to impress, provided Cohalan with a warm reception upon his arrival in Dún Laoghaire (formerly known as Kingstown). Desmond FitzGerald, minister for external affairs, and Diarmuid Lynch, who had preceded him to Ireland on an earlier sailing, formed part of the official welcoming party. After Cohalan, his wife Madge and three of their younger children had checked into the nearby prestigious Royal Marine Hotel, Cosgrave, General Richard Mulcahy, and the attorney-general Hugh Kennedy all paid courtesy visits.[35]

In the following days, Cohalan demonstrated that his support for the Free State government went far beyond writing newspaper columns and giving speeches in the United States. Cosgrave, who now headed the pro-treaty Cumann na nGaedheal party, was then in the midst of fighting yet another parliamentary election. The opposition anti-treaty party, who retained the name Sinn Féin, contested the election even though they still refused to take their seats in the Dáil. In his usual dynamic fashion, and despite still holding the office of a New York State Supreme Court Justice, Cohalan showed no hesitation in assisting the pro-treaty election campaign. A few days after his arrival, he appeared on the same election platform in Dublin's College Green as William Cosgrave, Richard Mulcahy and Kevin O'Higgins, the minister for home affairs. Tensions, in the aftermath of the Civil War, still ran high. The *Philadelphia Inquirer*, in a dramatic headline entitled 'Irish Election Row: Visiting New York jurist views free-for-all battle in Dublin', described in vivid prose how after Sinn Féin heckling, fistfights broke out at the College Green rally between rival groups. However, Cohalan, a veteran of many Tammany brawls in his younger days, emerged unscathed.[36]

The *Irish Times* also noted Cohalan's active participation in Ireland's 1923 election campaign. The newspaper records that Cohalan accompanied Cosgrave on a tour of the country and made several speeches on behalf of pro-treaty Cumann na nGaedheal candidates. Interestingly, Cohalan's involvement in this campaign coincided with the first use of aeroplanes in an Irish political setting. According to the *Irish Times* correspondent in Kilkenny, small aircraft 'conveyed the speakers from one centre to another'. Such a form of travel had its risks, as the reporter pointed out:

> Three aeroplanes left Ennis in the afternoon, the President travelling in one, Judge Cohalan in another, and Commandant O'Reilly in the third.

> The machines landed at Oakpark Carlow, shortly after 4 o'clock. The one in which Commandant O'Reilly travelled was slightly damaged on landing, but the occupants escaped with a few scratches.[37]

A reporter from the *New York Tribune* was on hand to photograph a shaken Cohalan and Cosgrave, both dressed in flying suits, after their dramatic landing in Carlow. The photograph appeared in the *Tribune*'s edition of 30 August 1923, carrying the caption: 'Proving that There's Nothing Slow about the Irish'. The *Tribune* saw the use of aeroplanes in election campaigns as a sign of Irish modernity. In fact, using aircraft on such a scale was not repeated in subsequent Irish elections. Their use in the summer of 1923 may well have been due to ongoing Civil War tensions which rendered travel by road dangerous, as Michael Collins had earlier found to his cost.

There is also evidence of government fears for Cohalan's safety, which may well have motivated this unusual mode of electioneering. This is contained in the diplomatic correspondence of Irish Free State 'envoy' to the United States Professor Timothy Smiddy. Professor Smiddy would not be officially appointed 'minister plenipotentiary and envoy extraordinary' to the United States until the following year.[38] In January 1923, Smiddy wrote to the then minister for external affairs Desmond FitzGerald expressing fears about collusion between New York-based Irish communists who he described as 'Reds' and 'Irregulars'. This latter term was then in common usage in Ireland to describe anti-treaty forces as distinct from the regular Free State army. Smiddy writes of using secret service agents to investigate a man called Cullen, described as 'one of the most violent of the Irish "Reds" in New York'. He also describes Cullen as a 'gunman ready to act' who had already been in touch with anti-treaty supporters 'in connection with the intention to shoot if opportunity presented itself Geddes [Sir Auckland Geddes, British ambassador], Judge Cohalan and your representative [Smiddy himself] after the execution of Mellows.[39] On the same occasion it was mentioned that this attempt would be carried out 'if de Valera was executed'.[40]

Such threats did not prevent Cohalan from speaking out in favour of the Irish Free State. In an interview with a reporter from the *New York Herald*, Cohalan, referencing the recent Civil War, claimed: 'It is the American opinion that the government which restores law and order should be returned to power by an overwhelming majority. America regards the issue as one between law and order and anarchy and chaos.'[41] As one might expect, the opposition Sinn Féin party resented Cohalan's participation in the election campaign and even produced a handbill critical of Cohalan entitled *Every Enemy of Ireland Is on the Side of the Free State, Enter Judge Cohalan*. This reminded its supporters that: 'In 1920 when President de Valera … was fighting for the cause of Ireland in America, it was Cohalan who bitterly opposed him.'[42]

In the election itself, Cosgrave's Cumann na nGaedheal party secured sixty-three seats while Sinn Féin obtained a respectable forty-four seats. Given that Sinn Féin continued to abstain from participation in the Dáil, Cosgrave's party could comfortably form a government and continue with the task of consolidating the new Irish state both economically and politically.[43] As we have seen, this had an international dimension.

Cosgrave appreciated Cohalan's efforts in his successful election campaign and in promoting the Irish Free State in the United States. A warm personal relationship developed between both men which extended beyond the political realm. In a 1923 Christmas greeting, Cosgrave, referring to Cohalan's support in both Ireland and the United States, thanked him 'for all you did for us last year'. The president also noted his appreciation for Cohalan's letter of condolence on the death of his brother Philip some months previously.[44] Coincidentally, the Cohalan family also suffered a tragic loss the following summer. Cohalan's little daughter Joan died from influenza in 1924. The only child of his second wife Madge, she had been born in 1917. In a letter to Cosgrave in July 1924, Cohalan remarked that: 'We have had much sickness in the family since her death and have come to realize the truth of the old saying that misfortunes never come singly.'[45]

The Irish government also sought Cohalan's help in securing a better deal for Ireland in the forthcoming 1924 Immigration Restriction Act, though it is important to note that Cohalan was one of many involved in these efforts and by no means the most significant player. Nativist groups in the United States, worried about immigration from Eastern and Southern Europe, had campaigned for more restriction. The measure introduced reflected these racial fears and limited annual immigration for any group to 2 per cent of that group's population according to the census of 1890. This, of course, discriminated against southern and eastern

Europeans but benefited the Irish and other northern European groups who had formed the bulk of immigration to the United States prior to 1890. Nevertheless, the Irish government wanted a separate quota for the Irish Free State, which would not only increase the Irish admission but would also symbolise Ireland's status as an independent state.

Professor Smiddy, as unofficial envoy to the United States at this time, knew that Cohalan was on friendly terms with two of the main sponsors of the act, Senator Hiram Johnson of California and Senator James A. Reed of Missouri. In a foretaste of similar Irish government contacts with influential Irish-Americans in later decades, Smiddy sought Cohalan's help in amending the Immigration Bill to suit Irish interests. In the following letter to Cohalan, Smiddy refers to a letter from Secretary of State Charles Evans Hughes to Hiram Johnson where Hughes had asked that an amendment be included to include a quota for the Irish Free State. According to Smiddy, the Hughes amendment 'just suits my requirements', as he indicated to Cohalan:

> My real object in writing to you is to solicit your influence with some of the influential members or members of the House and ask them to propose Hughes' amendment.
>
> Perhaps, you would also be good enough to have a word on the subject with Mr. Hiram Johnson who might help to ensure the necessary legislation which will warrant the Irish Free State having a separate quota.[46]

In the end the Immigration Act did contain a separate quota for the Irish Free State. It would be impossible to gauge whether Cohalan had any influence in this decision yet it is noteworthy that Smiddy thought fit to involve Cohalan and no doubt his 'word' with his old friend Hiram Johnson would not have hindered the Irish position. In other respects, Cohalan's efforts were less successful. Despite its diminished resources, the FOIF, in alliance with the AIHS, campaigned for a higher quota for Irish citizens to be allowed under the Immigration Act. In FOIF pamphlets and letters to members of Congress, Michael O'Brien, the historian of the AIHS, argued that on the basis of colonial records, the early colonial censuses had underestimated the number of Irish in the colonies. According to O'Brien, this entitled the Irish to a larger quota. Drawing on O'Brien's work, the FOIF published and circulated pamphlets to members of Congress, and other influential Americans.[47] Ultimately, this campaign had little impact and there was no adjustment to the size of the Irish quota.

Meanwhile, in the aftermath of the Irish Civil War, Cohalan continued supporting the Irish Free State in his public speeches. In April 1924, the *New York Times* reported on a Clan na Gael meeting at the Hotel Astor where Cohalan featured as the main speaker. In a speech to a large gathering which filled the main ballroom floor and gallery, Cohalan heaped praise on the achievements of the Free State government. He declared that the new state had 'performed a wonderful work in establishing a stable government. I do not endorse it as an end, but as a long step forward.' Knowing that his speech would be reported in the *New York Times*, Cohalan directed some of his comments to a wider American audience and stated that, while Ireland had not yet achieved the same degree of liberty as held by Americans, it was nevertheless 'the beginning of a condition of liberty such as the Irish people are entitled'.[48]

In another example of the high esteem in which Cohalan was held in the Irish Free State, John Heywood, the publisher of *The Voice of Ireland*, invited him to submit an article celebrating the connection between the newly independent Ireland and the United States. Cohalan entitled his article 'America's Advice to Ireland'. This choice of title was certainly appropriate for a man who had always excelled in the role of advisor. Predictably, Cohalan's article, in line with the other contributions to the volume, supported the Irish Free State but it also offers some insight into his thinking about Ireland's future relationship with the United States. Cohalan correctly recognised that America's focus on the 'Old World' would inevitably shift in the aftermath of the Great War and that this would have implications for Ireland: 'How far the Ireland of the future will continue to hold American interest as in the past must in large measure depend upon developments – economic, educational and social, as well as governmental – in Ireland during the next generation.'[49]

Secondly, Cohalan believed that a campaign of education in Ireland and the United States would promote greater bonds between both countries. As Cohalan put it:

> If Ireland is true to herself, America will be more than ever a friendly land … But in order to reap the full benefit of this disposition it is

> essential that the two countries, or active groups in each of them, shall inaugurate and carry through campaigns of education to make known to the other – not alone on sympathetic and racial lines, but also cultural, historic, commercial and economic – and above all, governmental – lines.[50]

Cohalan's correspondence with Cosgrave contained advice on a range of issues ranging from Irish relations with the US, Irish domestic affairs and Ireland's international standing. As we shall see in the next chapter, Cosgrave did not always accept such advice and, while Cohalan continued to support the Irish Free State, he increasingly found much to criticise.

10

Cohalan as Critic of the Irish Free State, 1924–30

COHALAN WOULD PROVE to be a supportive though not uncritical ally of the new Irish state. Always a man of action, he sought to promote links between Ireland and the United States. However, he often underestimated the difficulties involved in forging such links and the political and social constraints under which the new Irish state laboured.[1] He would also become increasingly disillusioned by what he perceived as the pro-British approach of the Irish government in a number of policy areas. At the same time, while often willing to fund democratic opposition voices within the Irish Free State, he never seriously contemplated supporting a de Valera-led alternative government.

In his letters to Cosgrave, Cohalan adopted an advisory tone. As we have seen in previous chapters, he had always excelled as a political advisor to a diverse range of individuals and organisations and may have hoped for a similar role with Cosgrave. In July 1924, he notified Cosgrave of his next visit to Ireland on the ship *Adriatic* in the following month: 'We shall probably go up to Glandore for a few days and I hope to have an opportunity of seeing you and going over several questions with you at some length.' In the same letter, Cohalan expressed a belief in the value of greater economic interdependence between the United States and Ireland: 'I have taken the liberty from time to time, as you asked me to, to give letters of introduction to you to distinguished Americans who were going to Ireland, and I hope you have had an opportunity to meet some of them as the effect of such meetings would be helpful in many ways to Ireland's interests in this country.'[2]

Cosgrave's letters to Cohalan suggest a willingness to take this advice seriously, especially in those policy areas related to furthering the trade interests of the Irish Free State in the United States. In this context, Cohalan corresponded with Lindsay Crawford, the Irish Free State's trade representative in New York. Crawford had been appointed in 1922 but previously had worked closely with Cohalan as leader of an organisation called the Protestant Friends of Irish Freedom, which was affiliated to the FOIF. While living in Canada in 1920, Crawford also led a 'Self-Determination for Ireland League' which again received financial support from the FOIF. Both men were on friendly terms and Crawford was a frequent visitor to the Cohalan household.[3]

Crawford's duties extended beyond the remit of trade and this correspondence indicates that Cohalan became privy to a wider range of issues impacting on the affairs of the Free State. In one such letter to Cohalan, Crawford complained about the British government's refusal to extend to the Free State consulate in Washington the right to issue passports. These still needed to be obtained at the British consulate. Crawford pointed out that: 'This is very humiliating and will, when made public, do the Govt. harm and aid D.V. [de Valera].'[4] Crawford must surely have known that Cohalan was powerless to alter this situation yet his willingness to confide in Cohalan on such sensitive matters is noteworthy. In the event, the appointment of Ireland's first minister plenipotentiary to Washington, Timothy A. Smiddy, in October 1924 helped to regularise this situation and Cosgrave too sought to reassure Cohalan that the 'passport question' would be put on a 'satisfactory footing' with the appointment of 'direct representation to Washington'.[5]

In a letter sent just prior to Cohalan's visit to Ireland in the summer of 1924, Crawford referred to the forthcoming report of the Boundary Commission. The Anglo-Irish Treaty provided for the setting up of this commission so as to delineate the border according to the wishes of the local inhabitants.[6] Given that these border areas contained a majority Catholic population, many nationalists believed that the findings of the commission would lead to such large transfers of territory to the Irish Free State that Northern Ireland would prove unviable as an economic and political entity. This may explain why the question of partition did not loom as large in the treaty negotiations as one might have expected.[7] However, by the summer of 1924 it was already clear that the commission would favour Northern Ireland rather than the Free State in its deliberations. Crawford feared that de Valera would exploit any negative outcome for nationalist Ireland in the United States and Ireland:

> Study well the Boundary Question, as this is reaching a grave crisis. Anything that would play into D.V.'s [de Valera's] hands at this time would be a grave blunder. The Govt. should re-assert the doctrine of the unity of Ireland in terms so clear that D.V. could take no advantage. You are going to Ireland at a most critical time, when C- [Cosgrave] will need some constructive advice. How to reconcile adherence to the Constitution with advances that are essential to the country should be carefully thought out on the way across.[8]

In early September 1924, in a five-page letter to Cohalan marked 'Strictly Confidential', Cosgrave sketched out his own fears about the outcome of the Boundary Commission's report. Cohalan was at this point staying in Glandore and Cosgrave began his letter with an apology, stating that he had originally intended to 'travel down' to west Cork but 'owing to a chill and more business decided to write to you instead'. Cosgrave's willingness to trust Cohalan's discretion at this point is apparent, since he points out: 'The harm which any quotations from this letter would do both in England and Ireland would be incalculable if published.'[9] Overall, Cosgrave expressed fears that the Irish nationalist voice on the commission would be marginalised in the decision-making process, given that the Northern Ireland prime minister James Craig had 'close associations and friendships in England and that political events follow to a considerable extent such associations'. Expressing fears for the 'legitimate national rights' of the nationalist minority in Northern Ireland, Cosgrave hoped that American opinion might force Britain to adhere to Article XII of the treaty, which 'was specially designed to secure that people were not placed under a Parliament against their will':

> We want propaganda in the U.S.A. of the type of British good faith under test; Signatories making statements which qualify or attempt to qualify their signed bond; Will England do its duty honestly, and so on.
>
> If this could be managed without associating your own name or that of Mr. Devoy it would be all the better. I do not mean that

> you should keep out but that the Press of America would show keen interest in the matter without direct interference by your people. I am sure that De V. or some of his following would commence operations (propaganda) if you were definitely to enter the lists and lead the way.[10]

Cohalan attempted to follow these instructions and corresponded with the editor of the *Boston Post* and other journals with a view to mounting the media campaign which Cosgrave had called for. He forwarded copies of his correspondence with the *Boston Post* to Cosgrave and indicated that he was 'very hopeful of having work along the same lines from many of the leading journals in other parts of the country'.[11] However, there is no evidence to suggest that this campaign had any impact on American opinion-formers. Since the end of the Civil War, Ireland had faded from the headlines and it would have been difficult in any case to generate a great deal of interest among American editors, let alone the American public, in such an obscure topic. Just as Cosgrave had feared, the report of the commission in November 1925 recommended little change to the existing boundary. Finally, in consultation with the British government and the administration in Northern Ireland, he decided to suppress the findings of the commission and allow the border line to remain unchanged.[12]

While Cosgrave willingly consulted Cohalan on matters related to Irish issues in the United States, he demonstrated a marked reluctance to accept Cohalan's recommendations in areas related to Irish domestic policy. This can be illustrated by Cosgrave's less than enthusiastic response to Cohalan's pleas for large capital investment in roads and infrastructure with a view to developing Ireland's tourist industry. Cosgrave recognised the value of 'tourist traffic' as a 'great source of revenue' but pointed to the economic and political conditions of the previous ten years which had hurt this industry.[13] Also, Cosgrave, who displayed a rigid adherence to economic orthodoxy, did not see how the costs involved in such expenditure on infrastructure could deliver an adequate return on investment. In a letter to Cohalan in February 1924, Cosgrave reflected this economic thinking:

> With reference to reconstruction, our economic fabric does not at present warrant any big development. We have not yet arrived at a

> normal economic basis. In other words – cost of works and output do not balance value received. Cost of works include organisation which is at the lowest ebb, and any scheme put into operation now would not get a fair chance of showing results.[14]

Cohalan also offered Cosgrave advice on domestic political issues and did not hold back from criticising what he saw as imperfections in the Irish electoral system. In a letter to Cosgrave, he referred to the 'absurd system of proportional representation … which would not be tolerated for a moment in our country'.[15] This system had been introduced so as to give adequate parliamentary representation to the Free State's Protestant minority. In fact, all smaller parties benefited, including the Sinn Féin opposition, who at this time refused to take their seats in the Dáil.

Cohalan's opposition to Irish membership of the League of Nations illustrates once again how his American loyalties coloured his views on Ireland's interests and brought him into conflict with the leaders of Irish nationalism. The *Gaelic American* set out these fears in an article entitled 'The Free State Makes Bad Blunder in Applying for League Membership'. The paper argued that Irish membership only strengthened the hand of 'Anglomaniacs' in the United States who were themselves plotting to bring the United States into the league.[16] Cosgrave seemed well aware of Cohalan's position and generally avoided getting into discussions about whether the US should or should not join. For Cosgrave, membership of the league offered proof that the Free State was a sovereign, independent and international legal entity.[17] In a letter to Cohalan, Cosgrave patiently explained how the league offered at least some protections for small nations in a predatory world where large, powerful nations dominated weaker ones:

> I do not want to go into the question of the advantage or disadvantage of membership, but I must say that one could but form one impression at last year's Assembly and that was the apprehension of the smaller nations and the opinion that while many imperfections might exist the League was really the only available machinery which the smaller nations had.[18]

Anxious to conciliate Cohalan, Cosgrave also attached to his letter a long report on the benefits of league membership for Ireland compiled by his then minister for education Eoin MacNeill. Predictably, there is no indication that this had any impact whatsoever on Cohalan's thinking and he remained deeply critical of Irish membership. Yet from Cosgrave's point of view membership of the league offered symbolic proof to its detractors that it was an independent nation.[19]

Cosgrave tolerated Cohalan's public criticisms of the Irish Free State on such issues in the interests of keeping his support on others. This again became evident during the so-called army mutiny in 1924 which for a time threatened the very existence of the Irish state. The origins of the mutiny are complex and lie outside the scope of this volume but a brief summary is necessary, since Cohalan became embroiled in the affair. The roots of the crisis lay in the inevitable army demobilisation at the end of the Civil War.[20] Some officers who had taken part in the Anglo-Irish war felt that the demobilisation process was unfair and that more recent arrivals, including former British soldiers, were being retained and promoted. They also resented the continued role of the IRB Army Council in the administration of the army. More fundamentally, these officers expressed dissatisfaction with the government's apparent reluctance to improve on the level of independence achieved in the treaty settlement. Many of those who supported the treaty had only done so out of loyalty to Michael Collins and in the belief that it would, in Collins' words, be a 'stepping stone' to the republic. They now felt betrayed. On 7 March 1924, senior officers, including Major General Liam Tobin and Colonel Charles Dalton, sent an ultimatum to President Cosgrave demanding the suspension of demobilisation and the removal of the Army Council from military decision-making.[21]

As the crisis escalated, over ninety officers resigned or deserted their posts, some with weapons and ammunition. The actions of the mutineers also attracted the sympathy of some members of the governing Cumann na nGaedheal party, notably the minister for trade, Joe McGrath, who acted as 'a mediator and spokesman for the mutineers'.[22] The government responded to the crisis in a confused way. Due to an illness, Cosgrave was unable to attend to his duties and his cabinet seemed divided on how to respond. At one point, in an effort to find stolen weapons, the minister for defence, Richard Mulcahy, ordered a raid on McGrath's home without President Cosgrave's knowledge. In the end, the decisive action of the minister for home affairs, Kevin O'Higgins, put a speedy end to the mutiny. O'Higgins asked Tobin and Dalton to resign and he made other administrative changes which satisfied the majority of the army. However, O'Higgins did not reinstate those officers who had already resigned their posts.[23]

While Cosgrave's government regained control of the situation, the affair had serious political repercussions. On 11 March 1924, McGrath resigned from the governing party citing his dissatisfaction with the government's handling of the crisis and indicating that he also shared the rebellious officers' dissatisfaction with the lack of progress on the national question. Subsequently, eight other TDs also withdrew from the governing party and under McGrath's leadership formed a so-called 'National Group' in the Dáil.[24]

McGrath, who had come to know Cohalan through his role as minister for trade, recognised that Cohalan's increasing dissatisfaction with the Free State government coincided with that of the National Group. The *Gaelic American* had previously criticised the pro-British policies of the Free State government and had accused the administration of not keeping faith with the republican ideals of Michael Collins. Indeed, in a telegram to Cohalan dated 2 April 1924 McGrath referred to a *Gaelic American* article which echoed such views: 'Gaelic American dated 13 March arrived today. Our policy coincides with your article "we keep faith" … our action I believe coincides with your views starting Republican Party in the Dáil with the object of interpreting Treaty as accepted writing.'[25]

Joe McGrath's papers in the archives of Dún Laoghaire Rathdown County Council, Dublin, also provide an intriguing insight into Cohalan's role in the crisis. These files, together with Cohalan's own papers in the AIHS, suggest that McGrath looked to Cohalan for both financial and political support. In a lengthy letter dated 4 April 1924, two days after his earlier telegram, McGrath provided a comprehensive report on the factors which led to the mutiny and the reasons for his own withdrawal from government. In his account of the crisis, McGrath praised the officers for taking a stand and accused the then minister for defence, Richard Mulcahy (who had resigned the previous month), rather than Cosgrave, of overreacting to the crisis. As McGrath pointed out to Cohalan: 'I have no doubt you will agree that the action of the officers concerned was big, manly and patriotic and deserving of the gratitude of the whole Irish race.'[26]

McGrath also expressed concern for the material welfare of the officers who had resigned their commissions and had not been reinstated. As he pointed out to Cohalan:

> I should say that their material sacrifices have been very great and I feel a personal responsibility for their future welfare. Consequently, I am forced to ask you if it would be possible to raise any funds for them – at least sufficient to tide them over their immediate difficulties.[27]

Cohalan responded generously to McGrath's pleas for assistance and in a letter dated 22 April 1924 enclosed a draft for 2,000 pounds. Diarmuid Lynch also indicates that the FOIF sent 10,000 dollars, ostensibly for the material welfare of the mutineers, though it is not clear if Cohalan's payment formed a component of this.[28] Nevertheless, these were considerable sums at that time and Cohalan's correspondence suggests that he recognised that this money would also have a political purpose. In his letter, Cohalan advised McGrath to use the money 'sparingly' and sympathised with his efforts to form a genuine opposition republican group in the Dáil which would be free from 'the curse of de Valera and his system of division and slander'.[29] Tellingly, he also informed McGrath that he had Devoy's support: 'Mr. Devoy, Mr. Lynch and Mr. Dalton join me in endorsing the establishment of an open Republican movement by you – as doubtless will the men who count throughout the United States when they get the word of what has happened.'[30]

McGrath, in turn, expressed delight at Cohalan's political and financial support and indicated that the money would be used not only to support the former officers but also to further the political ends of the National Group. Indeed, one of the members of the group, Sean Milroy, drawing on Cohalan's funds, started a short-lived newspaper called *The Nation*, which adopted a very critical stance on the government's orthodox economic policies.[31]

Cosgrave was well aware of Cohalan's support for McGrath's faction. In a confidential letter in July, he sought to reassure Cohalan that the crisis had passed and by implication, no intervention was necessary on his part. Referring to the mutiny as a 'big crisis', Cosgrave stated that: 'Our only consolation now is that the worst is over and things are shaping better.' He also wished that 'please God it is the last of our difficulties'.[32]

No doubt Cosgrave hoped that the crisis had ended but one could argue that Cohalan's material and political support for McGrath ensured that it would drag on for several more months. Matters became further complicated by John Devoy's first trip to the new Irish Free State in September 1924, his first since his clandestine visit in the 1870s during the Land War. The Irish government spared no effort in providing Devoy with a warm welcome and many official engagements were organised on his behalf. At the same time, Cosgrave knew from media reports of McGrath's contacts with both 'The Judge' and the old Fenian chief. According to a report in the *Irish Times* of 6 September 1924, Devoy, shortly after his arrival, journeyed to Glandore accompanied by McGrath to meet with Cohalan.[33]

The presence of both Devoy and Cohalan in the country and their known sympathies for the National Group encouraged Cosgrave to reach a reconciliation with McGrath. With Cohalan and Devoy agreeing to act as mediators, Cosgrave wrote to McGrath asking him to attend a conference with a view to securing 'unity and co-operation'.[34] Overall, the meeting appeared to have gone well and Cohalan left Ireland believing that a settlement between both parties had finally been reached especially with regard to the reinstatement of those officers who had resigned their commissions. Shortly after his return to the United States in late September, Cohalan wrote to Cosgrave hoping that the president would soon make an announcement to this effect and expressed fears that the disunity apparent in the wake of the army crisis could only be exploited by 'opponents' of the Free State both in Ireland and the US.[35]

> I have been anxiously awaiting the pronouncement from you that will bring into line the great majority of all those in Ireland who are honestly striving for progress and liberty. I suppose one thing or another may have delayed your statement but in the natural order of things, it ought to come soon in order to be really effective.[36]

Cosgrave made no such statement. Instead, Cohalan received a lengthy and anguished letter from McGrath indicating that all had not gone well once 'The Judge' and Devoy had left the country. In forthright terms, McGrath described a meeting he had with Cosgrave on 2 October where Cosgrave had not held to the promises he had made, including the one to reinstate the officers who had resigned:

> Portion of your optimistic statement on Ireland, as published in the 'Gaelic American', has been published here and was well received, but I am very sorry to have to relate that the principal plank on which, I know, you based your optimism has been smashed completely by the President turning a complete somersault …
>
> When pressed for a definite answer as to how he [Cosgrave] proposed to bring about the promised reinstatement, he trotted out the following: 'I was thinking of making Egan (of Tullamore) Minister for Defence and failing his acceptance, some other T.D. (unnamed) and I will recommend to him to take back these men as the occasion arises, but I cannot recommend to him to deal with them as a block. They will be dealt with when other cases, which I believe are just as deserving, are dealt with or along with those cases.' Now I simply asked, 'supposing the new Minister refuses, what will you do?' He replied, 'Oh! I can do nothing.'[37]

In his letter, McGrath stressed that Cosgrave had breached the agreement which Cohalan had helped to mediate in the interests of maintaining unity: 'I reminded him of his promise to both you and I and the reasons underlying same. His reply was, 'Is that so, I don't remember exactly.' McGrath informed Cohalan that he now believed the situation was 'hopeless':

> I am inclined to just leave them go ahead as they wish and whatever happens they can't say but we have done our part to bring about the unity so much desired and so very necessary … As to Cosgrave's action, the most charitable thing I can say is that I personally will never again negotiate with or trust him.[38]

In reply, Cohalan informed McGrath of his 'distress' that his intervention had not brought about the desired reconciliation. However, in truth, Cohalan overestimated his influence over Cosgrave in bringing a resolution to the crisis. Cosgrave's own hands were tied. Kevin O'Higgins, his powerful minister for home affairs, had acted with great decisiveness in the army crisis and had seen the actions of the mutineers as a direct threat to the authority of the civilian government. If Cosgrave had agreed to reinstate the officers, a clash between Cosgrave and O'Higgins would have inevitably ensued and might well have threatened the very survival of the government.

Following this latest dispute with Cosgrave, McGrath and the eight other TDs who formed the National Group resigned from their Dáil seats, thus provoking a series of by-elections.[39] Cohalan appeared optimistic that McGrath's party would do well in these election contests. In a confidential letter to Devoy, he expressed a belief that given the president's refusal to reinstate the officers involved in the original mutiny, McGrath had 'no other course left to him honorably and that the unselfish thing which he has done will greatly strengthen him with the thinking men of the country'.[40]

Cohalan may even have seen McGrath's faction influencing future government policy from the opposition benches. In a letter to McGrath in November 1924, just a week after his resignation, Cohalan returned to the idea of promoting strong tourist traffic: 'I hope you will press vigorously for the adoption of a platform that will include a strong campaign for American tourist traffic and for a system of fine hotels and of excellent roads in order to attract that traffic.'[41]

Again, Cohalan's hopes proved unfounded. Much to his disappointment, McGrath's group fared badly in the series of by-elections that followed their Dáil resignations. All lost their seats. The governing Cumann na nGaedheal party won two of the vacant seats and the remaining five went to de Valera's opposition Sinn Féin party, who were still boycotting the Dáil. At this point, McGrath retired from politics to focus on his business interests though he remained in contact with Cohalan, who acted as his legal agent in the United States for a number of business ventures.[42]

In the wake of the army mutiny, the editorials in the *Gaelic American* reflected Cohalan's increasing disillusionment with the Free State government. A January 1925 editorial stated that:

> With strong appreciation of what several of the present members of the Irish government have done for national ideals and interests, we deplore the weaknesses and instability shown by them on some recent occasions and we urge in the name of that section of the race which more than any other has been responsible for bringing to Ireland its present position among the nations that there shall be a closing up of the ranks along national lines, that there shall be an end to the petty bickering and small jealousies and that a strong position shall be taken against the forces of reaction and imperialism that of late have been gaining so strong a position in Ireland.[43]

Cohalan appears to have hardened his stance towards the Free State government in the wake of the events that surrounded the army mutiny. A National Council meeting of the Friends of Irish Freedom at the Hotel Astor, on 23 January 1925, expressed resentment at 'signs of reaction in Cosgrave's regime'.[44] The tone of the *Gaelic American* also became more critical of the Free State throughout the remainder of the government's life. A typical editorial in April 1927 complained of Irish 'dependence' on the British market and echoed Cohalan's call on the Irish government to develop more Irish trade with the United States. This criticism became a recurring feature of the paper's coverage of the policies of the Free State.

Irish government officials in the United States, in their reports to Dublin, often noted such criticism. In an April 1927 confidential report to Dublin, Timothy Smiddy, the Free State's minister plenipotentiary in Washington, noted in an exasperated tone that: 'On two occasions recently I took the opportunity, when I met Judge Cohalan, of introducing the subject of the attack on our Ministers by the Gaelic American. I failed to change his views though I endeavoured to make him realise that the Gaelic American had not all the facts …' In the same report to Dublin, Smiddy agreed that 'it is regrettable that our trade is not better distributed internationally' but noted that this was unlikely to change in the near future due to high American tariffs: 'In consequence of the high tariffs in this country against those articles which, with the development of modern efficiency on our part, we might export, I see at present little prospect of any substantial increase in our exports to the U.S.A.'[45]

Cohalan's willingness to support opponents of the government was especially apparent in the run-up to the 1927 election. In May of that year, he corresponded with members of the newly formed Clann Éireann party. Like the National Group, this party contained former government TDs who had grown disillusioned with the conservative nature of the Cosgrave administration. William Magennis, one of the founders of the party, had been critical of the Boundary Commission debacle and had also advocated abolition of the oath of allegiance. Contained in Cohalan's correspondence in the AIHS is a letter from Magennis acknowledging receipt of funds and expressing delight at Cohalan's financial support.[46]

Cohalan's papers also contain a surprising letter from his old enemy Patrick McCartan. In March 1927, some months before the election of that year, McCartan wrote suggesting that a grand alliance of Cumann na nGaedheal dissenters, Clann Éireann, Fianna Fáil, Sinn Féin, anti-treaty IRA and pro-treaty IRA could combine together to defeat the incumbent government. However, McCartan added that 'de Valera is the only man here around whom we can rally the country at the moment'. De Valera was at this time in the United States trying to raise funds for his newly established Fianna Fáil party, which had broken with Sinn Féin. McCartan tried to convince Cohalan of the merits of using de Valera as a figurehead to forge unity among the different Irish-American factions in the United States as well as in Ireland: 'You need unity in America as much as we need it here. You and de Valera must appear on the same platform before he returns. That is a tall order for you and perhaps as tall for him.'[47]

Cohalan's response to McCartan is not included in his records but Devoy received a similar request for support and no doubt spoke for Cohalan in making it plain that de Valera 'has no qualities of leadership and his record should bar him forever'.[48] In this context, the outcome of the 1927 election must have caused both Cohalan and Devoy some unease. While Clann Éireann failed to make any headway, de Valera's Fianna Fáil party made significant gains. Though they still remained in opposition, the party ended its boycott of the Dáil over the oath of allegiance with de Valera stating that the oath was merely an 'empty formula'.

Cohalan's rejection of McCartan's bid for support suggests that while he was increasingly critical of the Cosgrave administration, he never seriously contemplated supporting an opposition party which would include de Valera. Cosgrave appeared well aware of this, though he must surely have known about the various overtures Cohalan had made to disaffected members of his own party. The reality of this situation may explain why both men remained on cordial terms. Both shared a passionate opposition to de Valera and believed that his return to power had to be resisted at all costs. This common belief outweighed their other differences. During Cohalan's summer visit to Ireland in 1926, he invited Cosgrave to visit with his family in Glandore. Cosgrave graciously declined this offer in a letter to Cohalan's wife citing his wife's health and pressure of work, though the tone of Cosgrave's letter remained warm and friendly.[49] No doubt Cosgrave still recognised how Cohalan, despite his frequent criticisms of the Free State, could still provide valuable assistance to Irish interests in the United States. This became apparent during the president's visit to the United States in 1928. As Francis Carroll points out, this was the first official visit of an Irish head of state to the US. Cohalan formed part of the official welcoming committee, which greeted Cosgrave's ship in New York and hosted a luncheon for the president at the prestigious Lawyers' Club. The *Boston Globe* included a report on Cohalan's welcoming speech, which was fulsome in its praise for the Irish president:

> I present to you with pride and affection, as an example of Irish manhood and character, this modest man who is at once a dreamer and a realist; a fighter and a conciliator; an economist, a statesman and a man of action, who has done a man's share in bringing his people so far forward on the road to independence and prosperity.[50]

Yet despite his warm friendship for Cosgrave, Cohalan still remained critical of the Irish Free State. In the year following Cosgrave's successful visit, Michael MacWhite, who replaced Smiddy as minister plenipotentiary, noted the *Gaelic American*'s continued niggling criticism of the Free State and felt that Cohalan had a hand in this. In a report to Joseph P. Walshe, secretary in the Department of External Affairs, MacWhite cited as a source for this belief a conversation that he had with an Irish-American businessman, Robert E. O'Malley, who had spent time in Dublin and 'got to understand the position of the Saorstát [Irish Free State]'.

> He [O'Malley] says that when a member of the Executive Council [Irish government] makes a statement that appears friendly to England, Diarmuid Lynch, James Reidy of the Gaelic American, and other officials of the Clan want to launch an attack on the Saorstát right away in the Gaelic American. Judge Cohalan never tires of telling them that the Saorstát should adopt a more forward policy with regard to England, by which he means an aggressive anti-English policy irrespective of the consequences.[51]

In his letter, MacWhite implied that Cohalan and his associates lacked O'Malley's understanding of the position of the Irish Free State and the economic and political pressures it laboured under. He also pointed out to Walshe that the Clan na Gael was a 'dwindling force':

> I am told by representative Irish people in the various places I visit, that it is almost impossible to keep Irish organizations together in this country since the Free State was established … Young Irishmen coming to this country will not join the organizations, as they say, there is no necessity for them now, and American-born children of Irish parents who have been through high schools and universities have still a great deal of Irish sentiment but are not connected with any Irish movement the same as the young men of a generation or two ago.[52]

Irish-Americans themselves were aware of their declining power to influence events. In 1926, Edward McSweeney, a prominent member of the AIHS, wrote to Cohalan expressing these fears: 'I am sorry, but in my opinion, we are losing racial leadership, politically as well as morally. The Immigration Act of 1924 would not have been possible in 1920.'[53] The Friends of Irish Freedom organisation also continued to decline into the late 1920s and by the early 1930s numbered just a few hundred members. The organisation would eventually be wound up by national secretary Diarmuid Lynch in 1935 before he returned to Ireland.[54] Inevitably this undermined Cohalan's already dwindling power base both in relation to what he could achieve for Ireland and for Irish-America. As we shall see in the next chapter, the decline in membership of Irish-American organisations can also be seen in tandem with the decline in the power of the Tammany political machine, especially following the election of Republican New York mayor Fiorello La Guardia in 1934.[55]

Cohalan's approach to the army crisis and his criticism of the policies of the Free State government suggests that he believed that the government's pro-British policies had led to the increasing popularity of Sinn Féin and Fianna Fáil. This ignored growing dissatisfaction in the country with the social and economic policies of the Free State government, which tended to favour the more prosperous sections of Irish society.

In the 1932 election, Éamon de Valera's Fianna Fáil party secured sufficient seats to form a government with the minority Labour party. This brought Cosgrave's long administration to an end. Cohalan's contacts with the Irish government ceased at this point, though, as we have seen, these contacts had already lessened as his value to the Irish government declined.

Irish diplomat William J.B. Macaulay, in a March 1932 report to Dublin from the newly established Irish Consul General's Office in New York, noted 'great interest in the political situation in the Saorstát', but also 'apprehension lest a change in government might retard the progress of the country'.[56] Macaulay, who had been invited to speak at a number of Irish societies including the American Irish Historical Society, where Cohalan exercised considerable influence, stressed 'that all friends of Ireland should refrain from pre-judgement and hostile criticism' and that 'they should give at least their moral support to our new government in the hope that it will succeed in achieving our political, economic and cultural advancement'. Macaulay also noted with some trepidation that he expected a certain degree of hostility from Cohalan in the future:

> There was a meeting of the Clan na Gael on Sunday, 6 March, which I understand is dominated by Judge Cohalan and his group. The Judge made a long speech pointing out the difficulties which the new government will meet. This Organisation never entirely approved of the policy of the last Government and now appears prepared to be highly critical of the policy of the next one.[57]

In fact, Macaulay's fears were not borne out. True, Cohalan had expressed concern about the difficulties which the new government would face but at a later speech to a packed AOH annual banquet meeting at the Westminster Hotel in Boston he advised Irish-Americans to 'give the new regime in the Irish Free State a chance to prove its merits'. In a conciliatory speech, he also stressed that those now in power are 'inexperienced and need the patience of friends of Ireland until they have a chance to adjust themselves'.[58]

Cohalan's unexpectedly moderate response to de Valera's government must surely have come as a surprise to Macaulay. Yet for the pragmatic Cohalan, this speech reflected his recognition of the new realities of Irish politics over which he would have no control. Indeed, his decreasing ability to effect any change in Irish policy under Cosgrave had already been exposed during the army crisis and in the 1927 elections.

Cohalan was also aware of the declining importance of the Irish question in the United States. During his summer visit to Glandore in 1926 he noted in an interview with the *Cork Examiner* how Ireland had 'completely disappeared from the newspapers and in a large way from the public thought of America'.[59]

As if to symbolise the end of a dramatic era in Irish-American nationalist history, John Devoy passed away in September 1928 at the age of eighty-six. Cohalan remained in contact with Devoy to the end and even suggested editorial changes to Devoy's book *Recollections of an Irish Rebel* (1929). In the title page of the initial draft of his book, Devoy had described himself as 'Chief Organiser for the British Army'. Cohalan gently pointed out to Devoy that readers might draw the wrong conclusions from this and assume that he was an organiser of the British army rather than an organiser of Irish Fenian rebels within the army. Devoy took on board Cohalan's advice and an alteration was accordingly made to the title page to clarify this.[60]

For the remainder of his life, Cohalan increasingly focused his attention on American politics and upholding what he perceived as American 'liberty'. In his pamphlet entitled *Democracy or Imperialism, which?* (1925), published by the Friends of Irish Freedom, Cohalan emphasised his first loyalty to the United States and his concern for its welfare:

> What will happen in Ireland will largely depend on the people of Ireland … Let us help them in any way we can, I advise – by counsel, by example – but let us more than anything else recognise that these United States are and will continue to be our country … if liberty is blotted out in America, it is lost to the rest of the world.[61]

For Cohalan, defending American liberty meant upholding democratic principles at home and maintaining an isolationist stance towards the ongoing struggles of the 'Old World'. From previous chapters, we have seen that such objectives had always coloured his outlook on Ireland and the United States but, in the final two decades of his life, he would embrace these goals with renewed passion.

11

Defending Jeffersonian Democracy in the Great Depression

FROM THE MID-1920s until the end of his life, Cohalan focused most of his attention on both domestic American politics and foreign affairs. In particular, his long-standing battle against British intrigue in the United States overlapped with his campaign to maintain American isolationism in an increasingly unstable international order. This would become apparent in his opposition to American participation in the World Court and President Franklin D. Roosevelt's internationalist foreign policy. While Cohalan appeared somewhat out of step with popular support for Roosevelt's New Deal response to the Great Depression (1929–40), his isolationist rhetoric seemed more in tune with the popular mood of the 1930s. However, here too international events would render such views ambiguous and Cohalan's lifelong struggle to prevent American involvement in the struggles of the 'Old World' would end in failure.

In his professional life, Cohalan resigned from his Supreme Court post in 1924 and re-established his private practice. In his letter to Governor Alfred E. Smith informing him of his resignation, Cohalan cited financial reasons for his decision and indicated that he could earn more working in his private practice. This provoked some satirical comment from the press. The *New York Times* announced Cohalan's decision with the headline 'Cohalan Resigns, Salary Too Small'.[1] However, there were other factors which influenced his decision. As already noted, Cohalan's relations with Boss Charlie Murphy had cooled somewhat since the Connolly scandal of 1913. In 1922 the Tammany organisation turned down Daniel's brother John P. Cohalan for re-nomination as surrogate of New York County.[2] John had served in this position since 1909. Daniel Cohalan's own fourteen-year term as Supreme Court Justice was due to expire in 1925 and the Tammany decision in relation to his brother did not bode well for Daniel's own prospects for re-nomination.

According to a 1931 article written by Forrest Davis of the *New York World-Telegram*, Daniel Cohalan remained out of favour with the leaders of Tammany for much of the 1920s. Davis highlighted how, after Charlie Murphy's death in 1924, Cohalan supported John Francis Curry for the leadership of Tammany. However, Curry failed to gain sufficient support and an 'oligarchy which included Al Smith, Wagner and Foley' ruled Tammany in a dictatorial way for much of the 1920s. This did not prevent Curry from subsequently attacking what became known as 'New Tammany' in the press. According to Davis: 'The oligarchy detested Curry. Moreover, they accused Cohalan of inspiring the attack, indeed writing the singularly effective letters.'[3]

Despite the fact that most Catholic Irish-Americans supported the Democratic Party, Cohalan did not endorse the party's presidential candidate John W. Davis in 1924. Reflecting Cohalan's views, the *Gaelic American* objected to the fact that Davis 'favored the entrance of the United States into the League of Nations' and was president of the 'English Speaking Union' which allegedly sought to make the United States 'an integral part of the British Empire'.[4] Instead, both the paper and Cohalan supported the Progressive candidate Robert M. La Follette (1855–1925), who represented Wisconsin in both chambers of Congress.[5] La Follette had been an opponent of America's entry into the First World War and the League of Nations.

While Cohalan's opposition to John Davis can be explained by his isolationist sentiment, one might have expected his enthusiastic support for Al Smith's Democratic presidential election bid in 1928. Smith was the first American Catholic to run for the presidency and his mother was an Irish-American. Indeed, because of his Catholicism, he faced stiff opposition from Protestant groups including the Ku Klux Klan, who accused Smith of following the dictates of the papacy. In this instance, the *Gaelic American* endorsed Smith but Cohalan himself did not take any role in his campaign. In the summer of 1928, stricken with influenza, he left New York for Glandore and only returned, fully recovered, just prior to the election in early November. Forrest Davis in the *New York World-Telegram* has described Cohalan's support for Smith as merely 'perfunctory'. This view is borne out in Cohalan's interview with the *Gaelic American* just after his return from Glandore. While he praised Governor Smith for making a 'gallant fight' and condemned the anti-Catholic religious bigotry that had surfaced during the election campaign, he also praised both presidential candidates and indicated that 'of course the choice must be made by every voter'. Finally, he admitted, perhaps recognising the pro-Smith sentiment of the *Gaelic American*'s Irish-American readership, that he 'looked forward to seeing Governor Smith … win an outstanding victory on election day'.[6]

Cohalan's lukewarm support for Smith can be attributed to the infighting then taking place within the Tammany organisation. In any event, there was little Cohalan could have done to prevent Smith's defeat to Republican candidate Herbert Hoover. A booming economy favoured another Republican administration and the persistence of anti-Catholic feeling contributed to Smith's defeat. Smith's opposition to prohibition and his association with big city politics also alienated conservative voters, especially in America's rural heartlands.[7]

Paradoxically, Al Smith's defeat indirectly aided Cohalan's political ambitions. It undermined Smith's standing in local New York politics and, according to the *New York Tribune*, allowed Cohalan to mastermind the Democratic insurgent move which led to John F. Curry's return as leader of Tammany in 1929.[8] Cohalan was now in favour once again and not surprisingly Curry selected him as his special advisor and strategist. As Davis pointed out: 'He and Curry were united in their aversion to the New Tammany. Other interests, notably piety, teetotalism, reverence for the fabled glories of the Irish race, linked them. The Cohalan sign was up once again at Tammany after sixteen years.'[9]

As we have seen from previous chapters, anti-imperialism and isolationism had characterised Cohalan's approach to many of the international issues of the day. In his pamphlet *Democracy or Imperialism, which?* Cohalan saw the international order as a Great Power contest, where the strongest imperial powers sought to further their own interests and where 'the idea that the war was fought for democracy means nothing'. With the defeat of Germany and the weakening of France and Russia, Cohalan saw Britain as an even more dominant force in world affairs, ever anxious to extend its influence at America's expense.[10]

Cohalan's constant attacks on Britain sometimes upset former allies. In early 1924, George Sylvester Viereck, a German-American journalist who had worked closely with the Clan on anti-British campaigns in the past, wrote to Cohalan complaining about his apparent favourable attitude towards France. At this point, France had occupied the German Ruhr coalfields and was pursuing a vindictive campaign against Germany despite British calls for restraint. Viereck wrote: 'I am sorry if your hatred of England seems to make you all too lenient to the crimes of Poincaré [French premier]. France is the enemy of mankind.'[11] Cohalan in response defensively wrote:

> May I point out to you that you mistake my position entirely with relation to England. I have no hatred of England or any other country. But I have a hatred of imperialism whether embodied by England, France, Germany or any other country which will subject one people to the domination of another or permit one country to own a large section of the earth that is inhabited by other races. I say this with relation to both kinds of imperialism, whether they be Monarchical or so-called Republican in form. 'A plague on both your houses'.[12]

Despite this declaration, it must be said that, while Cohalan stood opposed to all forms of imperialism, he believed Britain posed the greatest threat to the United States. As discussed in previous chapters, he was of the opinion that sections of America's Anglophile elite identified with England's interests even more than they did with the interests of the United States. Cohalan exaggerated the extent of such cultural influences on American foreign policy but these views nevertheless shaped his beliefs. In 1922, in a letter to FOIF colleague James M. Burke, Cohalan declared: 'America … is rapidly recovering from the hysteria of sentimentality into which she was thrown by the war … Although we are still overrun with English propaganda in a hundred forms, the people are awakening to a realisation of the fact that England is bound to be our great and aggressive foreign competitor …'[13]

In his efforts to defend America against such threats, Cohalan took part in setting up a new organisation known as the All America National Council (AANC). The council emerged following a conference in Washington in February 1922. Correspondence relating to the organisation lists FOIF leader John D. Splain as its president, while Cohalan and other leading members of the FOIF served as national directors. The organisation operated from the same offices as the FOIF National Bureau in Washington, thus highlighting the overlap between both organisations. Mirroring the tactics of the National Bureau, the council distributed pamphlets and press releases to members of Congress and other prominent Americans.[14]

The AANC aimed to promote a policy of isolationism with its motto being 'America for all Americans'.[15] Cohalan invited like-minded senators such as William Borah and James Reed to address the organisation's meetings, which were again publicised. However, the evidence suggests that due to financial problems the AANC found it difficult to continue with its work despite subsidies from the already dwindling resources of the FOIF. In June 1922, the secretary of the AANC, G.A. Laffy, complained to Cohalan: 'As it is we cannot move one way or another on account of lack of $$. For instance: to show you in a practical way what is what – the last $1,000 the FOIF advanced us last week is nearly gone.'[16]

The absence of the Irish question in American politics, which had done so much to rally support for Irish-American nationalism during the years of conflict in Ireland, severely constrained the FOIF's ability to sustain other front organisations such as the AANC. The FOIF was now in rapid decline despite the best efforts of national secretary Diarmuid Lynch to hold on to members. In 1922 membership numbered about 20,000 but by 1928 this had fallen to 654.[17] Its capacity to support the AANC was therefore limited and there is no evidence in Cohalan's papers of any AANC activity beyond 1923.

The formation of the AANC took place against the background of the Washington Naval Treaty Disarmament Conference in 1921 and 1922. These deliberations between the five great naval powers – Britain, the United States, Japan, Italy and France – aimed to reduce the level of naval armaments in the world so as to help prevent future conflicts. As one would expect, disputes emerged as to the scale of disarmament each state was prepared to countenance. Cohalan, in a speech in New York, defended American interests and argued that: 'We are the next victim to be destroyed by England … she is now trying to get us to commit national suicide and to voluntarily destroy our great fleet.'[18] As a result of the conference, all the powers agreed to reduce naval construction but Cohalan felt that the United States had given up too much and had been 'dazzled' by British diplomats. As he pointed out in a letter to Senator William Borah: 'The whole scheme is a damnable one.'[19] However, with both the AANC and the FOIF at a low ebb, there was little that Cohalan could do to determine the outcome of these negotiations.

Cohalan remained deeply suspicious of Britain's intentions, especially after the Conservative Party victory in the British election of 1924. In a speech reported in the *Gaelic American* in January 1925, which referred to the 'brutal and arbitrary British exhibition of force and terrorism in Egypt and India', he remarked that: 'The return to power of the Tories in England and its immediate consequences in other parts of the world are indicative of the fact that a general fight against liberty is to be expected.' Again, Cohalan, in the same speech, linked this foreign threat to domestic conditions as he noted the 'stirring' in many ways of 'England's friends in the United States to entangle the US in imperialistic policies and commit us to schemes that will either weaken or embroil us'.[20]

In keeping with his isolationist approach to American foreign policy, Cohalan, in speeches and articles, also condemned international efforts by the other Great Powers to secure American participation in an international World Court. Article 14 of the Covenant of the League of Nations had envisaged the setting up of a Permanent Court of International Justice, or so-called 'World Court', to provide advice on the settlement of international disputes. The World Court began its work in 1921. As the United States had not joined the league, it did not recognise the verdicts of this international institution, though individual American jurists such as Charles Evans Hughes served on the World Court in Geneva.[21]

Throughout the 1920s and early 1930s, the US came under international pressure to formally join the court. For Cohalan this pressure represented yet another effort to embroil the United States in Old World struggles. In the *Gaelic American* and at FOIF meetings, Cohalan declared the court a 'menace'.[22] In 1931, the FOIF published a pamphlet entitled *Resolutions of the World Court* which enunciated Cohalan's objections to the treaty.[23] In 1934, Cohalan set out these objections once again in a hearing before the Committee on Foreign Relations in the United States Senate. Cohalan's lifelong friend and fellow isolationist Republican Senator William Borah of Idaho formed part of the committee.

Borah saw the value of having Cohalan with his rhetorical skills speak against the proposal and he was not to be disappointed. According to the committee's published report, Cohalan's testimony ran to several pages and, as he emphasised key weaknesses in the administration of the World Court, he drew applause from the audience:

> Why should we, after the dreadful experience we had when we were beguiled into the World War in 1917 and 1918, why should we again risk our ideals, our young men, our resources, by even taking a chance of getting mixed up in another Old World struggle?
>
> We are told that the body we are asked to join is a court. Nothing could be further from the fact if by a court we mean that which the word stands for in American life. The body which is called a court either has or has not the power to enforce its decrees and carry out its judgments. If it has, then it is a super-government which we are asked to join and to which we are asked to make submission; this against all the ideals and interests and traditions of our country. The people are in no mood to permit any such action on the part of those who represent them in office. [Applause.] If it has no force behind it to carry out those judgments, then it is a mere debating society from which nothing of any good can come …[24]

In the event, the United States Senate never ratified the protocol, which would have meant American recognition of the court. Cohalan's testimony represented but one of many opposition voices against participating in this international institution, so it would be impossible to judge the impact of his eloquent speech. Nevertheless, the decision to invite Cohalan to appear before this powerful Senate committee is evidence of his continued stature among isolationist members of Congress. His testimony also reflected the general isolationist mood of the 1930s and, in this context at least, Cohalan represented American mainstream opinion.

The election of President Roosevelt in 1932 caused Cohalan deep anxiety. On a personal level, Cohalan harboured a resentment towards Roosevelt going back to the convention of 1912. As we have seen in an earlier chapter, Boss Murphy had selected Cohalan as a possible Senate candidate but Roosevelt, with the support of a group of 'insurgent democrats', had blocked the nomination. According to his obituary in the *New York Times*, Cohalan 'never forgot' this slight to his ambitions.[25]

Yet Cohalan's antagonism towards Roosevelt went deeper than this and must be seen in the context of his deep-rooted isolationist ideology. Cohalan suspected Roosevelt of holding the same pro-British prejudice as that held by Woodrow Wilson. As the international crisis between Germany and Britain deepened in Europe in the 1930s, Cohalan feared that once again the United States would be drawn into a global conflict. In 1933, he wrote that America now appeared to be at a crossroads: 'Let Franklin Roosevelt declare under which banner we are to march during the term of his presidency. Is it to be under the banner of those who made America and preserved it, and made it great? Or is it to be under the banner of the man [Wilson] who shamelessly betrayed us and shockingly misled us?'[26]

Cohalan also vehemently opposed Roosevelt's response to the Great Depression, which had led to mass unemployment and hardship for millions of Americans. A deep-rooted social conservatism, which opposed 'big government', determined Cohalan's response. Indeed, his reaction to Roosevelt would be typical of the more monied sections of American society, and in this context Cohalan could be seen to represent a small but growing section of Irish-American opinion that was closer to the Republican Party viewpoint than the Democratic Party one.

Cohalan's opposition to Roosevelt seems also to have been motivated by the threat posed to the Tammany system by the New Deal. Though a Republican, Mayor Fiorello La Guardia, who took office in 1934, enjoyed a close working relationship with FDR. La Guardia replaced many of the older Tammany welfare programmes with federally funded New Deal projects, thus undermining the power base of the Tammany leaders. As Golway in his work on the Tammany machine points out, Roosevelt put 'La Guardia – not Tammany's bosses – in charge of federal funds for the massive public works projects of the Depression era'.[27] Federal relief measures for the unemployed also became a feature of New Deal expenditure and this naturally restricted the ability of the Tammany machine to exercise patronage in return for votes.

Cohalan's criticism of the New Deal is evident in the many speeches he made to Catholic societies of which he was a member. In March 1934, at a communion breakfast for 2,500 members of the Order of Seville, the Catholic guild of the Railroad Express Agency, held at the Hotel Astor in New York, Cohalan lambasted federal relief measures then carried out by the Roosevelt administration. According to a report in the *New York Herald Tribune*:

> Judge Cohalan switched suddenly from a general speech in praise of the industry and thrift of American Catholics to an unexpected attack on Federal relief measures. 'We will not tolerate long in this country,' he said, 'a government that attempts to support in idleness great masses of the people, who seem quite content to be amused and fed without any work on their part.'[28]

In a reference to public works projects, Cohalan also objected to the 'intrusion of Federal experimenters' in private business. In yet another effort to link domestic and foreign policy, Cohalan argued that the 'same type of arrogance on the part of public servants that forced us into the European war against our wills is now making plans for the support of a permanent unemployed class'.[29]

Interestingly, at the same gathering, Judge Robert V. Kinkead of the Court of Common Pleas, Hudson County, New Jersey, made a speech that supported the New Deal as well as relief measures for the newly unemployed. In a talk that received cheers from the audience, Kinkead argued that: 'The country I want to be ruled by is one that will stand between these innocent victims of industrial injustice and their desperate need.' Kinkead also argued, in direct opposition to Cohalan, that he could understand 'why we have people on relief': 'They were laid off by the hundreds of thousands by large companies, and they had a right to look to their country in their innocent emergency.'[30]

Cohalan's opposition to the New Deal was not shared by the majority of American Catholic workers, who looked to the federal government for a solution to the deepening economic crisis. Evidence of Roosevelt's popularity can be seen in his electoral success among the working class. This support for Roosevelt even extended to Cohalan's own immediate family. In an interview, retired State Supreme Court Justice Peter Fox Cohalan has described how his grandfather John (Daniel's brother) occasionally visited the Roosevelt home in upstate New York.[31]

Roosevelt's popularity did not prevent Cohalan from combining with other prominent Democrats to try to prevent the re-nomination of FDR as Democratic candidate for the presidency at the Philadelphia convention in June 1936. Along with Al Smith and three other prominent Democratic anti-New Dealers, Cohalan wrote an appeal to convention delegates to put aside President Roosevelt and nominate 'some genuine Democrat' for president.[32] The appeal to delegates criticised the New

Deal as maintaining twenty million Americans on the dole in a 'condition of semi-servility'. In strong language, it condemned Roosevelt's continued 'dictatorship' and alleged an attempt to 'buy the Presidency by the misuse of funds'.[33]

In the event, the appeal to delegates had little impact and Roosevelt was nominated as the Democratic presidential candidate. Undaunted, Cohalan maintained his attacks on Roosevelt in the run-up to the November election. In late September 1936, following a radio broadcast by Roosevelt at the Democratic state convention in Syracuse, New York, Cohalan broadcast his own critique of the president on the same radio station, WJZ. Cohalan spoke under the auspices of the National Jeffersonian Democrats, a loose alliance of conservative Democrats opposed to Roosevelt. In his broadcast, Cohalan claimed that there were millions of Democrats who refused 'to follow him into the quicksands of New Dealism'. Cohalan went on to accuse the president of trying to 'substitute America's economic system for some form of collectivism such as exists in several of the European countries today'.[34]

While some of Roosevelt's state-led efforts to create employment mirrored that of fascist Italy and Nazi Germany, Cohalan's allegation that Roosevelt wanted to collectivise the American economy had little foundation in fact. Also, there is no doubt that Roosevelt's efforts were widely popular, as evidenced by his election win in not only 1936 but also in 1940 and 1944. Yet Cohalan stubbornly clung to his convictions and, in line with Jeffersonian thinking, argued vehemently against 'big government' involvement in the American economy.[35]

Cohalan also held firm to his belief, throughout the 1930s, that America had been 'beguiled' into entering the war in Europe in 1917 and used this to argue against further American military interventions abroad. In a lengthy speech fully documented in the *Gaelic American* in November 1935, Cohalan warned against British intrigue in the United States aimed at forging an Anglo-American alliance.[36] In another speech, at a Clan na Gael meeting in 1936, Cohalan referred to the loss of over a hundred thousand American lives and financial losses of over forty billion dollars. He declared that this had come about as a result of Wilson's betrayal of George Washington's isolationist policy and that of successive American presidents.[37] Again in a speech to the graduating class of the Jesuit Xavier University, Cincinnati, Ohio, on 8 June 1938, Cohalan declared:

> Thomas Jefferson – keen student of human nature and of world history – warned us that Europe was a continent of eternal wars, and how right he was in that warning must be apparent to anyone who is acquainted with history since the time when he made that statement.[38]

During a summer visit to Glandore in 1933, Cohalan provided an interview to the *Southern Star* which underlined his isolationist perspective for an Irish audience. In this instance, his interview focused on the recent collapse of talks at the London Economic Conference.[39] This conference, which involved sixty-six nations, had as its objective the stabilisation of currency exchange rates and the revival of international trade as a means of combating the Great Depression. In the end President Roosevelt refused to contemplate currency manipulation or the abandonment of protectionism, which in turn contributed to the collapse of the talks. Cohalan in his interview blamed the First World War for disrupting the global economy and remained unconvinced that any co-ordinated international effort could solve the crisis:

> The internationalists in every country and especially in America rejoice that there has been so great a representative assemblage. The conference will be talked of as a symbol of goodwill and a promise of peace among nations …
>
> But there can be no disguising the fact that nationalism is pregnant and triumphant throughout the world, and that each of the great powers is resolved to look out for its own interests and take care of its own people.[40]

In his interviews with both Irish and Irish-American newspapers in the 1930s, Cohalan focused solely on American and international affairs and did not comment on political developments in Ireland. This attitude stood in stark contrast to that of Joe McGarrity, who continued to fund Irish republican activities in Ireland. McGarrity eventually broke with de Valera over what he perceived as the Irish government's failure to take a more robust stance on the partition issue. In the late 1930s, he helped fund the activities of the IRA, who launched a bombing campaign against British cities in a forlorn attempt to achieve a British withdrawal from Northern Ireland. Cohalan did not refer to this campaign in his speeches or interviews and even the *Gaelic American* devoted little coverage to these dramatic events. In its August 1939 edition it merely reported on de Valera's decision to invoke the Coercion Act against the IRA in Ireland in order to curb this campaign but offered no commentary on his actions. Like Cohalan, the paper seemed preoccupied with the deteriorating international situation and the danger that the United States would once again be drawn into a global conflict on the side of Britain.[41]

In May 1941, as war ravaged Europe and the United States supplied military equipment to Britain and imposed economic sanctions on Japan, Cohalan feared for the worst. In a letter to his old friend, former Senator James Reed, Cohalan wrote:

> As for our situation, I am almost in despair. Both the President and his late opponent are … hurrying us along the road to war … How I wish you could be back in the Senate to raise your voice against this horrible blunder and mistake … I fear that nothing can hold us back from action that will make us again the tool of England and her friends … Our only escape it seems to me would come because of a quick ending to the war and I see no great prospect of that at present.[42]

The *Gaelic American* echoed Cohalan's isolationist perspective. In an edition following the outbreak of hostilities between Britain and Germany in September 1939, the paper cited Senators Borah and Lodge's warning against American participation in 'Europe's ever-recurring wars'. However, following the Japanese attack on Pearl Harbour in December 1941, the paper did an about-turn. Its headline of 13 December 1941 declared: 'War with Japan! Irish here will fight to last man for honor and glory of United States.'[43] This change in stance mirrored the response of the newspaper in April 1917 and was not surprising given traditional Irish-American support for the US armed forces in time of war. At the forty-fifth annual banquet of the American Irish Historical Society at the Hotel Biltmore in May 1942, which was attended by Cohalan, the president general of the society praised the valour and heroism of the Irish to the United States in previous conflicts and in the current war. 'At this very hour it [Irish valour] is illuminating our path to victory in the island jungles of the Pacific as it flames with a fierce defiance in far away Eastern skies.'[44]

While Cohalan's Americanism ensured his support for the war effort, he may well have felt that his lifetime campaign to keep America free from the struggles of the 'Old World' had ended in failure. However, his prediction that American intervention in the war would only prolong the British Empire proved unfounded. Even though Britain emerged on the winning side, its material and financial losses paved the way for its post-war decolonisation and the loss of its 'Great Power' status. Indeed, after the Second World War had ended, it was the United States which emerged as the strongest global power and it was in no mood to return to its isolationist past. Its armies reigned supreme on several continents and the 'American Century', a phrase coined by publisher Henry Luce of *Time-Life Magazine* in 1941, was well under way by the time of Cohalan's death in 1946.[45]

12

Farewell to Glandore: The final decade, 1936–46

COHALAN'S LIFE IN THE 1930s was marked by both successes and failures. His prominence in public life had gradually diminished by the end of the decade and this was influenced by developments in both American domestic politics and by his own failing health. He still maintained an interest in Irish events and continued to visit Ireland until the mid-1930s. He also followed American domestic and foreign events closely and contributed frequently to the *Gaelic American* throughout this period. Like many prominent men who had devoted their lives to public service, he also became concerned about his legacy. Even before his death, Cohalan would be best known for his confrontations with de Valera during the latter's visit to the United States in 1919–20 rather than his contribution to the Irish nationalist cause or his active role in American politics.

By the late 1920s, the Cohalans still lived in their townhouse on New York's prosperous Upper East Side. The family remained relatively affluent compared to the majority of New Yorkers in a period marked by unprecedented economic upheaval and uncertainty. The Cohalans also maintained their deep attachment to the Catholic faith, a religion which still attracted considerable disdain in some sections of American society. Daniel Cohalan generously contributed his time to a host of Catholic societies, which frequently called upon him to make speeches at Catholic events. In February 1923 he agreed to serve on a reception committee to welcome the new apostolic delegate to the United States, the Most Reverend Pietro Fumasoni Biondi.[1] In 1930, Cohalan's daughter Aileen decided to become a nun and entered the Society of the Sacred Heart of Jesus convent at Kenwood, Albany, in upstate New York. Her father fully accepted her decision. The *New York Times* reported on Aileen's entry into the Kenwood convent, again highlighting the Cohalan family's importance in New York society.[2] Cohalan's son Patrick, who had trained as a lawyer, became a Jesuit priest in the late 1930s, while his other son Florence became a priest in 1938 and would later become monsignor for the Archdiocese of New York. In what must have been a proud moment, Pope Pius XI granted Cohalan an audience in August 1938 in the private papal residence at Castel Gandolfo, in recognition of his work in defending the Catholic Church in the United States.[3]

Clearly, the American media viewed Cohalan as a stalwart defender of conservative Catholicism. However, he also submitted articles to the press on a variety of social topics. Such articles reflected the attitudes of a well-heeled Irish-American Catholic, conservative on economic issues but socially liberal on issues such as prohibition. In an article entitled 'A New Civil War', which appeared in the German-American journal *American Monthly* in March 1930, Cohalan, though a teetotaller himself, condemned the impact of the Eighteenth Amendment which had introduced prohibition ten years earlier. He did not mention religion in his article, though it is likely that, when he referred to the 'well-intentioned fanatics' who pressured the government to introduce the amendment, he had Protestant evangelical pressure groups in mind. In his article, Cohalan asked: 'Is it an exaggeration to say that it has set the country by the ears; clogged the courts; filled the jails …?' Cohalan argued that the measure had 'diverted from the public revenue, into the pockets of bootleggers and high-jackers colossal sums almost equal to the entire Federal income tax'. He called on the majority of God-fearing, law-abiding, peace-loving Americans to take a stand against the small organised minority who had pressured the government to introduce the measure.[4]

Even though Cohalan must have had many pressing demands as a professional lawyer and as advisor to Curry in the early 1930s, he and his family still found time to visit their beloved summer home in Glandore. Such trips to Ireland often took in events in Dublin such as the Dublin Horse Show. In 1932 Cohalan attended the Eucharistic Congress held in Dublin's Phoenix Park. Such long absences in Ireland from his advisory duties in New York did not go unnoticed in the local press. Forrest Davis, in his series on Tammany 'War Lords' for the *New York World-Telegram*, commented amusingly on Cohalan's 'yearly pilgrimages' to Glandore:

'The Squire of Glandore, it must sadly be realised, is an absentee War Lord at this moment – helping to guide the high affairs of this metropolis in much the same neglectful fashion complained of by Cohalan in the English landlords of Erin.' In the same article Davis waxed lyrical about Cohalan's continuing emotional ties to Ireland.

> Cohalan who helped fight an Empire with plot and counter-plot, manifestoes, smuggled arms, liberty funds and all the purple trappings of revolution, meditates in his semi-tropical gardens high on a headland outside the thatched town of Skibbereen. The fog rolls in over that whole enchanting littoral from Cork city to Bantry Bay and the Lakes of Killarney.[5]

Cohalan's ability to visit his summer home in Ireland in the early 1930s suggests a relatively comfortable position at this time. Few Americans could afford to maintain a foreign residence, let alone spend so much time there. The US in the 1920s witnessed an economic boom and Cohalan's practice, like most legal financial institutions, benefited. Cohalan also directed a property investment syndicate, in which Joe McGrath and other wealthy Irish individuals participated. This syndicate hoped to secure for its members profits from the sale of Florida land. In a 1926 letter, Cohalan wrote to McGrath that the syndicate had purchased a large tract of land comprising 1,700 acres close to Miami. Like many investors at this time, Cohalan believed that the 'great prosperity in the United States' would continue and that he expected to see 'handsome returns upon the investment'.[6] Unfortunately for Cohalan, these investments went badly wrong following a dramatic fall in Florida land prices in the late 1920s. McGrath, who also acted as an advisor for a number of other wealthy Irish investors, somewhat unfairly blamed Cohalan for his advice, though Cohalan himself also suffered financially from these investments.[7]

This ended the business relationship between both men and may well explain why McGrath chose not to involve Cohalan in his Irish Sweepstakes venture, which began in 1930. Marie Coleman, in her work *The Irish Sweep*, notes that McGrath and his business partners chose Cohalan's arch-enemy Joe McGarrity as one of several 'special agents' for the Irish Sweepstakes in the United States. This alliance between erstwhile Civil War foes brought financial dividends to both parties and Coleman's research indicates that McGarrity earned an estimated 300,000 pounds in commission payments in the period 1930 to 1938.[8]

Compared to McGarrity, Cohalan fared less well financially in the 1930s but he was shielded from the worst effects of the Depression. In 1929, Boss John Curry appointed him as his special advisor and this position would have helped him secure legal contracts. In 1934 Boss Curry's term ended, thus terminating Cohalan's advisory role. However, Cohalan still had political connections and in 1935 he secured an appointment as a judicial referee. This ensured an adequate income, though not to the same level as he once earned in private practice during the prosperous 1920s. Around the time of Cohalan's death in November 1946, James McGurrin, the president of the American Irish Historical Society, commented in a letter to Diarmuid Lynch on the reduced circumstances of the Cohalans in their final years. According to McGurrin, Cohalan, as an 'Official Referee', was now on a salary of 16,000 dollars per year, 'which represents an income way below his average while at the Bar'.[9]

As a judicial referee, Cohalan could still maintain a private legal practice. However, as the economic depression intensified, this practice, like many other firms offering legal services, must have suffered greatly. According to one historian, many lawyers 'struggled to survive' and competition increased for the reduced amount of legal work caused by the steep contraction of the economy.[10] In a letter to Diarmuid Lynch after Cohalan's death, Richard Dalton, a senior member of the American Irish Historical Society, remarked that Cohalan's venture 'back into private practice in the face of a business-wrecking major depression had been a soul-wracking failure'. This undoubtedly had an impact on Cohalan's outlook on life. Dalton remarked that Cohalan 'had been a sick man since 1934' and was subject to 'terrible periods of introspective analysis and depression'.[11] Dalton went on to elaborate on the impact of these bouts of depression:

> Sure he snapped out of it from time to time. Sure he joined with the appeal to the Democratic Convention Delegates in 1936 of Al Smith and Bainbridge Colby and Governor Ely. Sure, he even wrote it. But at the time he was merely a resident of that usually comfortable haven for retired old Supreme Court Justices – an Official Refereeship.[12]

Dalton's reference to 1934 is significant, since Cohalan's position as advisor to Curry came to an end at this time. As noted in the previous chapter, the Tammany system was now in decline due to the impact of La Guardia's New Deal reforms. It appears that Cohalan, now aged almost seventy, had come to realise that his days in active politics were over. Reflecting these changed circumstances, the Cohalans moved in 1935 from their old house on 94th Street to an apartment at 21 East 82nd Street. Of course, it is important to note that, as a judicial referee, Cohalan still enjoyed a substantial income in Depression-era America compared to the majority of New Yorkers at this time.[13]

According to an obituary of Cohalan which appeared in the *Irish Press*, he ceased his visits to Ireland about ten or eleven years before his death. This would suggest that his last visits to Cork took place around 1935 or 1936. A report in the *Evening Herald* on 6 August 1938 indicates that his wife Madge and daughter Kathleen visited the Dublin Horse Show that year but the report also indicates that Daniel himself was on holiday in London at this time and had not yet made up his mind on whether to visit Dublin.[14] The reasons for his lack of interest in visiting Ireland at this time and in subsequent years are unclear and can most probably be attributed to his age and his failing health. The outbreak of war between Britain and Germany in 1939 would also have made transatlantic travel dangerous.

Cohalan may well have found the de Valera-dominated Ireland of the 1930s less congenial. Unlike the early 1920s, when he had enjoyed the adulation of Free State leaders, he had now become a marginal figure remembered only for his conflict with de Valera during the latter's mission to the United States in 1919–20. As if to reinforce this perception, Patrick McCartan published *With De Valera in America* in 1932. As we have seen, this work was critical of Cohalan's failure to support de Valera's mission to the US, though, upon close reading, it is also critical of de Valera's actions, especially with regard to the Irish leader's intransigent behaviour at the 1920 Republican convention in Chicago.[15] Reviewers of this work did not pick up on these critical references to de Valera and tended to focus on McCartan's criticism of Cohalan. Diarmuid Lynch, who had only recently returned to Ireland, sent copies of these reviews to Cohalan with sympathetic notations indicating, in his view, where McCartan had made serious errors of interpretation. However, there is no doubt that this book, and the accompanying reviews in the Irish media, damaged Cohalan's historical legacy in de Valera's Ireland.

In contrast, Cohalan's standing among the upper strata of Irish-American society in New York remained undimmed and he continued to be active in the affairs of the American Irish Historical Society. According to the society's journal: 'For more than twenty years before his death, he [Cohalan] was the society's guiding spirit.' His contribution to the work of the AIHS was recognised in 1941 when the medal of the society, awarded annually to a distinguished American of Irish blood, was presented to Cohalan 'in a tribute to his leadership in Ireland's cause'.[16]

Cohalan's last years were wracked with illness. He spent his final months in St Luke's Hospital in New York City, where he was visited by friends and family until his death on 12 November 1946. His old friend Dick Dalton, in a letter to Lynch, recalled seeing him some months before he died and remarked that he remained surrounded by his family to the end. Dalton's letter to Lynch following Cohalan's death conveys the keen sense of loss felt by his wife Madge as well as by his friends and family at his final passing: 'Madge said to a woman friend that every glass of water she placed to his lips was received by him with a graceful, appreciative gentleness which made her feel as though every slightest thing she had done for him was a token of love and was the occasion for a blessing.'[17]

Cohalan was buried in the family plot in Calvary Cemetery in Queens County, New York. According to a report on his death in the *Irish Press*, his beloved house in Glandore had been sold the previous year to the Sacred Heart Order. According to the *Southern Star*, the house functioned from 1947 as a novitiate for the training of Catholic nuns until its sale to a private buyer in 1999.[18] Doubtless, given his strong adherence to the Catholic faith, Cohalan would have approved of this usage.

Following Cohalan's death, the controversy over his relationship with de Valera once again briefly resurfaced. As one might expect, the *Gaelic American* published a glowing tribute which challenged the criticisms made in McCartan's work: 'Judge Cohalan was regarded by friend and foe as the outstanding leader of the Irish Race and rightly so; for no man ever served his people to greater advantage than did Justice Cohalan and no man was ever more unjustly accused or maliciously maligned.'[19]

Meanwhile, the de Valera-owned *Irish Press* adopted a more critical stance and noted his 'obstruction' to de Valera's mission to the United

States.[20] Nevertheless, the paper grudgingly acknowledged the valuable contribution of Cohalan to the Irish cause: '… there can be no doubt that Judge Cohalan was a sincere friend of Ireland's cause. Obstinate in his views and difficult to work with, he was, nevertheless, generous to a degree, and the help which he gave to the independence movement in America in the early years was of the greatest value.'[21]

Diarmuid Lynch, former national secretary of the FOIF and at this time living in Ireland, took issue with these comments. He immediately wrote a long letter to the *Irish Press* defending Cohalan's reputation, claiming: '… it is not fitting that any nationalist Irishman should assess in a grudging spirit the pre-eminent services rendered to Ireland's cause, long before 1916 and long after it, by that great American of Irish blood, Daniel F. Cohalan.'[22]

As Eileen McGough points out in her comprehensive biography of Diarmuid Lynch, this defence of Cohalan provoked a 'spate of hostile letters to the *Irish Press*'. One correspondent, Mrs Kitty [Katherine] O'Doherty, claimed that: 'The Devoy–Cohalan group engineered plots to destroy the Irish Republic.'[23] Lynch compiled a detailed response to these allegations, but to his dismay the editor refused to publish, claiming that the issue had already been 'thrashed out' already, 'and I do not propose to cover that ground again'.[24]

Lynch had at this point partially completed a manuscript history of the FOIF; it portrayed Cohalan in a favourable light and attacked McCartan's account of de Valera's mission to the United States. AIHS official Dick Dalton urged Lynch to publish the manuscript so that Cohalan's name could be cleared from 'McCartan's slurs'. However, Lynch thought otherwise.[25] Writing to Dalton, he claimed:

> You can appreciate the amount of work and worry which this letter to the I.P. [*Irish Press*] gave me, in my anxiety to make my remarks 'watertight'. And yet that only represents an infinitesimal fraction of what I'd have to go through were I to attempt to edit the entire FOIF material – even as written by myself – and get it into shape for publication.[26]

In the event, Lynch never completed his manuscript, and Cohalan's role in the Irish revolution and in Irish-American affairs largely faded from historical memory, except in so far as his actions impacted on de Valera's mission.[27] Such works would inevitably portray Cohalan as a key character in de Valera's drama rather than as a pivotal figure in his own right. In 1956, Katherine O'Doherty, who had responded to Lynch's letter in the *Irish Press*, published her own book on de Valera's mission to the United States. This work, entitled *Assignment America*, argued that de Valera would have secured American recognition for an Irish republic were it not for the actions of Cohalan and Devoy. This claim underestimated Wilson's opposition to such recognition, which even de Valera later admitted on his return to Ireland. Yet such works reinforced the perception that Cohalan had obstructed de Valera's mission.

Charles Tansill's *America and the Fight for Irish Freedom* (1957) represented an exception to those works critical of Cohalan's actions during de Valera's US visit. Tansill explored American involvement in Ireland's independence struggle from 1866 to 1922, though his work is mainly focused on the revolutionary decade of 1912–22. Tansill dedicated the book to Daniel F. Cohalan and John Devoy, describing them as 'Valiant Fighters for Irish Freedom'. Though not a biography of either Cohalan or Devoy, Tansill paid considerable attention to the problems which arose between both men and de Valera. The work provides a useful narrative of the Irish-American role in the Irish revolution and it is especially strong in its use of US congressional material, as well as Cohalan's own records in the American Irish Historical Society. In contrast, O'Doherty's work largely relied on de Valera's own account of his mission.[28]

In the preface to his book, Tansill referred critically to McCartan's account of de Valera's visit to the United States as a 'long tirade of misrepresentation', claiming that later works drew their 'inspiration from the McCartan volume and repeat obvious errors'. Tansill went on to claim that: 'In these books written by the de Valera court historians, the villain of the piece is always Judge Daniel F. Cohalan. There are many examples of this hysterical scholarship.' Tansill's hostility towards de Valera and his failure to countenance any criticism of the Irish-American leaders hampered his own work's objectivity and did little to restore Cohalan's standing in Irish-American history. Historical reviews of Tansill's work immediately picked up on this obvious bias. In a review article, Irish-American historian Thomas Brown pointed out that:

> Cohalan, whose papers were made available for this study, was admired by many nationalists but had the misfortune to run foul of Woodrow Wilson and Éamon de Valera. As a consequence, Cohalan has received the worst of it in accounts of the period. In this book, it is the judge's enemies who are roundly abused but an objective and thoughtful account of his work is not attempted.[29]

In his account of the dispute between Cohalan and de Valera, Tansill correctly recognised that: 'Cohalan was, above all, an ardent American whose loyalties to his native country were basic and compelling.'[30] However, he did not explore how this American orientation sometimes distorted his view of Irish issues and influenced his interactions with Irish nationalists, including allies such as William Cosgrave. Moreover, Tansill argued that Wilson's hatred of the Irish and support for Britain led to the failure to obtain self-determination for Ireland at the Paris Peace Conference. This perspective echoed Cohalan and Devoy's own perceptions and ignored other factors shaping Wilson's policy, such as his pursuit of American interests and his determination to create a new rule-based international order. Brown, in his review of Tansill's work, also points out that: 'Wilson was an Anglophile but Tansill makes too much of this and not enough of the practical difficulties raised by the doctrine of self-determination.'[31]

Tansill's own controversial profile as a historian would not have helped his efforts to rehabilitate Cohalan's reputation. One of Tansill's earlier works, *America Goes to War* (1932), had been deeply critical of United States involvement in the First World War and had been well received, in part because it tapped into widespread isolationist sentiment in 1930s America. However, unusually, Tansill also adopted a revisionist stance on America's entry into the Second World War. In retrospect, most Americans believed this conflict was a 'good war', since it helped liberate Europe from the tyranny of Hitler's Nazism.[32] Contesting mainstream opinion, Tansill took a more isolationist position and in his work *Back Door to War* (1952) argued that Roosevelt's provocative foreign policy had led to the Japanese attack on Pearl Harbor and forced Hitler to declare war on the United States. Tansill even took an isolationist view of later American policy and called for President Kennedy's impeachment because of American participation in what he termed the 'Soviet-controlled United Nations'.

Such sentiments, which called for an abandonment of US participation in global institutions and a retreat into isolationism, would not have been popular at this time.

In 1967, Sidney Albert Brown, a British graduate student at the University of Maryland, completed a well-researched master's degree entitled 'Daniel Florence Cohalan, 1865–1946: A study of an Irish-American leader'. This thesis put forward a more nuanced view of Cohalan's involvement in the Irish revolution and also dealt with aspects of his involvement in American politics. Like Tansill, Brown drew on Cohalan's papers in the AIHS and also benefited from interviews with Cohalan's son Monsignor Florence Cohalan. Brown recognised Cohalan's significance during this tumultuous period in Irish and American history, though he criticised his stance on American neutrality in the First World War and his opposition to the League of Nations. Brown attributes these policies to anti-Britishness which Cohalan inherited from his grandfather and father who fled Ireland during the Great Famine. However, as the present work has demonstrated, Cohalan's motivations were much more complex and were shaped by a variety of forces, not least his American patriotism and a belief in Jeffersonian principles of government.

Brown never published his master's thesis and his work on Cohalan has rarely been cited. Subsequently, Cohalan's significance as an Irish-American nationalist in his own right largely faded from historical memory, though he later featured prominently as a key player in works which documented Irish efforts to enlist American political and financial support during Ireland's revolutionary period. Notable works in this field include Francis Carroll, *American Opinion and the Irish Question* (1978), Alan J. Ward's *Ireland and Anglo-American Relations* (1969) and, more recently, Bernadette Whelan's *United States Foreign Policy and Ireland, 1913–1929* (2006). My earlier work, *Irish-American Diaspora Nationalism: The Friends of Irish Freedom 1916–1935* (2005), also examined Cohalan's leadership role in the direction of this significant Irish-American movement, but the scope of all these works was necessarily limited to the study of more general Irish and American interactions rather than the political life of a single individual.

In more recent decades, Cohalan has featured in numerous biographies of de Valera, which inevitably covered the Irish leader's mission to the United States. Such works provide an interesting guide to how Cohalan has been portrayed in Irish historiography, though they naturally focus on de Valera and events from an Irish perspective. Frank Pakenham, better known as Lord Longford, and his co-author Professor Thomas P. O'Neill completed what is regarded as de Valera's 'official biography' in 1971, which they entitled *Éamon de Valera*. Longford devoted two chapters to the American mission. De Valera made available his papers and participated in interviews with Lord Longford on the topic. Longford, who admired de Valera, accepted his account at face value and the resulting work largely reflects de Valera's desire to contribute to the historical record on his American mission but also to safeguard his own reputation.[33]

As one might expect, de Valera criticised Cohalan for obstructing the bond drive and frustrating his attempts to secure recognition of the Irish republic. He also alleged that, at the Democratic convention in Chicago in 1920, Cohalan, in return for a promise of high office, had struck 'some bargain' with his preferred candidate Hiram Johnson and deliberately undermined de Valera's own resolution. As noted in the introduction, de Valera also acknowledged that Irish-Americans like Cohalan had a different agenda to the Irish nationalists but did not explain how he might have done more to take this into account in his dealings with 'The Judge'.[34] In this context, Longford's work tended to reinforce McCartan's negative view of Cohalan, even more so since McCartan was often critical of de Valera's tactics and inflexible approach.

Later biographies such as Tim Pat Coogan's *Éamon de Valera: Long fellow, long shadow* (1995) have tended to be more critical of de Valera, reflecting changing public attitudes towards his legacy as a national leader. Even still, Coogan largely saw de Valera's dispute with Cohalan as a personality clash of two large egos. Other historians take a more nuanced view. Diarmaid Ferriter's *Judging Dev* (2007) interprets the conflict between the two men as a power struggle over who should lead Irish-America, while David Hannigan's *De Valera in America: The rebel president's 1919 campaign* (2008) has a more American focus and notes how Irish-Americans like Cohalan had a different political agenda, which contributed to the conflict. As we have seen, de Valera's desire to subordinate the Irish-American movement to Dublin certainly loomed large in his mission, though none of these works explore Cohalan's motivations in any great depth since, clearly, their primary focus is on de Valera himself.

David McCullagh's *De Valera, volume 1: Rise, 1882–1932* (2017) is again solely focused on de Valera's life but takes an interesting perspective on his feud with Cohalan. McCullagh notes that de Valera went to 'somewhat irrational lengths' in opposing Cohalan and because of an innate 'insecurity' tended to see any opposition as representing a conspiracy against him.[35] Interestingly, McCullagh notes how de Valera often used his dispute with Cohalan to explain the reasons for later political conflicts. In a letter to Joe McGarrity about tensions within Sinn Féin over the treaty, de Valera blamed Michael Collins for instigating conspiracies against him in the same manner as Cohalan had conspired against him in the United States: 'M.C. [Collins] had got the IRB machine working … It was a case of Cohalan and his machine over again … Curse secret societies.'[36] In the second volume of his biography (*Rule, 1932–1975*), dealing with de Valera's leadership role in government, McCullagh again refers to how de Valera likened the opposition of Republicans who did not support him to Cohalan's obstructionism: 'Those who are barring our path now are doing exactly what Cohalan and Co. did in 1919 to 1921.'[37] McCullagh's work, therefore, highlights de Valera's inflexibility in his dealings with Cohalan, which even McCartan admitted to.[38]

Until now, Sidney Brown and Tansill are the only historians to have focused more directly on Cohalan's life and role. However, these interpretations have neglected the social and political factors behind Cohalan's Americanism, which this biography of Cohalan's life has explored. Paradoxically, F.S.L. Lyons, in his review of Tansill's work in the *Irish Times*, came closer to an explanation for Cohalan's motivations than Tansill himself. Lyons goes beyond the role of personality and power politics to show how Cohalan's nationalism, like that of other Irish-American nationalists, was shaped not just by his Irish heritage but by an American environment which was itself undergoing massive change. As noted in the introduction, Lyons perceptively attributes Cohalan's 'dual allegiance' to both Ireland and the United States to the 'tragedy of the exile'. As Lyons points out: 'However nostalgically he may look back to the mother-country, however generously he may respond to her needs, he cannot help from forming fresh attachments and striking deep roots in a new soil.'[39] The present work has argued that his 'dual allegiance', more than any other factor, shaped Cohalan's motivations. In this context, a study of Cohalan's political life offers a fascinating insight into the ideology of Irish-American nationalism during a tumultuous period in Irish history.

EPILOGUE

Cohalan and American-Irish Nationalism

Daniel Cohalan was a man of action, a man who sought to transform his vision of how the world ought to be into reality. These efforts did not always bear fruit, yet there is no doubting the passion and determination he brought to every objective he sought to achieve. A study of Cohalan's life and work on behalf of Ireland and Irish-America is thus important for its own sake. He was a pivotal figure in the Irish-American nationalist movement, especially in the 1919–20 period, and he also played a significant role in American politics. His knowledge of the American political system and his political connections added to his value for Irish nationalists in the United States, though these very American aspects of his outlook led to friction with leading Irish nationalist figures such as de Valera and Patrick McCartan.

This study of Daniel Cohalan as an Irish-American nationalist is more than a reconstruction of his political life. It offers new insights into processes of Irish cultural integration into American society in the early twentieth century. Daniel Cohalan was a product of his time. The American domestic social forces of politics, religion, class and ethnicity interacted to shape Irish-American identity and, in turn, shaped Cohalan's brand of Irish-American nationalism. These forces were very different from those shaping Irish nationalism in Ireland. Cohalan was motivated by a desire to see Irish-Americans fully accepted into American life. From his perspective, this involved challenging a prevailing Anglo-Saxon dominance in American society and a resulting British influence on its foreign policy. He saw these goals as fully compatible with the interests of Ireland, since an America free from British influence could benefit both

Ireland and the United States. The achievement of these goals motivated Cohalan's involvement in Tammany Hall politics, the American Catholic Church, Clan na Gael, and the AIHS. These goals were not always understood by Irish nationalists from Ireland who believed that the perceived interests of Irish nationalism had to come before that of the Irish in the United States. As a case in point, both de Valera and Cosgrave saw membership of the League of Nations as vital to Ireland's security interests and an illustration of Irish sovereignty.

In this context, Cohalan's often tense relationship with Irish nationalists in the United States provides an insight into how nationalists in Ireland viewed Irish-America during the revolutionary period in particular. De Valera felt that Irish-Americans should follow the instructions of the leader of the Irish nationalist movement in Ireland. His assertion of this principle had the full backing of his Sinn Féin colleagues in Dublin. Michael Collins had, after all, declared in April 1920 that the interests of the 'Home Organisation' should take precedence over the interests of 'subsidiary organisations abroad'.[1]

Cohalan's contribution to our understanding of Irish-American nationalism is best analysed through the prism of three interconnected and overlapping themes: his role as an advocate of Irish nationalism within the United States; his role as a defender of the Irish race in America and opponent of domestic 'Anglo-Saxonism'; his isolationist role as a protector of the United States against British imperial interests. These overlapping roles in turn determined his relationship with Irish nationalists in both the United States and Ireland.

Throughout his life, Cohalan's actions demonstrated a strong allegiance to the cause of Irish independence and Irish economic prosperity. As Benjamin Reid pointed out in his biography *The Man from New York: John Quinn and his friends*, Cohalan was a member of a qualified Irishry: 'These were men of modest wealth who could still be depended upon to put their hands in their pockets for a hundred or five hundred dollars for almost any good Irish cause.'[2] Indeed Cohalan went beyond this to devote considerable amounts of his time and energy to the cause of republican Irish nationalism in the United States, despite his many other commitments as a New York State Supreme Court Justice.

In turn, Irish nationalists such as Douglas Hyde, Patrick Pearse, Éamon de Valera and William Cosgrave recognised how Cohalan's status in the United States and immense reservoir of goodwill for Ireland could be harnessed for their own particular objectives. In the immediate post-war period, 1919–20, Cohalan's political connections heightened his value to the Irish cause within the United States, especially with regard to fundraising and congressional support for the recognition of Irish independence. Cosgrave also exploited Cohalan's political contacts as he sought to forge economic and diplomatic links with the US and consolidate international acceptance of the new Irish state in the early 1920s.

Through his leadership roles in the Clan and the FOIF, his influence in the Clan newspaper the *Gaelic American* and his active role in numerous other Irish-American societies, Cohalan succeeded in bringing the Irish cause to US national attention and won important congressional resolutions in favour of Irish self-determination. Yet he failed to persuade President Wilson to apply his principles of self-determination to Ireland. Cohalan attributed this to Wilson's known pro-Britishness, but this work has explored how other geopolitical factors and practical considerations played a more significant role in Wilson's decision-making. Whether Cohalan would have persuaded the Republican Party to adopt a more interventionist policy towards Ireland if an Irish plank had been secured at the Chicago Republican convention remains an open question. Certainly, FOIF leader Bishop Michael Gallagher seemed to think so, though, as we have seen, Warren Harding had never identified with the Irish question prior to his presidency and the presence of such a plank might not have impacted a great deal on the traditional US policy of maintaining good relations with Britain.

The infighting between the various Irish factions in the US and the demise of the FOIF as an organised force weakened Cohalan's standing among Irish-American nationalists. Yet he still remained an influential figure in American politics. After the Irish treaty split and subsequent Civil War of 1922–3, when many of his fellow Irish-Americans turned away in disgust from Ireland, Cohalan still maintained a keen interest in Irish affairs in spite of the many accusations levied against him at the time of the split and before. He reluctantly supported the treaty, which brought Ireland's War of Independence to a close and led to the establishment of the new Irish Free State. While he would have preferred the establishment of a republic, he nevertheless believed that the degree of independence which Ireland had achieved offered a step towards greater independence. He echoed the views of most Irish-Americans in this regard.

Cohalan believed that a close economic connection between an independent Ireland and the United States would be of immense benefit to Ireland. His private papers at the American Irish Historical Society in New York reveal a close friendship with Irish Free State leaders such as President William Cosgrave and Minister Joe McGrath.[3] While always ready with advice and encouragement, Cohalan did not hold back from criticism of the progress being made by the new Irish state on a host of fronts. Feeling that the Cosgrave government was not doing enough to assert Irish independence, he actively supported breakaway groups with financial support and advice, though he always ruled out support for de Valera's opposition party.

Cohalan's work on behalf of the Irish state in the US highlights how the links between Irish government policymakers and the Irish-American diaspora have their origin in the very foundations of the Irish Free State. Yet the story of Cohalan's earlier relationship with Irish leaders also illustrates how misunderstandings on both sides can, in Patrick McCartan's words, bring 'ruin' to Irish nationalist hopes.[4]

As this biography has explored, there was an important American dimension to Cohalan's Irish nationalism which was shared by many prominent Irish-Americans at this time. Cohalan believed that the White Anglo-Saxon Protestant (WASP) character of the American host culture shaped the experience of the Catholic Irish ethnic group in America. In particular, he believed that there had always been a predisposition among some elite members of American society to equate the interests of America with those of Britain. Worse still, from Cohalan's perspective, this pro-British elite seemed to be gaining influence in America in the early twentieth century as social, political and cultural ties between England and the US increased.[5] This opposition to 'Anglo-Saxonism' was a constant refrain in his speeches and publications and shaped his strategy towards winning American support for Irish independence.

Not all Irish-American nationalists shared these fears, but considerable numbers did. FOIF president Bishop Michael Gallagher's commentary on de Valera's dispute with Cohalan represents an eloquent testimony to such beliefs among the higher echelons of the FOIF and the AIHS. Irish-American Catholics in particular sought acceptance as American citizens and wished to be recognised as such. They did not want to be seen as representing the interests of foreign leaders, since this would play into the hands of those who argued that Irish-Americans were not fully loyal to the United States.[6] Diarmuid Lynch, though a relatively recent immigrant from Ireland, agreed with Cohalan's approach. He began his ultimately unpublished manuscript history of the FOIF with a quotation from a famous Irish-American nationalist, John Boyle O'Reilly. O'Reilly had stated: 'We can do more good by our Americanism than by our Irishism.' This phrase neatly sums up Cohalan's ideological approach to promoting the Irish cause in the United States and it determined his attitude towards Ireland itself.[7]

Throughout his life, Cohalan witnessed enormous changes in perceptions of the Irish community in the United States. By 1946, the year of his death, the Catholic Irish ethnic group had become more integrated into American society, though it would still be another fourteen years before an Irish-American would be elected president of the United States. With the election of John F. Kennedy in 1960, it could now be argued that the ethnic defensiveness which characterised many of Cohalan's beliefs and actions in the early twentieth century was no longer warranted.[8] However, one cannot understand Cohalan's motives without reference to the cultural standing of the Irish ethnic group in early twentieth-century America and his own understanding of what perpetuated this status.

The defence of United States interests remained an important ingredient in Cohalan's American-centred Irish nationalism. He was first and foremost an American but he saw his allegiance to the United States and the Irish nationalist cause as perfectly compatible. He viewed Ireland's struggle against the British Empire in the same light as America's own revolutionary struggle against the same enemy. An independent Ireland, free from what he saw as Britain's tyrannical grasp, could also be a staunch friend of the United States.[9] Cohalan sympathised with other struggling nationalists and he peppered his speeches with references to the plight of India, Egypt and other parts of the British Empire struggling to obtain more freedom. As he explained in a pamphlet published in 1925 entitled *Democracy or Imperialism, which?*, 'If imperialism grows, it grows at the expense of freedom. If democracy grows, it grows at the expense of imperialism.'[10]

In his campaign to prevent American involvement in the struggles of the 'Old World', Cohalan maintained close contact with influential isolationist figures in Congress such as Senator William Borah and Senator James Reed. Given Cohalan's stature, mainstream publications such as the *New York Times* covered his speeches, and so his views reached a wide audience. This carried weight among the opinion-formers of the day. The Clan newspaper the *Gaelic American*, which Devoy edited, devoted considerable attention to foreign affairs, and Cohalan's ideas on this subject often featured on its front pages and in its editorials. In this way, Cohalan tried to shape Irish-American nationalist thought on international affairs, though with mixed success.

Cohalan voiced Irish-American fears about British intrigue in the United States. Somewhat naively, he felt that American presidents such as Woodrow Wilson and Franklin Roosevelt had a pro-British foreign policy agenda, given their Anglo-Saxon heritage. This perspective tended to ignore how other geopolitical and ideological motivations shaped their foreign policy objectives.[11] Nevertheless, the perception that these presidents had an inherent British bias shaped many of Cohalan's pronouncements on American foreign policy. He used his influence in the *Gaelic American*, and his leadership role in the Clan and later in the Friends of Irish Freedom (FOIF), to alert Irish-Americans about this perceived intrigue. However, Irish-Americans, as witnessed by their support in presidential elections for Wilson and Roosevelt, tended to vote on domestic economic issues rather than on foreign policy questions.

John J. Sheanan, writing for the *National Hibernian Digest* in 1948, headed his piece 'Daniel F. Cohalan, Defender of American Principles and an Ardent Lover of Ireland'.[12] This loyalty to both Ireland and the United States characterised Cohalan's life and actions, and, alongside an analysis of Cohalan's support for Irish revolutionary activities in the United States, this biography has explored how his sense of Irish nationalism was deeply influenced by his American patriotism. Cohalan's struggle as an Irish nationalist to secure Irish independence, his aim as an Irish-American to promote the status of the Irish community in the US, and his desire as an American to secure the interests of the United States were all intertwined. For Cohalan, these objectives were both compatible and mutually reinforcing.

Notes

Introduction: American Patriot and Irish-American Nationalist

1 In 1967, Sidney Brown completed a valuable MA thesis (unpublished) on Cohalan which is particularly strong on his nationalist activities during the Irish revolution, 1916–1921. Sidney Albert Brown, 'Daniel Florence Cohalan, 1865–1946: A study of an Irish-American leader', MA thesis, University of Maryland, 1967; Matthew Guterl, in a chapter entitled 'Bleeding the Irish White', recognises the significance of Cohalan in challenging the dominant conception of American identity in the early twentieth century. M. Guterl, *The Color of Race in America, 1900–1940* (Boston: Harvard University Press, 2002). See also Michael Doorley, 'Judge Daniel Cohalan: American Irish nationalist and crusader against British influence in American life', *New Hibernia Review*, vol. 19, no. 2, Summer 2015. Francis Carroll has also written an article on Cohalan for the comprehensive *Dictionary of Irish Biography* (Cambridge: Cambridge University Press/Royal Irish Academy, n.d.).

2 Éamon de Valera (1882–1975) was born in New York but was brought up in Ireland. He was elected president of the Irish nationalist party Sinn Féin in October 1917. He spent eighteen months in the United States, from June 1919 to December 1920, seeking funds and American diplomatic support for Irish independence. For a comprehensive account of his dispute with Cohalan, see Francis Carroll, *American Opinion and the Irish Question* (London: Macmillan, 1978), pp. 149–93. Most biographies of de Valera cover his American mission. See, for instance, David McCullagh, *De Valera, volume 1: Rise, 1882–1932* (Dublin: Gill Books, 2017), pp. 162–88.

3 De Valera to Arthur Griffith, 6 March 1920. Cited in T. Ryle Dwyer, *De Valera: The man and the myths* (Dublin: Poolbeg, 1991), p. 35.

4 Members of Tammany Hall, the Democratic Party's political machine in New York, often used Native American terms to describe aspects of their organisation. 'Sachem' meant chief, while the building where Tammany meetings were held was called the 'Wigwam'. Charles Francis 'Silent Charlie' Murphy (1858–1924), known as 'Boss Murphy', dominated Tammany Hall from 1902 to 1924. For more on the politics behind Cohalan's appointment to the New York Supreme Court, see Nancy Joan Weiss, *Charles Francis Murphy, 1858–1924: Respectability and responsibility in Tammany politics* (New York: Smith College, 1968), pp. 48–9. See also *New York Times*, 19 May 1911. For a more recent history of Tammany, see Terry Golway, *Machine Made: Tammany Hall and the creation of modern American politics* (New York: Liveright, 2014).

5 William Borah (1865–1940) became well known for his isolationist views and, like James Reed (1861–1944), opposed the League of Nations. Bainbridge Colby (1869–1950) was a powerful figure in the Democratic Party and served as secretary of state from 1920 to 1921 during the last year of President Woodrow Wilson's administration. He corresponded with Cohalan throughout his life: fl. 6, Box 3,

Cohalan Papers, AIHS. Frank Walsh (1864–1939) also served as joint president (with William Howard Taft, 1857–1930) of Wilson's War Labor Conference Board during the war. John Francis Curry (1873–1957) was from County Fermanagh and served as Tammany leader from 1929 to 1934.

6 *New York Times*, 22 June 1936.

7 Until his appointment to the judiciary in 1911, Cohalan was chairman of the New York Clan, known as District 1. Thereafter, he played a less formal but no less important advisory role. See Clan leader Jim Reidy's letter to Frank Robbins, 24 April 1949, Devoy Papers, MS 18,011/8/1, NLI. Frank Robbins had been a member of James Connolly's Citizen Army and had taken part in the 1916 Rising. Robbins had later spoken at Clan meetings in New York, where he met Cohalan and Devoy. Robbins' 'witness statement' to the Bureau of Military History (BMH) represents a fascinating account of interactions between so-called Irish 'exiles' and the Clan (BMH WS 585). For more on Cohalan's relationship with Devoy, see Terry Golway, *John Devoy and America's Fight for Ireland's Freedom* (New York: St Martin's Press, 1998).

8 Cohalan's disputes with Joseph McGarrity are covered in Sean Cronin, *The McGarrity Papers: Revelations of the Irish revolutionary movement in Ireland and America, 1900–1940* (Tralee: Anvil Books, 1972). Cronin takes an anti-Cohalan and pro-McGarrity line.

9 Michael Doorley, *Irish-American Diaspora Nationalism: The Friends of Irish Freedom, 1916–1935* (Dublin: Four Courts Press, 2005). This work covers Cohalan's leadership of the FOIF.

10 US Bureau of the Census, *Twelfth Census of the United States 1900: Population* (Washington, 1901), p. clxx; A.J. Ward, *Ireland and Anglo-American Relations, 1890–1921* (London: Weidenfeld & Nicolson, 1969), p. 126.

11 In the introduction to Cohalan's publication *The Indictment* (New York: FOIF, 1919), the Hon. John Rooney, former Chief Judge of the Court of Claims of New York State, declared that: 'Justice Cohalan is today the leader of the Irish Race and the Irish Cause in America.'

12 Patrick McCartan (1878–1963) from Carrickmore, County Tyrone, had emigrated to the United States as a young man. He later returned to Ireland and became involved in Sinn Féin activities prior to the 1916 Rising. For more on both McGarrity and McCartan, see Maura Anand, Andrew S. Hicks and Bryan Willits, 'The Man from Philadelphia: Joseph McGarrity and 1914', in Miriam Nyhan Grey (ed.), *Ireland's Allies: America and the 1916 rising* (Dublin: UCD Press, 2016), pp. 109–23. McCartan published an account of de Valera's mission to the United States in 1932 which was strongly critical of Cohalan. His work highlights tensions within the Irish-American nationalist movement prior to de Valera's arrival. Patrick McCartan, *With de Valera in America* (Dublin: Fitzpatrick Ltd., 1932).

13 Cohalan's papers are stored in New York in the American Irish Historical Society (AIHS). Refer to Box 3 and Box 18 for Cohalan's correspondence with William T. Cosgrave (1880–1965), the first president of the executive council of the Irish Free State. The correspondence of Irish diplomatic officials in the United States also highlights Cohalan's continuing influence in Irish-American affairs in the early 1920s. See *Documents on Irish Foreign Policy*, vol. 1, 1919–1922 (Dublin: Royal Irish Academy, 1998).

14 James Reidy, who had been a prominent member of the Clan in the early twentieth century, had enclosed a copy of this biographical sketch of Justice Daniel Cohalan from the *Digest*, with a letter, to Frank Robbins, 24 April 1949: Devoy Papers, MS 18,011/8/1. See also *National Hibernian Digest*, April/May 1948.

15 D. Lynch, 'Typescript History of the Friends of Irish Freedom and Associated Societies', Florence O'Donoghue Papers, MS 32597 (1–2). Diarmuid Lynch (1878–1950) was born in Cork and emigrated to the United States in 1896. Lynch returned to Ireland in 1907 and took part in the 1916 Rising. Deported to the US, he became national secretary of the Friends of Irish Freedom in May 1918. Lynch's manuscript on the FOIF was strongly supportive of Cohalan and in turn very critical of de Valera. Believing that his defence of Cohalan would not be understood in the Ireland of the 1940s, Lynch never proceeded with publication. The manuscript, running to 600 pages, is now in the National Library of Ireland and is a valuable source on Cohalan's leadership of the FOIF.

16 *Irish Times*, 24 January 1964. Padraic Colum (1881–1972) was born in County Longford and became a leading figure in the Irish literary revival. His article in the *Irish Times* was mainly about John Devoy but he also included background information on McGarrity and Cohalan. Colum described Devoy, Cohalan and McGarrity as the three 'chiefs' of the Clan in 1915.

17 Cited in Piaras Béaslaí, *Michael Collins and the Making of a New Ireland*, vol. 2 (Dublin: Phoenix Press, 1926), p. 9. De Valera's own account of his mission is also critical of Cohalan. See 'The American Mission: An account', dictated by de Valera to Marie Kelly, 19 November 1962, P150/1100, University College Dublin Archives (UCDA). See also David Fitzpatrick, *Harry Boland's Irish Revolution* (Cork: Cork University Press, 2003), p. 145.

18 Press release, McGarrity Papers, MS17445, NLI. See also de Valera Papers, 150/1155, UCDA, and *Irish World*, 30 October 1920.

19 Irish National Archives (INA), Crime Branch Special (CBS IGCI), Inspector General's monthly report for August 1906, Box 10. The Royal Irish Constabulary (RIC) policed Ireland on behalf of the British Crown and its intelligence division kept a close watch on the IRB and visiting Clan members.

20 Cohalan's message to Germany appeared in *Documents Relative to the Sinn Féin Movement* (London: HMSO, 1921) (Cmnd 1108), xxix, 429, p. 13. British intelligence had broken German codes and could read Clan messages to Germany. R. Doerries, *Prelude to the Easter Rising: Sir Roger Casement in imperial Germany* (London: Frank Cass Publishers, 2000), p. 58. See also German records entitled 'Operations and Incitements among the Irish against Our Foes', located in the German Foreign Office Archive on the World War, Weltkrieg, No. 11k, Das Politisches Archiv des Auswärtigan Amts (PAAA), Berlin.

21 Cited in James McGurrin, *Bourke Cockran: A free lance in American politics* (New York: Charles Scribner's Sons, 1948), p. 237. Arthur Brisbane was at this time a well-known newspaper editor and journalist. Brisbane was not an entirely unbiased observer of Cohalan. He was a close friend of newspaper tycoon William Randolph Hearst (1863–1951), who allied himself with Cohalan in opposing the League of Nations and the British Empire. See Hearst correspondence with Cohalan in fl. 2, Box 7, Cohalan Papers, AIHS.

22 Cited in D.T. O'Connell, 'Irish Influence on America's Foreign Policy: The work of our National Bureau in Washington', in W.G. FitzGerald (ed.), *The Voice of Ireland* (Dublin: John Heywood, 1923), p. 236. Henry Cabot Lodge (1850–1924) was Republican senator for Massachusetts and became an important ally of Cohalan in the FOIF battle against the League of Nations.

23 Cohalan's obituary, *New York Times*, 13 November 1946. James Beauchamp 'Champ' Clark (1850–1921) served in the US House of Representatives for twenty-six years and was speaker of the house from 1911 to 1919. John A. Garraty and Mark C.

Carnes, 'Clark, Champ', *American National Biography*, vol. 4 (New York: Oxford University Press, 1999).

24 Tumulty to Wilson, 1 March 1919, cited in J.M. Blum, *Joe Tumulty and the Wilson Era* (Hamden, CT: Archon Books, 1969), p. 176.

25 Edith Bolling Wilson, *My Memoir* (Indianapolis: Bobbs-Merrill Company, 1939), pp. 242–3. Edith Wilson was the president's second wife. See also *New York Times*, 10 March 1919.

26 Thomas Brown, *Irish-American Nationalism, 1870–1890* (Philadelphia: Lippincott, 1966); David Emmons, *The Butte Irish: Class and ethnicity in an American mining town, 1885–1925* (Champaign, IL: University of Illinois Press, 1989); Matthew Frye Jacobson, *Special Sorrows: The diasporic imagination of Irish, Polish and Jewish immigrants in the United States* (Berkeley: University of California Press, 2002). For an account of how historians have interpreted Irish-American nationalism, see David Brundage, 'Recent Directions in the History of Irish-American Nationalism', *Journal of American Ethnic History*, vol. 28, no. 4, Summer 2009, pp. 82–9.

27 David Brundage, *Irish Nationalists in America: The politics of exile, 1798–1998* (New York: Oxford University Press, 2016).

28 Kerby Miller, *Emigrants and Exiles: Ireland and the Irish exodus to North America* (New York: Oxford University Press, 1985), pp. 7, 277–8, 556; T.J. Meagher, *The Columbia Guide to Irish American History* (New York: Columbia University Press, 2005), pp. 198–213.

29 Gerardine Meaney, Mary O'Dowd and Bernadette Whelan, *Reading the Irish Woman: Studies in cultural encounters and exchange, 1714–1960* (Liverpool: Liverpool University Press, 2013), pp. 3–4, 87–105.

30 *Gaelic American*, 1 July 1911.

31 Joe Lee, 'Foreword', in Grey (ed.), *Ireland's Allies*, pp. xxix–xxxi. This work covers the many American links of those who took part in the rising. See also Robert Schmuhl, *Ireland's Exiled Children: America and the Easter Rising* (New York: Oxford University Press, 2016).

32 Cohalan's role in the rising is examined in Michael Doorley, 'Judge Cohalan and American Involvement in the 1916 Rising', in Grey (ed.), *Ireland's Allies*, pp. 151–64.

33 Kevin Kenny, *The American Irish* (London: Longman, 2000), pp. 195–6.

34 Bernadette Whelan, *United States Foreign Policy and Ireland: From empire to independence, 1913–1929* (Dublin: Four Courts Press, 2006).

35 This correspondence is available in the AIHS. Chapter 10 will draw on rarely used correspondence between McGrath and Cohalan in the Dún Laoghaire Rathdown County Council Archives (DLRCA) to explore Cohalan's involvement in the Irish army mutiny of 1924.

36 T.J. Sarbaugh, 'Ireland of the West: The development of Irish republicanism in California 1900–1916', *Pacific History*, vol. 28, no. 1, 1984, pp. 43–52.

37 Kenny, *The American Irish*, pp. 208–9.

38 Cited in A. Mann, *The One and the Many: Reflections on the American identity* (Chicago: University of Chicago Press, 1979), pp. 127–8. See also Madison Grant, *The Passing of the Great Race: Or, the racial basis of European history* (New York: Sandycroft Publications, 1916), pp. 58–9.

39 Guterl, *The Color of Race in America*, p. 69.

40 Ibid., pp. 68–99.

41 *Metropolis*, 15 March 1921.

42 Alison Kibler, *Censoring Racial Ridicule: Irish, Jewish and African American struggles over race and representation, 1890–1930* (Chapel Hill, NC: University of North Carolina Press,

2015), p. 30. See also Kibler, 'The Stage Irishwoman', *Journal of American Ethnic History*, vol. 24, no. 3, Spring 2005, pp. 5–30.

43 Kibler, 'The Stage Irishwoman', p. 7.

44 Ibid., p. 2.

45 Cohalan's role as fundraiser for the league is evident also in the John Quinn Memorial Collection, in the New York Public Library (NYPL). In her work on the Gaelic Revival in America, Ní Bhroiméil highlights how these objectives of the league in America sometimes led to conflicts with the home organisation in Ireland. Úna Ní Bhroiméil, *Building Irish Identity in America, 1890–1915: The Gaelic revival* (Dublin: Four Courts Press, 2003).

46 *Gaelic American*, 18 June 1904.

47 Kibler, *Censoring Racial Ridicule*, p. 33.

48 Interview with Justice Cohalan in *Metropolis*, 15 March 1921.

49 This was a constant theme in Cohalan's many speeches and writings, which are now archived at the American Irish Historical Society (AIHS), New York. See, for instance, Daniel Cohalan, *Andrew Jackson: Hero of New Orleans. An address before the American Irish Historical Society at its annual banquet, Hotel Astor, January 1930* (New York: Allied Printing, 1930).

50 Golway, *Machine Made*, pp. xx, xxiv. Golway also highlights the role of Tammany in assimilating the Irish, pp. 307–8.

51 Bourke Cockran (1854–1923) served as a Democratic congressman for New York for a number of terms, notably 1904–9 and 1921–3. Cockran turned against Redmond after the 1916 Rising.

52 Daniel Cohalan, *Democracy or Imperialism, which?* (New York: Friends of Irish Freedom, 1925).

53 Cohalan's speech to the First Irish Race Convention, *Gaelic American*, 11 March 1916.

54 This work is very partisan in favour of Cohalan. Charles Tansill, *America and the Fight for Irish Freedom, 1866–1922* (New York: The Devin-Adair Co., 1957), p. 194.

55 Carl Wittke, *The Irish in America* (Baton Rouge: Louisiana State University Press, 1956), p. 275.

56 Bradford Perkins, *The Great Rapprochement: England and the United States, 1895–1914* (New York: Scribner, 1968), pp. 296–314. For a contemporary account of the Irish question in Anglo-American relations, see David Sim, *A Union Forever: The Irish question and US foreign relations in the Victorian age* (New York: Cornell University Press, 2013).

57 H. Brogan, *The Penguin History of the United States of America*, 2nd edn (London: Penguin Books, 1999), pp. 438–9. For a comprehensive overview of how British and US diplomatic relations evolved in the nineteenth and twentieth centuries, see Kathleen Burk, *Old World, New World: Great Britain and America from the beginning* (New York: Atlantic Monthly Press, 2008).

58 Robert E. Hannigan, *The Great War and American Foreign Policy, 1914–24* (Philadelphia: University of Pennsylvania Press, 2016), pp, x, 4–6. Hannigan also argues that Wilson had little regard for the rights of small nations in Latin America and Europe in pursuing these global ambitions.

59 John Milton Cooper, *Breaking the Heart of the World: Woodrow Wilson and the fight for the League of Nations* (New York: Cambridge University Press, 2001), p. 416.

60 Whelan, *United States Foreign Policy and Ireland*, pp. 28–9.

61 M. Doorley, '"The Judge" versus "The Chief": Daniel Cohalan and the 1920 split within Irish America', *History Ireland*, vol. 23, no. 2, March/April 2015, pp. 44–7.

62 *DIFP* (*Documents on Irish Foreign Policy*), vol. 1, Document 30, National Archives of Ireland (NAI) DE 2/245, de Valera to Griffith, 17 February 1920.

63 The exchange of letters between de Valera and Cohalan, which Lyons refers to, is located in both Cohalan and de Valera's papers. De Valera to Cohalan, 20 February 1920; Cohalan to de Valera, 22 February 1920, de Valera Papers, P150/1134, UCDA; Cohalan Papers, fl. 1, Box 4, AIHS. F.S.L. Lyons, 'The Irish Americans: A dual allegiance', *Irish Times*, 3 December 1957.

1. The Making of an American-Irish Nationalist, 1865–1903

1 Letter from Monsignor Florence Cohalan to Brown, 23 June 1967, cited in Brown, 'Daniel Florence Cohalan, 1865–1946', p. 2. Florence Cohalan (1907–2001) was a monsignor in the Archdiocese of New York and served for over fifty years as leader of the American Irish Historical Society (AIHS). He was also official historian of the Archdiocese of New York and wrote *A Popular History of the Archdiocese of New York* (Yonkers: US Catholic Historical Society, 1983).

2 P. Hickey, 'The Famine in the Skibbereen Union (1845–51)', in Cathal Póirtéir (ed.), *The Great Irish Famine* (Cork: Mercier Press, 1995), p. 196.

3 In the Skibbereen area, while the mortality rate was 17 per cent, the emigration rate was only 2.4 per cent. Hickey, 'The Famine in the Skibbereen Union (1845–51)', p. 197. Those with little means either died, entered overcrowded workhouses or somehow made their way to England or Scotland.

4 Cormac Ó Gráda, *Black 47 and Beyond: The Great Irish Famine in history, economy and memory* (Princeton: Princeton University Press, 1999), p. 109. In an interview, Peter Fox Cohalan, grand-nephew of Daniel Cohalan, claims that the Cohalan family were relatively prosperous and their decision to leave was not motivated by hunger but by a desire for a better life in the United States. Peter Fox Cohalan is himself a retired New York State Supreme Court Justice, indicating the continuing links between his family and the New York judiciary down through the generations. Peter's son Pierce Cohalan became a district court judge in 2014 and is the sixth member of the Cohalan family over four generations to become a New York State jurist. Interview with Peter Fox Cohalan, Sayville, New York, 29 April 2017.

5 Gaelic American, 18 December 1909; Christine Kinealy, *The Great Irish Famine: Impact, ideology and rebellion* (New York: Palgrave, 2002), pp. 36–40.

6 *Cork Examiner*, 16 December 1846.

7 T.P. O'Connor, *Home Rule Movement* (New York: Benziger Bros, 1891), p. 117. The impact of Famine memories on Irish America is also discussed in James S. Donnelly, *The Great Irish Potato Famine* (Stroud, Gloucestershire: Sutton Publishing, 2001), pp. 228–9. One prominent political exile from Ireland, John Mitchel (1815–75), claimed that the Famine was a deliberate attempt to depopulate Ireland. The Mitchel view of the Famine as a British genocide thus became central to the ideology of many Famine immigrants and their descendants. John Mitchel, *The Last Conquest of Ireland (Perhaps)* (Glasgow: Washbourne, 1882).

8 Daniel Cohalan, *The Indictment* (New York: Friends of Irish Freedom, 1919), p. 1.

9 Donnelly, *The Great Irish Potato Famine*, pp. 171–8. US Bureau of the Census, *Twelfth Census of the United States 1900: population*, p. clxx.

10 *United States of America, Bureau of the Census, Eighth Census of the United States*, the town of Wallkill, Orange County, New York (Washington, DC: National Archives and Records Administration, 1860). *New York Times*, 19 May 1911. See also obituaries of Timothy Cohalan, *New York Times*, 9 December 1909, *Middletown Record*, 9 December 1909, and the *Gaelic American*, 18 December 1909.

11 James McGurrin, in his biography of Bourke Cockran, notes these connections between the Cohalan family and the American revolutionary war: McGurrin, *Bourke*

Cockran, p. 237. In the eighteenth century, many young Irishmen found service in foreign armies, especially those fighting against England.

12 Cohalan, *The Indictment*, p. 9. Irish-American support for Irish nationalism predated the Irish Famine. For more on the development of a 'diasporic nationalism' among the Irish in the United States, see Brundage, *Irish Nationalists in America*.

13 *Gaelic American*, 9 December 1909.

14 James W. Hurst, 'Fenian Brotherhood', in M.F. Funchion (ed.), *Irish-American Voluntary Organisations* (Westport, CT: Greenwood Press, 1983), p. 107.

15 For a comprehensive account of the 1866 invasion, see David Doolin, *Transnational Revolutionaries: The Fenian invasion of Canada 1866* (Oxford: Peter Lang, 2016).

16 *Gaelic American*, 18 December 1909, 1 July 1911. After Timothy's death, both the *Southern Star* and the *Middletown Record* provided a comprehensive account of Timothy's life: see *Southern Star*, 1 January 1910; *Middletown Record*, 9 December 1909.

17 Michael J. Cohalan, like his four brothers, entered the legal profession. Michael J. O'Brien et al. (eds), 'Michael J. Cohalan', *Journal of the American Irish Historical Society*, vol. xxv, 1926, pp. 317–18.

18 Brown, *Irish-American Nationalism*, p. xiv.

19 John Devoy, *Recollections of an Irish Rebel* (New York: Chase & Young, 1929), p. 393.

20 'A Notable Irish Nationalist Dead', *Gaelic American*, 18 December 1909. Many Clan branches were named after Irish revolutionary heroes. James Napper Tandy (1739–1803) had taken part in the 1798 Irish rebellion, which had been put down with great severity by the British government.

21 *New York World*, 7 May 1923; *Gaelic American*, 12 May 1923.

22 Brown, 'Daniel Florence Cohalan, 1865–1946', p. 2. *Southern Star*, 1 January 1910.

23 *New York Times*, 13 November 1946. There are no Cohalan letters written in Irish located in his extensive collection of papers, so this facility with the language may only have been oral. His parents would not have been taught to write Irish in school as the schooling system in 1830s Ireland was designed to encourage only literacy in the English language.

24 Aileen O'Leary Cohalan, RSCJ, 'Memoirs', ed. Claire Kondoff, RSCJ. Unpublished manuscript in the possession of Peter Fox Cohalan, pp. 4–5.

25 Kenny, *The American Irish*, pp. 112–20.

26 William E. Van Vugt, 'British and British Americans (English, Scots, Scots Irish, and Welsh), to 1870', in R. Barkan (ed.), *Immigrants in American History: Arrival, adaptation, and integration* (Santa Barbara, CA: ABC-CLIO, 2013), p. 19.

27 *New York Times*, 19 May 1911.

28 *Southern Star*, 1 January 1910.

29 Interview with Judge Cohalan in *Metropolis*, 15 March 1921.

30 *New York Times*, 9 December 1909; *Middletown Record*, 9 December 1909.

31 Brown, 'Daniel Florence Cohalan, 1865–1946', pp. 2–3.

32 Golway, *Machine Made*, pp. xxi–xxiv. Cohalan maintained his links with Manhattan College after graduation and served as president of its Alumni Association for a number of years. He later acted as the college's legal representative in various property deals in the 1920s. Cohalan Papers, AIHS, Box 9 and 18.

33 Brown, 'Daniel Florence Cohalan, 1865–1946', p. 2. *New York Times*, 19 May 1911. See also *New York Times* obituary of Daniel Cohalan, 13 November 1946.

34 Brown, 'Daniel Florence Cohalan, 1865–1946', p. 3.

35 *New York Times*, 18 May 1911. This newspaper report mentions that Timothy Cohalan had suffered reverses in his glass business at this time.

36 Miller, *Emigrants and Exiles*, p. 521.

37 *New York Herald Tribune*, 13 November 1946.
38 *New York Times*, 21 April 1919: 'Cohalan Assails England, Says She Exploits Ireland by Monopolising Foreign Trade'.
39 John R. McKivigan and Thomas J. Robertson, 'The Irish American Worker in Transition, 1877–1914', in Ronald Bayor and Timothy Meagher (eds), *The New York Irish* (Baltimore: Johns Hopkins University Press, 1997), p. 303.
40 The house is still standing and is listed in much of Cohalan's correspondence in the AIHS. Aileen Cohalan, 'Memoirs'. See also Hanna's obituary in the *New York Times*, 19 May 1911, and *Gaelic American*, I July 1911.
41 Meaney, O'Dowd and Whelan, 'The Emigrant Encounters the New World', p. 89.
42 *Gaelic American*, 1 July 1911.
43 Parnell, a Protestant landowner, led a constitutional nationalist movement which strove to attain home rule for Ireland within the British Empire. However, a scandal involving his relationship with a married woman, Kitty O'Shea, provoked a split within his party and most Catholic Church leaders in Ireland subsequently distanced themselves from him. Reflecting the complexity of Irish history, Hanna's brother, Major John O'Leary, served as a medical doctor in the British army and died in 1915 on active service in Egypt during the First World War. See Aileen Cohalan, 'Memoirs'. Interview with Peter Fox Cohalan, Sayville, New York, 29 April 2017.
44 See, for instance, *Southern Star*, 11 July 1914, which wished Cohalan a pleasant stay in the area. The Cohalan family continued their visits there until the 1930s.
45 'Cohalan's Daughter to Become a Nun Today', *New York Times*, 20 October 1930. Aileen's account of her decision to become a nun, which her father fully approved of, is contained in her memoirs.
46 Cohalan's visits to Ireland are documented in 'Passenger and Crew Lists of Vessels Arriving at New York, New York, 1897–1957' (National Archives Microfilm Publication T715 8892 rolls): Records of the Immigration and Naturalisation Service, National Archives, Washington DC.
47 Aileen Cohalan, 'Memoirs', p. 6.
48 Interview with Fachtna Hickey, 9 January 2019; photograph available in *Southern Star* archives; Coombes, *Utopia in Glandore*, p. 41.
49 Aileen Cohalan, 'Memoirs', p. 6.
50 *The Southern Star Centenary Supplement, 1889–1989*, p. 98; Aileen Cohalan, 'Memoirs', p. 20; Family Correspondence Bishop Daniel Cohalan, Cohalan Papers, Box 18, fl. 5, AIHS.
51 *Southern Star*, 28 September 1912.
52 Diarmuid Lynch, *The IRB and the 1916 Insurrection* (Cork: Mercier Press, 1957), p. 12. Alvin Jackson, *Ireland 1798–1998* (Oxford: Blackwell, 1999), p. 104.
53 Philip Fennell and Marie King (eds), *John Devoy's Catalpa Expedition* (New York: NYU Press, 2008), p. 41. See also 'Passing of Judge John Goff', *Gaelic American*, 22 November 1924. Goff served on the New York State Supreme Court bench from 1906 to 1918.
54 The IRB in Ireland had also opposed the Chicago wing's bombing of British cities in the 1880s. For more on this campaign, see Shane Kenna, *War in the Shadows: The Irish-American Fenians who bombed Victorian Britain* (Dublin: Irish Academic Press, 2014).
55 Carroll, *American Opinion*, p. 8.
56 Circular to members of the Clan na Gael, 10 October 1900, Cohalan Papers, Box 2, AIHS. Also cited in Brown, 'Daniel Florence Cohalan, 1865–1946', p. 16.
57 Clan circular, 10 October 1900, Cohalan Papers, Box 2, AIHS.
58 James Reidy to Frank Robbins, 24 April 1949, Devoy Papers, MS 18,011/8/1, NLI.

59 This is evidenced from Devoy's papers in the National Library of Ireland and Cohalan's papers in the American Irish Historical Society.

60 James Reidy to Frank Robbins, 24 April 194. Cohalan's chairmanship of the Clan is noted in the British government publication *Documents Relative to the Sinn Féin Movement*, PP 1921 (Cmnd 1108), xxix, 429, p. 13. The British authorities took a close interest in Cohalan.

61 Tom Clarke to Major McBride, 18 June 1901, cited in Gerard MacAtasney, *Tom Clarke: Life, liberty, revolution* (Sallins, Co. Kildare: Merrion, 2012), pp. 256–7.

62 James Reidy had enclosed this biographical sketch of Judge Daniel Cohalan with a letter to Frank Robbins, 24 April 1949, Devoy Papers, MS 18,011/8/1 NLI. *National Hibernian Digest*, April/May 1948. The *Digest* was the official organ of the Ancient Order of Hibernians (AOH).

63 Devoy to Joseph McGarrity, 16 April 1913, Box 7, MCIHP, NYPL.

64 Carroll, *American Opinion*, p. 3. These population figures, based on the 1900 census, did not account for second- or third-generation Irish-Americans.

65 F. Carroll, 'United Irish League of America', in M.F. Funchion (ed.), *Irish American Voluntary Organisations* (Westport, CT: Greenwood Press, 1983), pp. 272–6.

66 Apparently, the king had been well received by the Irish crowds but Keating in his speech at the Hoffman House denied this and claimed that the authorities had to 'guard with a policeman every flag decorated pole'. *New York Times*, 31 July 1903.

67 Ibid. Cohalan was probably referring here to the experience of 'Grattan's parliament' in 1782, where considerable freedom had been extended to the Irish Parliament at the time of the American Revolution. However, the Irish Parliament was then abolished by the Act of Union in 1801.

68 Clan na Gael circular, signed by Daniel F. Cohalan, DO1 (district officer, District One), Clan na Gael, New York, 26 October 1901, Cohalan Papers. Box 2, AIHS.

69 Ní Bhroiméil, *Building Irish Identity in America*, pp. 118–20.

70 Eileen McGough, *Diarmuid Lynch: A forgotten Irish patriot* (Cork: Mercier Press, 2013), pp. 22–3. McGough, drawing on a private collection of Lynch papers, highlights Lynch's largely forgotten role in Irish and Irish-American nationalist activities at this time.

71 Lynch, *The IRB and the 1916 Insurrection*, p. 10.

72 Ibid.

73 While O'Growney had died in 1899, the decision to move his body to Ireland was not taken until 1903. His funeral also provided an opportunity for the Clan to identify with the goals of cultural nationalism. For more on O'Growney, see Timothy McMahon, *Grand Opportunity: The Gaelic revival and Irish society, 1893–1910* (New York: Syracuse University Press, 2008).

74 Lynch, *The IRB*, pp. 9–10.

75 Ibid., pp. 10–11.

76 Ní Bhroiméil, *Building Irish Identity in America*, pp. 119, 121, 127.

77 *National Hibernian Digest*, April/May 1948.

78 Some of these share certificates are located in the McGarrity Papers, MS 17660, NLI.

79 'The Story of the Clan na Gael', *Gaelic American*, 6 June 1925.

80 Ibid.

81 Clan circulars, McGarrity Papers, MS 17660. Unlike the *Irish Nation*, the *Gaelic American* proved to be a financial success and outlived both Devoy and Cohalan. It continued publication until 1951, when it was taken over by its main rival, the *Irish World*. This success must surely be partly due to Cohalan's efforts.

82 Gannon to Devoy, 27 November 1905, Devoy Papers, MS 18005/14/11, NLI.

83 Whelan, *United States Foreign Policy*, p. 32; Ní Bhroiméil, *Building Irish Identity*, p. 53.

84 *Gaelic American*, 19 September 1903. This objective was outlined in banner headlines in Gaelic lettering under the title *Gaelic American*.

85 As an illustration of this traditional nationalist preoccupation, the centenary of the execution of famous Irish rebel Robert Emmet was covered on the front page of the *Gaelic American*, 19 September 1903.

86 *Gaelic American*, 20 November 1909. After much wrangling, a Home Rule Bill was introduced in 1912 by a Liberal government but, due to the opposition of the Conservative House of Lords, it would not become law until 1914. Even then, following the outbreak of the First World War, the measure was postponed.

87 McGarrity Papers, MS 17660, NLI. Guterl argues that Cohalan played a significant role in challenging the then dominant Anglo-Saxon perception of American identity: *The Color of Race in America*, pp. 80–1.

88 By 1900, according to the census of that year, 4,826,904 Americans were either Irish-born or had Irish parents. This was considerably lower than the 20 million the Clan claimed to represent but it was still higher than the actual number of Irish who lived on the island of Ireland. US Bureau of the Census, *Twelfth Census of the United States 1900; population* (Washington, 1901), p. clxx.

89 McCartan, *With de Valera in America*, p. 15.

90 McGarrity Papers, MS 17660, NLI.

2. Defending the Irish Race in America, 1903–11

1 Benjamin Reid, *The Man from New York: John Quinn and his friends* (Oxford: Oxford University Press, 1968), p. 110. See also Úna Ní Bhroiméil, 'An American Opinion: John Quinn and the Easter Rising', in Grey (ed.), *Ireland's Allies*, pp. 201–13.

2 *New York World-Telegram*, 21 August 1931.

3 Brown, 'Daniel Florence Cohalan, 1865–1946', p. 4.

4 As Terry Golway points out, Tammany also sought to enlist the support of other ethnic groups who increasingly occupied senior positions in their own wards: Golway, *Machine Made*, pp. 153, 165.

5 *The Outlook*, 21 February 1903.

6 Golway, *Machine Made*, p. 169. These urban reformers included Theodore Roosevelt and the then president of Columbia University, Seth Low, who later became a reform mayor of New York City.

7 James Bryce, *The American Commonwealth*, abridged (Philadelphia: John D. Morris, 1906), p. 241.

8 N.J. Weiss, *Charles Francis Murphy, 1858–1924: Respectability and responsibility in Tammany politics* (Northampton, MA: Smith College Press, 1968), pp. 28–9.

9 Golway also argues that Murphy, a devout Catholic, was influenced by Pope Leo XIII's 1891 encyclical on social justice *Rerum Novarum*, which 'gave tacit papal approval for specific social-welfare measures including the eight-hour workday: Golway, *Machine Made*, p. 199.

10 Edward T. O'Donnell, 'Tammany Hall and the New York Irish', in Michael Glazier (ed.), *The Encyclopedia of the Irish in America* (Notre Dame, IN: University of Notre Dame Press, 1999), pp. 887–9.

11 *New York Times*, 19 May 1911. For a contemporary history of Tammany Hall, see Gustavus Myers, *The History of Tammany Hall* (New York: Boni & Liveright, 1917).

12 Myers, *The History of Tammany Hall*, p. 353. *The New York Times* reported that Cohalan replaced Bourke Cockran as Grand Sachem on 26 May 1908. Previously Cohalan had been chairman of the Law Committee of the Hall. *New York Times*, 26 May 1908.

13 Cohalan's four brothers, John, Timothy, Michael and Denis, were all practising attorneys. John P. Cohalan (1873–1950) went on to become a New York State senator (1907–8) and surrogate of New York County (1909–22). In an interview, Peter Fox Cohalan, John P. Cohalan's grandson, reports that John and Daniel quarrelled over the legal costs of one case involving Con Edison and New York City in 1904. Relations between the two brothers became strained for many years afterwards. However, this did not impact on the other members of the two families, who continued to maintain close contact with each other. Interview, Saville, New York, 29 April 2018.

14 Devoy spent four months in Britain and Ireland in 1879 reviewing IRB operations in both countries. Demonstrating a pragmatism that would later be evident in the debate over the 1921 Anglo-Irish Treaty, he found time to meet with Home Rule League leader Charles Stewart Parnell and assured him of Irish-American support in an agreement later known as the 'New Departure'. Golway, *Devoy*, pp. 117–18.

15 McGough, *Diarmuid Lynch*, p. 22.

16 Cohalan purchased the magnificent house and secluded garden from a Church of Ireland clergyman, Dean Reeves. For information on Cohalan's visitors, see James Coombes, *Utopia in Glandore* (Cork: Butlerstown, 1970), p. 41.

17 Aileen Cohalan, 'Memoirs', p. 29.

18 Davis was writing a series of articles on prominent figures in the Tammany Hall political machine. 'Tammany's War Lords: Dan Cohalan, New York and Skibbereen, split attention of Yankee Squire of Erin', *New York World-Telegram*, 21 August 1931. George William Russell (1867–1935) was an Irish writer, poet and nationalist who wrote with the pseudonym AE; Denis Tilden Lynch wrote a biography of Tammany boss William Tweed (1823–78) in 1927 entitled *'Boss' Tweed: The story of a grim generation* (New York: Boni & Liveright, 1927). Tweed had earned notoriety for greed and corruption during his tenure as Tammany boss from 1866 to 1871. James (Jim) Reed (1861–1944) served as Democratic senator for Missouri from 1911 to 1929. In her 'Memoirs', Aileen notes that she often assisted at these large dinner parties, pp. 24–5.

19 Bulmer Hobson to Cohalan, cited in W. O'Brien and D. Ryan (eds), *Devoy's Post Bag*, vol. 2 (Dublin: Fallon Books, 1948), p. 412.

20 Pearse to Cohalan, 6 May 1914, FL 12, Box 13, Cohalan Papers, AIHS.

21 For more on Cohalan's friendship with Quinn, see Reid, *The Man from New York*.

22 'Irishmen Will Stamp Out the Playboy', *Gaelic American*, 14 October 1911; 'The Playboy must be suppressed', *Gaelic American*, 28 October 1911.

23 Devoy to Cohalan, 29 November 1911, MS15416 (1), Devoy Papers, NLI.

24 John Quinn to Cohalan, 3 February 1913, John Quinn Memorial Collection, NYPL. See also Ní Bhroiméil, 'An American Opinion: John Quinn and the Easter Rising', pp. 201–13.

25 See letter from Douglas Hyde to Cohalan, I January 1913, where Hyde extends 'a thousand thanks' to Cohalan for such advice: fl. 8, Box 7, Cohalan Papers, AIHS.

26 Cohalan's role as fundraiser for the league is also evident in John Quinn's papers in the New York Public Library. In her work on the Gaelic Revival in America, Úna Ní Bhroiméil highlights how these different objectives of the league in America sometimes led to conflicts with the home organisation in Ireland. Ní Bhroiméil, *Building Irish Identity in America, 1890–1915*, p. 134.

27 *Gaelic American*, 18 June 1904. See also Ní Bhroiméil, *Building Irish Identity*, p. 53.

28 Reid, *The Man from New York*, p. 64.

29 In 1912, Roosevelt had declared that: 'C.F. Murphy and his kind must, like noxious weeds, be pulled out.' Cited in Jean Edward Smith, *FDR* (New York: Random House, 2007), p. 78. In his work *Machine Made*, Golway points out that FDR came to see

Murphy in a more favourable light in his later career and also worked closely with Tammany's Robert Wagner during the New Deal. Golway, *Machine Made*, pp. 246–51. See also Mason B. Williams, *City of Ambition: FDR, La Guardia, and the making of modern New York* (New York: W.W. Norton, 2013), pp. 11–14.

30 Myers, *The History of Tammany Hall*, p. 354.

31 In June 1936, Cohalan, along with four other prominent Democrats, signed a message to the Democratic National Convention in Philadelphia calling on delegates to put aside President Roosevelt and nominate 'some genuine Democrat' for president. In a report on this dramatic development, the *New York Times* alleged that Roosevelt's opposition to his political ambitions in 1911 explained Cohalan's actions in 1936. 'Message Recalls Feuds of Signers', *New York Times*, 22 June 1936. This allegation was repeated in the *New York Times* obituary of Cohalan in 1946: 'Daniel F. Cohalan: Ex-Justice dies', 13 November 1946.

32 Reid, *The Man from New York*, p. 91.

33 *New York Times*, 19 May 1911.

34 Ibid.

35 Ibid.

36 Cited in Jonathan Lurie, *William Howard Taft: The travails of a progressive conservative* (New York: Cambridge University Press, 2014), p. 14.

37 Daniel Cohalan, 'Our Foreign Policy', *Forum*, vol. 65, 1921, pp. 187–96; Daniel Cohalan, *The Menace of Foreign Entanglements: Let us awaken before it is too late!* (New York: Friends of Irish Freedom, 1923).

38 Cited in John M. Mulder, *Woodrow Wilson: The year of preparation. Wilson supplemental volumes* (Princeton, NJ: Princeton University Press, 2015), p. 272.

39 Thomas Woodrow Wilson (1856–1924) had been the president of Princeton University before entering political life. He had earned his PhD in political science and history at Johns Hopkins University and his thesis was later published as *Congressional Government: A study in American politics* (1885).

40 'A News Report of an After-dinner Speech in New York, January 1904', in Arthur S. Link et al. (eds), *The Papers of Woodrow Wilson*, 69 vols (Princeton, NJ: Princeton University Press, 1966–94), pp. 15, 149.

41 Hannigan, *The Great War and American Foreign Policy*, p. 6. Richard Olney, 'International Isolation of the United States', *Atlantic Monthly*, vol. 81, May 1898, pp. 587–8; Bradford Perkins, *Great Rapprochement*, p. 29.

42 For a contemporary study of how these cultural ties influenced Anglo-American relations, see Paul A. Kramer, 'Empires, Exceptions, and Anglo-Saxons: Race and rule between the British and United States empires, 1880–1910', *Journal of American History*, vol. 88, no. 4, 2002, pp. 1315–35.

43 William Stead, *The Americanisation of the World or the Trend of the Twentieth Century* (New York: Horace Markley, 1902), p. 396.

44 Andrew Carnegie, 'A Look Ahead', *The North American Review*, vol. 156, no. 439, 1893, pp. 685–710. See also G.S. Clarke, 'A Naval Union with Great Britain: A reply to Mr Andrew Carnegie', *The North American Review*, vol. 158, no. 448, 1894, pp. 353–65.

45 Cited in Hannigan, *The Great War and American Foreign Policy*, p. 6.

46 Cohalan's address at the Hoffman House, New York, August 1900. Cited in Brown, 'Daniel Florence Cohalan, 1865–1946', p. 9.

47 Clan circular, McGarrity Papers, MS 17660, NLI.

48 In 1898, the Clan vigorously opposed a similar treaty and in alliance with a variety of 'Irish civic and military societies' sent resolutions to President Grover Cleveland, Secretary of State Richard Olney and the members of both houses of Congress

stating their opposition to this measure. See 'Printed Copy of a Resolution Passed by Irish Civic and Military Societies on the Anglo-American Alliance, 1898', Devoy Papers, MS 18070, NLI. See also 'Protest against Arbitration Treaty', *Gaelic American*, 27 May 1911.

49 *Gaelic American*, 14 October 1911.

50 Petition of the United German-American and United Irish-American societies of New York to the United States Senate, 1911, Devoy Papers, MS 18079, NLI.

51 *Gaelic American*, 10 February 1912.

52 Ibid., 15 November 1913.

53 Cohalan later celebrated this campaign against proposed arbitration treaties in a speech to delegates at the Irish Race Convention in March 1916. *Gaelic American*, 11 March 1916.

54 See Francis Carroll on Clan efforts to defeat the Anglo-American Arbitration Treaty, which came before the Senate in 1911–12. The Senate amended the treaty to such a degree that President Taft refused to sign it. Carroll, *American Opinion*, p. 28. The Clan worked closely with German-American groups in this battle. See 'Letter from James Reidy to John Devoy Regarding the Activity of the German American Alliance and the Relationship between the Irish and German Groups in General in the United States', 27 January 1912, John Devoy Papers, MS 18,011/8/3.

55 'The Triumph of the Clan na Gael', *Irish Freedom*, March 1912.

56 *Irish World*, 26 August 1911.

57 Cohalan's speech at the First Irish Race Convention, *Gaelic American*, 11 March 1916. Cohalan directed this speech towards the maintenance of American neutrality in the context of the war then raging in Europe.

58 Woodrow Wilson Papers, Library of Congress, Wilson MSS., Series vi, Box 89, File 61, 'Roman Catholic Affairs'.

59 *Gaelic American*, 23 May 1914, 7 October 1916.

60 Speech delivered in Carnegie Hall, 24 January 1917, Cohalan Papers, Speeches and Statements, 1916–1919, fl. 5, Box 23, AIHS.

61 Guterl, *The Color of Race in America*, p. 84.

62 *Journal of the American Irish Historical Society*, vol. 1, 1898; vol. 13, 1914; vol. 32, 1941. Besides historical articles, each volume includes records of society procedures and membership rolls.

63 W.D. Griffin, 'American Irish Historical Society', in Michael F. Funchion (ed.), *Irish-American Voluntary Organisations* (Westport, CT: Greenwood Press, 1983), pp. 40–3. Cockran's nationalist views became more militant after the 1916 Rising. See McGurrin, *Bourke Cockran.*

64 Michael J. O'Brien, 'How the Descendants of Irish Settlers in America Were Written into History as Anglo-Saxons and Scotch Irish', *Journal of American Irish History Society*, vol. 18, 1919, pp. 99–109. Cohalan felt that ordinary Americans needed to be made aware of the real contribution of the Irish in American history and this was a recurrent feature in his press interviews with mainstream media.

65 Irish loyalty to the United States in time of war was also a common theme in the *Irish World.* In 1911, the paper ran a series of articles on the exploits of the famous New York 69th Regiment during the American Civil War: *Irish World*, 29 April 1911. See also other editions in this month.

66 *Gaelic American*, 19 January 1907.

67 *Gaelic American*, 16 October 1909. Michael O'Brien's articles were incorporated into a two-volume work in 1979. Michael O'Brien, *Irish Settlers in America: A consolidation of*

articles from the Journal of the American Irish Historical Society (Baltimore: Baltimore Genealogical Publishing Company, Inc., 1979).

68 Daniel Cohalan, 'John Sullivan', *Journal of the American Irish Historical Society*, vol. 30, 1932.

69 Cohalan, *Andrew Jackson: Hero of New Orleans*; *Gaelic American*, 5 November 1904.

70 Devoy to Cohalan, 29 November 1911, Cohalan Papers, MS 15416 (1), NLI. Britain and the United States had last fought a war in 1812 and hostilities were formally concluded by the Treaty of Ghent in December 1814.

71 *Gaelic American*, 4 February 1911. The *Gaelic American* also denounced efforts to Anglicise American schoolchildren through the teaching of English history in the public schools: *Gaelic American*, 6 January 1912.

72 *Irish World*, 27 May 1911.

73 Devoy to Cohalan, 29 November 1911, Cohalan Papers, MS 15416 (1), NLI.

3. State Supreme Court Justice and Irish Rebel, 1911–16

1 *Gaelic American*, 27 May 1911. As noted in the previous chapter, Cohalan was elected for the full fourteen-year term.

2 Florence's twin brother Dermot Jeremiah later died in 1915. He is listed as age six in a report on Cohalan's second marriage in 1915 and died later that year: *New York Times*, 14 February 1915. See scrapbooks of condolence notes on the death of Dermot Cohalan, Cohalan Papers, Box 21, AIHS.

3 Aileen Cohalan, 'Memoirs', p. 15.

4 *Gaelic American*, 1 July 1911.

5 *Southern Star*, 15 July 1911.

6 Ibid., 3 August 1912.

7 The *Southern Star* of 3 May 1913 also carried a full report on his illness and wished him well.

8 Devoy to McGarrity, 16 April 1913, Box 7, MCIHP, NYPL. Cited also in Brown, 'Daniel Florence Cohalan, 1865–1946', p. 3.

9 Myers, *The History of Tammany Hall*, pp. 373–4; *New York World*, 25 May 1913; *New York Times*, 3 June 1913.

10 'Charges Served on Justice Cohalan', *New York Times*, 4 July 1913; *New York World-Telegram*, 21 August 1931.

11 *Gaelic American*, 14 June 1913; Reid, *The Man from New York*, pp. 156–7.

12 *New York Times*, 12 July 1913.

13 'Scoundrels Combine to Smirch Cohalan', *Gaelic American*, 31 May 1913.

14 Reid, *The Man from New York*, p. 157.

15 'Attack on Cohalan Evokes Cool Denial', *New York Times*, 26 May 1913; 'Connolly Insane Cohalan's Reply', *New York Times*, 1 June 1913; 'Cohalan Attack Shakes Connolly', *New York Times*, 10 July 1913; 'Cohalan Demolishes Connolly's Charges', *Gaelic American*, 7 June 1913.

16 'Votes to Acquit Justice Cohalan', *New York Times*, 12 July 1913. See also Reid, *The Man from New York*, p. 157. The media-shy Murphy disliked the negative publicity which the case had generated and Cohalan no longer served as his advisor even in an unofficial capacity: *New York World-Telegram*, 21 August 1931.

17 *New York Times*, 13 July 1913.

18 'Judge Cohalan's Enemies Routed', *Gaelic American*, 19 July 1913. The *Gaelic American* frequently accused the mainstream 'Anglomanic' press of presenting American readers with 'only the English version of the news': *Gaelic American*, 15 August 1914.

19 John Cohalan also held judicial office and was a surrogate of New York County from 1909 to 1922. He had earlier sued the *New York World* for libel when he was a state senator and won a 10,000 dollar verdict in 1908. Many Irish-Americans felt that the newspaper had unfairly targeted the Cohalan family. Interview with Peter Fox Cohalan, Sayville, New York, 29 April 2017.

20 'Justice Cohalan, Cleared by Legislative Committee, Is Passenger on the *Adriatic*', *New York Herald* (European edition), 18 July 1913; *New York World-Telegram*, 21 August 1931.

21 Carroll to Devoy, 7 February 1913, cited in William O'Brien and Desmond Ryan (eds), *Devoy's Post Bag*, vol. 2 (Dublin: Fallon Books, 1948–53), pp. 403–4. Michael J. Ryan was the leader of Redmond's support organisation in the United States, the UILA.

22 F.M. Carroll, 'America and the 1916 Rising', in G. Doherty and D. Keogh (eds), *1916: The long revolution* (Cork: Mercier Press, 2007), pp. 121–40.

23 Leon Ó Broin, *Revolutionary Underground: The story of the Irish Republican Brotherhood, 1858–1924* (Dublin: Gill & Macmillan, 1976), p. 140.

24 'Redmond's Bogus Home Rule', *Gaelic American*, 9 December 1911; Irish National Archives (INA), Crime Branch Special (CBS IGCI), Inspector General's Monthly Report for August 1906, Box 10.

25 Irish National Archives (INA), Crime Branch Special (CBS IGCI), Inspector General's Monthly Report for August 1906, Box 10.

26 Charles Townshend, *Easter 1916: The Irish rebellion* (London: Allen Lane, 2005), pp. 18, 22.

27 John Hutchinson, *The Dynamics of Cultural Nationalism: The Gaelic Revival and the creation of the Irish state* (Boston: Routledge, 1987), p. 283. See also Patrick Maume, *The Long Gestation: Irish nationalist life, 1891–1918* (Dublin: Gill & Macmillan, 1999).

28 Miller, *Emigrants and Exiles*, p. 542.

29 Cohalan's speech at the Hoffman House, 1902, New York, fl. 27, Box 2, Cohalan Papers, AIHS.

30 John L. Gannon to Devoy, 4 November 1905, Devoy Papers, MS 18005/14/10, NLI.

31 Golway, *Irish Rebel*, pp. 89–90.

32 Cohalan's speech at the Hoffman House, August 1900, cited in Brown, 'Daniel Florence Cohalan, 1865–1946', p. 9. See Golway on German-American alliance, Golway, *Irish Rebel*, p. 187.

33 Charles Townshend describes these events as 'the militarisation of politics': Townshend, *Easter 1916*, pp. 28–60.

34 *Gaelic American*, 25 July and 1 August 1914; Townshend, *Easter 1916*, p. 52.

35 Cited in Cronin, *McGarrity Papers*, p. 53. Wolfe Tone, also a Protestant Irish republican, had persuaded the French government to assist an Irish rebellion in the 1790s. Casement enlisted the help of his liberal friends in England, notably Erskine Childers, to raise funds for arms. In an unlikely combination, this money was supplemented by Clan funds.

36 Townshend, *Easter 1916*, p. 54.

37 *Gaelic American*, 1 August 1914; The *Irish World* also reacted with outrage: *Irish World*, 1 August 1914.

38 At this point it is unclear how many Ulster counties would be excluded from the measure but Carson had already indicated that he wanted six of the nine counties excluded as a minimum.

39 Clarke to Devoy, 7 July 1914, Box 7, McGarrity Papers, Maloney Collection of Irish Historical Papers (MCIHP), NYPL. Clarke addressed his letter to 'uncle', which was the code he used for Devoy. It is not clear what 'etc.' means but it may well relate to

Clan funds for the IRB. The *Irish Press* in its obituary of Cohalan in 1946 mentioned this meeting: *Irish Press*, 14 November 1946.

40 *Irish Independent*, 15 July 1914; Aileen Cohalan, 'Memoirs', p. 29.

41 *Gaelic American*, 15 August 1914. Poland and Finland were part of the Russian Empire and became independent following Russia's defeat in the war.

42 *Irish World*, 15 August 1914.

43 Note of Joe McGarrity, 5 October 1914, McGarrity Files, Box 2, MCIHP, NYPL.

44 Casement to Cohalan, 8 October 1914, Cohalan Papers, MS 22,463, NLI.

45 'Sinking Justified Says Dr Dernburg', *New York Times*, 9 May 1915.

46 Doerries, *Prelude to the Easter Rising*, p. 6. Doerries drew on German records on the Irish rebellion, located in the German Foreign Office archive in Berlin.

47 Cronin, *McGarrity Papers*, p. 53.

48 Ibid.

49 Cited in Doerries, *Prelude to the Easter Rising*, p. 8.

50 Casement to Cohalan, 12 November 1914, Cohalan Papers, MS 22463, NLI.

4. The First Irish Race Convention and 1916 Rising

1 The wedding was reported in the New York and Cork press. See *New York Times*, 14 February 1915; *Irish Examiner*, 3 March 1915; Aileen Cohalan, 'Memoirs', p. 27. Patrick O'Leary later became a monsignor and died in 1979: *Irish Examiner*, 4 July 1979.

2 Dermot was Florence's twin brother. Cohalan's files contain many letters of condolences on Dermot's death. See Box 21, Cohalan Family Papers, AIHS.

3 Because of the Irish War of Independence, which followed the Great War, Cohalan and his family did not travel to Ireland again until 1923.

4 Victor Herbert correspondence, fl. 3, Box 6, Cohalan Papers, AIHS; Daniel Cohalan, 'Victor Herbert', *Journal of the American Irish Historical Society*, vol. XXIV, 1925. According to Aileen Cohalan, Herbert told Cohalan on one such golfing trip that he would name his operetta *Eileen* after her: 'Memoirs', p. 33. However, according to historian Marion Casey, this title owes more to an old Irish air 'Eibhlín a Rúin' which had been Anglicised to 'Eileen Aroon', then a popular recital piece. Casey argues that this title enabled Herbert to link his operetta to an existing nationalist song tradition on both sides of the Atlantic. Marion Casey, 'Victor Herbert, Nationalism and Musical Expression', in Grey (ed.), *Ireland's Allies*, pp. 176–7. One could still argue that both factors played a role in Herbert's decision. As evidenced in Cohalan's papers, Herbert kept Cohalan closely informed of the 'route' of the successful *Eileen* American tour in March 1921. This would indicate that Cohalan had more than a passing interest in the success of this operetta.

5 After the news of Britain's entry into the First World War, Devoy remarked: 'What a long wait we've had for this.' See McGarrity's account of Casement meeting in Cohalan's house, 13 October 1914. Cited in Cronin, *McGarrity Papers*, p. 53.

6 The *Gaelic American* defended the German sinking of the *Lusitania* in 1915 and the loss of 128 American lives by describing the vessel as a 'floating arsenal': *Gaelic American*, 15 May 1915. The *Irish World* did not take the same pro-German line but continued to oppose Irish enlistment in the British army. Many of their front-page illustrations adverted to this theme. See, for instance, 'Why Should I Fight Your Battles?', *Irish World*, 24 October 1914; 'AOH against Recruiting', *Irish World*, 9 January 1915.

7 Quinn's papers in the New York Public Library (NYPL) indicate that this friendship was resumed in the early 1920s.

8 Doorley, *Irish-American Diaspora Nationalism*, p. 35.

9 Francis Carroll, 'The Collapse of Home Rule and the UILA', in Grey (ed.), *Ireland's Allies*, pp. 36–7. See also Ward, *Ireland and Anglo-American Relations*, p. 80.

10 McGinn to Devoy, 12 October 1915, cited in O'Brien and Ryan (eds), *Devoy's Post Bag*, vol. 2, p. 481.

11 Devoy to Joseph McLaughlin, 6 December 1915, MCIHP, fl. 8, Box 9, NYPL.

12 Devoy Papers, 'Minutes of Executive Meeting', MS 18017/20, NLI.

13 Clan circular, 29 December 1915, MCIHP, Box 9, NYPL. See also correspondence Irish Race Convention, fl. 10, Box 7, Cohalan Papers, AIHS.

14 For a full transcript of this invitation, see Doorley, *Irish-American Diaspora Nationalism*, Appendix 1, p. 177. See also 'To the Men and Women of the Irish Race in America', correspondence Irish Race Convention, fl. 10, Box 7, Cohalan Papers, AIHS.

15 Cohalan constantly stressed such themes in his publications. See, for instance, Daniel Cohalan, *The Freedom of the Seas* (New York: Friends of Irish Freedom, 1919), or *The Menace of Foreign Entanglements: Let us awaken before it is too late* (New York: Friends of Irish Freedom, 1923).

16 Cohalan's role in these bodies is covered in more detail in Doorley, 'The *Gaelic American* and the Shaping of Irish-American Opinion'.

17 'To the Men and Women of the Irish Race in America', correspondence Irish Race Convention, Box 7, fl. 10, Cohalan Papers, AIHS.

18 Devoy, *Recollections of an Irish Rebel*, p. 450.

19 *Gaelic American*, 11 March 1916. Judge William Goff (1848–1924) was born in County Wexford and was brought to the United States as a child. Goff had strong Clan sympathies and had been involved in the famous Clan rescue of Fenian prisoners from Western Australia in 1875. For more on this, see Peter F. Stevens, *The Voyage of the* Catalpa*: A perilous journey and six irish rebels' flight to freedom* (New York: Weidenfeld, 2002).

20 *Gaelic American*, 11 March 1916. The paper declared that: 'Everything moved like clockwork and not a cog slipped.' Cohalan's speech to the convention was also reprinted in the *Gaelic American* after his death in 1946: *Gaelic American*, 23 November 1946.

21 *Gaelic American*, 11 March 1916.

22 See Herbert's denunciation of Redmond as an agent of the British Empire in a press interview in the *New York American*, 23 April 1916. These views mirror those of Cohalan. Journalist John O'Neil, in researching an article on Herbert in 1964, claimed that Herbert's speeches were written by Cohalan: *Irish Press*, 25 August 1964.

23 Diarmuid Lynch, in his manuscript history of the FOIF, describes Cohalan as the leader of the FOIF and amusingly refers to Devoy as a 'member at large'. Even though he was not on the executive committee, Devoy consulted closely with Cohalan on FOIF policy: Lynch typescript, 'History of the FOIF', MS 32597, NLI.

24 Correspondence Irish Race Convention, Box 7, fl. 10, Cohalan Papers, AIHS. *Gaelic American*, 11 March 1916.

25 Ibid.

26 The United States' timely intervention on the Allied side ultimately convinced German leaders that victory could not be achieved. Robert Zieger, *America's Great War: World War I and the American experience* (Oxford: Rowman & Littlefield Publishers, 2000), pp. 113–14.

27 *Gaelic American*, 11 March 1916.

28 *Brooklyn Citizen*, 6 March 1916. See also Carroll, *American Opinion*, p. 53.

29 Joanne Mooney Eichacker, *Irish Republican Women in America: Lecture tours, 1916–1925* (Dublin: Irish Academic Press, 2003), pp, 34, 204. McWhorter later took de Valera's side in the Cohalan–de Valera dispute.

30 Lynch manuscript, MS 32597, NLI. See also Doorley, *Irish-American Diaspora Nationalism*. The appendix of this work contains information on FOIF branch development.

31 O'Brien and Ryan (eds), *Devoy's Post Bag*, vol. 2, p. 485; Cronin, *McGarrity Papers*, p. 69; Golway, *Irish Rebel*, pp. 211–13.

32 Golway, *Irish Rebel*, p. 215.

33 Doerries, *Prelude to the Easter Rising*, p. 58. Casement sent this message directly to Cohalan's Supreme Court office on 51 Chambers Street, New York.

34 *Documents Relative to the Sinn Féin Movement*, PP 1921 (Cmnd 1108), xxix, 429, 13. Curiously, the name Landy was spelled Lody in the British document. This was the name of an alleged German spy later executed by the British. The British authorities seemed convinced from this message that Lody was involved with Casement's mission when in fact Landy was the name of an American businessman that Casement had used as an alias on his journey to Germany via Norway.

35 Golway, *Irish Rebel*, pp. 223–34; Tansill, *America and the Fight for Irish Freedom*, p. 193.

36 Cited in Doerries, *Prelude to the Easter Rising*, p. 218. Cohalan's message to Germany also appeared in *Documents Relative to the Sinn Féin Movement*, p. 13. The British secured information on this via an intercepted German coded message and not from the American authorities. According to German diplomatic archives, Cohalan's message was not decoded until 21 April. Vol. R21163, AS 1401, Weltkrieg 11K (PAAA).

37 In a later statement issued to the *Gaelic American*, Cohalan compared the release of this document to the forged Pigott letters which British authorities had unsuccessfully used to try to incriminate Irish leader Charles Stewart Parnell: *Gaelic American*, 29 September 1917.

38 O'Brien and Ryan (eds), *Devoy's Post Bag*, vol. 2, p. 485.

39 McGarrity to Casement, MCIHP, Box 1, NYPL. The reference in Cohalan's message to landing German troops by airship may have been Cohalan's own innovation.

40 For an account of the confused situation in Kerry which led to Casement's arrest, see Townshend, *Easter 1916*, pp. 125–31. Casement was executed for high treason on 3 August 1916.

41 Cronin, *McGarrity Papers*, p. 62. Donard de Cogan argues that the coded message was sent first to Devoy. See Donard de Cogan, 'Ireland, Telecommunications and International Politics', *History Ireland*, vol. 1, no. 2, Summer 1993. See McGarrity, 'Memorandum on 1916', McGarrity Papers, MS17,550, NLI.

42 Michael Laffin, *The Resurrection of Ireland: The Sinn Féin party, 1916–1923* (Cambridge: Cambridge University Press, 2009), pp. 52–4.

43 *New York Times*, 3 May 1916. Spring Rice, the British ambassador to the United States, expressed fears that the executions would antagonise American public opinion. In his report to the Foreign Office he cited Cohalan's speech in this newspaper report: Spring Rice to Grey, 4 May 1916, NAUK, FO 115/2073, British National Archives. The *New York Times* was generally sympathetic to the Allied cause.

44 *New York Times*, 1 May 1916. The British army had suffered defeats at the hands of the Turks in Gallipoli in 1915 and Kut in 1916. Japan, for its own strategic reasons, chose to ally itself with Britain in the First World War but had its own long-term imperial ambitions in Asia.

45 T.J. Sarbaugh, 'Ireland of the West: The development of Irish republicanism in California, 1900–1916', *Pacific History*, vol. 28, no. 1, 1984, p. 49.

46 Sir Cecil Spring Rice to the Foreign Office, 10 May 1916 and 26 May 1916, NAUK, FO 95, 776.

47 H. von Bernstorff, *My Three Years in America* (London: Skeffington & Sons, 1920), p. 285.

48 Doorley, *Irish-American Diaspora Nationalism*, pp. 49–53. Spring Rice urged that Casement's life be spared, though this was ignored. Cited in B.L. Reid, *The Lives of Roger Casement* (New Haven, CT: Yale University Press, 1976), p. 389.

49 Robbins, to his later regret, did not take up Cohalan's offer but in his account of his experiences in New York he had nothing but praise for Cohalan's assistance: Frank Robbins, *Under the Starry Plough: Recollections of the Irish Citizen Army* (Dublin: Academy Press, 1977).

50 *Gaelic American*, 29 July 1916. The Catholic Church in New York also played a prominent role in relief efforts. See Kate Feighery, 'Timely and Substantial Relief: New York's Cardinal John Farley and the 1916 Rising', in Grey (ed.), *Ireland's Allies*, pp. 283–91.

51 Spring Rice to Grey, 9 June and 21 July 1916, NAUK, FO 800/86. Spring Rice complained that the extent of Irish suffering was exaggerated for propaganda purposes.

52 Ward, *Ireland and Anglo-American Relations*, p. 126.

5. Defending American Neutrality and the Flag, 1914–18

1 *Gaelic American*, 15 August 1915. See also Justice Goff's speech at the Irish Race Convention in praise of Germany as reported in the *Gaelic American*, 11 March 1916.

2 *New York Times*, 30 May 1916.

3 David Welch, *Propaganda, Power and Persuasion* (London: The British Library, 2013), pp. 37, 86. See also M.L. Saunders, 'Wellington House and British Propaganda during the First World War', *Historical Journal*, vol. 18, no. 1, March 1975, pp. 119, 130–1. This type of propaganda was more subtle than that used by Germany and targeted America's elite with material that did not on the surface appear as propaganda. For a definition of this so-called 'Gray Propaganda', see Nicholas J. Cull et al., 'Gray Propaganda', in *Propaganda and Mass Persuasion: A historical encyclopedia, 1500 to the present* (Santa Barbara, CA: ABC-CLIO, 2003), p. 152.

4 Lynch manuscript, 'History of the FOIF', MS 32597, NLI.

5 John Higham, *Strangers in the Land: Patterns of American nativism, 1860–1925* (New Brunswick, NJ: Rutgers University Press, 2002), p. 188. For more on the ethnic defensiveness of Irish-America during the Great War, see Thomas J. Rowland, 'Irish-American Catholics and the Quest for Respectability in the Coming of the Great War, 1900–1917', *Journal of American Ethnic History*, vol. 15, no. 2, Winter 1996, pp. 3–29.

6 Cited in Arthur S. Link (ed.), *The Papers of Woodrow Wilson*, vol. 35: 1915–1916 (Princeton, NJ: Princeton University Press, 1983), p. 172.

7 Woodrow Wilson, *Mere Literature and Other Essays* (New York and Boston: Houghton Mifflin, 1896). In his biography of Wilson, John Milton Cooper points out that Wilson accepted Burke's belief that behaviour and actions rather than institutions shaped politics: Cooper, *Woodrow Wilson: A biography*.

8 Cohalan interview, *Boston Daily Advertiser*, 20 April 1916.

9 For an overview of how this ideology shaped Cohalan's thinking, see Doorley, 'Judge Daniel Cohalan: A nationalist crusader against British influence in American life', *New Hibernia Review*, pp. 113–29.

10 Frank Walsh (1864–1939) served as joint president (with William Howard Taft) of Wilson's War Labor Conference Board during the war. Joseph Tumulty (1879–1954) was especially useful in helping Wilson to maintain close links with Irish-American elements in the Democratic Party.

11 Sir Cecil Spring Rice to Lord Robert Cecil, 13 April 1917: S. Gwynn (ed.), *The Letters and Friendships of Sir Cecil Spring Rice*, vol. 2 (New York: Houghton Mifflin, 1929), p. 393.

12 *Gaelic American*, 21 October 1916. See, for instance, Daniel Cohalan, *The Menace of Foreign Entanglements: Let us awaken before it is too late!* (New York: Friends of Irish Freedom, 1923). For a contemporary study of this issue, see Paul A. Kramer, 'Empires, Exceptions and Anglo-Saxons: Race and rule between the British and United States empires, 1880–1910', *Journal of American History*, vol. 88, no. 4, 2002, pp. 1315–35.

13 Charles Evans Hughes (1862–1948) served as a Supreme Court Justice and was a former governor of New York State. He later served as secretary of state from 1921 to 1925 under President Harding. See Ward, *Ireland and Anglo-American Relations,* for a detailed analysis of Irish-American involvement in the 1916 election.

14 Cohalan's friend Bainbridge Colby (1869–1950) campaigned for Wilson and later accepted the position of secretary of state during the final year of his administration from March 1920 to March 1921. This did not impact on his friendship with Cohalan, as evidenced by the correspondence between both men in the Cohalan Papers. See fl. 6, Box 3, Cohalan Papers, AIHS.

15 Golway, *Irish Rebel*, p. 239; *New York Times*, 30 September 1916, 1 October 1916. Wilson's advisor Colonel Edward House assured the president: 'Your message to O'Leary is the best thing so far in the campaign, and will do more good than you can imagine.' House to Wilson, 30 September 1916. Cited in Charles Seymore (ed.), *The Intimate Papers of Colonel House: From neutrality to war* (Boston: Houghton & Mifflin, 1926), p. 376.

16 Arthur S. Link and Richard L. McCormick, *Progressivism* (Arlington Heights: Harlan Davidson, 1983), p. 250.

17 *Gaelic American*, 18 November 1916. The paper argued that Wilson's 'pro-British policies' lost him the electoral college votes of New York, New Jersey, Illinois and Wisconsin. W.M. Leary, 'Woodrow Wilson, Irish-Americans and the election of 1916', *Journal of American History*, vol. 54, no. 1, June 1967, pp. 66–8.

18 Memo by British consul general Joyce Broderick, New York, 19 January 1917, enclosed in a letter from Spring Rice to Foreign Secretary Grey, 22 January 1917, NAUK FO 115/2244.

19 This speech was cited in the British government publication *Documents Relative to the Sinn Féin Movement*, pp. 27–8. This highlights Cohalan's importance in British eyes.

20 Cooper, *Woodrow Wilson: A biography*. Cooper points to the loss of American lives as a result of German submarine attacks on American shipping. See also Kendrick A. Clements, *Woodrow Wilson: World statesman* (Chicago: Ivan R. Dee, 1999), pp. 162–4.

21 Justus D. Doenecke, *Nothing Less than War: A new history of America's entry into World War I* (Lexington, KY: University Press of Kentucky, 2011), pp. 300–7. Wellington House may have played a role in inflaming American elite opinion against Germany. Welch points to British interception and release of the famous 'Zimmermann Telegram' as 'a perfect example of intelligence and propaganda working hand in hand' that in turn did much to bring America into the war as Britain's ally. Welch, *Propaganda, Power and Persuasion*, p. 86.

22 Hannigan, *The Great War and American Foreign Policy*, pp, x, 4–6.

23 Woodrow Wilson, 'Address to a Joint Session of Congress Requesting a Declaration of War against Germany', 2 April 1917, cited in Arthur S. Link (ed.), *The Papers of Woodrow Wilson, vol. 41: 24 January–6 April 1917* (Princeton, NJ: Princeton University Press, 1983).

24 *Brooklyn Tablet*, 21 April 1917.

25 *Irish Times*, 18 July 1918.
26 Aileen Cohalan, 'Memoirs', p. 37.
27 Cohalan would refer to this mistake in future speeches and publications. See, for instance, his press release 'America at a Crossroads' (1933), where he refers to Wilson's betrayal in 1917 in an attempt to garner support for American neutrality in the 1930s: Cohalan Papers, Box 18, AIHS.
28 *New York Times*, 9 April 1917. See also 'Petition to President and Congress', reprinted in the *Gaelic American*, 19 May 1917; Tansill, *America and the Fight for Irish Freedom*, p. 221.
29 The pro-Home Rule newspaper the *Freeman's Journal* was an enthusiastic supporter of the convention and reported its activities in full. See 'The Irish Convention: Its origin and purpose' in the *Freeman's Journal*, 25 July 1917.
30 Ibid.
31 For more on the Irish dimensions to the convention, see Laffin, *Resurrection of Ireland*, pp. 106–10.
32 *New York Times*, 18 May 1917.
33 *Gaelic American*, 9 June 1917.
34 Alan J. Ward suggests that the convention was a clever ploy by Lloyd George to conveniently shelve the Irish question for six months or more, by which time American opinion would be distracted by its own participation in the war. Ward, *Ireland and Anglo-American Relations*, p. 148.
35 For more on McGarrity and McCartan's role in 1916, see Maura Anand, Andrew S. Hicks and Bryan Willits, 'The Man from Philadelphia: Joseph McGarrity and 1914', in Grey (ed.), *Ireland's Allies*, pp. 109–23.
36 The memorial was dated 18 June 1917. Cited in Tansill, *America and the Fight for Irish Freedom*, p. 229. These signatures included Éamon de Valera and Diarmuid Lynch. Both of these men had occupied senior positions in the rising and both would later interact with Cohalan in the United States, though in very different ways.
37 McCartan, *With de Valera in America*, p. 13.
38 Ward, *Ireland and Anglo-American Relations*, p. 176.
39 In her letter, Sheehy-Skeffington referred to the *Los Angeles Times*, the *Portland Oregonian*, the *Bute Miner* and the *Anaconda Standard.* Devoy published this letter in the *Gaelic American*, 23 June 1917.
40 Spring Rice to Foreign Office, 14 June 1917, NAUK, FO 800/242.
41 Of their own accord, many branches outside of New York ceased activity entirely for the duration of the war. This included the FOIF branch in St Louis. See M. Sullivan, 'Fighting for Irish Freedom: St Louis Irish-Americans, 1918–1922', *Missouri History Review*, vol. 65, no. 2, 1971, p. 186.
42 Cohalan to McGuire, 21 July 1917, Box 6, Cohalan Papers, AIHS. See also Joseph E. Fahey, *James K. McGuire: Boy mayor and Irish nationalist* (New York: Syracuse University Press, 2014), pp. 151–3.
43 Publishing magnate William Randolph Hearst ran a chain of newspapers which had consistently advocated an American isolationist policy prior to American entry into the war.
44 'City's Most Complex Election', *New York Times, Sunday Magazine*, 4 November 1917; Golway, *Irish Rebel*, p. 244.
45 O'Leary to McGuire, 30 July 1917, reprinted in the *Gaelic American*, 4 August 1917. Some journalists on the *Gaelic American* such as Liam Mellows favoured a more active FOIF stance and may have sanctioned the publication of this letter.
46 *Gaelic American*, 1 September 1917, 15 September 1917. The police interrogated Moore about FOIF finances but he was later released.

47 *Gaelic American*, 1 September 1917.
48 Doerries, *Prelude to the Easter Rising*, p. 58. See also, Vol. R21163, AS1401, April 21, 1916 Auswärtiges Amt, Berlin.
49 The released information was entitled 'German Intrigue in America: Official exposé'; Ward, *Ireland and Anglo-American Relations*, p. 155.
50 *New York Times*, 23 September 1917; *New York Herald*, 23 September 1917.
51 This intercepted message is located in the British government publication *Documents Relative to the Sinn Féin Movement* (1921), p. 20. See also *New York World*, 4 October 1917; Tansill, *America and the Fight for Irish Freedom*, p. 289.
52 McCartan, *With de Valera in America*, p. 270.
53 Ibid.
54 Ibid., pp. 18–19.
55 Ibid. Maloney later published an account of his meeting with Cohalan in the *New York World*, 1 July 1921. In response, Devoy's *Gaelic American* challenged Maloney's account of his meeting with Cohalan and also questioned Maloney's loyalty to the Irish cause. See *Gaelic American*, 16 July 1921, 23 July 1921.
56 *Gaelic American*, 29 September 1917. The London *Times* newspaper had on 18 April 1887 published a letter, apparently in Parnell's hand, which suggested that he supported these murders. A Parnell commission of inquiry subsequently proved that the letter was a forgery. The forger Richard Piggott fled to Spain, where he committed suicide in a Madrid hotel room. Parnell successfully sued the *Times* for libel. Myles Dungan, 'Pigott v Russell: The Parnell Commission', in *Conspiracy: Political trials* (Dublin: Royal Irish Academy, 2009).
57 McCartan, *With de Valera in America*, p. 20.
58 Cited in Golway, *Irish Rebel*, p. 245; *Gaelic American*, 3 November 1917.
59 Record for Daniel Cohalan: Enemy activities – Arrest of alien enemies – Arrest of alien enemies in USA; Records of the War Department, 1917–18; Record Group 165; National Archives at College Park, MD, www.archives.gov [accessed 9 April 2019]. For photograph see National Archives Identifier (NAID) 31477748, NARA.
60 Golway, *Irish Rebel*, p. 244.
61 O'Leary, *My Political Trial and Experiences*, pp. 48–9.
62 *Gaelic American*, 28 September 1918.
63 Golway, *Irish Rebel*, p. 246.
64 Francis Carroll, 'The Irish Progressive League', in M. Funchion (ed.), *Irish American Voluntary Organisations* (Westport, CT: Greenwood Press, 1983), pp. 206–10; Doorley, *Irish-American Diaspora Nationalism*, pp. 79–80.
65 Éamon de Valera to Patrick McCartan, 7 February 1918, in O'Brien and Ryan (eds), *Devoy's Post Bag*, vol. 2, pp. 522–4.
66 Carroll, 'Irish Progressive League', pp. 206–10.
67 Ward, *Ireland and Anglo-American Relations*, p. 144.
68 Sheehy-Skeffington to Devoy, n.d., in O'Brien and Ryan (eds), *Devoy's Post Bag*, vol. 2, p. 250.
69 Townshend, *Easter 1916*, pp. 337–43.
70 FOIF Committee on Conventions, *To the Men and Women of the Irish Race in America* (1918), Records of the National Secretary, FOIF Papers, AIHS. See also Doorley, *Irish-American Diaspora Nationalism*, pp. 74–5.
71 Mellows' speech to the convention, quoted in Desmond Greaves, *Liam Mellows and the Irish Revolution* (London: Lawrence & Wishart, 2005), pp. 158–9.
72 For a full report of the speeches made at the convention, see *Gaelic American*, 1 June 1918.

73 Moore to Cohalan, 20 November 1917, Box 11, Cohalan Papers, AIHS.
74 Mellows to Golden, 8 August 1918, Golden Papers, NLI. In his unpublished draft manuscript history of the FOIF, Lynch championed Cohalan's role in leading Irish-America during the war years. Diarmuid Lynch typescript 'History of the FOIF', MS 32597, NLI.
75 Mellows to Golden, 8 August 1918, Golden Papers, MS 13141, NLI.
76 Carroll, 'Irish Progressive League', p. 208. See Peter Golden Papers for copies of such correspondence, MS 13141, NLI.
77 *Cork Examiner*, 23 October 1918.
78 Whelan, *American Foreign Policy and Ireland*, p. 180.

6. Supporting Irish Self-Determination but Opposing the League of Nations, 1919

1 In a later letter to Cohalan, de Valera actually referred to the 'great lever of American public opinion': de Valera to Cohalan, 22 February 1920, fl. 1, Box 4, Cohalan Papers, AIHS.
2 A report of the *Evening Mail* apology is contained in Cohalan Papers, fl. 9, Box 17. See also *Gaelic American*, 7 December 1918; Cardinal O'Connell to Cohalan, 3 December 1918, fl. 9, Box 18, Cohalan Papers, AIHS. Cardinal William Henry O'Connell (1859–1944), like many of his colleagues in the American hierarchy, was the son of Irish immigrants and became archbishop of Boston in 1907. He was elevated to the College of Cardinals in 1911.
3 Records of the National Secretary, Friends of Irish Freedom Papers, AIHS. See also Doorley, *Irish-American Diaspora Nationalism*, pp. 186–7.
4 Laffin, *Resurrection of Ireland*, pp. 164–8.
5 By the end of 1920, regular membership of the FOIF numbered 100,000 while associate membership numbered an estimated 175,000. See Records of the National Secretary, FOIF Papers, AIHS, and Doorley, *Irish-American Diaspora Nationalism*, Table 8, p. 188. The rise of Sinn Féin nationalism mirrored the development of an even more embattled unionism in north-east Ulster. This made a partition solution to the Irish question, which had already been envisaged in 1914, even more likely.
6 Matthew Cummings to Daniel Cohalan, 12 January 1919, fl. 19, Box 3, Cohalan Papers, AIHS.
7 *Dearborn Independent*, 5 July 1919. Henry Ford, the famous industrialist and car manufacturer, owned this newspaper.
8 Charles Whitman (1868–1947) was the Republican governor of New York from January 1915 to December 1918 and his presence on the platform indicated Cohalan's close ties with the Republican Party. Whitman lost his bid for re-election as governor to Tammany Democrat Alfred E. Smith, who served as governor from January 1919 to 1920 and later from 1923 to 1928.
9 Cited in Tansill, *America and the Fight for Irish Freedom*, p. 280.
10 Ibid., pp. 277–8; *Gaelic American*, 14 December 1918.
11 This speech is contained in Cohalan's papers in the FOIF, which suggests that Cohalan valued the cardinal's comments: fl. 9, Box 17, Cohalan Papers, AIHS.
12 Cohalan to John J. Splain, 12 December 1918, fl. 8, Box 16, Cohalan Papers, AIHS.
13 Lynch manuscript 'History of the FOIF', MS 32597, NLI.
14 This campaign had more success in some states than others. In Pennsylvania, eight congressional candidates from both the Republican and Democratic parties endorsed self-determination for Ireland. *Irish Press*, 26 October 1918.

15 US Congress, House Committee on Foreign Affairs, *The Irish Question*, 65th Congress, 3rd Session, 12 December 1918.

16 See 'Telegram from Thomas Gallagher to John Devoy Regarding a Foreign Affairs Committee Hearing, 5 December 1918', Devoy Papers, MS 18005/12/4, NLI.

17 Statement of Richard F. Dalton before the House Committee on Foreign Affairs, 12 December 1918, Hearings on H.J. Res 357, pp. 17–18, 55–6. Cited in Tansill, *America and the Fight for Irish Freedom*, p. 287. Ward points out the measure was ultimately watered down as a result of presidential pressure on more pliable Democratic senators: Ward, *Ireland and Anglo-American Relations*, p. 176.

18 *New York Times*, 2 March 1919.

19 Following the creation of Dáil Éireann or the Irish parliament in January 1919, de Valera was elected president of the Dáil in April 1919.

20 *New York Times*, 30 December 1918.

21 Matthew Cummings to Daniel Cohalan, 12 January 1919, fl. 19, Box 3, Cohalan Papers, AIHS.

22 Doorley, *Irish-American Diaspora Nationalism*, pp. 88–9; Carroll, 'The Irish Progressive League', pp. 206–10.

23 Cardinal James Gibbons (1834–1921) was born in the US to Irish parents but received some of his education in Ireland. For an account of his role in the convention, see J.T. Ellis, *The Life of James Cardinal Gibbons, Archbishop of Baltimore, 1834–1921* (Milwaukee: Bruce Publishing, 1952), pp. 226–7.

24 The *Gaelic American* provided full coverage of the convention and included on its front page a photograph of a proud Cohalan flanked by Cardinal Gibbons and Archbishop Dougherty of Philadelphia. Dougherty was yet another Irish-American cleric, reflecting Irish-American domination of the US Catholic hierarchy at this time: *Gaelic American*, 1 March 1919.

25 R. Downing, *A Report Presented to the Patrick H. Pearse Branch of the Friends of Irish Freedom, Washington D.C., by the President Rossa F. Downing at the Regular Meeting, 28 November1920* (Washington: AARIR, 1920), p. 5. This report was compiled by Downing after the split in November 1920. Downing took de Valera's side in his dispute with Cohalan.

26 Ibid.

27 McCartan, *With de Valera in America*, pp. 90–1.

28 Ibid., p. 82. *America* was a popular Jesuit weekly magazine.

29 Cited in Tansill, *America and the Fight for Irish Freedom*, p. 209.

30 McCartan, pp. 82, 93; Lynch manuscript 'History of FOIF', NLI.

31 Doorley, *Irish-American Diaspora Nationalism*, pp. 186–7.

32 The term 'dark Rosaleen' was a term used to refer to Ireland by Irish poets. Mary McWorther to Cohalan, 8 February 1919, Cohalan Papers, Box 9.

33 Cohalan had opposed Wilson's nomination. See Cohalan's obituary, *New York Times*, 13 November 1946.

34 'President Wilson and Ireland: Sinn Féin approval', *Irish Times*, 4 March 1919.

35 In statements to the press, Wilson explained his actions by reference to Cohalan's 'disloyal' activities during the war, though his enmity towards Cohalan dated to well before this. *New York Times*, 5 March 1919.

36 F. Carroll, 'American Commission on Irish Independence', in Funchion, *Irish-American Voluntary Organisations*', p. 18; Tansill, *America and the Fight for Irish Freedom*, p. 303.

37 'Mr. Wilson and the Irish', *Irish Times*, 6 March 1919.

38 *Gaelic American*, 15 March 1919; McCartan, *With de Valera in America*, p. 90.

39 Cohalan speech at the Metropolitan Opera House, 23 March 1919, Box 23, Cohalan Papers, AIHS.

40 McCartan to Devoy, 19 April 1919, cited in McCartan, *With de Valera in America*, p. 98.
41 Devoy to McCartan, 21 April 1919, fl. 4, Box 4, Cohalan Papers, AIHS.
42 Ward, *Ireland and Anglo-American Relations*, p. 176.
43 Carroll, *American Opinion*, pp. 131–6; Whelan, *United States Foreign Policy and Ireland*, pp. 205–9.
44 Polk to Wilson, 1 March 1919; Gilbert F. Close, confidential secretary to the president, to Polk, 3 March 1919, Polk MSS, Drawer 74, File 152, Library of Congress. Frank L. Polk was a counsellor at the State Department and advisor to Wilson.
45 Edward F. Dunne had served as mayor of Chicago from 1905 to 1907 and as governor of Illinois from 1913 to 1917. Michael J. Ryan, still active in Irish-American affairs after leaving the UIL, had served as city solicitor for Philadelphia. See Cohalan's correspondence with Ryan, fl. 16, Box 14, Cohalan Papers, AIHS.
46 The IPL had kept the Irish question alive during the war years but it had always been a minority voice with limited resources. Though affiliated to the FOIF, it remained outside the control of Cohalan and Devoy, who tended to regard their activities as too radical. Its leader Peter Golden and other members had been highly critical of Cohalan and Devoy.
47 Downing, *A Report*, p. 7.
48 For more on the work of the bureau, see O'Connell, 'Irish Influence on America's Foreign Policy', pp. 251–3.
49 There is much correspondence between both men on the league issue. See fl. 7, Box 2, Cohalan Papers, AIHS. See also Ward, *Ireland and Anglo-American Relations*, pp. 194–5.
50 Ward, *Ireland and Anglo-American Relations*, p. 182. The lone senator who opposed the measure was Democratic Senator Williams of Mississippi, who was well known for his pro-British views.
51 Ibid., p. 183.
52 Cohalan to Walsh, 28 March 1919, Walsh Papers, NYPL; *Gaelic American*, 12, 19 and 26 July 1919; F.P. Walsh, 'Impressions of Ireland', *The Nation*, 7 June 1919.
53 Whelan, *United States Foreign Policy and Ireland*, p. 213.
54 Cited in Kenneth Maxwell, 'Irish-Americans and the Fight for Treaty Ratification', *Public Opinion Quarterly*, vol. 31, Winter 1967, pp. 620–41. See also Ward, *Ireland and Anglo-American Relations*, p. 183. Despite the apparent failure of the mission, Cohalan welcomed the publicity which the actions of the American Commission had generated in the United States. In early June, he sent by cable his congratulations to Walsh and Dunne: Cohalan to Walsh and Dunne, 3 June 1919, Walsh Papers, MSS Col 3211, NYPL.
55 Ward, *Ireland and Anglo-American Relations*, p. 183.
56 Ibid., p. 201. Kendrick Clements in *Woodrow Wilson: World statesman* (p. 213) explores this disillusionment but does not mention Walsh specifically.
57 *Gaelic American*, 15 March 1919.
58 In 1823 President James Monroe had enshrined this doctrine, which called for non-intervention by European states in the western hemisphere in return for non-intervention by the US in European affairs. In the wake of American participation in the war in Europe, it would be difficult to argue that this doctrine still held.
59 Lynch typescript 'History of the FOIF', MS 32 597, vol. 1, NLI; Whelan, *United States Foreign Policy*, p. 225.
60 O'Connell, 'Irish Influence on America's Foreign Policy', pp. 236–7.
61 Senators differed over what these amendments should be and this group were further subdivided into 'Mild Reservationists' and 'Strong Reservationists'. Ward, *Ireland and Anglo-American Relations*, p. 198.
62 O'Connell, 'Irish Influence on America's Foreign Policy', p. 236.

63 Treaty of Peace with Germany, Hearing before the Committee on Foreign Relations United States Senate, Sixty-Sixth Congress, first session, part 17 (Washington, 1919). The members of the American Commission provided a graphic description of the conditions existing in Ireland during the ongoing Anglo-Irish war. See Whelan's discussion of the Irish testimony: Whelan, *United States Foreign Policy and Ireland*, p. 221–2.

64 Ibid. Because some of Britain's imperial dominions such as Canada and Australia had a vote in the League Assembly, Cohalan argued that this gave Britain six votes rather than just the one allocated to the United States. According to Ward's account, the Irish testimony took most of the day and the FOIF posted 100,000 copies of the final Senate report to prominent members of American society. This is further evidence to suggest that Irish-America exercised much more influence on the Senate deliberations than other ethnic groups. Ward, *Ireland and Anglo-American Relations*, p. 199.

65 Peter Fox Cohalan, Daniel Cohalan's grandnephew, has stated in an interview that his great-uncle hired hecklers, who stomped their feet during Wilson's speeches. Interview, 29 April 2017, Sayville, New York. Wilson was suffering from nervous exhaustion at this time and such tactics must surely have worsened his mental state: see Cooper, *Breaking the Heart of the World*, p. 422.

66 The Senate voted three times on the treaty, two with Lodge reservations and one without reservations. All votes were defeated. Carroll, *American Opinion*, p. 147. The lack of United States involvement in the league more than likely crippled its effectiveness in the interwar period.

67 Cohalan to Borah, 19 November 1919; Borah to Cohalan, 22 November 1919, fl. 7, Box 2, Cohalan Papers, AIHS.

68 *Gaelic American*, 29 November 1919.

69 Cited in Schmuhl, *Ireland's Exiled Children*, p. 115. The letter from Dodd is located in the president's published papers edited by historian Arthur S. Link: see Link, *Papers*, vol. 67, p. 44. Dodd went on to become US ambassador to Germany.

70 Cooper, *Breaking the Heart of the World*, p. 422.

71 See correspondence between William Randolph Hearst and Cohalan on the league question, fl. 2, Box 7, Cohalan Papers, AIHS. See also Whelan's discussion of the important role played by the FOIF in the campaign against the league: Whelan, *United States Foreign Policy and Ireland*, pp. 223–5.

72 Sean Cronin, 'Wilson Cracks Down on the Irish', *Irish Times*, 16 April 1969. We shall see in the next chapter how Irish nationalist representatives, including de Valera, wanted to take a more bipartisan approach to American politics and were in favour of a reformed league.

73 Victor Herbert to Cohalan, 13 September 1919, fl. 3, Box 3, Cohalan Papers, AIHS.

7. Cohalan and de Valera: 'The Judge' versus 'The Chief'

1 The Anglo-Irish war had begun in January 1919 and by the summer had intensified into an all-out guerrilla war between members of the IRA and police and British army units stationed in Ireland. Sinn Féin also established a parallel system of courts and administration in Ireland. A. Mitchell, *Revolutionary Government in Ireland, 1919–22* (Dublin: Gill &Macmillan, 1995), pp. 68–77.

2 Harry Boland (1887–1922) had taken part in the 1916 Rising. He was a leading member of the IRB and a member of the Irish Dáil. David Fitzpatrick covers his mission to the United States in considerable detail in *Harry Boland's Irish Revolution* (Cork: Cork University Press, 2003). De Valera was known as 'The Chief' to many of his supporters.

3 'Cohalan and Company Hold Irish Funds', McGarrity Papers, MS 17521 (2), NLI.

4 The IPL also opposed Cohalan on this issue, though, like other American progressive movements, they too opposed the League of Nations: see Carroll, *Irish Progressive League*, pp. 206–10. See also letters from Peter Golden, IPL Secretary, to McCartan, Patrick McCartan Papers, MS 17,688, NLI.

5 Harry Boland to Griffith and de Valera, 4 June 1919, de Valera Papers, P150/1132, UCD.

6 Boland to de Valera, 4 June 1919, cited in Frank Pakenham Longford (Earl of) and Thomas P. O'Neill, *Éamon de Valera* (London: Hutchinson, 1970), p. 97. See also de Valera typescript article 'The American Mission: An account', dictated by de Valera to Marie Kelly, 19 November 1962, P150, 1100, UCD. For a comprehensive survey of de Valera's mission to the United States, see Dave Hannigan, *De Valera in America: The rebel president and the making of Irish independence* (New York: Palgrave Macmillan, 2010).

7 For a comprehensive account of the role of American money in Ireland's revolutionary struggle, see Francis Carroll, *Money for Ireland: Finance, diplomacy, politics, and the first Dáil Éireann loans, 1919–1936* (Westport, CT: Praeger Publishers, 2002).

8 Lynch typescript, MS 32 597, vol. 1, pp. 298–303. Cohalan also contributed to other pamphlets on Ireland such as *Ireland and Secession: An answer to Lloyd George* (1920). Many of these pamphlets were published by the FOIF and are located in the AIHS, New York.

9 Sean T. O'Kelly to Judge Cohalan, 27 June 1919, Cohalan Papers, fl. 4, Box 13, AIHS.

10 O'Brien and Ryan (eds), *Devoy's Post Bag*, vol. 2, pp. 534–5.

11 *Gaelic American*, 28 June 1919.

12 The American press commonly referred to de Valera as the 'Irish President' throughout his tour. This added to his appeal. See, for instance, *The Butte Daily Bulletin*, 26 July 1919.

13 Carson had been speaking at a twelfth of July Orange festival at Belfast where he also denounced the 'campaign going on in America, fostered by the Catholic Church and soon to be joined by the Germans and their friends to create a great anti-British feeling'. See full report in *Life* magazine, 24 July 1919, which was critical of both Carson and Cohalan, accusing the latter of having no right to speak for the United States.

14 'Cohalan Replies to Sir Edward Carson', *New York Times*, 14 July 1919.

15 Ibid.

16 Tansill, *America and the Fight for Irish Freedom*, p. 347.

17 Cockran to Cohalan, 14 July 1919, fl. 3, Box 3, Cohalan Papers, AIHS.

18 McCartan, *With de Valera in America*, p. 144. McCartan argues that William Maloney and Joe McGarrity helped to resolve these difficulties. Franklin Delano Roosevelt, then a lawyer in New York, also provided vital assistance. Hannigan, *De Valera in America*, pp. 62–3.

19 Splain to Bourke Cockran, 17 February 1920, Cockran Papers, Box 17, NYPL. J.J. Splain was one of eighteen FOIF national vice-presidents. According to a later report in the *Irish World*, Cohalan had wanted American trustees to take charge of the money: *Irish World*, 6 June 1920.

20 Lynch typescript, MS 32 597, vol. 2, p. 304, NLI.

21 Lynch, *The IRB and the 1916 Insurrection*, p. 209. Despite the fact that the bond certificate drive raised over five million dollars, this 100,000 sum became the subject of legal action between different parties. See Doorley, *Irish-American Diaspora Nationalism*, pp. 155–6.

22 De Valera also visited more remote parts of the country which had large Irish-American populations. Over 10,000 turned out to welcome the 'President' in Butte, Montana: *The Butte Daily Bulletin*, 26 July 1919. See also Hannigan, *De Valera in America*, for a comprehensive survey of his tour.

23 Carroll, *American Opinion*, p. 154. Splain continued to argue that Cohalan should take over its management: Splain to Walsh, 17 September 1919, Walsh Papers, Box 124, NYPL.

24 McCartan, *With de Valera in America*, p. 149; *News Letter*, 12 March 1920. See also Brown, 'Daniel Florence Cohalan, 1865–1946', p. 101. The bond drive was officially launched on 17 January 1920.

25 *Dáil Éireann, Minutes of Proceedings, 1919–1921: Official record* (Dublin, undated), p. 290 (10 May 1921). See also Fitzpatrick, *Harry Boland's Irish Revolution*, p. 76. Ironically, the FOIF later condemned de Valera for wasting American money at the Chicago convention in 1920. This is explored in the next chapter. About half of the five million collected was lodged in American banks, to become the subject of litigation after the establishment of the Irish Free State. See Francis Carroll, *Money for Ireland*, for more on this.

26 Fitzpatrick, *Harry Boland's Irish Revolution*, p. 143, pp. 183–4; Harry Boland to Michael Collins, 22 September 1920; Michael Collins to Harry Boland, 15 October 1920, de Valera Papers, P150/1125, UCDA.

27 Devoy to de Valera, 6 September 1919, Cohalan Papers, MS 15416 (3), NLI.

28 McCartan, *With de Valera in America*, p. 149.

29 Ibid.

30 Ronan Brindly, 'Woodrow Wilson, Self-determination and Ireland, 1918–1919: A view from the Irish newspapers', *Éire-Ireland*, vol. 23, no. 4, Winter 1988, p. 79.

31 De Valera to Griffith, 9 July 1919, de Valera Papers, P150/727, UCDA.

32 O'Connell, 'Irish Influence on America's Foreign Policy', p. 253.

33 Ward, *Ireland and Anglo-American Relations*, p. 207.

34 De Valera to Collins, January 1921, cited in Piaras Béaslaí, *Michael Collins and the Making of a New Ireland*, vol. 2 (Dublin: Phoenix Publishing Company, 1926), p. 145. When prime minister in the 1930s, de Valera upheld the actions of the league and condemned Italy's invasion of Ethiopia.

35 Devoy to Cohalan, 9 October 1919, Devoy Papers, MS 15416 (3), NLI.

36 The FOIF resolution was reprinted in the *Gaelic American*, 8 November 1919.

37 Frank Walsh, in common with other progressives, had also become more disillusioned with the idea of a League of Nations, seeing it as a means of perpetuating colonialism.

38 *Gaelic American*, 20 December 1919.

39 *Westminster Gazette*, 7 February 1920. The issue of British security had surfaced during debates on the Mason Bill. McCullagh, *De Valera, volume 1: Rise, 1882–1932*, p. 173.

40 Cited in Howard Zinn, *A People's History of the United States* (New York: Harper & Row, 2001), pp. 311–12.

41 Cronin, *McGarrity Papers*, p. 77.

42 *Gaelic American*, 21 February 1920.

43 De Valera to Griffith, 17 February 1920, de Valera Papers, P150/727, UCDA. See also *DIFP*, vol. 1, Document 30, NAI DE2/245.

44 Ibid.

45 De Valera to Cohalan, 20 February 1920, de Valera Papers, P150/1134, UCDA. See also fl. 1, Box 4, Cohalan Papers, AIHS.

46 Interestingly, in April 1921, Bishop Michael Gallagher, then president of the FOIF, issued a statement, published in pamphlet form, which elaborated on this theme of

Irish-American loyalty to American principles of liberty and ironically accused de Valera of being a foreign potentate. Rt Rev. M.J. Gallagher, *Statement Dealing with Matters that Arose out of the Visit to the United States of America of the Hon. Éamon de Valera*, Detroit, 1921, McGarrity Papers, Villanova University Archives.

47 Cohalan to de Valera, 22 February 1920, de Valera Papers, P150/1134, UCDA. See also fl. 1, Box 4, Cohalan Papers, AIHS. The exchange of correspondence between Cohalan and de Valera was also reproduced in the booklet published by Bishop Gallagher, so FOIF members would have been aware of Cohalan's stance in this dispute.

48 Tansill, *America and the Fight for Irish Freedom*, p. 365; Golway, *Irish Rebel*, p. 273. According to Lynch, Archbishop Hayes, Governor Alfred Smith, Mayor John Hyland and Police Commissioner Enright joined Cohalan and de Valera on the reviewing stand. Lynch typescript history of the FOIF, NLI. *News Letter*, 26 March 1920.

49 Cronin, *McGarrity Papers*, p. 79.

50 Ibid., pp. 79–80.

51 Ibid.

52 J.J. Splain, 'Under which King? The story of de Valera's tour in the United States', in Fitzgerald (ed.), *The Voice of Ireland*, p. 260.

53 Grace to Andrew J. Ryan (secretary to Central Council of Irish County Associations, Boston), 28 June 1920, fl. 6, Box 6, Cohalan Papers, AIHS.

54 McCartan, *With de Valera in America*, pp. 168–9; McCullagh, *De Valera, volume 1: Rise, 1882–1932*, p. 177.

55 Boland, McCartan and other Sinn Féin representatives in the United States shared this view.

56 Lynch typescript, 'History of the FOIF', MS 32 597 (1–2), NLI.

8. Cohalan and the Split within Irish-America, 1920–1

1 De Valera to Griffith, 25 March 1920, de Valera Papers, P150/727, UCDA. De Valera wrote this letter just seven days after his apparent reconciliation with Cohalan at the Park Avenue Hotel meeting.

2 Boland to Collins, 25 March 1920, de Valera Papers, P150/1125, UCDA.

3 Collins to Boland, 5 March 1920, de Valera Papers, P150/1125, UCDA.

4 Michael Collins to Harry Boland, 26 April 1920, de Valera Papers, P150/1125, UCDA. See also Fitzpatrick, *Harry Boland's Irish Revolution*, pp. 156–8.

5 Ibid.

6 Michael Collins to Harry Boland, 26 April 1920, de Valera Papers, P150/1125, UCDA.

7 Ward, *Ireland and Anglo-American Relations*, p. 220. See also Resolutions of the National Council of the FOIF, Box 10, MCIHP, NYPL.

8 Cohalan's views on the international order have been set out in many of his pamphlets and newspaper interviews. See 'Articles, Pamphlets, and Reprints Written by DFC', Box 25, Cohalan Papers, AIHS.

9 Cohalan to Senator Hiram Johnson, 23 March 1920, fl. 15, Box 7, Cohalan Papers, AIHS.

10 Hannigan, *De Valera in America*, p. 155. See also Desmond Ryan, *Unique Dictator: A study of Éamon de Valera* (London: Arthur Barker, 1936), p. 129. McCullagh argues that this was more than just a demand for sympathy, as de Valera later alleged. McCullagh, *De Valera, volume 1: Rise, 1882–1932*, pp. 181–2.

11 McCartan, *With de Valera in America*, p. 191.

12 'Campaign for American Recognition of the Irish Republic, (Chicago) Republican National Convention, and Other Material Related to de Valera's Mission', McGarrity

Papers, MS17652/3, NLI. Sir Auckland Campbell Geddes (1879–1954) was British ambassador to the United States, 1920–4.

13 *Chicago Tribune*, 12 June 1920.

14 McCartan, *With de Valera in America*, p. 191.

15 Piaras Béaslaí, *Michael Collins and the Making of a New Ireland* (London: G.G. Harrap & Co., 1926), p. 16.

16 McCartan, *With de Valera in America*, p. 193; O'Connell, 'Irish Influence on America's Foreign Policy, pp. 251–3.

17 'Campaign for American Recognition of the Irish Republic, (Chicago) Republican National Convention, and Other Material Related to de Valera's Mission', McGarrity Papers, MS17652/3, NLI.

18 Ibid.

19 Ibid.

20 Ibid.

21 Ibid. This statement by Cohalan was underlined presumably by McGarrity himself, who had included handwritten notes on the document.

22 Lord Longford, in what is considered the official biography of de Valera, echoes the view that Cohalan wanted de Valera to return to the United States: Longford, *De Valera*, pp. 105–9.

23 Ibid.

24 *Chicago Tribune*, 11 June 1920.

25 Doorley, *Irish-American Diaspora Nationalism*, pp. 127–30; Golway, *Irish Rebel*, p. 278.

26 There was also no competitive pressure on the Democrats to adopt a stronger measure that would outdo the Republicans. Golway, *Irish Rebel*, p. 279.

27 McGarrity notes that this statement had been intended for publication in the *Gaelic American* but it had been withdrawn because of fears that tensions would be inflamed further. 'Campaign for American Recognition of the Irish Republic, (Chicago) Republican National Convention, and Other Material Related to de Valera's Mission', McGarrity Papers, MS17652/3, NLI. This point is also made in Lynch's typescript, 'History of the FOIF', MS32597, vol. 1, NLI.

28 Ward, *Ireland and Anglo-American Relations*, p. 233.

29 McCartan, *With de Valera in America*, p. 232. Béaslaí, *Michael Collins*, p. 145.

30 Gallagher's lengthy statement was printed by the FOIF and released in pamphlet form. Rt Rev. M.J. Gallagher, *Statement Dealing with Matters that Arose out of the Visit to the United States of America of the Hon. Éamon de Valera* (New York: Friends of Irish Freedom, 1921).

31 Geddes to Curzon, 16 June 1920, FO 371/4550, NAUK.

32 McCartan, *With de Valera in America*, p. 195. Tansill argues that the failure to secure a Republican or Democratic convention resolution in support of Irish self-determination allowed Lloyd George to unleash a 'reign of terror' in Ireland: Tansill, *America and the Fight for Irish Freedom*, pp. 403–9.

33 De Valera to Bishop Gallagher, 6 August 1920, de Valera Papers, P159/987, UCDA.

34 Cohalan to Devoy, undated but contained in correspondence from Devoy from the summer of 1920, MS 15416, NLI. Devoy corresponded with Cohalan almost daily during this period.

35 Devoy to Cohalan, 12 August 1920, Devoy Papers, MS 15416(3), NLI.

36 *New York Times*, 1 October 1923.

37 Helen Golden to Margaret Hickey, 11 August 1920, Golden Papers, MS 13141 (2), NLI.

38 Carroll, 'American Association for the Recognition of the Irish Republic', in Funchion, *Irish-American Voluntary Organisations*, pp. 9–12. Its first president, Edward Doheny, was a California oil millionaire who later had to resign due to his support for the Anglo-Irish Treaty. Doheny was later implicated in the Teapot Dome scandal, 1922–3, a corruption case involving oil money which damaged the Harding administration.

39 Press release, 22 October 1920, McGarrity Papers, MS17445, NLI. However, this declined with the ending of the Anglo-Irish war and outbreak of civil war in Ireland as Irish-Americans began to lose interest in Ireland. Doorley, *Irish-American Diaspora Nationalism*, pp. 134–5.

40 Florence O'Donoghue, 'Diarmuid Lynch as National Secretary', in Lynch, *The IRB and the 1916 Insurrection*, p. 241.

41 Carroll, 'The Irish Progressive League', p. 209.

42 According to the British embassy report, a member was paid between 25 cents and 50 cents for every new person he or she brought into the organisation. This may well have accounted for an inflated membership list: British Embassy Washington Report, FO 371/5632, NAUK. Unlike the FOIF, the AARIR lacked influence in Congress and merely acted as a collection agency for Sinn Féin in the United States. Membership collapsed during the Irish Civil War.

43 Records of the National Secretary, FOIF Papers, AIHS.

44 Golway, *Irish Rebel*, p. 280.

45 'Cohalan and Company Hold Irish Funds', McGarrity Papers, MS 17521(2), NLI.

46 Golway, *Irish Rebel*, p. 280; *Gaelic American*, 31 July 1920.

47 Cited in Kathleen O'Doherty, *Assignment America: de Valera's mission to the United States* (New York: De Tanko Publishers, 1957), pp. 142–3.

48 Correspondence, Glandore, fl. 3, Box 6, Cohalan Papers, AIHS.

49 Interview with Fachtna Hickey of the Rosscarbery and District History Society, 9 January 2019.

50 Gallagher, *Statement Dealing with Matters …*

51 Dr W.P. Slattery to Frank Walsh, 3 January 1921, Walsh Papers, Box 127, NYPL.

52 McCartan, *With de Valera in America*, p. 198.

53 McCartan to McGarrity, 12 July 1920, cited in Cronin, *McGarrity Papers*, p. 83. See also McCartan to Irish Free State diplomat Gavan Duffy, where McCartan states that Ireland's representatives in America should try to influence Irish-Americans not dictate to them. McCartan to Gavan Duffy, 23 January 1922, MCIHP, Box 21, NYPL.

54 Lynch, *The IRB and the 1916 Insurrection*, p. 209.

55 *Gaelic American*, 30 October 1920.

9. Supporting the Treaty and the Irish Free State, 1922–3

1 Francis Carroll, 'American Committee for Relief in Ireland', in Funchion, *Irish-American Voluntary Organisations*, pp. 26–31. See also 'Circular Letter from Diarmuid Lynch to Branch Secretaries of the Friends of Irish Freedom … asking that all money collected be forwarded to the American Committee on Relief in Ireland', Irish Relief Fund, MS 17658/3/1, NLI.

2 Laffan, *The Resurrection of Ireland*, p. 295.

3 Golway, *Irish Rebel*, p. 295.

4 Devoy kept Cohalan fully informed of the outcome of McHugh's mission: Devoy to Cohalan, 26 July 1921, fl. 4, Box 6, Cohalan Papers, AIHS.

5 Ward, *Ireland and Anglo-American Relations*, p. 249.

6 Laffan, *Resurrection of Ireland*, pp. 351–5. Irish nationalists on both sides of the treaty debate believed that a proposed Boundary Commission, which would later delineate the border according to the wishes of the local inhabitants, would grant so much territory to the Free State that Northern Ireland would prove unviable as a political and economic entity.

7 *New York Times*, 7 December 1921.

8 Ibid., 8 December 1921. The term 'Irish Free State' was used in the treaty to refer to that part of Ireland which would be given dominion status. After 6 December 1922, the new Irish state became known as the Irish Free State.

9 *Gaelic American*, 10 December 1921. In the following week's edition, the *Gaelic American* denounced the treaty as a 'surrender'. *Gaelic American*, 17 December 1921.

10 Dáil Eireann Official Report, *Treaty Debate*, 34 (Dublin, 1922).

11 Laffan describes the divide as one between 'purists' and 'pragmatists': *Resurrection of Ireland*, pp. 350, 360. For more on de Valera's role in the treaty debates, see David McCullagh, *De Valera, volume 1: Rise, 1882–1932*, pp. 249–86.

12 'Minutes of the National Council of the FOIF', 22 January 1922, FOIF Papers, AIHS.

13 Cronin, *McGarrity Papers*, p. 161.

14 Denis McCullough (1883–1968) played a key role in helping to revitalise the IRB prior to the 1916 Rising, though he did not take part in the rising itself. A northerner, he supported the treaty, believing that Sinn Féin needed to stay united in the face of unionist threats to northern nationalists. George Gavan Duffy (1882–1931) was a qualified solicitor who defended Sir Roger Casement during his trial. He also took part in the treaty negotiations in London and served as minister for home affairs from January to July 1922.

15 *DIFP*, vol. 1, Document 282, McCullough to Gavan Duffy, 8 May 1922.

16 Ibid.

17 Ibid.

18 Ibid.

19 Tom Garvin, *1922: The birth of Irish democracy* (Dublin: Gill & Macmillan, 1996), pp. 134–7.

20 Golway makes the point that Devoy, despite his militant reputation, had a record of pragmatism and flexibility. He was willing to work with Parnell's constitutional home rule campaign and supported Michael Davitt's land agitation in the 1880s. Golway, *Irish Rebel*, p. 301.

21 Debate on treaty, *Dáil Éireann Debates*, vol. T, no. 15, 7 January 1922.

22 Carroll, 'American Association for the Recognition of the Irish Republic', pp. 9–12; AARIR Membership Figures, July 1925, Frank Aiken Papers, P104/2520 (55), UCDA. The 'reorganised' Clan also declined but republican immigrants from Ireland helped to sustain the organisation and it numbered 5,000 in 1927. An Timithire (AT), Clan na Gael, 20 May 1927, Moss Twomey Papers, UCDA, P69/183 (47).

23 Irish-American support for the treaty was not universal. Along with a much-diminished AARIR, Joe McGarrity's wing of the Clan lent their weight to the anti-treaty side. The *Irish World* newspaper, which had taken de Valera's side in his dispute with Cohalan, also denounced it as a 'Treaty of surrender': see *Irish World*, 10, 17, 31 December 1921. An unseemly wrangle also developed between the pro-treaty and anti-treaty side over ownership of the remaining bond certificate money that lay in American banks. This received extensive coverage in the American press and further alienated American opinion. The issue was not resolved until 1936. See

Francis Carroll, *Money for Ireland: Finance, diplomacy, politics and the First Dáil Éireann loans, 1919–1936* (Westport, CT: Greenwood Publishing Group, 2002).

24 Daniel Cohalan to Matthew Cummings, 13 March 1922, fl. 19, Box 13, Cohalan Papers, AIHS.

25 This role was equivalent to the role of prime minister. Collins was also the minister for finance. Once the Civil War began in June 1922, Collins asked the cabinet if he could become commander-in-chief of the army and W.T. Cosgrave took over as acting chairman of the Provisional Government. T. Ryle Dwyer, 'Michael Collins and the Civil War', in J. Crowley et al. (eds), *Atlas of the Irish Revolution* (Cork: Cork University Press, 2017), p. 727.

26 Collins to Devoy, February 1922, cited in Golway, *Irish Rebel*, p. 302; Collins to Devoy, 2 March 1922, Devoy Papers, MS 18001(14), NLI.

27 'Michael Collins', *Pearson's Magazine*, September 1922. Refer also to 'Articles, Pamphlets, and Reports', fl. 1, Box 25, Cohalan Papers, AIHS.

28 McSwiney to Mulcahy, 24 April 1922, Mary McSwiney Papers, P48a 235/236, UCDA. Mary McSwiney was the sister of Terence McSwiney, the former mayor of Cork who died on hunger strike in 1920. See also Marie Coleman, *The Irish Revolution, 1916–1923* (London and New York: Routledge, 2014), p. 112.

29 During the treaty negotiations, de Valera sought to bridge the gap between both sides by proposing an alternative formula known as Document No. 2. This envisaged a form of 'External Association' which involved recognition of the British king as head of an 'Association' between a 'Sovereign Irish Nation' and the British Commonwealth. However, the British government, unwilling to reignite divisions within their own cabinet, refused to reopen negotiations on such an issue. This proposal also caused unease in anti-treaty circles. For an account of how de Valera sought to bring the conflict to an end, see David McCullagh, *De Valera, volume 1: Rise, 1882–1932*, pp. 317–28.

30 The Civil War impacted on the fortunes of the AARIR. James E. Murray (1867–1961), who replaced Edward L. Doheny as leader, tried to use the new organisation to bring about a reconciliation between both factions in Ireland. When this failed, he too resigned and later became Democratic senator for Montana from 1934 to 1961. Many disillusioned Irish-American members left the AARIR. Carroll, *American Opinion*, pp. 180–1.

31 Cohalan to Bishop William Turner, 15 September 1922, Cohalan Papers, Box 10, AIHS.

32 Liam Lynch, the commander of the anti-treaty forces, was shot dead in April 1923 and on 24 May 1923 his successor Frank Aiken (1898–1983) ordered a ceasefire. Coleman, *The Irish Revolution*, p. 115.

33 Francis Carroll, 'The Irish Free State and Public Diplomacy: The first official visit of William T. Cosgrave to the United States', *New Hibernia Review*, vol. 16, no. 2, Summer 2012, p. 78.

34 Ibid.

35 'Judge Cohalan's Visit to Ireland', *Irish Times*, 18 August 1923.

36 'Irish Election Row', *Philadelphia Inquirer*, 12 August 1923. The *Irish Times* also carried a report on the same meeting, describing it as 'the largest crowd brought together in Dublin for many years'. The paper also noted Cohalan's presence, describing him as 'the well-known Irish-American'. 'Election Campaign in Full Swing', *Irish Times*, 18 August 1923.

37 'President Flies to Carlow. Three Aeroplanes for His Party', *Irish Times*, 20 August 1923.

38 For more on Smiddy's diplomatic career, see Eda Sagarra, *Envoy Extraordinary: Professor Smiddy of Cork* (Dublin: Institute of Public Administration, 2018).

39 Liam Mellows was executed by Free State forces in December 1922 as a reprisal for the killing of a government TD. He was one of seventy-seven republicans executed by the Free State government. Even though Mellows had once worked for the *Gaelic American*, the paper supported his execution, blaming de Valera for his death. *Gaelic American*, 16 December 1922.

40 *DIFP*, vol. II, 1923–1926 (Dublin, 2000), Document 18, Smiddy to Fitzgerald, 15 January 1923.

41 *New York Herald Tribune* (European edition), 21 August 1923; *New York Tribune*, 30 August 1923.

42 *Every Enemy of Ireland Is on the Side of the Free State: Enter Judge Cohalan*, ILB 300p [Item 60], NLI. The first part of the title of this pamphlet may well have been drawn from a speech made by the anti-treaty Australian Archbishop Daniel Mannix in Melbourne on St Patrick's Day in 1923. Mannix declared: 'Every enemy of Ireland is on the side of the Free State.' See copy of speech, ILB 300p [Item 19], NLI.

43 Michael Hopkinson, *Green against Green: The Irish Civil War* (Dublin: Gill & Macmillan, 1988), p. 262.

44 Cosgrave to Cohalan, 24 December 1923, Cohalan Papers, Box 18, AIHS.

45 The death of little Joan caused untold grief in the Cohalan household, as described by Aileen Cohalan in her 'Memoirs', pp. 41–3; Cohalan to Cosgrave, 18 July 1924, Cohalan Papers, Box 18, AIHS.

46 Smiddy to Cohalan, 14 February 1924, fl. 2, Box 16, AIHS. The Free State was given a yearly temporary quota of 28,567 until 1929 and this was then reduced to a permanent quota of 17,853. Whelan, *United States Foreign Policy and Ireland*, p. 492.

47 See FOIF pamphlet *A Protest against the Immigration Law of 1924* (New York: FOIF, 1924), Cohalan Papers, Correspondence FOIF, AIHS.

48 *New York Times*, 21 April 1924. The *New York Times* still viewed Cohalan's comments as newsworthy and frequently included portions of Cohalan's speeches in their columns. This meant that Cohalan's pronouncements on Irish affairs went far beyond those who attended such meetings.

49 Daniel Cohalan, 'America's Advice to Ireland', in FitzGerald (ed.), *The Voice of Ireland*, pp. 233–5. Whelan notes a declining interest in Irish affairs in America after 1924. Whelan, *American Foreign Policy and Ireland*, p. 466.

50 Cohalan, 'America's Advice to Ireland', pp. 234–5.

10. Cohalan as Critic of the Irish Free State, 1924–30

1 In his Hotel Astor speech in April 1924, Cohalan criticised the overdependence of the Irish economy on England and advocated 'a closer commercial contact between Ireland and the United States'; *New York Times*, 24 April 1924.

2 Cohalan to Cosgrave, 18 July 1924, Cohalan Papers, Box 18, AIHS. Cohalan's papers contain copies of many of these letters of introduction, including one for businessman James McGurrin, who later became president general of the AIHS in the early 1930s.

3 Robert Lindsay Crawford (1868–1945) was a Northern Ireland Presbyterian and a founding member (1903) of the Independent Loyal Orange Institution of Ireland. However, he later turned against unionism and embraced Irish republican politics. Pauric J. Dempsey and Shaun Boylan, 'Crawford (Robert) Lindsay', in *Dictionary of Irish Biography* (Cambridge: Cambridge University Press/ Royal Irish Academy, n.d.). Peter Fox Cohalan states that Crawford was a frequent visitor to Cohalan's home for

social events. Interview with Peter Fox Cohalan, Sayville, New York, 29 April 2017. See also Mary C. Kelly, 'The Hand of Friendship: Protestants, Irish-Americans, and 1916-era nationalism', in Grey (ed.), *Ireland's Allies*, pp. 229–37.

4 Crawford to Cohalan, 2 August 1924, fl. 16, Box 3, Cohalan Papers, AIHS.

5 Cosgrave to Cohalan, 12 July 1924, fl. 1, Box 18, Cohalan Papers, AIHS. For more on how the question of issuing Irish passports became a symbol of Irish sovereignty, see Joseph P. O'Grady, 'The Irish Free State Passport and the Question of Citizenship, 1921–4', *Irish Historical Studies*, vol. 26, no. 104, November 1989, pp. 396–405; and Mary E. Daly, 'Irish Nationality and Citizenship since 1922', *Irish Historical Studies*, vol. 32, no. 127, May 2001, pp. 377–407.

6 Crawford to Cohalan, 2 August 1924, fl. 16, Box 3, Cohalan Papers, AIHS. Lloyd George had cleverly used the idea of a Boundary Commission to temporarily put to rest the Ulster question during the treaty negotiations.

7 David McCullagh points out that even de Valera seems to have accepted the Boundary Commission clause in the treaty: *De Valera, volume 1: Rise, 1882–1932*, p. 233.

8 Crawford to Cohalan, 2 August 1924, fl. 16, Box 3, Cohalan Papers, AIHS.

9 Cosgrave to Cohalan, 11 September 1924, Box 18, Cohalan Papers, AIHS.

10 Ibid.

11 Cohalan to Cosgrave, 1 October 1924, Box 18, Cohalan Papers, AIHS.

12 Enda Staunton, 'The Boundary Commission Debacle 1925: aftermath and implications', *History Ireland*, vol. 4, no. 2, Summer 1996. In a 1926 interview with the *Cork Examiner*, Cohalan noted 'how Ireland had completely disappeared from the newspapers and in a large way from the public thought of America': *Cork Examiner*, 28 July 1926.

13 In an interview, Cohalan, criticised the poor landing facilities available to American tourists coming to Queenstown in contrast to those available in Bremen and Cherbourg. 'Ireland's Prosperity: Views of Judge D.F. Cohalan', *Irish Times*, 29 July 1926; Cosgrave to Cohalan, 12 July 1924, fl. 1, Box 18, Cohalan Papers, AIHS.

14 Cosgrave to Cohalan, 18 February 1924, fl. 1, Box 18, Cohalan Papers, AIHS. Cosgrave later became more enthusiastic about how tourism could benefit the economy. In 1927, in a speech to the Irish Tourist Development Association reported in the *Irish Times*, Cosgrave described how improvements in infrastructure such as roads, railways and hotels had made tourism now much more viable: 'The Tourist Traffic', *Irish Times*, 6 April 1927.

15 *Gaelic American*, 29 September 1923.

16 FOIF pamphlet, *Free State Makes Bad Blunder in Applying for League Membership*, reprinted from *Gaelic American*, 28 April 1923. See also FOIF Papers, AIHS. The *Gaelic American* did not list the author of this piece, but there is no doubt that it had Cohalan's approval, since the FOIF subsequently reprinted and distributed this article in pamphlet form. See also John P. McCarthy, 'The Friends of Irish Freedom and the Founding of the Irish Free State', *The Recorder*, vol. 6, no. 2, Fall 1993.

17 Ciara Meehan, *The Cosgrave Party: A history of Cumann na nGaedheal, 1923–1933* (Dublin: Prism, 2010), p. 51.

18 Cosgrave to Cohalan, 28 August 1924, Cohalan Papers, Box 18, AIHS.

19 Gerard Keown, 'Taking the World Stage: Creating an Irish foreign policy in the 1920s', in Michael Kennedy and Joseph Skelly (eds), *Irish Foreign Policy 1919–1966: From independence to internationalism* (Dublin: Four Courts Press, 2000), p. 25.

20 By the end of the Civil War in the summer of 1923, the Irish army had expanded to 55,000. This represented an enormous financial burden on the Irish Free State.

Maryann Valiulis, *Almost a Rebellion: The Irish army mutiny of 1924* (Cork: Tower Books, 1985), p. 31.

21 These officers had formed part of Michael Collins' intelligence unit, or 'squad' as it became known, during the Anglo-Irish war. Ibid., pp. 32, 116.

22 Ibid., p. 116.

23 Historian John McCarthy highlights O'Higgins' powerful role in the Free State government: *Kevin O'Higgins: Builder of the Irish Free State* (Dublin: Irish Academic Press, 2006), p. 161.

24 'Mr. J. McGrath: Resignation from the Dáil', *Irish Times*, 30 October 1924. Joseph McGrath (1887–1966) was a colourful figure who earned notoriety for his ruthlessness in rounding up opponents of the Free State government during the Civil War. He later became involved in setting up the Irish Sweepstakes. See Marie Coleman, *The Irish Sweep: A history of the Irish Hospitals' Sweepstake, 1930–87* (Dublin: UCD Press, 2009).

25 McGrath to Cohalan, 2 April 1924, fl. 1, Box 10, Cohalan Papers, AIHS. See also *Gaelic American*, 13 March 1924.

26 McGrath to Cohalan, 4 April 1926, LA 6, Joe McGrath Papers, DLRCA. Richard Mulcahy resigned from government in March 1924 in response to criticism of his handling of the crisis. McCarthy, *Kevin O'Higgins*, pp. 139–42. For more on Mulcahy's role in the Irish Free State, see Risteárd Mulcahy, 'The Mulcahy Tapes and Papers', *History Ireland*, no. 1, vol. 8, Spring 2000.

27 Ibid.

28 Cohalan to McGrath, 22 April 1924, Joe McGrath Papers, LA 6, DLRCA. At this point, de Valera and his Sinn Féin party were still boycotting the Dáil over the oath of allegiance issue. Lynch typescript, 'History of the FOIF', MS 32597 (1–2), pp. 539–40.

29 Cohalan to McGrath, 22 April 1924, Joe McGrath Papers, LA 6, DLRCA.

30 Ibid. Richard (Dick) Dalton, a native of Tipperary, was a senior figure in the FOIF and in the AIHS. The *Gaelic American*, 10 May 1924, praised Tobin and McGrath as the saviours of Ireland.

31 McGrath had a number of business interests and would also have helped fund this enterprise. See copies of *The Nation* in LA 6, 177, Joe McGrath Papers, LA 6, DLRCA.

32 Cosgrave to Cohalan, 12 July 1924, fl. 1, Box 18, Cohalan Papers, AIHS.

33 *Irish Times*, 6 September 1924.

34 The *Irish Times* later reported on Cohalan's role as mediator in the crisis: *Irish Times*, 30 October 1924. John McCarthy, in his biography of Kevin O'Higgins, also notes Cohalan and Devoy's role as 'intermediaries' in the dispute: McCarthy, *Kevin O'Higgins*, p. 161.

35 Cohalan to Cosgrave, 1 October 1924, Box 18, Cohalan Papers, AIHS.

36 Ibid.

37 McGrath to Cohalan, 13 October 1924, Box 10, Cohalan Papers, AIHS.

38 Ibid. McGrath left Irish politics at this point and engaged in a variety of business ventures. In 1925, he became labour advisor to the German Siemens Company, who were then engaged in building a massive hydroelectric plant on the Shannon river at Ardnacrusha in County Clare. McGrath acted ruthlessly in supressing workers' strikes for more pay but in early 1926 Cohalan praised McGrath in having 'succeeded so well in handling the labor problems'. Cohalan to McGrath, 16 February 1926, Box 10, Cohalan Papers, AIHS. For more on McGrath's involvement in the so-called Shannon Scheme, see Michael McCarthy, *High Tension: Life on the Shannon Scheme*

(Dublin: The Lilliput Press, 2004). In an interview with the *Irish Times* in July 1926, Cohalan expressed admiration for the Shannon Scheme: 'Irelands Prosperity: Views of Judge D.F. Cohalan', *Irish Times*, 29 July 1926. See also praise for the scheme in *Gaelic American*, 10 November 1928.

39 *Irish Times*, 30 October 1924.

40 Cohalan to Devoy, 25 November 1924, fl. 4, Box 4, Cohalan Papers, AIHS.

41 McGrath to Cosgrave, 7 November 1924, Joe McGrath Papers, LA 6, DLRCA.

42 See McGrath to Cohalan, 15 December 1929, DLRCA, Papers of Joseph McGrath, LA 6/71-110. According to correspondence between both men, Cohalan acted as McGrath's legal advisor for some property investments in Florida. Because of a dramatic fall in Florida land prices in the late 1920s, these investments went badly wrong. See also Cohalan to McGrath, 29 April 1927, Box 10, Cohalan Papers, AIHS. In this letter Cohalan laments that: 'Things in Florida are not going well …'.

43 *Gaelic American*, 31 January 1925.

44 Ibid. The meeting was reported in full in the *Gaelic American*, 31 January 1925.

45 Confidential report from Timothy A. Smiddy to Desmond FitzGerald (Dublin), 5 April 1927, *DIFP*, No. 76, NAI DFA EA 231/1/1929. The United States became even more protectionist following the introduction of the Hawley-Smoot Tariff in June 1930. The *Gaelic American* ran a series of critical editorials in April 1927 accusing the Free State government of lacking the 'courage' to tackle Ireland's economic problems. *Gaelic American*, 2 April 1927, 9 April 1927, 16 April 1927.

46 William Magennis to Cohalan, 27 May 1927, fl. 21, Box 8, Cohalan Papers. William Magennis (1867–1946) was one of the founders of Clann Éireann and had for a time held the chair of metaphysics at University College Dublin.

47 McCartan to Cohalan, 12 March 1927, fl. 1, Box 9, Cohalan Papers, AIHS.

48 Cited in Golway, *Irish Rebel*, p. 317.

49 Cosgrave to Madge Cohalan, 14 August 1926, Box 18, Cohalan Papers, AIHS.

50 *Boston Globe*, 4 February 1928. Cohalan later organised a reception at his home on East 94th Street to which prominent Irish-Americans were invited. See Francis Carroll, 'The Irish Free State and Public Diplomacy: The first official visit of William T. Cosgrave to the United States', *New Hibernia Review*, vol. 16, no. 2, 2015, p. 85.

51 Confidential Report from Michael MacWhite to Joseph P. Walshe (Dublin) (M.P.1008-42-29), *DIFP*, No. 320, NAI DFA EA 231/1/1929. James Reidy had replaced Devoy as editor of the *Gaelic American* following Devoy's death in 1928. Reidy was also a member of the Clan na Gael executive.

52 Ibid.

53 Edward McSweeney to Cohalan, 5 December 1926, Cohalan Papers, AIHS. Bernadette Whelan has noted the decline in Irish-American nationalist organisations following the establishment of the Irish Free State. Whelan, *United States Foreign Policy and Ireland*, p. 566. With the onset of the Great Depression in 1929, emigration from Ireland declined and this too would have impacted on Irish-American organisations. Mary E. Daly, 'Nationalism, Sentiment, and Economics: Relations between Ireland and Irish-America in the post-war years', in Kevin Kenny (ed.), *New Directions in Irish-American History* (Madison, WI: University of Wisconsin, 2003).

54 The once-powerful Friends of Irish Freedom had declined to just a few hundred members by the early 1930s. See membership numbers in Doorley, *American-Irish Diaspora Nationalism*, appendix.

55 For an account of La Guardia's impact on Tammany, see Williams, *City of Ambition*.

56 Confidential Report from William J.B. Macaulay to Joseph P. Walshe (Dublin) (54/100/32) (Secret), 8 March 1932, *DIFP*, No. 644, NAI DFA 19/9.

57 Ibid.

58 *Boston Globe*, 13 March 1932. According to this report, over 500 people attended, including Boston FOIF leader Matthew Cummings.

59 *Cork Examiner*, 28 July 1926.

60 Golway, *Irish Rebel*, p. 318. Devoy's body was retuned to Ireland to be given a state funeral by the Free State government. He was buried in Glasnevin Cemetery on 16 June 1929. Lynch typescript, vol. 2, p. 586, MS32597, NLI.

61 D.F. Cohalan, *Democracy or Imperialism, which?*, pp. 3–18.

11. Defending Jeffersonian Democracy in the Great Depression

1 *New York Times*, 29 December 1923; Cohalan to Smith, Cohalan Papers, Box 17, fl. 17, AIHS. According to the *New York Tribune*, the New York Bar Association hosted a large party for Cohalan at the Metropolitan Club to welcome him back to private practice. The large number of judicial and political figures in attendance is an indication of Cohalan's high standing in New York society. See attendance list in 'Justice Cohalan Welcomed Back to Practice by the Bar', *New York Tribune*, 6 February 1924.

2 *New York Times*, 17 August 1922.

3 *New York World-Telegram*, 21 August 1931. Forrest Davis was a well-known New York journalist who later wrote *The Atlantic System* in early 1941. Davis anticipated US entry into the war on Britain's side because of geopolitical considerations. Forrest Davis, *The Atlantic System: The story of Anglo-American control of the seas* (New York: Reynal & Hitchcock, 1941). Alfred Emanuel Smith (1873–1944) served as governor of New York four times and won the Democratic nomination for the presidential election in 1928. Smith lost to Republican candidate Herbert Hoover. Robert F. Wagner (1877–1953) was a German-American who later served as Democratic US senator for New York. Unlike Cohalan, he became a strong supporter of President Franklin D. Roosevelt on labour issues. 'Big Tom' Foley (1852–1925) was a prominent Tammany Hall district leader and local saloon owner.

4 *Gaelic American*, 3 November 1928.

5 McCarthy, *The Friends of Irish Freedom and the Founding of the Irish Free State*, p. 126.

6 *New York World-Telegram*, 21 August 1931; *Gaelic American*, 3 November 1928. In his interview with the *Gaelic American*, Cohalan attributed his recovery to the fresh air of 'good old Glandore'.

7 For more on Al Smith, see Christopher M. Finan, *Alfred E. Smith: The happy warrior* (New York: Hill & Wang, 2002). In the 1920s, while Irish-Americans could gain control of local urban political machines, the chance of securing the presidency still eluded them. Even in the much more secular era of the 1960s, Irish-American John F. Kennedy encountered similar anti-Catholic prejudice and only barely secured victory in his own presidential campaign.

8 *New York Tribune*, 13 November 1946. In this obituary of Cohalan, the *Tribune* described him as an Irish-American leader and 'strategist' of Tammany Hall.

9 *New York World-Telegram*, 21 August 1931.

10 Cohalan, *Democracy or Imperialism, which?*, p. 6.

11 Viereck to Cohalan, 17 January 1924, fl. 1, Box 17, Cohalan Papers, AIHS. Raymond Poincaré (1860–1934) served as prime minister of France from January 1922 to June 1924 and from July 1926 to July 1929.

12 Cohalan to Viereck, 18 January 1924, fl. 1, Box 17, Cohalan Papers, AIHS. Viereck was later arrested as a German agent and convicted for treasonable activities. *New York Times*, 9 October 1941.

13 Cohalan to James M. Burke, 18 June 1922, Cohalan Papers, AIHS. Cited in Brown, 'Daniel Florence Cohalan, 1865–1946', p. 122.

14 Some of these pamphlets, published by the FOIF, consisted of Cohalan's speeches and included Daniel F. Cohalan, *The Menace of Foreign Entanglements: Let us awaken before it is too late! Speech of Justice Daniel F. Cohalan at the Hotel Astor New York, May 25, 1923* (New York: Friends of Irish Freedom, 1923).

15 Brown, 'Daniel Florence Cohalan, 1865–1946', p. 128. There is much correspondence related to the AANC in Box 15, Cohalan Papers, AIHS.

16 G.A. Laffy to Daniel F. Cohalan, 2 June 1922, Cohalan Papers, AIHS. Cited in Brown, 'Daniel Florence Cohalan, 1865–1946', p. 128.

17 Records of the National Secretary, FOIF Papers, AIHS. See also Doorley, *Irish-American Diaspora Nationalism*, p. 200.

18 Cohalan speech, 'Is America the Next Victim?', Brooklyn Academy of Music, New York City, 25 November 1921, Cohalan Papers, AIHS. This speech was later circulated in pamphlet form by the FOIF: *Is America the Next Victim?* (New York: FOIF, 1921).

19 Cohalan to Borah, 29 November 1921, Borah Papers, cited in Brown, 'Daniel Florence Cohalan, 1865–1946', p. 130.

20 *Gaelic American*, 31 January 1925.

21 Cohalan's opposition to the World Court was noted by the *Irish Times*, which commented sarcastically that this made him an ally of the Ku Klux Klan who also opposed American involvement in this institution. 'Opposition to the World Court: Curious position of Judge Cohalan', *Irish Times*, 15 January 1926.

22 *Gaelic American*, 28 November 1925 and 26 December 1925. Minutes of the Meeting of National Council, Friends of Irish Freedom, 25 May 1923, Box 8, fl. 9, FOIF Papers, AIHS.

23 Cohalan Papers, Box 25, fl. 3, AIHS.

24 Statement of Judge Daniel F. Cohalan, Former Justice of the Supreme Court of the State of New York, *The World Court, Hearings before the Committee on Foreign Relations United States Senate*, Seventy-Third Congress, Second Session Relative to 'The protocols concerning the adherence of the United States to the Permanent Court of International Justice', May 16, 1934, Part 2, pp. 197–9.

25 *New York Times*, 16 November 1946.

26 Cohalan statement, 'America at a Crossroads', Box 24, fl. 2, Cohalan Papers, AIHS.

27 Golway, *Machine Made*, p. 294. These projects included the Triborough Bridge, one of the biggest construction projects of the 1930s.

28 'Cohalan Assails, Kinkead Lauds the New Deal', *New York Herald Tribune*, 23 March 1934.

29 Ibid.

30 Ibid.

31 Interview with Peter Fox Cohalan, 29 April 2017, Sayville, New York.

32 *New York Times*, 22 June 1936; *Daily Boston Globe*, 26 June 1936. Besides Smith and Cohalan, the three other Democratic critics of the New Deal included Bainbridge Colby, who had served as secretary of state under Wilson; former US senator James A. Reed of Missouri; and former governor Joseph B. Ely of Massachusetts.

33 *New York Herald Tribune*, 22 June 1936. According to Richard Dalton, a close associate of Cohalan at the American Irish Historical Society, Cohalan wrote the appeal to delegates, though it was signed by all five men. Dalton to Diarmuid Lynch, 26 November 1946, Lynch Papers, Private Collection.

34 The *New York Herald Tribune*, 22 June 1936 provided a full report on Cohalan's broadcast on WZB, which highlighted his importance as a spokesman for the small but

vocal anti-Roosevelt wing of the Democratic Party. According to Peter Fox Cohalan, following Daniel Cohalan's broadcast, Roosevelt cleverly persuaded Daniel's brother Judge John Cohalan to broadcast a message in support of the New Deal, which caused Daniel much annoyance. As noted earlier, Daniel and John Cohalan had become estranged due to a dispute over legal fees in 1904. Interview with Peter Fox Cohalan, Sayville, New York, 29 April 2017.

35 Roosevelt's Public Works Programs faced opposition from Republicans and conservative Democrats, who saw the massive expenditure as wasteful. Williams, *City of Ambition*, pp. 209–11.

36 'Judge Cohalan Exposes British Intrigue', *Gaelic American*, 23 November 1935.

37 Cohalan speech at Clan na Gael meeting at the Hotel Astor on the twentieth anniversary of the rising, *New York Times*, 13 April 1936.

38 Cohalan Papers, Box 17, fl. 8, AIHS.

39 *Southern Star*, 9 September 1933.

40 Ibid.

41 *Gaelic American*, 26 August 1939.

42 Cohalan to Reed, 12 May 1941, cited in Brown, 'Daniel Florence Cohalan, 1865–1946', p. 134.

43 *Gaelic American*, 9 September 1939 and 13 December 1941.

44 'Irish Heroism Reaches Lofty Heights in Times of Trial, Declares James McGurrin', *Gaelic American*, 9 May 1942.

45 *Time-Life Magazine*, 17 February 1941.

12. Farewell to Glandore: The final decade, 1936–46

1 Cohalan to Martin Conboy, 26 February 1923, fl. 10, Box 3, Cohalan Papers, AIHS. Conboy was president of the Catholic Club of New York.

2 'Cohalan's Daughter to Become a Nun Today; Will Enter Convent at Kenwood, Near Albany', *New York Times*, 20 October 1930.

3 'Pope Receives Daniel Cohalan', *New York Times*, 13 August 1936. See also *New York Herald Tribune*, 13 August 1936.

4 'A New Civil War', *American Monthly*, March 1930. Cohalan also contributed articles to the *Gaelic American*, usually on topics related to American foreign policy.

5 *New York World-Telegram*, 21 August 1931.

6 Cohalan to McGrath, 16 February 1926, Cohalan Papers, Box 18, AIHS.

7 McGrath to Cohalan, 15 December 1929, Joe McGrath Papers, NA6, DLRCA.

8 Coleman, *The Irish Sweep*, pp. 90, 124. Coleman suggests that McCartan may have introduced McGarrity to McGrath, since he was friends with both men.

9 McGurrin to Lynch, December 1946, Lynch Family Collection.

10 Eli Wald, 'The Economic Downturn and the Legal Profession: The great recession and the legal profession', *Fordham Law Review*, vol. 78, no. 2051, 2010.

11 Dalton to Lynch, 26 November 1946, Lynch Family Collection.

12 Ibid.

13 McGurrin to Lynch, November 1946, Lynch Family Collection.

14 *Irish Press*, 14 November 1946; *Evening Herald*, 6 August 1938.

15 McCartan, *With de Valera in America*, p. 191.

16 Anonymous, 'Daniel Florence Cohalan, 1865–1946', *The Recorder: Journal of the American Irish Historical Society*, vol. 10, December 1947, pp. 2–5; 'Cohalan to be Honored', *New York Herald Tribune*, 30 April 1941.

17 Dalton to Lynch, 26 November 1946, Lynch Family Collection.

18 *Irish Press*, 14 November 1946; *Southern Star*, 9 October 1999.
19 *Gaelic American*, 16 and 23 November 1946.
20 *Irish Press*, 14 November 1946. Cohalan's death was also noted in a lengthy article in the *New York Times*, 13 November 1946, and in the *New York Herald Tribune*, 13 November 1946.
21 *Irish Press*, 14 November 1946.
22 Lynch letter, *Irish Press*, 26 November 1946.
23 *Irish Press*, 29 November 1946. It seems likely that this correspondent was Katherine O'Doherty, *Assignment America: De Valera's mission to the United States.*
24 Editor of *Irish Press* to Diarmuid Lynch, in Lynch Papers, cited in McGough, *Diarmuid Lynch*, p. 207.
25 Dalton to Lynch, 26 November 1946, Lynch Family Collection.
26 Cited in McGough, *Diarmuid Lynch*, p. 207. Lynch's manuscript history never went beyond draft form but it nevertheless represents a fascinating pro-Cohalan view of events in America during the revolutionary period. The manuscript, running to 600 pages, is now in the Irish National Library. D. Lynch, 'Typescript History of the Friends of Irish Freedom and Associated Societies', Florence O'Donoghue Papers, MS 32597 (1–2), NLI.
27 Guterl, in his work *Color of Race in America*, recognises the significance of Cohalan in challenging the dominant conception of American identity in the early twentieth century. In her work *Diarmuid Lynch*, McGough also gives prominence to Cohalan's central role in supporting the Irish cause in America. See also Doorley, *Irish-American Nationalism*, for coverage of his central role in the FOIF.
28 Tansill also corresponded with James McGurrin, president of the AIHS, and appears to have also made use of Lynch's manuscript notes on the FOIF.
29 Thomas N. Brown, 'Irish-American Nationalism', *The American Historical Review*, vol. 63, no. 4, 1958, pp. 1010–11.
30 Tansill, *America and the Fight for Irish Freedom*, p. x.
31 Brown, 'Irish-American Nationalism'.
32 The term 'The Good War' was used by Studs Terkel in his award-winning work *The Good War: An oral history of World War II* (New York: New Press, 1984). For more on Tansill's analysis of American foreign policy, see Charles Tansill, *America Goes to War* (New York: Little Brown & Company, 1938) and *Back Door to War: The Roosevelt foreign policy, 1933–1941* (Chicago: H. Regnery Company, 1952).
33 Longford, *De Valera*, pp. 105–9. For an account of de Valera's obsession with his own place in history, see Patrick Murray, 'Obsessive Historian: Éamon de Valera and the policing of his reputation', *Proceedings of the Royal Irish Academy*, vol. 101C, no. 2, 2001, pp. 37–65.
34 Longford, *De Valera*, pp. 109, 112.
35 McCullagh, *De Valera, volume 1: Rise, 1882–1932*, p. 415.
36 De Valera to McGarrity, 27 December 1921, de Valera Papers, P150/1560, UCDA. See also McCullagh, *De Valera, volume 1: Rise, 1882–1932*, pp. 258–9.
37 De Valera to McGarrity, 31 January 1934, McGarrity Papers, MS 17 441/19, NLI. See also David McCullagh, *De Valera, volume 2: Rule, 1932–1975* (Dublin: Gill Books, 2018), p. 68.
38 See Ryle Dwyer's review of McCullagh's work *De Valera, volume 1: Rise, 1882–1932* in the *Irish Examiner*, 25 October 2017.
39 F.S.L. Lyons, 'The Irish Americans: A dual allegiance', *Irish Times*, 3 December 1957.

Epilogue: Cohalan and American-Irish Nationalism

1 Michael Collins to Harry Boland, 26 April 1920, de Valera Papers, P150/1125, UCDA. See also Fitzpatrick, *Harry Boland's Irish Revolution*, pp. 156–8.

2 Reid, *The Man from New York*, p. 110.

3 Cohalan Papers, Box 3, 18, AIHS. See also McGrath Papers, DLRCA, County Dublin.

4 McCartan, *With de Valera in America*, p. 198.

5 Doorley, *Irish-American Diaspora Nationalism*, pp. 23–5.

6 Gallagher, *Statement Dealing with Matters ...*, pp. 3–5.

7 John Boyle O'Reilly was a one-time radical Irish nationalist who later earned respectability as editor of the *Boston Pilot*. Cited in William V. Shannon, *The American Irish: A social and political portrait* (Boston: University of Massachusetts Press, 1989), p. 135. Like Cohalan, O'Reilly took an active interest in American affairs. See Ian Kenneally, *From the Earth a Cry: The story of John Boyle O'Reilly* (Cork: The Collins Press, 2011).

8 Kennedy had to overcome some anti-Catholic bias in his election campaign but this was in no way comparable to Al Smith's bid in 1928. For more on this topic, see Nicole Anderson Yanso, *The Irish and the American Presidency* (New York: Routledge, 2017), pp. 105–65.

9 These views are evident in his speeches and publications. Many of Cohalan's publications were issued in pamphlet form by the FOIF and the American Irish Historical Society. Given his status, his speeches were also covered in mainstream newspapers such as the *New York Times*. These pamphlets include: D. Cohalan, *The Menace of Foreign Entanglements: Let us awaken before it is too late!* (1923); D. Cohalan, *Political Isolation Is Independence: World Court a danger to our liberty* (1923).

10 Cohalan, *Democracy or Imperialism, which?*, p. 7.

11 In 1798 the 'Alien and Sedition Acts' of the Adams administration had discriminated against Irish Presbyterian immigrants in the late eighteenth century. For more on this, see Kevin Kenny, *The American Irish*.

12 *National Hibernian Digest*, April/May 1948.

Bibliography

MANUSCRIPT SOURCES AND OFFICIAL PUBLICATIONS

United States

American Irish Historical Society, New York

Daniel F. Cohalan Papers

Friends of Irish Freedom Papers

New York Public Library

William Maloney Papers

John Quinn Papers

Frank Walsh Papers

New York State Library

New York (State). Legislature. Senate. Standing Committee on the Judiciary. LEG 894.6-2: Proceedings of the joint committee on the Judiciary of the Senate and Assembly in the matter of the investigation demanded by Honourable Daniel F. Cohalan, a Justice of the Supreme Court of the State of New York, in and for the First Judicial District: June 25, 1913

Glucksman Ireland House, Bobst Library, NYU

Archives on the Irish in New York

Library of Congress, Washington

Borah Papers

Wilson Papers

National Archives and Records Administration

Record for Daniel Cohalan: Enemy activities – Arrest of alien enemies – Arrest of alien enemies in USA; Records of the War Department, 1917–18; Record Group 165; National Archives at College Park, MD, www.archives.gov [accessed 9 April 2019]

US Congress, House of Representatives, Committee on the Judiciary, *To Punish Espionage and Interference with Neutrality: Hearings before the committee on the judiciary*, 64th Congress, 2nd Session, 22 February 1917

US Congress, House of Representatives, Committee on Foreign Affairs, *The Irish Question*, 65th Congress, 3rd Session, 12 December 1918

US Congress, Senate, Committee on Foreign Relations, *Treaty of Peace with Germany: Hearing before the Committee on Foreign Relations,* 66th Congress, 1st Session, part 17, Washington, July 1919, S. Doc. 106, S159-0

US Congress, House of Representatives, Committee on Foreign Affairs, *To Provide for the Salaries of a Minister and Consuls to the Republic of Ireland,* 66th Congress, 2nd Session, 12 December 1919

US Congress, Senate, Committee on Foreign Relations, *The World Court: Hearings before the Committee on Foreign Relations,* 73rd Congress, 2nd Session, Relative to 'The Protocols Concerning the Adherence of the United States to the Permanent Court of International Justice', 16 May 1934, Part 2, pp. 197–9

Ireland

National Archives of Ireland
    Crime Branch Special (CBS IGCI), Inspector General's Monthly Reports
National Library of Ireland
    Daniel Cohalan Papers
    John Devoy Papers
    Peter Golden Papers
    Diarmuid Lynch Papers
    Patrick McCartan Papers
    Joseph McGarrity Papers
    Florence O'Donoghue Papers
    Hanna Sheehy-Skeffington Papers
Dún Laoghaire Rathdown County Council Archives
    Joseph McGrath Papers
University College Dublin Archives
    Frank Aiken Papers
    Harry Boland Diaries
    Mary MacSwiney Papers
    Éamon de Valera Papers
    Moss Twomey Papers

Britain

British National Archives, *Foreign Office Papers: Reports and papers of the British ambassador and the British consuls in the United States,* 1916–1922, FO 115

British National Archives, *Foreign Office Papers: Dispatches, instructions, memoranda, and minutes relating to United States affairs,* 1916–1922, FO 371

British Library, *Documents Relative to the Sinn Féin Movement,* PP 1921 (CMND 1108), xxix, 429

Germany

Das Politische Archiv des Auswärtigen Amts (The Political Archive of the Federal Foreign Office), Berlin: Operations and Incitements among the Irish against our Foes. PA-R 21153–21166.

Private Papers

Justice Peter Fox Cohalan, Sayville, Long Island, New York
- Aileen Cohalan, RSCJ Memoirs
- Newspaper cuttings, family correspondence and photographs

Diarmuid Lynch Papers
- Granig House, Cork County, Lynch Family Archives

Authors Interviews

Justice Peter Fox Cohalan (grandnephew of Daniel Cohalan), 29 April 2017, Sayville

John Hamilton, former assistant editor of *Southern Star*, 6 March 2019, by telephone

Fachtna Hickey, Rosscarbery and District History Society, 9 January 2019, by telephone

Newspapers and Periodicals

America: A Catholic review of the week
American Monthly
Boston Daily Advertiser
Boston Globe
Boston Post
Brooklyn Citizen
Brooklyn Tablet
Butte Daily Bulletin
Chicago Citizen
Chicago Tribune
Cork Examiner
Dearborne Independent
Friends of Irish Freedom News Letter
Gaelic American (New York)
Irish Examiner
Irish Independent
Irish Press
Irish Times
Irish World (New York)
Metropolis
Middletown Record
National Hibernian Digest
New York Herald Tribune
New York Times
New York World
New York World-Telegram
Pearsons Magazine
Philadelphia Inquirer
Southern Star
The Evening Mail
The Outlook
Time Magazine
Westminster Gazette

SECONDARY WORKS

Anand, M., Hicks, A., Willits, B., 'The Man from Philadelphia: Joseph McGarrity and 1914', in Miriam Nyhan Grey (ed.), *Ireland's Allies: America and the 1916 Rising* (Dublin: UCD Press, 2016)

Anderson, B., *Imagined Communities: Reflections on the origins and spread of nationalism* (London: Verso, 1981)

Anonymous, 'Daniel Florence Cohalan, 1865–1946', in *The Recorder: Journal of the American Irish Historical Society*, vol. 10, December 1947

Béaslaí, P., *Michael Collins and the Making of a New Ireland*, 2 vols (Dublin: Phoenix Press, 1926)

Blessing, J., 'Irish Emigration to the United States, 1800–1920: An overview', in P.J. Drudy (ed.), *Irish Studies 4: The Irish in America – emigration, assimilation and impact* (Cambridge: Cambridge University Press, 1981)

Blum, J.M., *Joe Tumulty and the Wilson Era* (Boston: Houghton Mifflin, 1951)

Brindly, R., 'Woodrow Wilson, Self-determination and Ireland, 1918–1919: A view from the Irish newspapers', *Éire-Ireland*, vol. 23, no. 4, Winter 1988, pp. 62–80

Brogan, H., *The Penguin History of the United States of America*, 2nd edn (London: Penguin Books, 1999)

Brown, S.A., 'Daniel Florence Cohalan, 1865–1946: A study of an Irish-American leader', MA thesis, University of Maryland, 1967

Brown, T.N., 'The Origins and Character of Irish-American Nationalism', *Review of Politics*, vol. 18, no. 3, July 1956, pp. 327–57

—, *Irish-American Nationalism, 1870–1890* (Philadelphia: J.B. Lippincott, 1966)

Brundage, D., '"In Time of Peace Prepare for War": Key themes in the social thought of New York's Irish nationalists, 1899–1916', in R.H. Bayor and T.J. Meagher (eds), *The New York Irish* (Baltimore, MD: Johns Hopkins University Press, 1996), pp. 321–34

—, 'Recent Directions in the History of Irish-American Nationalism', *Journal of American Ethnic History*, vol. 28, no. 4, Summer 2009

—, *Irish Nationalists in America: The politics of exile, 1798–1998* (New York: Oxford University Press, 2016)

Bryce, J., *The American Commonwealth*, abridged (Philadelphia: John D. Morris, 1906)

Buckley, J.P., *The New York Irish: Their view of American foreign policy, 1914–1921* (New York: Arno Press, 1976)

Burk, K., *Old World, New World: Great Britain and America from the beginning* (New York: Atlantic Monthly Press, 2008)

Burns, R.B., 'D'Arcy McGee and the Fenians: A study of the interaction between Irish nationalism and the American environment', *University Review*, vol. 4, no. 3, Winter 1967, pp. 266–73

Carnegie, A., 'A Look Ahead', *The North American Review*, vol. 156, no. 439, 1893, pp. 685–710

Carroll, F.M., *American Opinion and the Irish Question, 1910–1923* (Dublin: Gill & Macmillan, 1978)

—, American Commission on Irish Independence', in M.F. Funchion (ed.), *Irish-American Voluntary Organisations* (Westport, CT: Greenwood Press, 1983)

—, 'American Committee for Relief in Ireland', in M.F. Funchion (ed.), *Irish-American Voluntary Organisations* (Westport, CT: Greenwood Press, 1983), pp. 26–31

—, 'United Irish League of America', in M.F. Funchion (ed.), *Irish-American Voluntary Organisations* (Westport, CT: Greenwood Press, 1983), pp. 272–6

—, 'The Irish Progressive League', in M.F. Funchion (ed.), *Irish-American Voluntary Organisations* (Westport, CT: Greenwood Press, 1983)

—, 'American Association for the Recognition of the Irish Republic', in M.F. Funchion (ed.), *Irish-American Voluntary Organisations* (Westport, CT: Greenwood Press, 1983)

—, *Money for Ireland: Finance diplomacy, politics, and the first Dáil Éireann loans, 1919–1936* (Westport, CT: Praeger, 2002)

—, 'America and the 1916 Rising', in G. Doherty and D. Keogh (eds), *1916: The long revolution* (Cork: Mercier Press, 2007)

—, 'The Irish Free State and Public Diplomacy: The first official visit of William T. Cosgrave to the United States', *New Hibernia Review*, vol. 16 no. 2, Summer 2012

—, 'The Collapse of Home Rule and the UILA', in Miriam Nyhan Grey (ed.), *Ireland's Allies: America and the 1916 Rising* (Dublin: UCD Press, 2016)

Casey, M., 'Victor Herbert, Nationalism and Musical Expression', in Miriam Nyhan Grey (ed.), *Ireland's Allies: America and the 1916 Rising* (Dublin: UCD Press, 2016)

Clarke, G.S., 'A Naval Union with Great Britain: A reply to Mr Andrew Carnegie', *The North American Review*, vol. 158, no. 448, 1894, pp. 353–65

Clements, K.A., *Woodrow Wilson: World statesman* (Chicago: Ivan R. Dee, 1999)

Cohalan, D.F., *The Freedom of the Seas* (New York: Friends of Irish Freedom, 1919)

—, *The Indictment* (New York: Friends of Irish Freedom, 1919)

—, *Is America to be the Next Victim?* (New York: Friends of Irish Freedom, 1921)

—, 'Our Economic Interest in Ireland', *Forum*, vol. 65, 1921, pp. 59–67

—, 'Our Foreign Policy', *Forum*, vol. 65, 1921, pp. 187–96

—, 'The Freedom of Ireland', *Forum*, vol. 67, 1922, pp. 317–47

—, 'America's Advice to Ireland', in W.G. Fitzgerald (ed.), *The Voice of Ireland* (Dublin: John Heywood, 1923), pp. 233–5

—, *Political Isolation Is Independence: World Court a danger to our liberty* (New York: Friends of Irish Freedom, 1923)

—, *The Menace of Foreign Entanglements: Let us awaken before it is too late!* (New York: Friends of Irish Freedom, 1923)

—, *Democracy or Imperialism, which?* (New York, 1925)

—, 'Victor Herbert', *Journal of the American Irish Historical Society*, vol. 24, 1925

—, *Andrew Jackson: Hero of New Orleans* (New York: Allied Printing, 1930)

—, 'John Sullivan', *Journal of the American Irish Historical Society*, vol. 30, 1932

—, *Senator Lodge Past and Present* (Washington, n.d.)

Cohalan, F., *A Popular History of the Archdiocese of New York* (Yonkers: US Catholic Historical Society, 1983)

Coleman, M., *The Irish Sweep: A history of the Irish Hospitals' Sweepstake, 1930–87* (Dublin: UCD Press, 2009)

—, *The Irish Revolution, 1916–1923* (London: Routledge, 2014)

Coogan, T.P., *De Valera: Long fellow, long shadow* (London: Arrow, 1995)

Coombes, J., *Utopia in Glandore* (Cork: Butlerstown, 1970)

Cooper, J.M., *Breaking the Heart of the World: Woodrow Wilson and the fight for the League of Nations* (New York: Cambridge University Press, 2001)

—, *Woodrow Wilson: A biography* (New York: Alfred A. Knopf, 2009)

Cronin, S., *The McGarrity Papers: Revelations of the Irish revolutionary movement in Ireland and America, 1900–1940* (Tralee: Anvil Books, 1972)

Cuddy, E., 'Irish-American Propagandists and American Neutrality, 1914–1917', *Mid-America*, vol. 49, no. 4, 1967

Cull, N.J., et al. (eds), 'Gray Propaganda', in *Propaganda and Mass Persuasion: A historical encyclopedia, 1500 to the present* (Santa Barbara: ABC-CLIO, 2003)

Daly, M.E., 'Irish Nationality and Citizenship since 1922', *Irish Historical Studies*, vol. 32, no. 127, May 2001, pp. 377–407

Davis, F., *The Atlantic System: The story of Anglo-American control of the seas* (New York: Reynal & Hitchcock, 1941)

De Cogan, D., 'Ireland, Telecommunications and International Politics', *History Ireland*, vol. 1, no. 2, Summer 1993

Dempsey, P.J., and Boylan, S., 'Crawford (Robert) Lindsay', in *Dictionary of Irish Biography* (Cambridge: Cambridge University Press/Royal Irish Academy)

Devoy, J., *Recollections of an Irish Rebel* (New York: Chase & Young, 1929)

Doenecke, J.D., *Nothing Less than War: A new history of America's entry into World War 1* (Lexington, KY: University Press of Kentucky, 2011)

Doerries, R., *Prelude to the Easter Rising: Sir Roger Casement in imperial Germany* (London: Frank Cass Publishers, 2000)

Donnelly, J.S., *The Great Irish Potato Famine* (Stroud, Gloucestershire: Sutton Publishing, 2001)

Doolin, D., *Transnational Revolutionaries: The Fenian invasion of Canada 1866* (Oxford: Peter Lang, 2016)

Doorley, M., *Irish-American Diaspora Nationalism: The Friends of Irish Freedom, 1916–1935* (Dublin: Four Courts Press, 2005)

—, 'The Friends of Irish Freedom: A case study in Irish-American nationalism, 1916–1921', *History Ireland*, vol. 16, March/April 2008

—, 'The *Gaelic American* and the Shaping of Irish-American Opinion, 1903–1914', in W. Everham and V. Schelbert (eds), *Probing the Past: Festschrift in honor of Leo Schelbert* (New York: Peter Lang, 2015)

—, 'Judge Daniel Cohalan: American Irish nationalist and crusader against British influence in American life', *New Hibernia Review*, vol. 19, no. 2, Summer 2015

—, '"The Judge" versus "The Chief": Daniel Cohalan and the 1920 split within Irish America', *History Ireland*, vol. 23, no. 2, March/April 2015, pp. 44–7

—, 'Judge Cohalan and American Involvement in the Easter Rising', in Miriam Nyhan Grey (ed.), *Ireland's Allies: America and the 1916 Rising* (Dublin: UCD Press, 2016)

—, 'The Friends of Irish Freedom and the Irish Revolution', in J. Crowley et al. (eds), *Atlas of the Irish Revolution* (Cork: Cork University Press, 2017)

Downing, R., *A Report Presented to the Patrick H. Pearse Branch of the Friends of Irish Freedom, Washington D.C., by the President Rossa F. Downing at the Regular Meeting, 28 November1920* (Washington: AARIR, 1920)

Dungan, M., 'Pigott v Russell: The Parnell Commission', in *Conspiracy: Political trials* (Dublin: Royal Irish Academy, 2009)

Dwyer, T.R., *De Valera: The man and the myths* (Dublin: Poolbeg, 1991)

—, 'Michael Collins and the Civil War', in J. Crowley et al. (eds), *Atlas of the Irish Revolution* (Cork: Cork University Press, 2017)

Eichacker, J.M., *Irish Republican Women in America: Lecture tours, 1916–1925* (Dublin: Irish Academic Press, 2003)

Ellis, J.T., *The Life of James Cardinal Gibbons, Archbishop of Baltimore, 1834–1921* (Milwaukee: Bruce Publishing, 1952)

Emmons, D.M., *The Butte Irish: Class and ethnicity in an American mining town, 1875–1925* (Urbana, IL: University of Illinois Press, 1989)

Fahey, J.K., *McGuire: Boy mayor and Irish nationalist* (New York: Syracuse University Press, 2014)

Fanning, R., *A Will to Power: Éamon de Valera* (London: Faber & Faber, 2015)

Feighery, K., 'Timely and Substantial Relief: New York's Cardinal John Farley and the 1916 Rising', in Miriam Nyhan Grey (ed.), *Ireland's Allies: America and the 1916 Rising* (Dublin: UCD Press, 2016), pp. 283–91

Ferriter, D., *Judging Dev* (Dublin: Royal Irish Academy, 2007)

Finan, C.F., *Alfred E. Smith: The happy warrior* (New York: Hill & Wang, 2002)

Fitzgerald, W.G. (ed.), *The Voice of Ireland* (Dublin: John Heywood, 1923)

Fitzpatrick, D., *Harry Boland's Irish Revolution* (Cork: Cork University Press, 2003)

Gallagher, Rt Rev. M.J., *Statement Dealing with Matters which Arose out of the Visit to the United States of America of the Hon. Éamon de Valera* (New York: Friends of Irish Freedom, 1921)

Garraty, J.A., and Carnes, M.C., 'Clark, Champ', in *American National Biography*, vol. 4 (New York: Oxford University Press, 1999)

Garvin, T., *1922: The birth of Irish democracy* (Dublin: Gill & Macmillan, 1996)

Golway, T., *John Devoy and America's Fight for Ireland's Freedom* (New York: St Martin's Press, 1998)

—, *Machine Made: Tammany Hall and the creation of modern American politics* (New York: Liveright, 2014)

Grant, M., *The Passing of the Great Race: Or, the racial basis of European history* (New York: Sandycroft Publications, 1916)

Greaves, D., *Liam Mellows and the Irish Revolution* (London: Lawrence & Wishart, 2005)

Griffin, W.D., 'American Irish Historical Society (AIHS)', in M.F. Funchion (ed.), *Irish-American Voluntary Organisations* (Westport, CT: Greenwood Press, 1983)

Guterl, M., *The Color of Race in America, 1900–1940* (Boston: Harvard University Press, 2002)

Gwynn, S. (ed.), *The Letters and Friendships of Sir Cecil Spring Rice*, vol. 2 (New York: Houghton Mifflin, 1929)

Hannigan, D., *De Valera in America: The rebel president and the making of Irish independence* (New York: Palgrave Macmillan, 2010)

Hannigan, R.E., *The Great War and American Foreign Policy, 1914–1924* (Philadelphia: University of Pennsylvania Press, 2016)

Hickey, P., 'The Famine in the Skibbereen Union (1845–51)', in Cathal Póirtéir (ed.), *The Great Irish Famine* (Cork: Mercier Press, 1995)

Higham, J., *Strangers in the Land: Patterns of American nativism, 1960–1925* (New Brunswick, NJ: Rutgers University Press, 2002)

Hurst, J.W., 'Fenian Brotherhood', in M.F. Funchion (ed.), *Irish-American Voluntary Organisations* (Westport, CT: Greenwood Press, 1983)

Hutchinson, J., *The Dynamics of Cultural Nationalism: The Gaelic Revival and the creation of the Irish state* (Boston: Routledge, 1987)

Jacobson, M.F., *Special Sorrows: The diasporic imagination of Irish, Polish and Jewish immigrants in the United States* (Berkeley: University of California Press, 2002)

Kelly, M.C., 'The Hand of Friendship: Protestants, Irish-American, and 1916-era nationalism', in Miriam Nyhan Grey (ed.), *Ireland's Allies: America and the 1916 Rising* (Dublin: UCD Press, 2016), pp. 229–37

Kenna, K., *War in the Shadows: The Irish-American Fenians who bombed Victorian Britain* (Dublin: Irish Academic Press, 2014)

Kenneally, I., *From the Earth a Cry: The story of John Boyle O'Reilly* (Cork: The Collins Press, 2011)

Kenny, K., *The American Irish: A history* (London: Longman, 2000)

Keown, G., 'Taking the World Stage: Creating an Irish foreign policy in the 1920s', in M. Kennedy and J. Skelly (eds), *Irish Foreign Policy 1919–1966: From independence to internationalism* (Dublin: Four Courts Press, 2000)

Kibler, A., *Censoring Racial Ridicule: Irish, Jewish and African American struggles over race and representation, 1890–1930* (Chapel Hill, NC: University of North Carolina Press, 2015)

Kinealy, C., *The Great Irish Famine: Impact, ideology and rebellion* (New York: Palgrave, 2002)

Kramer, P.A., 'Empires, Exceptions, and Anglo-Saxons: Race and rule between the British and United States empires, 1880–1910', *Journal of American History*, vol. 88, no. 4, 2002, pp. 1315–35

Laffin, M., *The Resurrection of Ireland: The Sinn Féin party, 1916–1923* (Cambridge: Cambridge University Press, 2006)

—, *Judging W.T. Cosgrave* (Dublin: Royal Irish Academy, 2014)

Leary, W.M., 'Woodrow Wilson, Irish-Americans and the Election of 1916', *Journal of American History*, vol. 54, no. 1, June 1967

Lee, J.J., and Casey, M. (eds), *Making the Irish American: History and heritage of the Irish in the United States* (New York: New York University Press, 2006)

Link, A.S., *The Papers of Woodrow Wilson*, 69 vols (Princeton, NJ: Princeton University Press, 1966–94)

Longford, Earl of, and T.P. O'Neill, *Éamon de Valera* (London: Hutchinson, 1970)

Lurie, J., *William Howard Taft: The travails of a progressive conservative* (New York: Cambridge University Press, 2014)

Lynch, D., *The IRB and the 1916 Insurrection* (Cork: Mercier Press, 1957)

Maume, P., *The Long Gestation: Irish nationalist life, 1891–1918* (Dublin: Gill & Macmillan, 1999)

Maxwell, K., 'Irish-Americans and the Fight for Treaty Ratification', *Public Opinion Quarterly*, vol. 31, Winter 1967, pp. 620–41

McCartan, P., *With de Valera in America* (Dublin: Brentano, 1932)

McCarthy, J.P., 'The Friends of Irish Freedom and the Founding of the Irish Free State', *The Recorder: The Journal of the American Irish Historical Society*, vol. 6, no. 2, Fall 1993, pp. 116–28

—, *Kevin O'Higgins: Builder of the Irish Free State* (Dublin: Irish Academic Press, 2006)

McCarthy, M., *High Tension: Life on the Shannon Scheme* (Dublin: The Lilliput Press, 2004)

McCullagh, D., *De Valera, volume 1: Rise 1882–1932* (Dublin: Gill Books, 2017)

—, *De Valera, volume 2: Rule, 1932–1975* (Dublin: Gill Books, 2018)

McGee, O., *The IRB: The Irish Republican Brotherhood from the Land League to Sinn Féin* (Dublin: Four Courts Press, 2005)

McGough, E., *Diarmuid Lynch: A forgotten Irish patriot* (Cork: Mercier Press, 2013)

McGurrin, J., *Bourke Cockran: A freelance in American politics* (New York: Charles Scribner's Sons, 1948)

McKivigan, J.R., and Robertson, J.T., 'The Irish-American Worker in Transition, 1877–1914', in Ronald Bayor and Timothy Meagher (eds), *The New York Irish* (Baltimore: Johns Hopkins University Press, 1997)

McMahon, T., *Grand Opportunity: The Gaelic Revival and Irish society, 1893–1910* (New York: Syracuse University Press, 2008)

Meagher, T., *Inventing Irish America: Generation, class and ethnic identity in a New England city, 1880–1928* (Notre Dame, IN: University of Notre Dame Press, 2001)

—, *The Columbia Guide to Irish-American History* (New York: Columbia University Press, 2005)

Meaney, G., O'Dowd, M., and Whelan, B., *Reading the Irish Woman: Studies in cultural encounters and exchange, 1714–1960* (Liverpool: Liverpool University Press, 2013), pp. 3–4, 87–105

Meehan, C., *The Cosgrave Party: A history of Cumann na nGaedheal, 1922–1933* (Dublin: Prism, 2010)

Miller, K.A., *Emigrants and Exiles: Ireland and the Irish exodus to North America* (New York: Oxford University Press, 1985)

Mitchel, J., *The Last Conquest of Ireland (Perhaps)* (Glasgow: Washbourne, 1882)

Mitchell, A., *Revolutionary Government in Ireland, 1919–22* (Dublin: Gill & Macmillan, 1995)

Mulcahy, R., 'The Mulcahy Tapes and Papers', *History Ireland*, vol. 8, no. 1, Spring 2000

Mulder, J.M., *Woodrow Wilson: The year of preparation. Wilson supplemental volumes* (Princeton, NJ: Princeton University Press, 2015)

Myers, G., *The History of Tammany Hall* (New York: Boni & Liveright, 1917)

Ní Bhroiméil, U., *Building Irish Identity in America, 1870–1915: The Gaelic Revival* (Dublin: Four Courts Press, 2003)

O'Brien, M.J., 'How the Descendants of Irish Settlers in America Were Written into History as Anglo-Saxons and Scotch Irish', *Journal of American Irish History Society*, vol. 18, 1919, pp. 99–109

— et al. (eds), 'Michael J. Cohalan', *Journal of the American Irish Historical Society*, vol. xxv, 1926, pp. 317–18

—, *Irish Settlers in America: A consolidation of articles from the* Journal of the American Irish Historical Society (Baltimore: Baltimore Genealogical Publishing Company, Inc., 1979)

O'Brien, W., and Ryan, D. (eds), *Devoy's Post Bag*, 2 vols (Dublin: Fallon Books, 1948–53)

Ó Broin, L., *Revolutionary Underground: The story of the Irish Republican Brotherhood, 1858–1924* (Dublin: Gill & Macmillan, 1976)

O'Connell, D.T., 'Irish Influence on America's Foreign Policy: The work of our national bureau in Washington', in W.G. FitzGerald (ed.), *The Voice of Ireland* (Dublin: John Heywood, 1923)

O'Connor, T.P., *Home Rule Movement* (New York: Benziger Bros, 1891)

O'Doherty, K., *Assignment America: De Valera's mission to the United States* (New York: De Tanko Publishers, 1957)

O'Donnell, E.T., 'Tammany Hall and the New York Irish', in Michael Glazier (ed.), *The Encyclopedia of the Irish in America* (Notre Dame, IN: University of Notre Dame Press, 1999)

Ó Gráda, C., *Black '47 and Beyond: The Great Irish Famine in history, economy and memory* (Princeton, NJ: Princeton University Press, 1999)

O'Grady, J.P., 'The Irish Free State Passport and the Question of Citizenship, 1921–4', *Irish Historical Studies*, vol. 26, no. 104, November 1989, pp. 396–405

Olney, R., 'International Isolation of the United States', *Atlantic Monthly*, vol. 81 (May 1898)

Perkins, B., *The Great Rapprochement: England and the United States, 1895–1914* (New York: Scribner, 1968)

Reid, B.L., *The Man from New York: John Quinn and his friends* (Oxford: Oxford University Press, 1968)

—, *The Lives of Roger Casement* (New Haven, CT: Yale University Press, 1976)

Robbins, F., *Under the Starry Plough: Recollections of the Irish Citizen Army* (Dublin: Academy Press, 1977)

Rowland, T.J., 'Irish-American Catholics and the Quest for Respectability in the Coming of the Great War, 1900–1917', *Journal of American Ethnic History*, vol. 15, no. 2, Winter 1996, pp. 3–29

Ryan, D., *Unique Dictator: A study of Éamon de Valera* (London: Arthur Barker, 1936)

Sagarra, E., *Envoy Extraordinary: Professor Smiddy of Cork* (Dublin: Institute of Public Administration, 2018)

Sarbaugh, T.J., 'Ireland of the West: The development of Irish republicanism in California, 1900–1916', *Pacific History*, vol. 28, no. 1, 1984

Saunders, M.L., 'Wellington House and British Propaganda during the First World War', *Historical Journal*, vol. 18, no. 1, March 1975

Schiller, N.G., 'Long-Distance Nationalism', in *Encyclopaedia of Diasporas: Immigrants and refugee cultures around the world*, vol. 2, 2004, pp. 570–80

Schmuhl, R., *Ireland's Exiled Children: America and the Easter Rising* (New York: Oxford University Press, 2016)

Seymore, C. (ed.), *The Intimate Papers of Colonel House: From neutrality to war* (Boston: Houghton & Mifflin, 1926)

Shannon, W.V., *The American Irish: A social and political portrait* (Boston: University of Massachusetts Press, 1989)

Sim, D., *A Union Forever: The Irish question and US foreign relations in the Victorian age* (New York: Cornell University Press, 2013)

Smith, J.E., *FDR* (New York: Random House, 2007)

Splain, J.J., 'Under which King? The story of de Valera's tour in the United States', in W.G Fitzgerald (ed.), *The Voice of Ireland* (Dublin: John Heywood, 1923)

Staunton, E., 'The Boundary Commission Debacle 1925: Aftermath and implications', *History Ireland*, vol. 4, no. 2, Summer 1996

Stead, W., *The Americanization of the World or the Trend of the Twentieth Century* (New York: Horace Markley, 1902)

Stevens, P.F., *The Voyage of the* Catalpa*: A perilous journey and six Irish rebels' flight to freedom* (New York: Weidenfeld, 2002)

Sullivan, M., 'Fighting for Irish Freedom: St Louis Irish-Americans, 1918–1922', *Missouri History Review*, vol. 65, no. 2, 1971

Tansill, C., *America Goes to War* (New York: Little, Brown & Company, 1938)

—, *Back Door to War: The Roosevelt foreign policy, 1933–1941* (Chicago: H. Regnery Company, 1952)

—, *America and the Fight for Irish Freedom, 1866–1922* (New York: The Devin-Adair Co., 1957)

Terkel, T., '*The Good War: An oral history of World War II* (New York: New Press, 1984)

Townshend, C., *Easter 1916: The Irish rebellion* (London: Allen Lane, 2005)

Valiulis, M., *Almost a Rebellion: The Irish army mutiny of 1924* (Cork: Tower Books, 1985)

Van Vugt, W.E., 'British and British Americans (English, Scots, Scots Irish, and Welsh), to 1870', in R. Barkan (ed.), *Immigrants in American History: Arrival, adaptation, and integration* (Santa Barbara: ABC-CLIO, 2013)

Von Bernstorff, H., *My Three Years in America* (London: Skeffington & Sons, 1920)

Wald, E., 'The Economic Downturn and the Legal Profession: The great recession and the legal profession', *Fordham Law Review*, vol. 78, no. 2051, 2010

Ward, A.J., *Ireland and Anglo-American Relations, 1890–1921* (London: Weidenfeld & Nicolson, 1969)

Weiss, N.J., *Charles Francis Murphy, 1858–1924: Respectability and responsibility in Tammany politics* (New York: Smith College, 1968)

Welch, D., *Propaganda, Power and Persuasion* (London: The British Library, 2013)

Whelan, B., *United States Foreign Policy and Ireland, 1913–1929* (Dublin: Four Courts Press, 2006)

Williams, M.B., *City of Ambition: FDR, La Guardia, and the making of modern New York* (New York: Norton & Company, 2014)

Wilson, D.A., *Thomas D'Arcy McGee: Passion, reason, and politics, 1825–1857* (Montreal: McGill-Queen's University Press, 2008)

Wilson, W., *Mere Literature and Other Essays* (New York and Boston: Houghton Mifflin, 1896)

Wittke, C., *The Irish in America* (Baton Rouge: Louisiana State University Press, 1956)

Yanso, N.A., *The Irish and the American Presidency* (New York: Routledge, 2017)

Zieger, R., *America's Great War: World War I and the American experience* (Oxford: Rowman & Littlefield Publishers, 2000)

Zinn, H., *A People's History of the United States* (New York: Harper & Row, 2001)

Index

Illustrations are indicated by page numbers in **bold**.